CLASSROOM
Kaleidoscope

Lizzy Sutton

CLASSROOM
Kaleidoscope

Lizzy Sutton

TABLE OF
Contents

Introduction

CLASSROOM
KALEIDOSCOPE

As I have organized and re-organized and re-re-organized this book to try to create a reasonable approach that makes sense and is useful, I have constantly been searching for a name that would describe this collection of information, ramblings, and teaching tools. I have considered several, which I thought were brilliant at the time, but as I ran them past people, the looks on their faces told me to keep searching. Well, as far as I am concerned, the search is over! No amount of frowning or face scrunching is going to get me to change my mind about the title this time, because *CLASSROOM KALEIDOSCOPE* is such a great metaphor for what I am trying to say. It sounds catchy too...

Like a kaleidoscope, a classroom should be an ever changing scene that is made up of an infinite number of ever changing pieces. There is not just one "best" combination. There are a gazillion! Each turn of the tube creates a new arrangement whose pieces work together in harmony. Best of all, if the pieces do not seem to fit just right, they can be changed and re-arranged to create another scene.

What I have tried to do in this book is give you many pieces that you can pick and choose from until you have created a pleasing array for your classroom. In the beginning, your compositions should be relatively simple. As you gain more experience, however, your compositions should become more complex and you should turn the tube more often, constantly adding shiny pieces of "glass" to your creation. With time, you will become a master at the art of composition and your classroom kaleidoscope will be a joy to look through!

I have divided this book up into eight chapters that I would like to briefly describe for you. Often, the chapters seem to overlap, but in trying to find the right place for each topic I have chosen to use a paraphrase of Max Lucado's book *It's Not About You* to describe each section. Feel free to read the book in any order if you would like to go straight to a particular chapter!

The first chapter is titled "It's All About The Teaching" and provides a general introduction and overview of some general teaching observations. It also includes some personal ramblings and several disclaimers.

The second chapter is "It's All About Us" and continues to be a collection of personal teaching experiences and advice to all of us teacher types. The "Us" in the title assumes that those reading this book are teachers. (I can not imagine that anyone who is not a teacher would want to read this book, unless they were related to me and felt that they had to.) In this section I get down and dirty about some old-fashioned professionalism that I believe helps you become a better teacher. I might as well go ahead and apologize now, because I know that I am going to step on some folks' toes.

The third chapter is "It's All About Them" and is dedicated to the students. This section focuses on understanding where the kids are coming from and how we can best relate to them. It also identifies certain "student types" and offers advice on how to most gently "deal" with them. The concept of teaching the "whole child" is explored in this section.

The fourth chapter is "It's All About Classroom Management". I find it is hard to separate classroom management from the other sections because good classroom management usually creates an atmosphere where all the other parameters fall into place. Yet there are so many classroom tools that have little to do with the other topics, that I felt that they deserved their own section. The ideas in this part will help you manage your classroom time. It also contains some neat tricks that make your life simpler.

The fifth chapter is "It's All About Discipline". This section explores good classroom behavior as a necessary element for learning to take place, and provides practical advice in maintaining it. It is packed with specific scenarios and possible solutions. It also provides you with "humorous" tools to help you control your class in unusual ways that will win the hearts of your students. The emphasis in this section is on positive reinforcement and "painless" extinction.

The sixth chapter is "It's All About Instruction" and centers on the delivery of information in the classroom. The main theme of this section is to help you create a "data base" of options to vary your presentations and keep your instruction alive and your students awake.

The seventh chapter is "It's All About Communication" and focuses on communication with parents. Dealing with parents is a very important skill for every teacher.

The eighth chapter in this book is "It's All About Over". By this point, I am sure that you will be ready for a summarization and the wordiness to end! This section is designed to encourage you and inspire you, especially if you have been teaching for many years. In "book" language it is the conclusion.

At the beginning of each chapter you will find a dedication. From the beginning, when this book was just an idea and the first word had not been written, I had so many people that I wanted to dedicate it to that I knew I would never be able to choose just one. So I decided to have a dedication in each chapter. That way I only had to narrow it down to a list of eight! Following the dedication, you will find my thoughts, philosophy, and practical ideas woven in with my ramblings. Ramblings offer "real life" examples of classroom situations and lots of editorializing on my part. You will recognize them because they are in a more fanciful font. Some of the sections include what I have titled "bits of glass. " They are a very random list of quotes, notes, and practical advice that I have collected over the years.

I hope that you will find this book pleasant to read, practical in helping you teach, and inspirational in your quest to educate.

Respectfully,

Lizzy Sutton

MAY I WRITE MY OWN BOOK REVIEW?

I wonder if other authors fantasize about the book they are writing. Do they waiver, like me, from thinking what they are doing is good and that lots of people will want to read it, to thinking that no one will even want to pick it up? If nothing ever becomes of my book except that I pay more money than I can afford to have several copies bound, I will never regret writing it. At the least, I will pass it out to a few of the students that I have taught who plan on teaching and hope it will be helpful to them.

But no matter what happens, please allow me to fantasize the best and dream that my book will be a success. I will open the cover of my professionally published book and read book reviews that proclaim what a great and useful book it will be for teachers, especially new ones. But most of all I want those reviews to say that my book is practical, encouraging, honest, and humorous.

I don't know which way my book will go. I know one thing for sure, however; I had to write it.

Chapter One
IT'S ALL
ABOUT TEACHING

IT'S ALL ABOUT TEACHING

I READ IN SOME ARTICLE that there was a contest to see who could write the best first sentence for a book. This magical first sentence needed to be something special as it would set the tone for the whole book and might even be the determining factor as to whether the reader would purchase and read the entire book. The article I read, I think it was in Reader's Digest, also gave the winning sentence of the contest. Wow, was that one great sentence! In fact, it was so great that the first sentence lasted long enough to make up the first paragraph. I don't remember much about it, except that it was long and did leave me spellbound and wanting more. I wish that I could do that for you (the spellbound and wanting more part). As a writer, unfortunately, I am not that talented with words. So what I must do is leave you spellbound in a very different way. I want to share with you the joys of teaching in a very positive and practical way. I want to stomp on all of the negative people who discourage young people from becoming educators. I want to put joy and enthusiasm back into the teaching profession for those who are burned out and I want to give practical advice and common sense for those of you just beginning. And for those of you who already love what you do, I would like to spark your own creativity with a bundle of new ideas.

Before we begin our journey, however, I think it is important to make sure that this book is for you. I hate it when I buy a book, get it home, and find out it was not at all what I thought it to be. Therefore, I want to let you know very early what this book is about and how it can help you in your day-to-day teaching. If all goes as planned, and it rarely does when I start writing, this book will be a light hearted, practical look at teaching. It will be full of my personal thoughts and experiences. I am very passionate about teaching and I cannot separate who I am from what I do. Although I want it to be witty and easy reading, more than that I want it to be "down to earth" and full of teaching ideas that will help you in your classroom. I have tried to include all of the "teacher tools" that I have created or discovered over the years and I have also tried to include enough "ramblings" so that this book can be real to you and not just a lot of ideas that sound great but won't work. There are no easy answers to many of the challenges that we face in everyday teaching, but with a little common sense, a lot of prayer, and advice from those who have gone before us, we can know that we gave it our best. So if you haven't dog-eared the pages, and you are not interested in where I am leading you, you can still get your money back for this book. Did you save the receipt?

NOT JUST ANOTHER DIET BOOK

Have you ever gone into a book store and looked in the health section for a good diet book? I have. In fact, I have spent many hours looking through titles that claim to have all of the answers. My favorite ones are ones that claim to be the last diet you will ever need or the one that will get you skinny in two weeks. I was always smart enough not to fall for those claims, but in the back of my head I always wondered... The one thing I am sure of is that there is no one diet that works for everyone. We are all very unique individuals and we all need different approaches to managing our eating habits. I for one, have been struggling with mine for many years and find that my best approach is taking what works for me out of several diet plans and customizing them to my needs. So why in the world am I starting a book on the craft of teaching with a discussion on the vast number of diet books available? It is all about choice.

IF YOU DON'T CHOOSE, YOU LOSE

If you go in any good book store or on-line you will also find a vast array of books on teaching. I have read many of them. I encourage you to do the same. My book is no better or worse than any of the others; it is just another collection of things that have worked for me. It is your job to discern what is workable for you. That is what I want you to do with the information in this book, choose carefully. No teaching method works for everyone. You need to read this book with an open mind and an attitude of adventure! Highlight what you think might work for you and try it. If it doesn't work, modify it and if it still doesn't work throw it out! The great thing about teaching is that you get a new start every year. Even better, you get a new start every day. If something doesn't work at all, quickly get rid of it. Don't hang on to a bad idea because you don't want to be a "quitter". It may be a good idea for someone else just not for you. That kind of "do or die" mentality reminds me of the times I tried to switch my eating habits from pizza and cake to broccoli and dried beans. After much digestive discomfort I knew that I had tried to do too much too fast. Don't let that happen to you. Have you ever gone to a professional conference and come home with lots of great ideas? Two things happen to me when I get too much "inspiration" at once. I am either overwhelmed by the quantity of it and never try anything, or I try it all and it becomes obvious to my students that I have been to a teacher's conference. They usually just roll their eyes, hang on, and ride out the storm until I calm down and things get back to normal.

SLOW DOWN, YOU MOVE TOO FAST

Once you go through this book and highlight what you would like to try, take it slow. If you are a future teacher, start with the basics and just put a few of the other strategies in for flavor. Add a few more each year until you are a "mean, lean, teaching machine". If you are an experienced teacher, just add a few tricks at a time. Trying to do too much at once is not only overwhelming for the students, it will also be overwhelming for you. Any strategy that is going to succeed and become a permanent part of your teaching style has to have time to mature or it will not feel right in your classroom.

WHAT SHAPE ARE YOUR CLOSETS IN?

Many of these strategies require a certain level of organization and a few of them require you to be almost obsessive compulsive. I understand OCD in a very personal way. If I had not become a teacher, I am convinced I would have made a great efficiency expert or closet organizer. There are many areas of my life that I find it inconvenient to possess this personality trait, but managing my classroom is not one of them. If you are like me and already separate your socks into five categories and have all of your earrings in separate containers so as not to mix the colors, you will probably enjoy some of my organizational ideas. All of you normal people will probably laugh, but you may get some unique ideas, so I encourage you to read on. I would also like to say that there are many un-organized teachers out there who are excellent teachers, dearly loved by their students.

ACQUISITION OR GRANDTHEFT?

In this book you will find general teaching tips that everyone should know and most probably do. You will also find stuff that I have "acquired" from years of listening to other teachers, watching others perform their craft in the classroom, and reading a gazillion books. My biggest fear in writing this book is that I am giving the impression that all of these ideas are mine. They are not. The problem is that I do not know where all of them came from. Many of them are mine and are the result of years of trial and error. Many are from other sources. I used to think that all of those politicians who conveniently forgot all those facts when they went before the Senate Investigation Committee were all lying. Now I realize that they were just over fifty. So, I begin this book with an apology to anyone whom I have not credited properly. It is the nature of all professions that we learn best from each other. This is not stealing ideas; it is honing our craft.

I DON'T DO CRAFTS!

Some of you are thinking that you don't do crafts. Oh yes you do! I assume that if you are reading this book, you are a teacher or you want to be a teacher. Good teaching is as much of an art form as composing a symphony or performing a triple by-pass. Good teaching is the ability to put together the best of what you know to create a classroom that is conducive to learning. It does not happen overnight and it is a skill that is created by a willingness to learn and change and practice. If you already have all of the answers, you should be writing this book, not me. At this sitting, I have taught for 40 years and I learn new tricks all of the time. I consider myself a collector. I collect new teaching ideas and in my opinion you can never have enough. I also stand firm in my statement that teaching is indeed a craft. This book will be an attempt to share the tools that I have found useful. It will show how a little skill, dedication, and creativity will result in a classroom atmosphere that will be welcoming and beneficial to the students and enjoyable for you.

FORGIVENESS VERSUS PERMISSION

You need to know early on that I am a math teacher. I am not very good at grammar, punctuation, or spelling. I have a terrible time with first person, second person, and heaven forbid if I use third person! If this book ever makes it to publication, I am hopeful that the publisher will have had the good sense to hire some English teachers to fix my work. So why am I so bold as to think that I can write a book? It is very simple. I am dying. Don't feel sorry for me, we are all dying, we just don't know when. I am just probably closer to that final yearbook dedication than you are! It occurred to me around the age of fifty that I had almost "figured out" this teaching "thing" and I had a lot of neat tricks that would be useful to other teachers. I needed to write them down. I do not want to take all of these ideas to the grave with me. I remember all of the things I would have liked to have learned from my parents and grandparents. My grandmother made wonderful fried chicken that I have never been able to duplicate and my mom made the best potato salad! How hard can it be to re-create potato salad? I can't even spell recipe, how am I going to follow one that does not exist any more? I wish my Mom had written it down or I had paid more attention to the cooking part and less to the eating part. Therefore, I want to write down what I have learned about being an effective teacher in the hopes that it will help other teachers deal with the challenges of the classroom. As a result, I will seek forgiveness in being so bold as to think that I can write a book. I do not have all of the answers, and I do not pretend to be an expert. I do have some experiential wisdom and a love for the classroom.

BORN TO TEACH

I truly believe that some teachers were so "born to teach" that as children they were pre-programmed and entered into the world calling the roll and lining up their lesson plans for the next three weeks. They knew at an early age what they wanted to do with the rest of their lives and started watching those who taught them to note the good and the bad. Their desire was so strong that the discouragement of others because of mediocre salaries, long working hours, and often difficult working conditions did not influence them. Teaching was their passion from the beginning and will be until the end. I am one of those people, and I thank God everyday for the joy that teaching brings to my life. Okay, I don't thank him everyday. Some days I wish I flipped hamburgers or washed cars for a living because it seems so much simpler. Imagine never having to take any work home… But, most days I am grateful for my profession and know that it is a gift from God. How about you? Is teaching your passion or just a way to get a long vacation in the summer? (I know you are not in it for the money.) Maybe you fit somewhere in between. Wherever you fit in that spectrum, fear not. Not only are great teachers born, they are made! The question is how do you become a great teacher? The answer is that you start with a big dose of common sense, a little humor, and then lots of PRACTICE, PRACTICE, PRACTICE...

GOD NEVER LEFT THE BUILDING

When I first began teaching, God was in my classroom. The Supreme Court, in its infinite wisdom decided to remove him. I did not. I am such a rebel! ! ! He is still in my classroom and always will be. I will make statements later about how I am in control of my classroom and at a human level that is true, but God is in control and any success I have experienced as a teacher has been because of what he has enabled me to do. It is impossible for me to write a book about teaching without mentioning Him, so please do not be offended. In public education, I had to be very cautious about my outward dependence on Him. There were no public prayers and I kept my comments guarded. This did not stop my prayers for the students and for the learning. After 30 years of teaching in public schools, I entered Christian education. Not only was I allowed to pray and speak of the Lord, I was required to do so. Oh what a difference His acknowledged presence makes!

BAD POETRY

If you think that the grammar and spelling is bad, just wait until you get a sample of my poetry. Over the years, I have written a lot of bad poetry. I can't tell an iambic pentameter from a sonnet. I know it stinks, but it is very much a part of my teaching strategy and alas, must be exposed to public scrutiny. I have included some of it in this book, not for its literary merits, but for its lighthearted humor.

SOAP BOX

This section might be a good one to skip because it is just me on my soap box... I have a real problem with teacher education. The problem is that colleges don't usually have a course entitled Common Sense 101 or Humor for the Classroom Teacher. Yet, I am convinced that there are certain "basic skills" that all teachers should learn before they can become truly effective in the classroom. These skills are not taught in education courses. Colleges do a great job of teaching us how to create curriculum, write lesson plans, and create educational power points, but they usually fall short on practical classroom management. So where do most teachers learn these "teaching success gems"? It is sad to say, but these skills are learned on the job, often at the expense of the students and the teacher's sanity and self-esteem. Would you be comfortable with a surgeon who was allowed to learn his craft while operating on you? Do not think for one minute that poor teaching does any less damage than that novice surgeon. It may take a little longer to murder the patient, but the end result can be similar.

180 DAYS TO MAKE A DIFFERENCE

Some of us are fortunate, some of us are not. The fortunate among us have more than 180 days to make a difference in the lives of a student. We teach them more than one year or we maintain our relationship in some other manner. The less fortunate of us only have 180 days to accomplish whatever needs to be done by us for each student. Never underestimate the power we each have to influence a student's life and never take that power for granted. It does not matter where you teach or how good or bad you are, you are changing the course of history one young mind at a time. No teacher ever knows the future of the ones they teach. Some will be a positive influence on our world, some of them will be negative, and some of them will fall somewhere in-between!

We often get discouraged because we see in a student so much that we believe needs changing and we feel that we are making no progress whatsoever with them as the year progresses. All we can do is plant the seeds. Some of them will never germinate, and some of them will bring forth very productive fruit. We just rarely get to see the end result.

If you have the privilege of teaching in a smaller school, you may be able to teach the students for more than one year. I was in a situation at a small magnet school where I taught some of the students their entire math curriculum from Algebra I thru Calculus. It was amazing to watch them grow in intellectual and emotional maturity. I had five "180 day" chances! I was privileged to see some of those differences, yet there were many students that I was sure that I had not "touched". However, as the years have gone by, I have gotten some unexpected calls and emails from these young people letting me know that something I said or did was influencing their lives.

Through the years, I have taught literally thousands of students in all sorts of situations and there is no way to remember them all. My teaching career began in middle school with three years in an old facility on the "wrong side of the tracks", followed by seven years in a new facility in a semi-rural community. I then made the jump to high school and ten years were spent in a large comprehensive high school. Amazingly enough, I then found myself in a small K-12 magnet school. Presently, I have retired from public education and teach full time in a Christian school. So far that is 7200 days that I have had to make a difference and I am not through yet! If I estimate 125 students a year that means I have had 900,000 chances to make a difference.

My prayer is that in some way, big or small, I have positively impacted the young people that I have had the privilege to teach. Teaching is a privilege not to be taken lightly.

JOB OR MINISTRY?

At the beginning of each year, the Christian school where I teach has a Spiritual Emphasis Week that is designed to motivate the students and offer them spiritual nourishment as they start the new year. There are sessions for students and faculty and one of the teacher sessions was on helping our students make Godly decisions. Dr. Timothy Dowdy, Pastor at Eagles Landing Church in Atlanta began with a wonderful comparison of a job and a ministry. I want to share this with you because I believe that every good teacher, whether they are a Christian, Jew, Buddhist, or an atheist, should treat their vocation as a ministry. They may not call it that because it sounds too Protestant, but they must still believe in what they do. Some refer to it as passion, or calling, but they all know that the label is not important, the outcome is. Since this is Dr. Dowdy's presentation, I will use his term of ministry.

Job	Ministry
Obligation	Opportunity
Teaches the subject	Teaches the student
Weight of a chore	Weight of a call
Fills time	Invests time
Neglects responsibility (minimum to get by)	Accepts responsibility (maximum able)
Does what is required	Does what is needed
Sees success at graduation	Sees success at expectation
Occupation	Mission
Product	Passion

I like this and I wanted to include it because teachers who teach as if they are working in a "mission field" receive a lot more than a monthly paycheck and a retirement package. I am grateful the Lord did not call me to teach in Africa or South America because I am very spoiled by air conditioning and I do not like sharing my living quarters with bugs and reptiles. I have never even been called into the inner city, yet I know that wherever I have taught there are many hurting students who need my presence in their life. I teach every day like it is a call from God and when I have taught my last, I know that at least a small difference was made.

DEDICATED

Once in a while I have one of those moments that I categorize as "big affirmation." As a teacher, I know how hard I work and I know that much of what I do goes unnoticed and unappreciated. Nevertheless, I get enough "little affirmations" that it is all worth my energy. Little affirmations are those daily moments when a student says thank you, a parent tells you that you are doing a good job, or you get a note in the mail from a former student. They also come in the form of students "catching on" to the material and enjoying what goes on in the classroom.

Occasionally it goes beyond "little" and at the beginning of the 2010 school year it went way beyond for me. If I remember correctly, I have had three yearbooks dedicated to me and I have been chosen as a star teacher 9 times. I even was selected as faculty homecoming queen once, but I don't think that can count because I wowed them with my Dolly Parton impersonation so that might have been cheating. I have received other awards and recognitions and as wonderful as they were, they all got topped by a former student in a simple act of love that I will never forget.

Teaching at a private Christian school affords opportunities for spiritual renewal that are not allowed in public schools. At my school, one way we stay spiritually grounded is a yearly event called "Spiritual Emphasis". The activities are a combination of praise and worship music, a speaker who keeps the theme going, and break-out sessions geared to individual topics or groups of kids. This year's event was great and you could feel the kids getting caught up into the theme of how "amazing" they are in the eyes of God.

On the second day a band called "The Less" put on a concert for the students. It was a five man band and four of the five were graduates of my school. I had taught three of them; Zac, Michael, and Adam. Adam was a good student, but he was one of those students that could not conceptualize mathematics. He was willing to work, but he was very frustrated that his efforts were not always rewarded with good grades. Adam was my most regular "customer" at before and after school tutoring and we spent many hours together trying to unravel the intricacies of math. He never gave up and on one occasion he actually made a 98 on a test. I was so proud of him that I made a big announcement at lunch and presented him with a cheap plastic medal on a red, white, and blue ribbon that said "math star". During their high school career the boys did "praise and worship" for our school chapels, hoping they would have a career as a Christian rock band. I was a little skeptical that they would be able to support themselves in that manner, but not wanting to discourage such a noble dream, I just smiled and kept my mouth shut. Now here it is four years later and I am sitting listening to that band that I thought was just a dream. They have recorded C. D. 's, written original songs, one of which was used in a movie, and play all over the area. That just proves how well my crystal ball is working!

Adam was always very special to me, but I never realized how special

I was to him until he sat down at the keyboard that day and dedicated his next song to me. He is the lead singer and he took a good two minutes before the song started telling the entire school how patient and untiring I was in helping him before and after school. He even said that he still had the medal! I was trying so hard to be humble, but sometimes you glow so bright that it is obvious that you are pleased. I will never forget that moment. The fact that a student remembers me because I never gave up on them and was patient and kind means the world to me.

THE OLD CEDAR CHEST

One of the biggest problems I am having with writing this book is finishing it. Every time I think I am close to being done, I think of something I have left out that I want to say or I find something that I want to add. I thought this section was complete until I started digging in my Mom's old cedar chest where I keep all of my keepsakes and old papers. I was looking for something I needed for some documentation and I came across a couple of things that summed up my vision of what a great teaches should be and I could not resist throwing them in. The first was my application for the state teacher of the year competition. It was written in 1995 and when I read it I was amazed at how my basic approach has stayed so constant over the years. I think that proves my point when I say that the basics to teaching are timeless. Below are two questions that I answered in 1995 that I would answer exactly the same today.

BASED ON YOUR KNOWLEDGE OF HOW CHILDREN LEARN, WHAT ARE THE MOST CRITICAL ELEMENTS OF YOUR CLASSROOM PRACTICE?

I like to concentrate on what I call "The Four C's," Caring, Consistency, Creativity, and Common Sense. I find that when I stick to these four words, learning happens! Caring is probably the most important of the four, because if my students know that I truly care about them and what I am trying to teach, they will forgive me for my human imperfections. I must care about them enough to remember that they do not all learn with the same learning style or rate. I must vary my approaches to instruction enough so that each child has an opportunity to internalize the information in the way they do it best. I must care enough to praise the good, and correct the not-so-good, and make sure that the punishment fits the crime. I must care enough to get the facts before I jump to conclusions. I must greet every student with a "good morning". I must let them know that I will never give up on them, even if they have given up on themselves.

Consistency is also a critical element in my classroom. The environments that my students come from and the world we all live in have gotten very inconsistent and young people today are getting many mixed messages. A classroom should be a place of safety, where students know what to expect. They should not be threatened or feel that they are not being treated fairly. Rules, organizational methods, and expectations should be consistently enforced. Surprises should be saved for the subject matter! Consistency in high expectations is especially important. If a child receives continual messages from me that I have faith in his/her abilities, eventually it will pay off.

Creativity goes without explanation. The creative classroom keeps the students on their toes! So much of high school math seems so very boring and uninteresting to the students that it takes real creativity just to keep them awake at times.

Common Sense is the balm that helps everything else work smoothly. Consistent enforcement of rules is critical but common sense moves in when a child, who has just lost a parent to death or divorce, breaks a rule. Caring about finishing the curriculum is critical, but common sense takes over when a teachable moment arrives and the day's lesson plans go out the window to grab the opportunity. Common sense tells me very quickly when a method I am using to teach a skill is not working and despite my best efforts, I must start over with a new plan. Common sense lets me know that no matter how old a student gets, they all learn best if they are not bored, and the lesson has some meaning to them, so I try to create a new approach.

WHAT IS TEACHING IN A NUTSHELL?

Teaching is not just teaching. It is performing, counseling, playing the role of a college admission officer, and being a surrogate mother, even if you are a male. If a class gets bored or off task, it is becoming a comedian or a Marine drill sergeant and knowing when to do which.

Teachers today have a lot of electronic competition and therefore must be even more creative in their presentation and approach.

Teaching is not isolated to the classroom either. It is communicating with parents, and taking part in the school community. It is giving 200% and still maintaining a balanced personal life, so you can face each day with a minimum of personal problems. It is maintaining a sense of humor when there is little to laugh at.

I found the second "treasure at the very bottom of that old cedar chest. It was a take home final exam that I had in my last education class before I began my teaching journey. For the essay part, I took the song The Impossible Dream and rewrote the words. I was passionate about teaching before I ever began and I always will be. I know it is a little corny but it tells where my heart was and is.

The Quest
To dream the impossible dream
To love the unlikeable child
To help with that search for tomorrow
To stay when the cleaning crews gone

To find right, when there's so much wrong
To laugh, when it is easier to cry
To grade, when your eyes are too weary
To teach the unreachable child

This is my quest
To strengthen their hope
To hang on to success, no matter how small
To work for their trust-without magic, just prayers
To be willing to start all over when your lesson plan fails

And I know, if I'll only hold out
And they learn just to think
That they can do whatever they need
To make their life complete

And the world will be better for this
That one kid, scorned and hopeless for years
Found trust and new hope for tomorrow
To reach his impossible dream.
~ Lizzy Sutton

GOOD TEACHING IS LIFE TIME LEARNING

In forty years of teaching I have been to so many teacher in-services and read so many "teacher" books that I cannot begin to remember them all. No matter how long we teach, it is imperative that we keep on learning. If you look on my nightstand or in my "library" you will usually find a "teacher" book. Presently you will find a copy of *The Falconer: What We Wish We Had Learned in School* by Grant Lichtman and *50 Ways to Improve Student Behavior* by Annette Breaux and Todd Whitaker. I have learned something from all of the books that I have read and I will probably keep reading "teacher" long after I have been "put out to pasture"! I will share some of the books that I have found most helpful later. Now, however, I would like to share two very special in-service opportunities that I will never forget. Generally, when I attend an in-service, I try to keep my expectations low and if I come away with one or two "jewels" that I can use in my classroom, I count it a good day. There have been three in-services, however, that have rocked my teaching world and changed my paradigm forever. I am going to share two of these experiences in this section and then one later. I came away from all three of these days with a renewed sense of energy that would be rarely dampened by the day to day routine of teaching.

THE CONFRONTATIONAL EXPERT

In January of 2010, I attended a workshop that was sponsored by The Professional Association of Georgia Educators The speaker, Grant Wiggins, was enthusiastically confrontational, and there were very few dull moments. Wiggins is the co-author of a book entitled *Schooling By Design* with Jay McTighe. His presentation was thought provoking and the responses from some of the other teacher's in the room indicated that it was "otherwise" provoking. I liked him very much and was challenged

by his comments. Unfortunately, everyone in the room did not feel that
way and some verbal arguments ensued. At one point, I thought the
teacher across the table from me was going to have a stroke. She was
shaking and turning red and taking everything that he said personally. I
could understand where she was coming from because, there used to be
a day when I felt the need to defend all of my moves. With age has come
wisdom, and I know that I can always improve and learn more.

When a teacher works as hard as they can and some "expert" comes
along and knocks the blocks out from under them, it is very easy to get
defensive. I think everyone in the room started out on the defensive
when he told us not to use conditional statements in our comments for
the day. For instance; "I could teach the curriculum if we just had more
time", or "I could get more critical thinking skills done if I didn't have
to concentrate on improving standardized test scores", etc. Wiggins was
more into the "where there is a will, there is a way" mentality, and he
would not back down for anything. In a time of furloughs, cut-backs,
and strained budgets, some of the teachers in the room were not in the
mood for a "sky is the limit" motivational talk. I, however, was, and was
enjoying myself immensely. Here was a guy who was not afraid to tell
it like he saw it. It was not sugar coated and it was directed at the teachers. It was not about putting the "blame" in the proper place; it was a
plan for making education real and in my opinion doable. His presentation, simply put, was: "It's all about the teaching. "

I do not want to plagiarize any of his ideas, but I do want to share
my perception on some of the things that he said. I have since read all
of his books on backwards design and I encourage you to read them
also. If I understand it correctly, the basic premise that he tried to communicate to us is that a school must carefully develop a mission statement and then design their school program and curriculum around that
statement. So many schools are running on habit and tradition that if
asked the purpose of a course they would start listing the topics taught
in the course. They would be hard pressed to state a bottom line purpose. Our curriculums are often developed by textbook companies as
we just blindly go through the table of contents of the books. Critical
thinking is thrown out the window as short term content drives teaching
today. He picked on the math teachers all day and his last comment be-

fore we left was that if the kids don't learn math it is the math teacher's fault. One of his most explosive comments was when he quoted research that proved that classroom feedback and instruction outweigh home environment in the learning process. That comment got a lively discussion going.

He stated that a "vision/reality" gap analysis is the engine of change. He believes that this must happen regularly and explicitly as part of everyone's job. He used the example of coaches throughout the day. A coach evaluates his talent and continually reevaluates and makes adjustments. The teachers immediately responded with; "we don't get to pick our teams and everybody has to make the team and gets to play". He shot back with the comment: "that is what recreation league coaches do all of the time"! It seemed that he had an answer for everything and the teachers had an excuse for everything. He was shooting down all of our "buts" and I was beginning to think that here was a guy that might actually have something. Much of what he said, I had heard before, but somehow he brought it all together and pushed us to "make it happen".

Here are my notes from his workshop. They are un-edited and a little scrambled, but they made a major impact on me. Some of them I already knew and just needed to be reminded; some of them made perfect sense but I never thought of them that way; and a few of them were debatable in my opinion. Nevertheless his workshop shifted my paradigm and reinforced my belief that no matter how long you teach, you are never too old to change.

- Good is the enemy of the best. What do you use as an incentive to keep improving?

- We are measuring what is easy to measure, not what matters.

- Don't tell people what to do. Give them the problems and ask for the solutions.

- You have to be so completely committed that you optimize your resources and time.

- Just knowing the truth does not make the truth happen because habit trumps truth.

- When students get more tests and feedback they do better.

- You are the "causer" of results...

- They need to know what excellence looks like.

- Our kids are going to college where no one is going to teach them anything. They must know how to learn.

- Do your courses and programs have clear and defensible long term learning goals? Or are courses just designed around topics and textbook content?

- Stop telling them, giving them graphic organizers, and asking them to spout it back.

- Stop hinting, helping, and scaffolding. We have to teach them to learn on their own. We teach them to drive so that they can drive alone.

- Students need to develop a flexible understanding of when, where, why, and how to use their knowledge to solve new problems. They must learn how to extract underlying principles and themes from their learning exercises.

- They can't learn at high levels if they are instructed at low levels.

- Excessive front load of material will fail if not used with application.

- Make things problematic for students and see what they do.

- More feedback not more teaching is what the students need.

- Do important things two or three ways.

- I do, you watch. I do, you help. You do, I help. You do, I watch.

- Make it clear to the students that the goal is inquiry not passive learning of knowledge.

- My job as a teacher is not to simply cover the material, teach my favorite topics, cover content standards, use engaging activities, or practice for the state test.

- My job as a teacher is to cause learning, teach for understanding, help students make meaning of big ideas, use engaging and effective learning that causes transfer, help students "do" the subject.

- Don't confuse learning with covering.

Now I know that all of the tidbits above will not make sense to you because they have been taken out of context but they were what I needed to be reminded of. I hope they spur you to read about backward design as well as any other educational trend that comes down the pipeline. Take what is good and make it work for you. When you teach long enough, you begin to get too comfortable, yet one of the greatest qualities of a good teacher is the willingness to let our pride take a back seat to our effectiveness in the classroom. A lot of teachers got their pride stepped on that day and a few of us were glad for the stomping.

OH WHAT A GLORIUS DAY

As wonderful as Grant Wiggins was, the most memorable in-service I ever experienced in my entire teaching career was a day spent at the Ron Clark Academy in Atlanta. I was vaguely introduced to Ron Clark when I saw his first book *The Essential 55*. I purchased the book and enjoyed reading it very much. I knew a lot of adults that could benefit from his rules. Several years after reading his book, one of my parents asked me if I knew who he was and was I interested in going to his academy to watch him teach. She brought me a brochure and I started reading and researching. Ron Clark and another amazing teacher, Kim Bearden, have founded The Ron Clark Academy in a socio-economically challenged section of Atlanta. They have converted a very old, dilapidated warehouse into a school of dreams! I strongly encourage you to read *The End of Molasses Classes,*which gives the complete story of Ron and how he brought his vision to reality. Thankfully, this parent

was very insistent that I be exposed to Ron, and she next showed up
with an autographed copy of his "molasses" book. I could not read it
fast enough and I knew that I had to find a way to experience his school.
I used departmental money to buy a copy of the book for everyone in
my department and the principal. I gave the principal about two weeks
to read the book and then I went to him and asked if some of us could
go to Ron's Academy. He had not read the book, but I think he was
bowled over by my enthusiasm and agreed to use staff-development
funds to send me, him, and one other teacher. I quickly did the paper
work before he could change his mind! Thus began the process of anticipation. I went on his website and researched test scores; I went on
Amazon and ordered his movie; and I went back and read *The Essential
55* again. I was enamored with Ron Clark, his story, and his drive. What
struck me most, however, was his commitment to making his dream
happen. No one threw money at him. The proceeds of his books allowed him to build his dream but much of what he has accomplished
comes from his hard work. Having worked myself into an "anticipation
frenzy", I was looking forward to the big day in the same way I always
looked forward to Christmas morning when I was young and still believed that Santa existed solely to fulfill my every wish.

March 30th will always be a special day in my heart. It was the day that
my batteries were recharged enough to last me at least ten years! I cannot
adequately describe my experiences that day but what I saw was "overboard" teaching that was supported by high expectations and a "whole
child" approach. We ate lunch with the students and I asked one of the
students how they felt about the three and half hours of homework
they had every night. They were quick to answer that they did not like
it, but it was worth it. I saw fifth graders doing math that my calculus
students would have struggled with and filling in a periodical table with
amazing accuracy. I participated in a literary discussion on Tony Morri-
son's *Blue Eyes* with eighth graders that could have been conducted in a
college classroom. I watched Ron Clark teach math with a disco ball
and kids dancing on top of their desks! The expectations are incredibly
high and we were told over and over again to teach to the top and the
others will rise. All day we were instructed to make every moment count,
don't sit down, move more, smile more, look them in the eye, create a

sense of urgency, constantly mix it up, and be a pocket of passion!

I know that some people might be thinking that what we saw was a "dog and pony show" put on for visitors. My response to that is "maybe". Do I really believe that those teachers can maintain that level of energy every day, all year long? Probably not; but I do know that if they display fifty percent of their energy when no one but the students are present in the room, they are still expending more energy than I have ever seen in one school in all of my teaching career. We wonder why school is so boring for so many. Students today have so much stimuli around them that zings and zaps. We need to zing and zap in the classroom. The Ron Clark Academy is all about that and for all of those doubters, check out the test scores on the internet and be sure to check how many of their graduates have scholarships to the finest secondary high schools in the nation.

When it was time to leave, our exit was even magical. In the middle of the lobby area is a large spirally blue slide that connects the second floor to the first. If you dare to slide down you do so in front of an enthusiastic crowd of well wishers! You are then immediately presented with a large sticker that says that you are "blue slide certified". Needless to say, I was not leaving without that sticker and my day of a lifetime ended with a slide of a lifetime and a renewed "energy".

A PROFESSION FOR SUCKERS
We work so hard and get paid so little.
With parents and students we're always in the middle.
There is so much paperwork our eyes are fading fast!
We teach, reinforce, and drill, but the knowledge does not last.
Are we a bunch of suckers, giving our "all" for naught?
Are we wasting our talents on those who would rather not be taught?
Comparing teachers to suckers is an analogy that does have merit.
But so far I have missed the point and now I would like to share it.
A sucker lasts a long, long time and so can what we do and say.
We never know far down the road, the difference we have made on any given day.
A sucker may be gone when the stick is empty and the mouth is closed.
But when you stick your tongue out the evidence is still there and always shows!

Teaching is a lot like that, our results are never clear.
Students come and go through our lives,
Of their futures we rarely hear.
But we know our influence (as small as it may be) is like that tell, tell
tongue.
And if teaching is a job for suckers, boy, I'm glad I'm one!
~ Lizzy Sutton

THE ELEMENTS OF GOVERNING POWER

Below you will find a long quote from *Manual of Methods for Georgia
Teachers 1911*. I just could not resist sharing this "timeless jewel" with
you. It is in a section entitled School Management which was written
by C. B. Gibson, Superintendent of Columbus Public Schools.

A word of caution: get out a large Webster's dictionary and prepare
to read in language that needs a little "dusting off. " It is a little like reading Shakespeare! There are parts that are not clear to me, like the boy
sitting with his teacher on the log, but as I read this I smile and am grateful for the wisdom of the ages. I hope that you will agree with me that
there are a lot of things about teaching that never change! If you can
wade through this section, you will have a wonderful, very old fashioned
summarization of good teaching. If you find it difficult to get through,
skip it; most of my proof readers did. They suggested that I eliminate
it, but I like it too much! I think it is a great way to end this section.

"In a certain schoolroom the author has in mind are thirty pupils
from the best homes of the place. The room is equipped with good
furniture and appliances for teaching. The teacher is a cultured lady of
experience in teaching. She aims at good order, but she must draw
largely on her time and attention from the beginning until the end of
the school day if she has no more than quiet. The pupils are listless and
indifferent to the recitation, noisy and nagging, ready to drop a book
or slate if the teacher's eye be not on them, rebellious in their spirits, in
short, young anarchists. If the teacher leaves the room, pandemonium
reigns. At the end of the day the teacher is worn out; at the end of the
session she feels like going to her reward. No wonder she despises
teaching. "

In another schoolroom not far away are forty-six pupils from inferior homes. The school furniture is poorer, the appliances more limited. The teacher's methods of conducting the recitation are perhaps not so good, and yet the children get far more good out of it than in the first school. They freely and yet courteously and in the most orderly manner ask questions of the teacher and of the pupil reciting or of any other pupil in the class. A beautiful spirit of harmony and consideration and self-control is manifest. If the teacher leaves the room the work goes quietly and earnestly on. There is not a constant strain on the teacher. At the end of the session she has energy left with which to work during the vacation. Naturally the teacher loves her work.

Why this difference? One has the true element of governing power; the other has not. What are the elements of governing power?

LOVE. The easy government of most schools means the control of a comparatively few pupils of unhappy dispositions. To these the teacher must give most attention; why not win their esteem and confidence, bring yourself to take a warm interest in them, and as an easy natural consequence, love them? It is not impossible to love even the unlovely. They are usually those who have least love at home, and are therefore quite susceptible to genuine love of a teacher – not declared but manifested. Love is one of the strongest incentives to good, as well as restraints from evil, that can be used.

CONSISTENCY. The teacher cannot govern properly without the respect of his pupils. He may have order, but order of a low degree. He cannot have the respect of his pupils unless his living be consistent with his teachings. Pupils are as quick to discover inconsistencies in a teacher's living and teachings as the world is to discover them in the minister of the gospel. Not only will pupils lose their respect for the inconsistent teacher, but the more thoughtful ones will be forced to despise him. A teacher ought to be the embodiment of the high ideals placed before his pupils. Then indeed is it good for a boy if he is allowed only to sit on the end of a log with his teacher. Not only should he be consistent in his living and teaching, but he should be consistent in his daily requirements of his pupils. To be rigid one day and lax the next, makes it the more difficult to be rigid on the day following. Consistency in the teacher is a rare jewel.

CHARACTER. Unconscious tuition is stronger than eloquent ex-hortation. Not only should the teacher's character not be smirched with vice and polluted with corruption, but, in its purity and nobility, it should stand out boldly, and impress itself on the life of the pupils. A strong moral influence, emanating from a high moral character, will do more to lead pupils into right conduct than all the rods and rules that can be plied upon their backs and brains. Order may be had by force, but the vitalizing influence of the teacher's inner life is necessary to secure good government. Character means absolute truthfulness, it means good temper, it means good habits, it means purity of life.

GOOD JUDGEMENT. This is the child of common sense and the parent of tact, both of which should be found in every school governor. The ability to handle judiciously, tactfully, skillfully, special cases of misconduct and real or imaginary grievances of patrons is the secret of many a teacher's success in government. Judgement in dealing with the little everyday affairs of the schoolroom is a good preventive of the greater, more serious problems of school government. By finding the pupil's true motive for the troublesome conduct with which he may be changed, and dealing judiciously with him, he may be saved from being a rebellious young anarchist.

VIGILANCE. Alertness with eye and ear is an essential element in governing power. The school impressed with the fact that the kind, consistent, faithful teacher sees and hears all that goes on in the schoolroom, even while having his attention centered mainly on the recitation, will be found to be an orderly room. Constant fault-finding and nagging are not necessarily comcomitants of vigilance. Nor is it necessary that the pupils should regard the teacher as suspicious and distrustful of them. If they feel that the teacher is always looking for mischief they may be obliging enough to see that he is not disappointed. If the teacher's vigilance is not seasoned with sympathy and love, there is apt to be frequent occasion for fault-finding. Never should a violation of a moral principle be passed unnoticed. The vigilance of the teacher should extend to the little details of the schoolroom-the condition of the furniture, apparatus and appliances, the seating of the pupils-all those things that bear on easy control.

SCHOLARSHIP. A broad margin of ripe scholarship, giving the teacher confidence in himself and increasing the confidence of pupils in their teacher; will go far towards rendering control an easy matter. If the teacher is able, or undertakes, merely to keep school and incidentally to hear what the children learn from the text-books, control is a burdensome business. Thorough, fresh scholarship and a good store of ready information will awaken in pupils an interest in the pursuit of knowledge; interest begets application: application drives away mischief. A liberal amount of scholarship is not sufficient unless it be fresh and appropriate to the topics of that day. To keep it fresh and appropriate one must study daily. Daily study means not only increased scholarship, but it means ready and appropriate methods of teaching; and all this makes school government easy.

BITS OF GLASS
Teaching

*** Teaching is like sailing. We have to adjust our sails based on the kids who walk in the door. We decorate, we plan, then the kids walk in and the adjustment starts.

***All teaching is transformational. The question is what are we transforming them into?

***We are going to have to learn and retool the rest of our lives. We are always teaching and always learning.

***No Excuses Allowed for Poor School Performance: Performance will be the key. Problem solving instead of excuse building will be the ethic. "Can do" will be the attitude and excuses will be unacceptable. Excuses will be unacceptable, not because they don't explain a set of circumstances, but only because they contribute nothing to changing these circumstances. Grant Wiggins

***The most demoralizing thing we can do to a human being is to expect nothing.

***Education is not the filling of a bucket, but the lighting of a fire.

***To teach is to draw out.

***To teach them you first have to reach them.

***I can be a tool of torture or an instrument of inspiration.

***Common sense is not common.

***From the internet: After being interviewed by the school administration, the prospective teacher said: "Let me see if I've got this right. "You want me to go into that room with all those kids, correct their disruptive behavior, observe them for signs of abuse, monitor their dress habits, censor their T-shirt messages and instill in them a love of learning. You want me to check their backpacks for weapons, wage war on drugs and sexually transmitted diseases, and raise their sense of self esteem and personal pride. You want me to teach them patriotism and good citizenship, sportsmanship and fair play and how to register to vote, balance a checkbook and apply for a job. You want me to check their heads for lice, recognize signs of antisocial behavior, and make sure that they all pass the final exams. You also want me to provide them with an equal education regardless of their handicaps, and communicate regularly with their parents in English, Spanish or any other language, by letter, telephone, newsletter, and report card. You want me to do all this with a piece of chalk, a blackboard, a bulletin board, a few books, a big smile, and a startling salary that qualifies me for food stamps. You want me to do all this and then you tell me not to pray. "

***How wonderful it is that nobody need wait a single moment before starting to improve the world. Anne Frank

***The dream begins with a teacher who believes in you, who tugs and pushes and leads you on to the next plateau, sometimes poking you with a sharp stick called truth. Dan Rather

***Email from a parent: I wanted to take a minute to thank you for your hard work and efforts this year to ready the students for their exams and their future in math. I have watched many teachers "kill" time at the end of this semester with movies or other things, but you have really stayed on task with them and I really appreciate it. ...

Chapter Two
IT'S ALL
ABOUT US

Dedication

This section of my book is dedicated to my dear teacher friend Terry. He allows me to whine and then helps me re-focus and remember that it really never is about us!

IT'S ALL ABOUT ME

WHY ME? IF THIS were a book of fiction, it seems to me that knowing a little bit about the author would not be important. (I can hear my fellow English teacher, who by the way is one of the best teachers I have ever met, disagreeing with me, but I move onward...)

This is non-fiction, and I think that if I am to convince you that anything I say is worth saying, you need to know where I am coming from. I am no Ron Clark, Jaime Escalante, or Christa McAuliffe. (If you aren't familiar with those names, look them up. They were exceptional teachers.) I am a very good teacher and I love what I do. I will never be famous, and I haven't accomplished anything that will ever attract the national news. But I am a great example of a teacher who shows up every day, teaches her heart out, and has learned a lot about teaching over a long period of time. How I learned these things was through trial and error and a lot of divine inspiration. Some of the most important things I learned came from life experiences that changed my whole perspective. I need to share these with you before we get more practical. I have had a lot of "moments" in my teaching career. I always wanted to do this teaching thing and I have only rare desires to be a Wal-Mart greeter. Yet there are six moments in my life that I will call my defining moments that impacted who I am as a teacher. They taught me what no education course or book could have and I would like to share them with you.

DEFINING MOMENT NUMBER ONE

Shortly before the birth of my son, I returned to college to begin working on my master's degree. I was teaching during the day and going to school a couple of nights a week. I was doing well and headed for a degree in middle school education. I needed one more math class before graduation and the one I really needed was not to be taught that semester. My advisor convinced me that with my GPA, I was smart enough just to skip that class and take the next one. So without the pre-requisite course, I charged into the second course of some kind of Boolean Algebra. (It wasn't really Boolean Algebra, but I just love to say that word and I can't remember what kind of class it really was!) I was convinced that if I tried hard enough, I could learn anything. Well, I couldn't. Most of the content was formal proof and it was a little like trying to prove a geometry theorem without knowing any of the postulates. I really tried! I would go to class and try to pay attention, but none of it made sense to me and I had a hard time staying awake. I would study at home, but just ended up crying and whining. I actually failed the class! I had never failed anything academic in my life. I had always been a good student. Obviously it was the instructor's fault! It was one of those moments in life that seems devastating when you are going through it and of no positive value at all, yet it was one of the most instructive experiences of my life. Admittedly, it took me several years to find the silver lining in that situation. But it existed, and it was critical for my further improvement as a teacher.

So what did I learn from that academic crisis? That it is very difficult to keep paying attention to a teacher and trying hard when you are clueless as to what is going on. I also learned that staying awake in a class where the teacher might as well be talking in a foreign language is not that easy. But it did much more for me than that: It quenched my preconceived notions that all students who fail are not trying and all students who sleep in class are bored, tired, or apathetic.

DEFINING MOMENT NUMBER TWO

I had been teaching in a middle school on the "wrong side of the tracks' on the outskirts of Atlanta for five years. I was doing a great job. (I was full of humility.) My classroom was well managed, my lessons were creative and interesting, and I was sure that I had figured out all of that teaching stuff. It was the glory days of teaching when a good spanking did the trick, a phone call home got action, and the teacher was always right. It was in this state of happy euphoria that I had my first child. Right on schedule, I was back in the classroom after my allotted six weeks of pregnancy leave. But something had changed. It would never be the same again. Did I mention that I am an only child? Did I mention that I was all about managing a classroom and creating lesson plans? Did I mention that I was more into order than kids? Did I mention that I am bossy and have a control problem? Did I mention that before I had my son I never saw those students as individuals that needed me on a personal level just as much as my new son did? My perspective had changed. I had become a parent and I was no longer the center of the universe. I went from being a classroom-centered teacher to a student-centered teacher. It didn't happen overnight. I still had to work at making time to listen and wipe tears when I needed to be filing and grading papers. Becoming a parent created a major paradigm shift in my approach to teaching. It created an attitude in me that should have been there in the beginning. Sometimes I still struggle to stop what I am doing and give my full attention to a relationship issue when I would rather be dealing with a paper work issue. But I can now identify when that is happening, go against the grain, and be the teacher that I need to be for my students.

DEFINING MOMENT NUMBER THREE

After teaching middle school for ten years, I decided to give high school a try. My family was moving from North Georgia to South Georgia and it seemed a good time to try out my upper level mathematical skills. This switch from middle school to high school provided me with another very important "ah-hah" moment.

As I made the transition, I went from ten years of teaching seventh graders to two General Math classes of Juniors and three Sophomore classes of Geometry. At the middle school level, my teaching style included a lot of hands-on activities and entertaining. I constantly used peer competition and rewards. I was certain that this approach was too juvenile for high school students and began my year with seriousness and a dedication to prepare my students for the rigors of college. By Christmas break, I am not sure who was more miserable, the students or me. This new approach just wasn't my style and I had not ignited an enthusiasm for learning in my students. Second semester, I went back to entertaining and "bribing" and I was much happier and so were my students. They were a little concerned that an alien had taken over my body during the break, but they did not miss the serious side of me and were glad for the invasion! So what am I trying to say here? Everyone, no matter what their age, wants to be entertained. Nobody wants to be bored. Seniors in high school will work very hard just to get a peppermint if there is competition involved. They still like to dress up in costumes and sing silly songs. I thought that older kids did not need to have fun in the classroom. I was so wrong. The enthusiasm that young children have for learning is stifled by the notion that we need to get more serious and less "playful" as the child ages. I needed to get that "playfulness" back if I was going to succeed. You would have thought that I had learned my lesson, but twenty years later I retired from teaching in public schools and began teaching in a Christian academy. This was really new territory for me. I had no problems with the Christians, since I was one, but I did not know how serious I would have to be. My son advised me that if I wanted to hang on to the job, I better "lay low" for a year. Well I managed to lay low for about two weeks, before I realized that Christians like to have fun too. Never fear, I think I have it figured out now!

DEFINING MOMENT NUMBER FOUR

I was fourteen years into my teaching career, and I was well aware that I had made a positive difference in a few of my students' lives. (There is that humility again.) I was too young to think about the word legacy, much less to try to define mine. Then my husband of fifteen years died. He was one of those marvelously devoted teachers that taught with all cylinders wide open! His organizational skills were questionable and his penchant for properly spelled words was bordering on dogmatic and got him into trouble on more than one occasion! But oh, did he love to teach. Until he was gone, I never realized what an impact one teacher can have on so many. His legacy was the hearts and minds of the young people he had touched. After his death, I received many calls, cards, and letters from his students telling me what an impact he had on their lives. They continue to this day. The amazing thing about all of those communications is they had one common thread. Each one of those students was convinced he or she was my husband's favorite. He made them all feel like teacher's pets! I soon began to try to make my students feel that way. It couldn't always be done in class; just a wink, a nod, or a smile, might be all time would allow. The legacy my husband left was not only for the kids, it was also for me. I am a better teacher because of his example.

DEFINING MOMENT NUMBER FIVE

I was going into year number 21 and you would think that I would have it all figured out. Yet, I had so much to learn. I was attending one of those infamous teachers' conferences and I wish I could tell you what it was all about, but I can't. (This is that third in-service that I mentioned before that rocked my world.)What I do remember was the tables in the conference room. Each table had a nice tablecloth, glasses, pitchers of ice-water, complementary notepads and pens. There were even peppermints and chocolate. As I sat there, it occurred to me that when adults gather, we do everything we can to create a welcome environment. We don't fuss at them because they forgot their pencil or paper or textbooks. I had been trying every trick in the book to get my students to be prepared for class. At that conference it occurred to me that

I had never created a "user friendly" classroom. As usual, I went overboard at first. I had a classroom with flat top desks and separate chairs.
I arranged them in teams of four, and put brightly colored tablecloths
on them. I then put a cheap plastic pitcher and small disposable cups in
the center of each. The kids really thought that I had lost my mind. As
they entered the room, there were pencils for the borrowing and notebook paper for the taking. There were also extra textbooks. Well, the
water lasted about three days. (I should have seen that coming!) I do-
nated those pitchers to the cafeteria. Amazingly enough, however, the
table cloths lasted for several years, and I will always continue to provide
notebook paper and pencils. Later in the book, we will discuss this "user
friendly" classroom idea more. I know that some of you are thinking
that this does not teach students responsibility. I am all about responsibility and I agree. But there are other ways to do that and I vote for
spending my time on more important issues than forgotten writing instruments. It is all about choosing your battles.

DEFINING MOMENT NUMBER SIX

I taught middle school for ten years. Then I taught Geometry, Algebra II, and Trigonometry for twelve years. After ten years of middle
school math, I had to study a little to be able to teach the higher math
topics, but it was not too much of a struggle. Then in my 23rd year of
teaching, I had to teach Calculus! I had not had Calculus since I was a
Sophomore in college. There were no other Calculus teachers at my
school to learn from! It was me, Sir Isaac Newton and the textbook. I
reasoned that it would not be too hard since I had made "A's" in all four
of my college Calculus courses. Yet, I could not seem to get all of my
little brain cells working together. This was my, oh so personal realiza-
tion of that famous saying: "use it or lose it". It doesn't matter how
good you are at something, if you do not practice and review it, you
will not remember it. I hear that does not apply to riding a bike, but
trust me, I tried it and I can't do that now either. I had always tried to
review my students constantly but at this point in my teaching career, it
seemed even more critical. A continual repetition of what I wanted my
students to remember became an integral part of my teaching. I began

to review daily, not just before the test.

I need to make one other point here. I worked very hard that year and managed to teach Calculus, but I did not do a very good job. Every year I taught Calculus, I got better. I wish I had that first class back so that I could do some things differently, but they are gone for good. I do not think that any of them suffered permanent damage because I did not do a stellar job of teaching them. They knew my heart was in it and how hard I tried. Because I was real with them and did not try to cover my total lack of understanding, they worked with me and we all taught each other. I have found that as I have aged, my brain is not as sharp as it once was. I am now much wiser and know a whole lot more than I did when I started teaching, but I can't always pull facts out of my memory banks when I need them. I am getting especially bad at names. I have two choices, I can get bitter about growing old or I can admit my flaws, enlist the help of my students during my "senior" moments and move on. I choose to ask for help and continue my craft. If you have the respect of your students, you can overcome brain lapses and old age!

IN SUMMARY I HAVE LEARNED:

1. Be a "student-centered" teacher. They are why you do what you do. The paper work and bulletin boards will get done in their time!

2. It is hard for a student to concentrate and focus on what they are clueless about. Apathy sometimes just means a lack of understanding.

3. No matter how old they are, students still want to have fun. Make your classroom an exciting place to be.

4. Treat every student in a way that will make each one of them think that he or she is your favorite.

5. Make your classroom user friendly. Provide supplies and concentrate on the teaching.

6. Review important concepts constantly. If they don't use it, they lose it!

7. You won't be perfect, and as you get older you will be less perfect. Never take yourself too seriously. Laugh at yourself and keep on "keeping on".

PRE-PLANNING PONTIFICATING

It is the end of the first day of pre-planning and I am very tired. I hate it when I get like this but my feet hurt because they are not used to being in "real" shoes all day and my neck hurts because the stress has already started.

When I got out of bed this morning, I was excited and ready to face a new year and change the world. This will be year number 37 for me. I still get excited. I am always ready for the year to be over in May, but about July 10th I am ready to start again. I miss the structure and most of all I miss the interaction with the kids.

So I began the day with great enthusiasm and a faculty breakfast. The usual "teacher rituals" began. I thought I would croak if another person asked me "how my summer was", and yet, amazingly enough, I found myself asking others the same question! (I am not sure if it is habit or just not knowing what else to say.) I was so ready to go hide in my room and play with my bulletin board letters. I did redeem myself on my hall as I genuinely inquired about the other teacher's families and what was going on in their lives

Fortunately, I teach at a Christian school and after breakfast, we begin with praise and worship. I find it very difficult to remain irritated when I am praising the Lord! My attitude was now adjusted and things were going fine with the first few "motivational speakers". Every faculty needs to start their year off with a word of encouragement, but we were all getting a little antsy after a couple of hours. It never ceases to amaze me how educators who train teachers to give kids breaks and to never "talk" too long, expect teachers to sit still for two hours for a meeting. My ADD was kicking in bad at the end of the first hour. Like most of the folks being held captive by speakers, I just wanted to get back to my room and do my own thing. I had already spent a couple of days before pre-planning getting my room in order but there was so much left to do and the looming open house was weighing heavily on my mind. My enthusiasm was still pretty high and the potential for accomplishment was still there until I hit my first source of real irritation. I have a great deal of patience with the kids, but I seem to have a real short fuse when it comes to adults. It was almost time for us to be dismissed for some much coveted "room time", when the predictable faculty "questioner" kept asking those irritating questions that hold every one up and make you want to commit pre-meditated murder. I guarantee you that there will always be one on each faculty and if that person goes away, someone will pop up to take their place; kind of like a class clown!

Okay, so now I am irritated at anything that I perceive is wasting my precious time! That certainly includes the announcement that came next. We were all to schedule an appointment with an insurance salesmen and annuity representative. "Benefits" are wonderful and I would never want to have to do without them, but why do we have to listen to the same speeches and sign the forms even if we have no changes or do not want them?

Once again we are presented with a wonderful meal and I see real hope for a productive afternoon since my appointments with the "Benefits Brigade" are not until Wednesday. My first order of business was to make sure that everyone in my department has all of the textbooks that they need. It seems that everyone did, except me. No books for my AP Calculus class or my SAT Prep class. Oh well, Socrates and Plato didn't use textbooks either. My request in, the only thing left to do was to hope that "UPS" was swift.

Having run into one snag and surviving with relatively little damage, I decided to work on some paperwork. Unfortunately, that was a serious mistake on my part. My laptop had been replaced with a desk top but no one had time to transfer my files from the old hard drive to the new one. My "floppy" wouldn't talk to the new computer and the computer wouldn't talk to the network and therefore no printer.

By this point, I was wondering how I was going to change the world when I couldn't even change computers. It just seemed like everything I tried to do was running into a dead end on that first day of pre-planning. All of that sparkle and enthusiasm was being crushed by reality. I had two and a half days until open house and what I shall fondly refer to as the parent stampede. (More on that later.)

PRE-PLANNING PONTIFICATION DAY TWO

I arose this morning determined that nothing was going to downgrade my attitude, not even that pesky computer. We had a great breakfast, the kind that sticks to your ribs. How could the day go sour after that? Two words: in-service! (Or is that one word?) Once again in-service was scheduled before we had time to finish our rooms. The meeting before lunch did not go well because the presenter let everyone do their own thing during computer training and for most of them that meant just talking. I felt that they were being downright rude! Have you ever noticed that teachers are some of the worst listeners? I did learn that I could go into Google and punch in a math topic with Power Point and download some great ideas. I had my one good idea, but it took two wasted hours to get it!

Praise the Lord for administrators that understand the primal need of a teacher to get their room ready for open house! The afternoon in-service session was canceled and we got to work in our rooms! I am almost finished decorating and organizing and ready to start on paperwork. I prepared my syllabi during the summer and Xeroxed them during lunch so I would not have to wait in line. With my room almost ready and my syllabi done, I can relax a little. The stampede is imminent but the cavalry is ready!

Twas the Week before School Starts

(I wrote this poem so long ago that I cannot remember why in the world I wrote it but I think it does a good job of explaining the atmosphere during pre-planning.)

Twas the week before school starts
And all thru the school
Not a teacher was ready
The principal was losing his cool.

The bulletin boards were hung
By the teachers with care,
In hopes that the students
Wouldn't re-arrange the letters there.

The counselors were cornered
In their offices with fear
Fifty new students to register
And Monday is almost here.

And Ms. Jones with her gold star
And Mrs. Todd with her phone,
Were calming the faculty
Who threatened to go home!

When out in the hall
There arose such a clatter
The entire 300 wing came out
To see what was the matter.

Away to the hallways
They flew like a flash
Science teachers jumped over desks
And stumbled over trash.

The commotion in the hall
Of the new polished floor
Gave the sound of a disaster
As they looked for the nearest door.

When, what to their curious eyes
Did appear,
But four rooms, when last year
Only two had been there!

But out in 100 hall,
An even more startling sight
A neglected old bookroom
Turned into offices overnight.

More rapid than consolidation
The changes they came.
New places, new people, and
All those kids names.

Now syllabus, now textbooks,
Now plan book and correlations,
Now lockers, now insurance
Now aspirin, and heart palpitations.

From the rear of the campus
To the 400 hall
Moaning and Groaning
Could be heard by all.

As clean floors before the students shoes do die,
The Tuesday smile has turned to a sigh.
Back and forth to the classroom the teachers do fly
With memos and lists and new things to try.

And then, in a twinkling
When things finally get done
Another task appears
An even bigger one.

As homeroom lists are checked
And so are duty rosters
Down the tubes go good spirits
What hostility it fosters!

Dressed not in shorts,
Professional from head to foot
Teachers clean and scrub
Hauling bookcases and shoveling soot.

A bundle of textbooks
Flung on their back
They look like neatly dressed bag ladies
Getting ready for the pack!

Their eyes how they water
Their feet how they swell
Their calves are like jelly
And the new gray hairs do tell!

Their brave little mouths
Are drawn up in a pout!
If the fire alarm rings
What's the quickest way out?

The stump of the pencil
Thrown carelessly behind their ear,
Roll books and rosters are filled
For another year!

They have such broad shoulders
And try to bear the load
But the promises made last year
Have turned into a toad.

It's discouraging and tiresome
When all doesn't go well
But they keep it in perspective
In spite of themselves.

A wink of their eye
And a twist of their head
Soon helped them remember
They had nothing to dread.

They spoke many a word
But got on with their work.
And filled the rooms with great learning
Even if their knees did jerk!

And laying their palms
Under their chin
They all secretly admitted
They'll do it again and again!

They sprang to their rooms
And to their classes they'll teach
The chalk dust will fly
And excellence they will all reach.

And they're heard to exclaim
As they bow down and pray
Happy Monday to all
But when is pay day?
~ Lizzy Sutton

"P" DAY

Today is "P" day; "P" standing for parent! Most people call it open
house but that is so boring. My room was ready. This is the day that the
teachers have to keep enthusiastic body language going for at least five
hours and juggle three conversations at once without hurting anyone's
feelings. If the truth be known, I am sure that the parents aren't looking
forward to "it" either. Some of them have several kids at the school and
it must be a nightmare for them to get around to all of those teachers

and get all of those supply lists and fill out all of those forms.

In preparation for the big day, I gave some thought about the appropriate thing to wear. I want it to be professional yet not too dressy. I don't want it to look like I am trying too hard. I wear my regular pre-planning clothes with the intention of changing about an hour before open house begins. There are two flaws in this plan which I did not anticipate. Flaw one is that so many parents came early this year. There were at least ten that were not able to bask in my true beauty! The second flaw was the fact that I did not try my pantsuit on ahead of time. How silly of me to think that gaining six pounds over the summer would not affect the fit of my outfit. This dilemma could not be corrected and although I was uncomfortable all day, I did not embarrass myself. (When you are teaching, good quality comfortable shoes and clothing cannot be underestimated as a teaching tool!) I was not alone in my discomfort. Many of the younger teachers who have spent the last four years of their lives in flip-flops were in real pain.

Open house began and the race was on. It was really great to see all of my former students and meet lots of knew ones. The attendance was great and now I am sorry that I dreaded it so much. I guess it is just the pressure of the whole thing that sets me on edge. It was supposed to be over at 4:00 but the parents were having so much fun that they did not leave until 4:40. I was tired with a capital "T" and went home and took a two hour nap.

MY CLASSROOM BUBBLE

Today should have been really good. It is the last day of pre-planning with no open house pressure and the morning free to work on lesson plans. I got to school early to finish my last minute Xeroxing and the machine did not even jam once. It was going to be a great day! ! ! After four days of unnecessary preplanning worry and stress, all of which I created for myself, I was calm and just enjoying the day. I got out my "first day file" and went over my list. I have a check off list so that I can remember what I need to do for each class. Once I get back into the rhythm of my teaching, I don't need daily reminders, but a "cheat sheet" never hurts until my procedures get "tattooed" back on my brain.

At lunch the math department met. It is easier to discuss business over Chinese food and we have made it a tradition. It almost makes you look forward to a department meeting. The meeting was good and once again ended in a timely manner. Could the day get any better? Yep! It was 1:30 and I was totally prepared for the first day with kids. All of that panic and "poor me" was for nothing. It is every year; you think that I would learn...Every year I have gone thru the same ritual of pre-planning. I show up a week early, worry as hard as I work, and create undue stress for myself. I am always ready by the first day and no parent has ever refused to put their child in my class because I did not have time to put up that last poster!

I should have known not to get smug about being ready because at 1:30 all of those stress-free thoughts and that blue bird of happiness pooped right on my head. It was a case of lack of planning on the part of someone else creating a crisis for me and I was really irritated. Let me explain. I am very blessed to be at a Christian school and I do not take lightly the importance of time spent with God. Nevertheless, I am very protective of my Advanced Placement Calculus time. I will leave out all of the gory details, but the administrator in charge of chapel came by my room and told me that a pilot discipleship program at our school would require a 50 minute lunch every Friday. This is a good thing. It, however, cuts 20 minutes off of my AP Calculus class every week. This may not seem like a lot but we have already lost ten minutes a week because of modified block scheduling and we are about to lose another 20. In other words, that would be 18 hours a year or three and a half weeks of instruction missed. That is a huge chunk of time from a class as intense as AP Calculus. I could not believe that we had not been told this sooner. I was so mad, I was about to burst so I just did what any dedicated adult female would do, when he left, I cried. (I think part of this was the fact that I was 58, it is the end of the week, and I got up at 4:30am.) I was like a toddler that was mad and tired all at the same time.

I declared myself useless for the rest of the day and went home. I am sure that this will get fixed somehow, but I get so discouraged that things have to be fixed when with a little fore-thought they would never have broken. I am very type "A" and have very little patience with other educators that are type "Z", especially when they are making decisions that impact what I do in the classroom.

Therefore I have vowed to get into my "classroom bubble" and teach with my whole heart and just do what I am told. I so believe that faculty input is important before administrative decisions are made, and get so frustrated when no input is requested in the planning stages. It is even more frustrating when input is given, agreed upon, and then ignored! But for my own mental health I am going to try very hard to mind my own business and stay out of the politics! (I wonder how long that will last?)

DAY ONE, 2009

It is the first day of the year and I am always so excited and ready to go. At least I was on Friday, but today I am lacking the passion for my profession that I so believe in. I am still reeling from getting the wind kicked out of me on Friday afternoon when I found out that the Chapel coordinator wants to take 20 minutes out my AP Calculus class each week. My blood pressure climbed all weekend. I know that I have to let it go. All day I kept saying 'classroom bubble", "classroom bubble"... (When general things about school drive me crazy, I try to form a classroom bubble and just focus on the good I can do in my classroom without worrying about the rest of the school.) It is much healthier in that bubble! If I can't get out of this funk what I do isn't fun anymore. I need it to be fun because I plan on teaching forever! I have always been excited on the first day of school so I really needed to buck up and not let other people steal my joy! ! !

Not being able to shake my irritation at Friday's events did not relieve me of my responsibility to appear to be excited and perky as my first class entered the room. One of the most important things a teacher should be is a good actor. I did indeed put on an academy award performance. As the day wore on, I began to feel better and the light began to appear at the end of the tunnel. I perked up and soon it wasn't an act anymore. Now I am sure that you are wondering why I am sharing my deep inner thoughts and problems with you. It is very simple. Being a good teacher is very complex and involves so many factors. One of the most important is not letting how you feel get in the way of what you are supposed to be doing.

Good mood or bad mood, I still needed to be efficient as I got thru the first day. To help me stay organized, I had several "cheat sheets" prepared. I always post a bell schedule somewhere that I can easily see. It takes me 180 days to learn one and then they change it! I really think that they do it to irritate me! ! ! I also have a first day check off sheet that I use to keep up with what I should tell each class. It is simply a list of items like: introduce self, call roll, issue textbooks, pass out syllabus, discuss number one rule, etc. By each item is a slot for each class so I can check it off as I do it. I try to stay away from all of the rules on the first day. It is boring for them and I want to start new material. We discuss my rule number one: Mrs. Sutton must have fun. After that, when someone breaks a rule, we stop class and discuss it and they get mercy because they are the first rule breaker on that particular offense. The first week is full of a lot of grace and mercy. I don't get mean until week two!

I have not established my rhythm yet and it is a bit awkward, but I will get in the swing of things. I teach five different classes and on the first day I can not even remember who is walking in next with out my cheat sheet so I refer to it often. The rhythm will come with time.

First Day Butterflies

Actors get them when they enter stage right.
Gardeners love them when they come into sight.
Children are delighted and squeal with such glee.
In a good teacher's tummy they often run free.

They usually start in the middle of July.
When the holiday is over, and the heat begins to fry.
They signal the beginning of a new year ahead.
When enthusiasm is high and only a little is to dread.

The kids really have mixed feelings.
The first day of school is coming quite soon.

For some it will be wonderful.
Some are already counting the days until June!

So how many years will you actually teach?
Before the butterflies stop and calmness you reach?
Will they ever go away and leave you alone?
Will you ever be calm on that first day you teach?

Of course not, you silly! What fun is in that?
Those butterflies mean more than you know!
They mean you care about what you are doing,

And not just putting on a show!
So take several deep breaths and say a quick prayer.
Put your enthusiasm on high and try not to stare.
Only one or two will walk thru the door
with purple tattoos and red spiked hair!
And as the years roll by...
And you look back to the beginning...
The butterflies will still be flapping...
Only now you will be grinning...
~ Lizzy Sutton

THROUGH THE CLASSROOM DOOR

As I walk down the hall of my school and peek thru the windows in the classroom doors, I get a quick glimpse of what is happening, at that moment, in each classroom. I quickly form impressions in my mind, some of which are true and some that aren't. As I walk by, I see a student sleeping in the back of the room. You know, the one with drool on his paper and his watchband imprinted on his forehead. In another room I see students raising hands, anxious to be the one to offer the correct answer! In another room, I see a lot of glazed looks as the students watch a DVD. The last room on the left looks like a zoo. They are all out of their seats, throwing paper air planes around the room! And is it possible that the teacher in E-6 is just sitting at her desk while her students are passing notes and experiencing "free time"? The students in another room appear to be spellbound, while the teacher demonstrates a concept with manipulatives. Yet, further down the hall, I am shocked to see two or three students with I-Pods plugged into their ears or outwardly text-messaging, while an oblivious teacher lectures.

If you were an administrator what conclusions would you draw? Could you make a judgment call by just walking down a classroom hall and looking thru the classroom doors on one occasion? Of course not! !! But if you walked down that hall day-after-day, and had the same impressions, would your judgment be more appropriate? A paper air-plane experiment in a science class may appear very non-productive from the window, but it is a wonderful activity for gathering data and analyzing aerodynamics. Maybe the student with the drool on his paper is usually a very attentive student who spent the night in the emergency room with a younger sibling and the teacher is just trying to cut him some slack.

What makes chaos in one classroom meaningful, while the same activity in another room is ineffective? I think that the answer is determined by the "teacher persona" of the instructor in the classroom. Two teachers could be given exactly the same lesson plan and one presentation could be a disaster while the other is wonderful. Moreover, two teachers could be given exactly the same lecture notes, and one lecture would hold the students' attention, while the other would put them to sleep. So what is the difference? It is that "teacher persona" again! You will see the phrase "teacher persona" pop up several times in this book. It is a hard thing to define, but I am going to try as I discuss the many different "jewels" that makes up the personality of an effective teacher. Teaching persona is almost like one of those things that it is hard to describe but you know it when you see it!

In an effort to find this illusive "persona", let's make the journey down that hall again and again and peek thru the classroom doors on several occasions. Let's take what is good and share it with all of our peers and let's take what is bad and see that it doesn't become part of our teaching repertoire. Let's learn from each other and be all that we can be for our students. Let's get rid of the glazed eyes and the I-Pods and fill those classrooms with a level of instruction that is compelling and rewarding. Let's make chaos work for us, not against us, and let's reclaim the classroom!

CLAIMING THE AUTHORITY

One of the most important parts of developing your "teacher persona" is to establish your authority. It is very critical that you are the master of your ship, the king or queen of your castle, the benevolent dictator of your small island... You get the picture. Do not let anyone steal your position of authority! There are very obvious thieves of this very important abstract commodity, but there are also subtle ones. The subtle ones come in every shape and size and are often in disguise. Your authority in your classroom is what allows the learning to take place. If you have absolute authority and cannot teach a single concept, you are not an effective teacher, but you will have an orderly classroom. If you could teach anything to a "brick wall", but you have no authority in your classroom, chaos will reign and very little learning will occur. Finding the proper balance is critical to your success. There are four major thieves of authority: students, administration, other teachers, and the most insidious of all, yourself.

STUDENTS

The most obvious stealers of authority are the students. They are the grand masters. They have had lots of practice and if you are teaching high school, some of them pretty much have the "art" perfected. Undermining the teacher's authority is "job one" for some of these kids. The problem is that they have so many ways to break us down. The bravest openly challenge us in class. They question our every move and try to "attack" every "system" we have. They are probably the least dangerous to us, because they define the battle so easily. We begin by talking to them individually and drawing the "line in the sand". They usually just bide some time, waiting for us to dare them to cross it. And cross it they will! At that point we must soundly defend our ground. The "gauntlet" has been thrown and the whole class is watching. We must act swiftly, decisively, and firmly. Whether it is detention, a trip to the office, or a phone call to the parent, swift, public action must be taken. An overt challenge to our authority must not be coddled or ignored.

The less obvious thieves are those students who are not so brave. They whittle away at your strength a nick at a time. Some of them even do it by "niceing" you into oblivion. The best example I can think of is that of a young fellow named Chuck. I previously had him as a student in Algebra I and then he had a first year teacher in my department for Advanced Math. Chuck is a good kid that everybody loves. He is an average math student and a very kind soul. Nevertheless, he is somewhat of a practical joker and has a talent for distracting the class and the teacher. The new teacher was frustrated because Chuck was making a game out of making things "disappear" in her classroom. It started with one insignificant thing that managed to re-appear later, and had mushroomed to an almost daily event that made her question her own sanity. His joy and skill was that he was so good he was able to remove things right from under her nose, without being caught! She had been patient with him for much longer than I would have and it was getting worse. She finally talked to him, let him know his "joke" had gone too far and not to touch her "stuff". He stopped for a while and the issue seemed to be resolved. Then Chuck got brave and took her cell phone and used it to call his number. At this point she assigned him detention and called his parents. Chuck had not heeded her warning, and had definitely crossed the line. She had tried to nip his little "occurrences" in the bud before they became big, but he had to learn the hard way.

Young teachers have to make a special effort to maintain authority. Students often see them as "fair game" and in-advertently undermine their authority by trying to make them friends. The smaller age difference makes this the natural thing to do, but it is very dangerous ground to walk on. Teachers should be caring mentors, but they should not be friends.

ADMINISTRATION
Another "authority breaker" comes from the direction of the administration. Sometimes the problem arises as the result of direct intervention, and sometimes it is just a lack of proper communication.

Requested intervention occurs when a teacher requests that an administrator come into his/her classroom to "talk to the class". This is a clear admission by the teacher that he/she has lost control and is out of options. It should always be an absolute last resort. A teacher has so many discipline tools at his/her disposal that administrative intervention should be avoided if at all possible. If the administration is taking it upon itself to enter the teacher's room to correct problems, without invitation, this is even worse. I always believe that a teacher should be consulted if there is a problem, before an administrator tries to fix it. How bold you are in handling an administrator in this situation depends on the receptiveness of the administration and how much you need the job! There is really little you can do besides respectfully talking to your superiors and hoping that it will stop. If it will not, you need to create such a managed classroom that they do not see the need for intervention.

Communication is another authority stealer, especially, if it breaks down between the administration and the faculty. A good example of this is rule enforcement and dress code issues. At every school that I have ever taught, there have been so many un-resolved dress code issues that it makes you want to make the students come to school in choir robes. Rules are clearly printed in the handbook, yet no matter how hard you try, the students are able to "interpret" them to their advantage. When the adults do not communicate, the kids end up "playing" one of us against the other and we all end up looking like idiots. Over and over again, a faculty member has sent a student to the office for a dress code violation and the kid wisely corrected it on the way. The student is then sent back with no consequences because the principal or the secretary said the student was "fine. " Teachers must be backed up and communication should be so clear among the faculty and staff that the students get consistent responses and do not play one adult against another. To do otherwise undermines the authority of the teacher.

OTHER TEACHERS

Other teachers do not usually intentionally try to create situations that undermine your authority, but some of their well-meaning actions end up doing just that. I have a first year teacher in the math department that I have been mentoring this year. She is a good teacher on her way to being a great teacher... She works hard, is anxious to learn, and seeks the advice of veteran teachers. In a middle school team meeting, a discussion on discipline was going on and she brought up the fact that she had one class that was having some behavioral issues. One of the veteran teachers present, who teaches the same kids in another subject, proceeded to go back to her classroom and tell the students in that class that they needed to behave for the new teacher. This was so wrong on two counts. First of all the veteran teacher broke a confidence. A teacher should be able to say anything at a staff meeting, without worrying that it "gets out. "

Can you imagine how the new teacher felt when her kids found out that she had been talking about them? Secondly, how did that teacher feel about someone trying to manage her classroom behavior from outside? I am sure that the veteran teacher meant well, but had she thought it through, she should have offered advice and let the new teacher handle it.

If you have watched any television at all, you know that when law enforcement does a chase scene and gets into another jurisdiction, they always alert the proper authorities in that city, county, state, etc. Each agency has its own jurisdiction and they usually co-operate and do not take over each other's territory. That is the way it should be for teachers. I am afraid that I must admit that I am guilty of breaking this rule. If I see an infraction in the hall, I am likely to follow the student into a classroom and if I see other bad behavior in the classroom, I am likely to deal with it myself. Every teacher is responsible for all behavior in the entire school, but it should be done properly with due respect for the teacher in that "territory". For instance, if I see a student chewing gum in the hall between classes, and catch up with him in Mrs. Smith's classroom, it is appropriate for me to ask the student to "spit out the gum". It is not appropriate for me to then turn around and ask all of the students in her class to spit out gum. It is never appropriate for me to interrupt her class and directly address a student. It is appropriate, if it is urgent, to ask her to step outside, tell her the problem, and then ask her if she would like for me to talk to her student.

Probably the most hurtful of all is when students want to talk about another teacher in your presence. It is natural for us to want to hear what the kids think about other teachers, and as long as the conversation is complimentary, it is okay to listen. When the discussion becomes negative, however, it is time to put an end to it. Let the kids know that if they are going to bash other teachers, they are not going to do it in front of you. Also, encourage them to go talk to the teacher(s) they are complaining about and see if the situation can be resolved. You do not model mature behavior when you encourage students to "bad mouth' other teachers. It is setting a terrible example for the students and undermining the authority of that teacher.

YOURSELF

The difficult part about us undermining our own authority is that we fail to recognize that we are doing it. Every time we lose our temper, start nagging, or let the students know that they have gotten on our last nerve, we are putting another chip in the granite façade known as authority. Your authority means your ability to not only control others but to also control yourself. And as we all know, it is usually easier to control others. It was Peter the Great who said: "I've conquered an empire, but I've not been able to conquer myself. " With that in mind, let's look at some areas where we need to exhibit our self control.

Controlling our tempers is absolutely necessary if we are to maintain our authority. Some students make a career out of "pulling a teacher's chain". If you can be manipulated by your students, you are not in control. I am not talking about righteous anger here. There are times when we all need to let the students know that we have had enough and we cannot be tested anymore. But it is very important that we model how to manage anger for our students. Losing our tempers becomes a sideshow for them, not a lesson in anger management.

Nagging students is just about as effective as nagging our husbands or wives. Sooner or later, they will just learn to tune us out. Basically they have heard it all before and didn't listen the first time. It is like all of those Charlie Brown cartoons where the teacher is talking in nonunderstandable utterances. That is what our students are hearing when we keep nagging about the same things. I fight against this all of the time. We need to save our "nagging" for what is most important so they won't tune us out before we start.

Another very subtle way that we sabotage our own authority is when we "take care of business" on school time. I once knew a middle school teacher who was so addicted to romance novels that she could not leave them at home. She would teach a concept, assign a worksheet, and read while the students did the work. She read her books during tests, breaks between classes and at lunch. I have seen teachers write their bills, make "business" calls during class, and do work for their graduate classes. What kind of message does this send the students? If you are trying to teach them to multi-task and do several things in a mediocre manner, you will probably make your point. But you are also showing them that they are not your first priority and that you are not totally dedicated to teaching them, and their education is not really important.

I remember when I was in high school, I had an English teacher who had been a soldier in France during WWII. The course was supposed to be half grammar and half literature and it ended up being two-thirds WWII and one-third literature-mostly European. The goal of the students in the class was very simple. When Mr. Ross starts teaching English, especially grammar, ask him a question that will get him started on his "war stories". With some teachers it is getting them off track talking about their children or grandchildren. With other teachers it is begging for free time, or a study period or to put the test off another day. The basic premise is the same. Your authority is being subtly challenged when the students can get you off the course you had planned for the class period. Don't let students dictate what will happen in your class during any given time frame. They will see you as weak and under their control. You are in charge of your room and responsible for how that precious time is used. Use it wisely.

THE PERFECT TEACHER

The word perfect implies a level of teaching that we can only hope to reach and is probably the improper term to use because no teacher is perfect. Nevertheless it is the word I use when seeking the opinions of others as to the desirable characteristics of a teacher. It says so much in so little space.

I have used this terminology on several occasions in hopes of putting together a profile of the perfect teacher. I believe that it is very important to seek opinions from several sectors and therefore I have grouped my research into four categories:

1. The perfect teacher according to present students.
2. The perfect teacher according to college students. (referring to their primary and secondary teachers)
3. The perfect teacher according to parents.
4. The perfect teacher according to administrators.

I asked about 350 teachers, students, and parents at several workshops and meetings what they felt a perfect teacher was. I posted large sticky notes around the room and asked them to respond to all four categories. I knew that I would get both serious and silly answers but I wanted them to have the freedom to respond however they wanted. You can imagine that there were many repeats. Below you will find some of their unedited responses:

THE PERFECT TEACHER
ACCORDING TO PRESENT STUDENTS

free days
loves me unconditionally and gives no homework
no homework
no tests, makes learning fun
sense of humor
lots of recess
fun
always fair, curves every test and only counts homework that I did
respects, loves, and listens to them-won't shame/embarrass them
listens and is available
likes me best

THE PERFECT TEACHER
ACCORDING TO COLLEGE STUDENTS

accountability
teaching me to write

making me prepared
thoroughness
teaches study skills
made sure I learned-didn't let me fall behind
proud of me
hard, but I really learned
loving enough to push them always to the next level
made them work hard to get good grades and knew they were loved
even when pushed
held them accountable and made them work

THE PERFECT TEACHER
ACCORDING TO ADMINISTRATORS
flexible-adaptable
dependable
competent
organized
loves children
consistent
on time
innovative
paperwork on time
excellent with PR. with parents and students
does what they are asked
goes over and beyond
available and consistent

THE PERFECT TEACHER
ACCORDING TO PARENTS
cooperative
passionate
understanding
giving 100%
fair
no homework

stays in communication
nurturing
loves my child
competent
gives everybody an A

No teacher will ever be perfect, but if we resist the qualities our present students jokingly posted, and try to emulate what our former students, parents, and administrators want, we will be as close as we can get.

CIRCA 1968

When I was in high school, I began making a list of the things that I was and was not going to do when I became a teacher. I watched my teachers and took copious notes. I was making plans for my classroom, four years before I had a classroom. I lost those notes and those lists sometime between high school graduation and college graduation. Oh how valuable they would have been to me if I had hung on to them!

Fortunately for me, I still remembered the very good teachers and the very bad teachers. Those are the ones that teach you the most about teaching. I remember very clearly my math teacher in the ninth grade. Her name was Mrs. Matthews and she was a preacher's wife. The valuable lesson she taught me was to never wear the same outfit more than once in a week. There were some times during my poverty stricken first years that I could barely scrape up five outfits, but I always managed to do so because of Mrs. Matthews. She always wore dry clean only suits and she would wear them three consecutive days, and then send them to be cleaned. You could set your calendar by her outfits. I don't remember anything else about her or her teaching style but I do remember those suits. The most important lesson she taught me was that the kids will remember you so make it positively memorable.

Then there was Mrs. Kaiser, who taught chemistry. She was a delicate little creature that could not control her class. She taught chemistry that year and I learned nothing. She let the students run all over her and spent too much time with her back to the class, oblivious of what was going on in her room. She was a very sweet lady. She taught me some very valuable lessons about what not to do in a classroom. Lesson number one was not to talk to a class until you have their attention. Lesson number two is that without control, there is no respect. Lesson number three, face the class as much as possible.

My favorite high school teacher was Mrs. Shumate. She was my senior math teacher and she was all business. She was tall and slender and wore those glasses on the end of her nose with the chain around her neck. She always wore a shirtwaist dress and was always neat and clean. She was pleasant and kind but she was all business. I learned a great deal of math from her and a great deal about being an effective teacher. She expected much from her students and she usually got it. There was no doubt in her classroom who was in charge and she could look at you down her nose, through those glasses, and you would tremble in her presence. Very few were brave enough to cross her. She taught me that a little healthy fear is a good thing if it is backed up with love and concern.

Another memory that pops up very distinctly is when one of my female teachers was in front of the class and her slip fell down! I do not remember her name, but I do remember her composure as she quickly pulled it back up and continued teaching. No one dared laugh or say anything and she kept on like nothing had happened. I have used this technique on several occasions, fortunately never with a wardrobe malfunction. But I have, however, run into furniture, spilled things, and had inappropriate comments come out of my mouth. I have learned to keep on teaching like nothing happened.

There is one teaching technique that I could never use, but sometimes I would love to. I had a band director named Mr. Luke. He was an excellent director, and the band won many awards. He was very serious about the performance of his bands and directed with a passion. The band members, however, did not always take their practices seriously. Once in a while there would be laughter from the band, usually from the percussion section. Mr. Luke would give them one warning and when they did not cooperate he would send his baton sailing thru the air aimed straight at the offender. I never saw him hit anyone but he always came too close for comfort. What if he aimed to miss and missed his aim and hit someone? When I think of this now, it makes me cringe. I don't think he could get away with that today. I tried something similar during a quizbowl practice one day thinking it was harmless and it backfired. I used a water bottle and sprayed my kids that would not be quiet during practice. I found the most perfect water bottle squirter that had a long steady stream, I did not see how anyone could get hurt. Unfortunately when I used it on Chris, he got water under his contact and had to leave practice to fix his "eye". I took the water bottle home to spray my plants. Unlike Mr. Luke, I learned my lesson and I never attack students with anything but my orange bat (more on that later). Trust me, I would like to throw that baton and hit a few of them between the eyes, but I don't.

YOU NEED THREE THINGS

"To succeed in life, you need three things: a wishbone, a backbone, and a funnybone. " (Reba McIntyre)

When I read this quote, I knew that I had to put it in the book, because it says so much. I am sure that she did not mean it especially for teachers, but it says so much about the "perfect teacher" in so few words that I cannot resist adding it to my never ending quest to find out how to talk about the perfect teacher. I was always a little bit confused when the Bible quoted Jesus as saying we should be perfect and then turning around and telling us that we are all sinners and can never be perfect. Then I was taught that the definition as Christ used it meant more about gaining spiritual maturity than being "without flaw. "

Being the "perfect teacher" is more about growing into professional maturity when dealing with students and content, than never making a mistake. If no mistakes made a perfect teacher, there would be none and I know several perfect teachers. I now think of perfect more like an old beat up hammer or screwdriver. They have paint chips and dents and scratches on them, but they are "perfect" for their job. You would never put up drywall with a wrench or use a hammer to turn a pipe. The actual tool may not be in perfect shape, but it is the best one for the job.

So why the quote? I strongly believe that the three things in the quote are essential for a great teacher. The wishbone is all about a vision for our students. It is about believing in our students and what we can do for them. It is "knowing" that what we have to offer is more than just the material that we teach them. It is high expectations and knowing that what we do now will have a positive impact on our students' future.

Backbone is critical to teaching as long as you know when to use it and when to lose it. There are so many issues that it is important to stand strong on. Academics is one of them, and yet even with curriculum there are times to back down. I think one of the most important skills that a teacher can develop is to know when to stand their ground and when to be flexible. Every situation is uniquely different because every person is unique. There can be no exact list and no one word of advice that fits all situations. The closest that I have ever heard to good advice on standing your ground and having "backbone" is to come down hard on what challenges your authority and take everything else with a grain of salt.

There are many good teachers lacking in the area of sense of humor who are still effective in the classroom. I believe, however, that a well developed sense of humor, is a very valuable trait for teaching success. When you are very good at it, it becomes spontaneous and even better! It diffuses difficult situations and adds life to the classroom.

When you have the right combination of wishbone, backbone, and funnybone, and know how to mix them, you are close to being the perfect teacher!

TEACHER BLOOPERS

It is so hard trying to maintain a perfect façade. It takes up so much energy that I learned a long time ago to give it up. It wears you out and irritates everybody else. I would like to share with you one of my many erroneous instances.

The first example concerns an academic class where we had been discussing a questionable problem. I like to call it a "math fight. " They insisted that something was a rule and I insisted that it wasn't. After the class was over I tried to find a counter example to help me win my side of the "math fight". I got out my textbook and not only could I not find a counter example, I was wrong about it not being a rule listed in the book. It was plain as day. I felt like a real idiot. Sometimes I do not know why they let me teach! I admitted my stupidity to my class the next day. I have found it much smarter to fess up than try to pretend that you did not make a mistake or worse yet, make excuses. I knew that some of them had spent time trying to find a counter-example and I wanted to reward them. I asked everyone who had spent any time working on the problem to stand up. About seven kids stood up and I asked each one how much time they had spent. Five of them had just spent a few minutes and I asked each of them to fill out a SHAZAAM (more on those later)! The other two had spent almost an hour and I gave them both, ten points on their next test grade. When you make a major mistake, I find it helpful to make-up for it in a major way.

THE DAY I TAUGHT SPANISH

Mrs. Ole was out today and a substitute was found who could cover every period but fourth. I have a planning period fourth and therefore I found myself teaching Spanish I. I took four years of Latin in high school but that was 200 years ago and I was not real good at it then. The instructions for the class came to me on a sticky note and even though they were not written in Spanish, they had been written hurriedly and were a scrambled up mess. They were not even all written facing the same way! I was handed an overhead transparency with about 30 Spanish words and the sticky note. There was no roll and I did not even know who was going to show up for the class. Now don't get me wrong, I like a challenge, but this was more of a challenge than I felt comfortable with. It was definitely testing my "who is in control here" mentality. Nevertheless, if I were to succeed, I had to give the appearance of knowing what I was doing.

28 students showed up for class. I have 26 desks in my room! I scrambled for some folding chairs and we continued. I passed around a piece of paper and had everyone sign it so I could give Mrs. Ole a roll. While this was happening we played the name game so I could learn some of their names. This took about ten minutes and let them see that I could be fun, yet task oriented. I collected the roll and instructed the students to clear off their desks except for a writing instrument and two clean

pieces of notebook paper. (Once again this process made it look like I knew what I was doing and established my control despite my ineptitude with the subject matter. It also used up at least two minutes!) I then placed the transparency on the overhead and turned it on. I instructed the students to copy down the words, skipping one line between each word. I then told them that I would set my timer for 10 minutes and they must be finished copying the words by then. I would not leave the overhead on for more than 10 minutes. (I did not tell the students, but I was not willing to donate my overhead bulb time to the foreign language department.) Students who complained that they could not see, were allowed to sit on the floor in the front of the room until they had the list copied. (This activity made a great stalling tactic while I continued to try to interpret the rest of the instructions off of the aforementioned sticky note.) When the timer went off, two students had not finished copying the words and the rest of the class was working quietly on homework for another class or dozing.

At this point, I gathered everyone back together and handed the first kid who had not finished copying the words the transparency with the instruction to pass it onto the second kid when he had finished. (I proudly called them by name because of the name game!) I then walked around the room to make sure that everyone had done what I asked and skipped a line between each word.

I then asked each student to take each vocabulary word and write a sentence with it using one of each of the verbs that were given to me on the sticky note. I didn't now what the word meant since it was on the sticky note, but we were going to use it because we were told to and the kids helped me figure it out. The next crisis came when the kids said that they needed their Spanish Dictionaries, which were in their classroom. I did not want them to go get them because they would be too noisy and take too much time so I told them to look up the ones that were in their book and leave the other ones blank. They worked well. Those who finished early, continued to work on homework for another class. No one was brave enough to ask to go to the bathroom and they generously allowed me to bask in the illusion that I was in charge and that I had taught Spanish!

I am sure that at this point you are asking yourself: "What is the point?

" The point is that even though I did not know what I was doing, I quickly took control of the class and maintained order throughout the period. I claimed the authority and gained the respect of students that I did not know by showing them that I was in charge and firm but flexible. I sought their help and respected their knowledge of the situation. I showed them that I cared enough to learn their names. I established a reputation with them that will be helpful when I teach them in the future.

FIRST IMPRESSIONS

If I were a student who did not know me, and I saw me for the first time, I would not be impressed. I am old, short, plump, and I have three very prominent moles on my face. In fact, once I found a caricature of myself in a student desk and the moles were bigger than my nose! No one has ever called me beautiful and about the best they come up with is "cute". I am very careful about my appearance, but once again "neat and clean" is about all I can muster. (In my defense, I do have some drop dead eyelashes.) To add to my less than admirable physical characteristics, I am the dress code Nazi and kids duck into doorways when they see me coming. I am a strict rule enforcer and kids who I do not teach, start out fearing me. They perceive me somewhat as the wicked witch of Hansel and Gretel fame.

Once a student is in my classroom, however, the problem solves itself as I dazzle them with my winning personality and sparkling persona. There is usually one or two in each class that I cannot win over, but I work on them all year and hope that I can soften their hearts towards me. If I have taught their brothers and sisters, they fear me less because they have heard about my antics and that I am mostly bark and little bite.

The key to my success in gaining respect with those inside and outside my classroom is reputation. The first year that you start at a school you do not have "it" and you have to build "it". "It" takes time. You gain a good reputation by coming up with the right combinations of fair and firm; consistent and flexible; passionate and calm. You communicate well and often with parents. You do little things to let the students and parents know how much you care about them. You are kind to the maintenance men, the secretaries, and the cafeteria workers. You participate in activities and you show your human side. You teach well and encourage. You watch out for the teacher's lounge. It can sometimes be a negatively charged atmosphere of whining and gossip. You speak positive things and try to give Little Miss Mary Sunshine a run for her money. You resist the temptation to be a "know it all". There is very little as annoying as someone who thinks they have all the answers. Humility is beautiful. Be reasonable in your expectations.

As the years go by, your reputation builds and if you stay at a school long enough your job gets easier because if you have done your homework and built a good reputation, a lot of problems are solved before they are ever conceptualized in the student brain. The kids learn quickly who not to mess with. A good reputation becomes a special blessing when you mess up, and you will. Once you have developed a history of caring, dedication, and competence you will be blessed with a great deal of forgiveness when you "slip off of your pedestal. "

TRUE CONFESSIONS

One of the most dangerous pitfalls that I still experience as a teacher is the need to make up for the perceived wrongs done to me when I was in school. I think that this is a very important issue to address because I suspect that I am not the only teacher to have to overcome the negative impacts of my school career. You may not have that problem, but I urge you to pay attention to your own management techniques and see if there might be something in your behavior towards your students that lurks from your past! To explain this concept fully, I need to tell you a little more about myself. I will "confess" a shortcoming and then I will tell you how it has affected my teaching. I believe that some of these characteristics have made me a better teacher, but most of them have not and I have to be very careful. Let me start with a positive:

PAST: I was never popular in school. I was short, wide, and shy with my peers. I was an only child who did well around adults, but struggled at socialization with other kids. I had a few friends, but never felt like I really belonged to any group. I was always a "good" girl and was very much a people pleaser. (I still am!) I was never picked on or given a hard time, I just never felt significant.

PRESENT: I usually cheer for the underdog! I watch out for the kids who seem "insignificant" and I try to be their encourager. I make sure that, in my classroom, they get as much positive attention as possible. I pay special attention to kids who seem to fit the profile of "Footprints in the Snow", and try to be especially kind to them and make them feel important. This is one place where I think my experience as a teenager, makes me a more compassionate teacher. A teacher friend of mine, Marvene, put it this way: "If you have ever been the underdog, you never forget what it feels like to be one. "

PAST: In high school, I never dated and I had already started my career as a "work-a-holic". I was envious of kids who chose to have fun instead of working hard. I did not know how to loosen up! Mind you, the kind of fun I am talking about here is good, clean, legal fun. I resented the fact that my perfectionist tendencies required me to spend hours on a project while I knew that others threw theirs together at the last minute and still received an "A". They were having "fun" while I was slaving away and they still got an "A"! What was wrong with that teacher? Didn't she know quality when she saw it? ? ? ? Oh how I wish that I had spent more time having fun and less time trying to be perfect!

PRESENT: I would like to tell you how much I have changed since my school years but I can't. As I have aged I am relaxing a more, but I still have a long ways to go. I tend to be very jealous of my class time. I am way too serious sometimes and hate it when kids miss my class for school activities and family trips. I think that my class is more important than pep-rallies, walk-a-thons, and class meetings. Students who miss my class because they were "having fun" usually get the evil eye on their return. I have to work hard on managing this… The other day in Advanced Placement Calculus, two of my seniors were called to the office near the beginning of the period. They did not come back until class was over. I had developed a new concept and was very irritated that they missed class. If you think I am serious about my other classes, you should see my level of intensity in an Advanced Placement class. It is downright scary. One of the young men who missed class sent his girlfriend back to get his book bag, because he did not want to "face" me! (I wrote him a note later, letting him know that he would be allowed to live!) I think it is important that I not waste class time and that we work hard, but I do not want my students to be scared of me. I work on this constantly. I can usually loosen up on the outside, but sometimes I am still seething on the inside that "fun" is more important than "work" to the average teenager. IMAGINE THAT!

PAST: I was very much a rule follower. I dotted every "i" and crossed every "t". It always bothered me that some students "got away" with so much and never got caught. I had a great deal of judgment in my heart and I was too immature to realize that it was hurting me a lot more than the people I was judging. It just seemed so unfair to me that I worked so hard and did everything "right" and those who were lazy or broke the rules got away with it more often than not.

PRESENT: As I have matured, I realize what a horrible personal trait judging is and I try desperately to overcome it, but it is still a struggle. Although it is hard to argue that following rules is a bad thing, I can see that my obsession with this has not always been a good thing in my dealings with students. Kids who don't follow the rules really irritate me! I am very picky about gum chewers, litterers, and sidewalk ignorers! Those students who think that the rules do not apply to them drive me crazy and I have a tendency to over enforce the rules. I must say in my defense that I treat every student the same, I expect them all to "toe the line. " To a degree this is good. The students know that I am consistent and I do hold them to a high standard. Yet, I do go overboard at times. I give lots of warnings, yet I sometimes have trouble picking my battles. I know that some "rule breakage" has to be ignored, especially in some unusual discipline situations. (We will talk about those in the discipline section.)

So much for my inner battles; I hope that you get the point. We all have baggage and we do not need to bring the negative aspects of it into the classroom. I still struggle with this, but age and wisdom have helped me identify my "demons" and I am very conscious of the way they guide my perception of my student's behavior. I work diligently to keep them under control.

The Wow Factor

I have just experienced one of those events in life that I like to categorize as "one of the hardest things I have ever had to do". It can't top burying my husband at the ripe old age of 43 or delivering my only child into the arms of the Marine drill sergeant on Paris Island, but it sure is high on the list. I watched a teacher lose her job because she did not have the "WOW" factor.

As a department head, I found myself in a situation where I was asked to be present when a teacher was informed by the principal that she would not be receiving a contract for the coming year. Understandably, she wanted to know why. He told her that her instruction was good but she did not communicate well with the parents and that there was the perception that she did not care about the students. She asked for specific instances and he could not give her any, just a string of parental requests that their children not be placed in her class. She wanted to know what she was doing wrong and let him know that she was willing to fix "it". Unfortunately, he could not tell her what "it" was.

It was all I could do to keep from crying as I watched her struggle to understand what she had done wrong. It was difficult enough to hear the words "your contract is not being renewed", but I think it would have been a little easier if there had been something more concrete to offer her when she asked why. After she left the room, the principal looked at me with sad eyes and said: "She just doesn't have the WOW factor." The wow factor seems to be the new "buzz" word on our campus, and I have been told by the principal that I have "it." I am glad that I have "it" because I sure do want to continue to teach!

So what is the WOW factor and how can one get "it" if you do not already have "it" and how do you know if you have "it" and why is "it" so hard to define? The last question is probably the easiest to answer so I shall start there and work my way backwards. First, I will try to define the wow factor, then I am going to try to explain how you know if you have "it".

I was not going to look it up because I doubt that Mr. Webster defines the WOW Factor, but then I decided that it would not hurt to look up wow and see what the dictionary says. Wow is an interjection, "an expression of surprise, wonder, pleasure, pain, etc". It is a noun; something very amusing or a great success. That seems to be an appropriate definition, since I think that most teachers are a combination of pleasure and pain, but I don't think that was what the principal was talking about.

I think what the principal was talking about was the idea of wonder and surprise. In my class it is usually wrapped up in two statements: I *wonder* what she is going to do next. And there is always a great deal of *surprise* that I do not hurt myself falling off the step that allows me to reach the top of my Promethian Board.

Wonder in a classroom is a little more complicated than curiosity about what will happen next. No matter what subject you teach, you need to find those things in your curriculum and technique that create the element of wonder. Every lesson should have some element of the mysterious or "aha" factor. It might be a little bit of "math magic" that you can perform with your "magic cape" or it can be a history fact about which president got stuck in the bathtub. If there is nothing in your lesson that can be "wonderful" and sometimes there is not, then your presentation needs to add the wonder. (I would like to say here that I believe that almost every lesson has some bit of history of the development of the topic or something catchy to make it more interesting to the students, but it takes a great deal of time to research. Would that be a great thing for the students to do?)

The more I think about it the harder it is to separate wonder and surprise. Isn't surprise, just wonder that has caught you off-guard? Isn't surprise a great way to keep students on their toes and engaged? Surprise does not always have to be a pleasant experience either; it can be a wake up call! If my class is looking bored and sleepy, I usually surprise them with a quizlet, a "stand-up", or a bad joke. (Bad joke does not need an explanation and "quizlets" and "stand-ups" will be explained later.) I have a book of the corniest riddles imaginable and once in a while when things are at a lull, I just pull it out to get them focused on what I am saying again!

Wow is not only in the classroom, it is also in your handling of the students all of the time. It is surprising them once in a while by showing them a little more of yourself, without falling into the trap of being distracted from the lesson to talk about your dog or your children. It is showing up at ball games and plays and spelling bees. It is picking up something that they dropped and letting them see the passion that you have for what you do. It is admitting you are wrong and saying you are sorry. It is never losing your temper and knowing when to take action and when to just take note. It is being predictable and yet spontaneous.

There is so much more to being a WOW teacher and I hope that you will find lots of "it" in the rest of the book...

BAD HAIR DAY

I had a department meeting this afternoon and we were discussing observations. As the department head, it is my responsibility to observe all of the members of my department, fill out an evaluation form, and discuss my visit with them. In the past I have always asked them when they want to be observed and they knew when I would be coming. This is nice, but almost anyone does a good job teaching when they know in advance that they are going to be observed. If we all planned and taught every day like we knew we were going to be observed, education would be a beautiful thing! ! !

I asked my department how they felt about surprise observations. You could tell by the looks on their faces that unannounced observations were about as popular as rattlesnakes at a baby shower! One of the braver members asked: "What if we are having a bad hair day? " My reply: "There are no bad hair days for a teacher. " They still were not thrilled about the idea, but knowing that they had no ground to stand on and that every day should be a "stellar" performance, they agreed that I could "pop in" any time. In all fairness to them, I invited them to do the same, and come visit my classroom whenever they liked.

Is it possible to teach 180 days a year and never have a bad day? Of course not; life throws too much at us to expect that we would be able to be wonderful all of the time. Nevertheless, as teachers, we have an obligation to "put aside" our personal issues and teach as many days as we can with "gusto". If the "gusto" is just not there, let the kids know, and do the best that you can, but still teach.

About once a year, the flu goes around and everyone just holds their breath and waits their turn. I learned a long time ago to get a flu shot and ride out the storm. After many years of teaching, I have a very strong immune system and I usually only get a small dose of digestive discomfort when it is "my turn". Unfortunately for me, my small dose came in a week that I just could not miss school. I had a big quiz bowl tournament on Saturday that involved the state championship and my school was hosting the tournament. No one could make the plans and orchestrate them but me. (O. K. that statement is not true, but it was the way I felt at the time.) I had two major tests scheduled for the week in honor's classes and as Ricky told Lucy: "I still had a lot of "splanin" to do. " I just could not be sick! ! ! On my planning period I ran to the store and bought Ginger-ale and saltine crackers and determined myself well. I was nauseated and weak but I forged on. I have found that desperate times call for desperate measures and I did the un-thinkable. I sat the whole time during each class period. It would have been a terrible day to be observed but the point is that no instruction was missed, even if it was delivered with no enthusiasm. I picked problems and sent the kids to the board. I sat in a student desk in the back of the room and directed. I ate saltines and sipped Ginger-ale. I went home and went to bed and the next day I was still on my strange diet, but I was back in front of the class and manned it with a little bit of enthusiasm.

The point here is that even though instruction was poor for a brief time, it was still instruction. No matter what is going on in our lives, our job is to teach and teach we must. We should be like the mailman in our dedication; neither sleet, nor snow, nor dead of night, nor bad hair days…

GOOD HABITS, BAD HABITS

I like to lead teacher in-services and am delighted when I am given an opportunity. I have sat through so many of them that tell you how to teach, but do not model what they preach. I do not like being bored anymore than the kids and I resent an in-service where I feel that my time is being wasted. It is always a challenge to me to teach my workshops in a way that is both entertaining as well as informative. I want the participants to be so mentally involved that when it is over, they want more and cannot imagine where the time went. As difficult as that is, it is how our classes should be. One workshop that I did was entitled

"Breaking Teacher Habits". It was based on the work of Grant Wiggins and Jay McTighe. To get their brain juices flowing I gave my faculty some homework before we met as a group. I requested that they fill out a form which asked them to list their five best teaching habits and their five worst teaching habits. I instructed them to just come up with the first things that they thought of and I would not tell them what we were going to do with them. I did promise anonymity. The workshop turned out great and we had fun looking at their best and worst. I am not going to take the time to analyze their responses because most of these, good and bad, are discussed somewhere in the book. I just thought it was very instructive how their responses turned out.

GOOD HABITS

Using bell to bell instruction

Ability to mesh humor and good questions and ideas into my classroom "talks" (not lectures)

Lots of formative assessment-not allowing students to "just fail" a quiz; I have lots of "learn from it" assignments

Providing organized, detailed presentation of info

Giving students "thought" questions to expand their thinking skills

Encouragement

Using power point for notes

Using vocabulary through speaking and testing it with quizzes

Questioning students to help them connect previous knowledge or ideas

Questioning students, trying to include all students

Asking frequent questions about previously taught material

Keeping the students engaged

BAD HABITS

Using writing assignments to assess a students' level of proficiency

Not assessing student understanding often enough

The assumption that the kids know a key concept/idea/person/

event w/o my explanation of it prior to beginning a new topic
Apathy toward student engagement in class (they're 18! They
have to take ownership of their own education eventually).
Spending too much time on one concept or idea
Getting into a "rut" or routine.
Answer my own questions before giving time for students to answer
Poor judgment of time. Thinking we can accomplish more than
is realistic.
Impatience with things that interfere with classroom time
Students reading aloud is boring. I don't do this as much as I used
to however students need to read.
Lack of toleration
Teaching the same way all of the time

I have not cleaned any of these up. They are recorded as written. I
think it is always valuable for us to assess ourselves in terms of what
we are doing right and what we are doing wrong. I encourage you to
make a similar list for yourself. Analyze it and make another list of what
you can do to correct your bad habits and enhance your good ones.
There is no purpose in identifying our weaknesses if we are not going
to try to improve on them.

If you are really brave, have your students evaluate you. At the end of
every year, I pass out a form giving the students an opportunity to evaluate me. I created the questions myself but I leave space for them to
write comments. I ask them not to put their names on it and I have a
student pick them up and put them in a manila envelope so that they will
be more willing to be honest. If you choose to try this, and I encourage
you to give it a try, get ready to have your feelings hurt. As I read through
my evaluations I find a lot of good things, but I also find comments that
are unkind and unfair. The good outweighs the bad, but it still hurts. I
take all of the comments and use them to see what I can do to improve
my classroom. If a comment is negative, I analyze it carefully to see if
there is any truth in it and if I find some, I immediately try to figure out
how I can change my behavior. Often, I have gotten the bonus of general
information such as what kind of cheating is going on in my room or if
it is time to highlight my hair as my roots are offending someone! Re-

gardless of the possible pain, student evaluation is a valuable tool for improving classroom management and instruction.

IS IT ME OR IS THIS WORKSHOP BORING?

I attended a teacher institute that I was really excited about. It was at a state university; it was sponsored by a respected professional educators' organization; and it featured a nationally known speaker. I figured it had to be good; not to mention the fact that it was a treat for me to be treated like a business executive. On arrival I was greeted by a very gracious lady, given a nametag, and the neatest "satchel" that I have ever received as a freebie. I got a copy of the speaker's book, a great pen-highlighter combination, and best of all a pad of sticky notes. I was then treated to a great breakfast buffet, a great lunch, and two great snack breakouts. The restrooms were great. (I was really impressed because if you wanted a little flush you pulled the handle up, but if you needed a big flush, you pushed the handle down!) I enjoyed being on campus and the general atmosphere. I enjoyed talking with my peers and sharing ideas.

My problem was that I was not impressed with the speaker or his topic. In my opinion he was too "big picture" and I did not feel like I took much "of substance" away with me. I will admit that he had great jokes. My real problem is that I did not sense that anyone else was dissatisfied with his presentation. Usually when I am in a workshop and the speaker, in my opinion, is not effective, there is agreement communicated among the participants in very subtle body language during the presentation and then outright complaints during the break-outs. Not so today. No eye rolling, no heavy sighs, no negative comments during breaks. I even went so far as to peek at other peoples evaluations at the end of the day to see if they were all that happy with what was presented. They were. The ones I looked at gave him excellent all the way. I wasn't sure what to do, because if I was the only one in the room that felt like he had not delivered the goods, maybe it was I who had the problem. I gave him "very good" on everything, even though I didn't believe it.

On the way home I began to question myself. Maybe he was great and I expected too much. Maybe I am getting old and grumpy. Maybe I am getting befuddled and confused. Maybe I have lost my zest for learning.

Maybe all of that food, affected my thought processes. Maybe the rest of the crowd was impressed because he was nationally published and it takes more than that to impress me. Maybe he was too abstract and full of educational jargon and I am all about the practical and the useful.

By the time I made it home, I convinced myself that it was the latter. It couldn't have possibly been me…

PERSONALITY

Once again, I am going to defer to Mr. Webster and his definition of personality. I rarely go wrong with him, and being a math teacher, I find it wise to check his definition, before plunging forward like I know what I am talking about. Webster defines personality as the complex of characteristics that distinguishes an individual. Your personality often sets the tone for your classroom and more or less sets the boundaries for your approach to teaching.

Before I get into teaching personalities too deep, I would like to share an excerpt from a wonderful little antique book entitled *The Teacher's Speech* (pgs 15-17).

> Let us dismiss at once the unworthy notion that your personality is already fixed by nature or by habit and cannot be altered. There is not defense for the person who excuses all his faults and deficiencies with "I'm always like that," or "That's just my way. " Why should you be like that? All the patterns of your behavior can be modified in any direction you choose. A sour, acid temper can be sweetened. An annoying mannerism can be eliminated. An evil tendency in character can be corrected. Even that most integral aspect of your personality-your voice can, by patient practice, be altered and improved.
>
> But, you may say, would you have me pretend to be what I am not? Would you have me adopt a manner that is unnatural for me? Would you have me be insincere?
>
> Distinguishing your "real" self from your pretended self is by no means so simple a matter as you may think. Of the

various fronts which you show the world, how is it possible to tell which is "real", which is most genuinely you? Is it that ingratiating, cultured, efficient-seeming personality you present to a superintendent when applying for a position? Is it that sweet and playful self that emerges when you are romping with your neighbor's baby? Is it that savage disposition that erupts in the heat of athletic competition or of some bitter quarrel? Or is it that relaxed and informal and careless self that emerges in the privacy of your family circle? We cannot say. Perhaps all these selves are real. In any case there is not insincerity in putting forward your best self in the classroom. There is not harm in pretending to be sympathetic and patient when you don't really feel that way.

We all practice poses and pretenses, and many of them are quite legitimate and even desirable. Would you condemn the polite fictions which we all practice on our hosts or guests: "So glad you called. Do come again," and "How do you manage such marvelous dinners? " To refuse to pretend is often to be discourteous and unsocial...

...Our task is to discover the ideal personality for teaching, and then sincerely try to make ourselves into its likeness. Remembering her responsibility for the reputation of her profession before the world, as well as the proneness of children to imitate their elders, and the effect of personality upon efficiency, every conscientious teacher, whether recruit or veteran, ought daily to ask herself, "What kind of personality do I wish to present before my pupils and before the community? "

I love this quote. It may be a little too old fashioned and for some, but I think it gets to the heart of what I am trying to communicate about teacher personality. The critical issue lies in the fact that there is no one personality type that makes a good teacher. I have done so many workshops where the participants will tell me that what I suggest is wonderful, but it just does not fit their personality. My answer to that is always do what works for you, but be willing to take a few risks. One of the best teachers I have ever worked with never did anything I would label "exciting" or "out of the box". He lectured all of the time. He was a military veteran who taught history and managed to keep them attentive through engaging narrative and his love of his subject. No one ever accused him of having a sparkling personality but the students loved him, respected him, and learned a lot.

As the quote suggests, however, it is important to "tweek" your personality to become a more effective classroom teacher. My personality is not always what I want to portray in the classroom. Sometimes my personality is too judgmental, controlling, and organizationally obsessive. These are not character traits that I am proud of and I certainly do not want to project them into the classroom. Therefore, I have developed a classroom persona that "overrides" the things about my personality that are not attractive. I have plenty of good personality traits, so I do not feel that I am being "untrue" to myself, I am just "making adjustments".

SLEEP DEPRIVATION

Last night I got three hours of sleep. My home has finally sold after an eight month wait and I have less than three weeks to move out. Although not totally unprepared, I am in rush mode and I spent most of last night packing boxes and making lists in my head. I am very stressed about the move and all of the details and I have not slept well for a while. I feel awful and I probably should have stayed home but my kids need me and here I am. At the beginning of each class I explained to my class why my cell phone would be on all day. I was waiting for a word from my realtor. I believe that I should follow the rules just like the kids. I do not walk on the grass, drink coffee in class, or use my cell phone at school unless it is my planning period. I know that I am a dinosaur and most other teachers do not agree with this, but I believe that the kids respect me more because of it.

In AP Calculus I knew that I would not be able to think straight. I announced at the beginning of class that all I wanted to do was cry! That got their immediate sympathy because I NEVER have said that and they are used to seeing me as a pillar of strength. I told them that I knew how to take the derivative of a polar equation when I left school yesterday and that I will know how again tomorrow, but right now I am staring straight at the formula and my brain will not wrap around it. I wrote it on the board and they helped me! They were great and even came up with a neat way to remember it that I would have never thought of. I struggled all period to focus but THEY KEPT ME ENGAGED! I am so proud of them and very glad that I had confessed my state of mind. We got a lot accomplished and I feel like we did not waste time just because I was a lousy teacher today.

PERSONA

Every teacher has a persona. It is how we act in the classroom and how we appear to our classes. Webster defines persona as an individual's social facade or front. It is how our personality is interpreted by those around us. As a teacher, it is very important to start on your persona early and develop it as you gain experience.

Persona helps us cover up our "inward awkwardness", and a lot of other things that we need to "not reveal" to our students. Sometimes we have to overcome our personalities and let our persona take over. I think that the best way to communicate my point is to use a specific example of how persona has had to mask personality for me. It is painful for me to share my failings in print but I believe it is very important for everyone to understand that no matter how good a teacher you are, you will have issues to overcome.

Let me begin with "justice". It is critical to your effectiveness that students perceive you as "just". The problem is that some teachers have a vague sense of what is "just" and some have an overactive need to see justice dispensed in every situation. I am in the last category. As a young teacher, I believed it my mission to be sure that all transgressions were identified and dealt appropriate consequences. I was working so hard on being "just" that I was sucking the fun out of being a teacher. I had to tell my personality to back off and let my persona reflect a little more common sense in this area. I could not "catch" every wrong and I had to learn what to let go. This works in the other direction too. If you are so laid back and lacking in justice enforcement that your classroom is a zoo and everyone is having too much fun, you better start dispensing some consequences. We all need to consider that we might have an area where our personality needs to take a back seat to a new persona.

Persona is not only a "cover-up" for our insecurities and personality flaws, it is also what makes us unique and creates our reputation among the students. You can develop a good persona or a bad one, but trust me you have created one. I have deliberately created a persona of "tough and firm" for my classes, but when I work with individual students, they know what a softy I really am. I just don't want to appear that way before the class.

In *Up The Down Staircase* (pg. 76) there is a note written to the new teacher that is simply signed "dropout":

> In my 16 year life span so far I've had my share of almost every type of teacher but one I shall ne'er forget was in elementary (6th grade) because with her I had to watch my peas and ques. She was so strict she gave us homework every night and tried to pound it into our heads, but it's the way she did the pounding that makes her different. She took a real interest and brought out our good and bad points. She stayed in every day after school so we could come in and ask her questions about the work. She militarized us and sometimes whacked us, but for all of her strictness a strange thing happened at the end of the term: every one gathered around her and kissed her. But high school seems harder, speeches, speeches, that's all we hear.
>
> Dropout

Now here is a teacher with the right kind of persona! She was tough and yet loved. Her persona is something that she has created and that has evolved with her teaching experience. Your personality is what you bring to the table, your persona is what you develop. It is also important to note the last sentence of this note. Students don't pay near as much attention to what we say as how we act. They get tired of "being talked to".

Your persona is the attitude that you create, which in turn creates the attitude that the students have towards you. Paying attention to your persona can go a long way to adjusting your personality. And the best news is that we have a chance every year to start over and create the type of persona we want, though we may have some reputation to overcome. I love this passage from the book *The Heart Is The Teacher* (pg 94):

> It has always seemed to me that discipline, at least in part, depends on the attitude that teacher brings to the classroom. My attitude-whether good or bad, sound or fallacious-might be phrased as follows: "I am the teacher. I am older, presumably wiser than you, the pupils. I am in possession of knowledge which you don't have. It is my function to transfer this knowledge from my mind to yours. For the most efficient transfer of knowledge, certain ground rules must be set up and adhered to. I talk. You listen. I give, you take. Yes, we will be friends, we will share, we will discuss, we will have open sessions for healthy disagreement-but only within the context of the relationship I have described, and the respect for my position as teacher which must go with it. " This attitude was instinctive to me. It was not until late in my teaching career that I ever thought to put it into words.

Every year I start out with a similar "speech" to my classes. I am no longer a sharp, young, whipper-snapper. My brain cells are slower than they used to be and I have never been the smartest in the room. But I make sure that they know that I am wiser and in charge! As I age, I find that my sense of humor compensates for most of my miss-steps. I do not have to be predictable, just reliable. I think that every teacher should teach in a room that has a large wall of mirrors in the back of the room like a ballet class. If we could see how we appear to our students, we might be more willing to make changes in our delivery!

I would like to end this discourse with one word of caution. You can spend years developing a persona that works for you and lose it in a moment. I once worked with a wonderful science teacher who is dedicated to her students and works very hard at her craft. The students love her and understand that she has a passion for teaching science. They view her as smart, hardworking, and a caring teacher. One of her low level classes, despite her best efforts, was not working hard and showed no willingness to put in the effort to pass. On one occasion, she lost her cool and blurted out in class: "This class disgusts me. " She knew the minute that it had escaped her lips the damage that it had done, but it was too late. She never "got that class back". They still viewed her smart, and hardworking but their view on her caring, before the slip of the tongue, would never be the same again. All she could do was treat them with respect the rest of the year and start over with a new group in the fall.

Persona is a fragile, evolving façade that should be carefully cultivated by all teachers. It presents to the students the best that we have to offer! I saw a Verizon commercial on TV that says a lot about a teachers' persona. "You are not here to fill up space, you are here to fill the room. "

BIFF VALIDATES MY EXISTENCE

I just got off the phone with Biff. I taught him Algebra II, and Trigonometry several years ago. He is still in graduate school at The University of Georgia. He majored in history, but was told by some educators that he would have more success in finding a job if he would add math education to his repertoire. Before he could add middle school math to his diploma he had to pass a "middle school" math test. He decided to try to take the test "cold-turkey" just to see how he did. He called to let me know that he had passed the test on the first try and that the things that I taught him in Algebra II came back to him as he took the test. He remembered the radical monster and my funny pictures of LIOF after all of that time!

It does my heart good to hear success stories from my former students. Biff's story even gets better. He called me about a year later and asked me for advice. He was hired as a long term substitute and we spent a lot of time on the phone helping him with his Pre-algebra and Algebra 1 classes. After about two weeks of teaching, the principal called him in and asked him to interview for a position for next year. He called me and we practiced some interview questions. He got the job and then there were several calls with more questions. He was trying to pick my brain for as many classroom control tips as I could think of. He is very happy as a middle school math teacher and he had no idea when he was in school that he would ever be teaching math.

I constantly get the question, "what is this stuff good for? ". I try to answer them honestly but much of what I teach will not be used by the students after they take their last math course in college. In fact in class today, one of my students asked me what logarithms are good for and I went through my usual speech of how we really don't use them as much as we used to because of the calculator. I showed them the one kind of problem that you could only solve with logs, realizing that most of them would never have to use that skill in life. I then continued my speech stating that the discipline of mathematics helps them learn to think logically, a skill which will transfer to all of life. They usually don't buy it and one of them made a comment about how sad my life must be, torturing teenagers with useless information. I then tell them that my existence is not sad and the story of Biff... You never know when you are going to become a math teacher.

DIGNITY LOST AND REGAINED

Today is one of the days during the year that the younger students love, the upperclassmen endure, and I dread to see coming. It is the Walk of Faith. It began many years ago as a fund raiser. The kids used to get pledges and then walk to earn them, thus the name "Walk of Faith. " It has evolved into a huge fundraiser where letters are sent out, relatives and friends send in donations and we take off a day of school and play. We have the first two classes as usual, but since I teach seniors, they do not come to classes as they are helping with the elementary students. We then proceed to the football field where we spend the day on big jumpy things and playing.

The faculty is told to be out on the field and to supervise. This year we had to reschedule the Walk of Faith Day twice because of the weather and it messed up our parent volunteers and we all had to help with the different activities. I am just not cut out to help students strap themselves in and out of a harness that allows them to jump on a small trampoline and flip in the air while being held up by an octopus "arm". I spent two hours doing this and then walking around picking up litter. I was pretty much miserable. I know that I should be a better sport about days like this but I just pray to get through them quickly. When I was younger, I actually enjoyed days like this, so I try very hard to pretend that I am having a good time and I hope that I put on a good act. In fact last year, I actually did have fun for a little while anyway.

There were plenty of parents last year and all that the faculty had to do was walk around and generally supervise. A few of us "teacher types" decided to be supportive and have fun and we tried a few of the larger jumpy things. I was really having fun without acting, until we came to a huge blow up slide that we felt relatively safe in climbing up and sliding down. Several of us got on at once, and lined up horizontally at the top of the slide. Just as we were about to go down, one of the employees of the jumpy thing company yelled at us and told us that there was too much weight on the slide and for us to get down immediately. Just let me say that he did not use his polite voice. Now this "employee" must have been almost 19 years old and I am confident that he did not even have a two year associate's degree. He was talking to five teachers who had bachelors and masters degrees and treating us like we were ignorant juvenile delinquents. This did not bring out the Christian side of me. My immediate response was to put him in his place and let him know that we did not know there was a weight limit and we were just trying to have fun. I was well aware that there were a lot of students around and it was very important how I reacted. Therefore, against all instincts, I looked the young man in the eye and said "yes sir". I felt that this was a very important way to react in front of so many students whom I am trying to influence to react in the appropriate way to authority. After I did my best to reclaim any shred of dignity that I had left, I stayed on the ground and vowed to start a new diet on Monday.

OLD DOG, NEW TRICK

For you to understand my enthusiasm for the day, I have to give you a little background. Our school got a new headmaster. He had a strong desire to empower his teachers to dream big and teach innovatively. Being the Calculus teacher, I was approached about having a Promethian Board hung in my classroom. Not knowing what a Promethian Board was, I inquired, and found out that it was a "smart board" with an attitude. If you believed the sales pitch, it practically taught without the teacher. I was not in favor of this particular innovation because I did not want to be replaced in any way and I was not interested in any device that would have me turn my back on the class. I expressed my concerns and as a result, in August there were four Promethian Boards in the school, but not in my room.

I thought that I had escaped the technology wave until pre-planning when we were all corralled into an in-service on the boards. For about an hour we were shown the glories of the "board". None of this enlightenment included its value in a mathematics classroom. I was not motivated and was glad when the in-service was over. Now don't get me wrong, I am not one of those old dogs that cannot be taught a new trick, but this old dog needs to be convinced that it is worth the brain cells needed to adapt and so far no one had succeeded in convincing me that this new-fangled board was for me.

I was totally content in my ignorance and I was taken unawares when I received an email from my principal letting me know that on October 1st I would be going to an all day in-service for the Promethian Board. Now there were basically two things wrong with that email. Thing number one is that I don't like to miss out on a day of instruction with my kids. I am rarely out and never by choice. The second thing wrong with this email was that I had thought that I had made it perfectly clear that I did not want anything to do with these boards because I would have to turn my back on the students and here I was being shipped off to "board boot camp". In a very respectful way, I let my principal know that I did not believe that I was the right person to go and offered to let someone else take my place. That ruse did not work, so I tried the "I will just embarrass you with my lack of technology skills" approach, but he was on to me on that one too and I couldn't think up another excuse.

So on October 1st there I was on school day 37, not at all where I wanted to be. I did manage to teach my College Algebra class before we had to leave the campus. I did enjoy the ride with my colleagues and it was nice to see how the real world functioned while I was in school all day. On arrival, I was given a menu to select what I wanted for lunch and encouraged to pick out anything. This day was not going to be too bad after all. The presenter was very personable and the morning went very well. I was very impressed by her presentation and the highlight came when an accessory sheet was passed around and there was a special device called a "tablet" that would allow me to work with the board without having to turn my back on the students. From that moment on they had my complete and undivided attention. The Promethian Board became a technological wonder to behold and I could not get enough of it. I knew that I would not be able to remember everything, but that was O. K. also, because they passed out manuals that we could keep. I was in love.

At lunch I called my principal and apologized profusely for my original lack of enthusiasm. I told him how wonderful the training was and that the "tablet" would solve all of my reservations. I also told him that I needed one of these "marvels" in my room by next Monday! I was just being silly, because I knew that I had missed my opportunity and I was just hoping that I would be on top of the list for next year. He said give him until Tuesday and I assured him that would be adequate. On my return, the I. T. man was in my room measuring the wall, and I had a board within the month.

PROMETHIAN ADJUSTMENT

I got my Promethian board three days ago and I cannot get anything else done. Learning this "new trick" is taking more of my time than I anticipated and everything else has gone to the back burner. I have just felt like I was spinning my wheels and I was afraid that this day was going to be like the last three with lots of effort and no results. I got to school early and started on the pile that I had left on my desk. I was making real progress when a mother that really likes to talk came in and started chatting. I hope that I did not look as anxious for her to leave as I felt. It is a very important part of a teacher's job to listen to parents and I am still learning to be patient when they need to talk, especially when it does not concern their child! I was polite and she finally left. I could only hope that this trend of interruptions over the last three days would not continue. Fortunately one of my classes was not meeting today and I would have three planning periods to catch up on all of those papers.

As first period planning began, I continued to work on the mound of paper work, being sure to have all make-up tests graded and then answering my emails. Sometimes I wonder what we did with our time before computers, but then I remember the time I used to spend on the phone with parents and I am grateful for email. I was making some real progress and decided to stop and set up my Promethian Board with the Mean Value Theorem. I had found a web site that had a ready made power point and all I had to do was pull it up. I got out my manual and began the process. The training lady made it seem so simple. I, however, made it so complicated and the time got away from me and I still did not have it loaded on the board when the guidance counselor came to talk to me to get input on some school goals and morale issues that he needed to address at an administrative meeting. I am always honored and humbled when my opinions are sought and we spent most of the rest of the period discussing school issues.

With a little help from a student I was able to rescue my presentation on the Mean Value Theorem and it went very well. I spent my lunch time with two teachers in the math department that were teaching Advanced Math for the first time. We needed to talk about what to teach and what to skip. Fourth period in Honors Advanced Math I did a bad job of teaching maximums and minimums because I got stuck on evaluating some x values. I finally gave up and told them that I would straighten them out tomorrow. I am still getting frustrated using the Promethian Board and it is affecting my confidence and my teaching. I am improving and I keep telling myself that. Fifth period was my planning period again and I decided to bite the bullet and start rearranging my room to go from overhead projector mode to Promethian Board mode. I had two aides who helped and we moved furniture until we had exhausted all possibilities. By the time the next class came in, I felt that I had made all of the necessary adjustments to use the Board and still get to all of my stuff. I was feeling better about being in control of my classroom. I must have order to function properly!

Seventh period I did not have a class and I thought I might be able to get some more accomplished on that stack. It was not to be. As soon as it started one of the members of my department was at my door asking me to go with her to the principal's office. He had requested a meeting on Friday because she was having some difficulties with some parents and she wanted me to be there for her. She had spent a very difficult weekend not sleeping and worrying about the situation. She had prepared some notes for the meeting and was eager to get it out of the way. I wanted to be there for her but hoped it would not take all period. Well it did. It was a good conference, where she stood up for herself, and let the principal know how she felt about the parents labeling

her. She made it clear how much she cared and he was apologetic that
he had been a little in-sensitive in his handling of the situation. Everyone
was fine when we finished. My only problem was that it took all period.
As soon as the bell rang to finish seventh, I dashed to the restroom and
hurried back down the hall to accomplish wonders in the last few minutes of the day before it was time to leave. As I rounded the corner into
my room I spotted Tabatha. Oh well, so much for getting anything done
today. Tabatha is one of last year's graduates and a very special young
lady. There was no way that I was going to put her off. She was home
for fall break and checking in with her teachers. I was anxious to hear
about her year and she was interested in how my year was going. We
ended up talking the entire time. Oh well, there is always tomorrow…

GO WITH THE FLOW

Our school has a program where seniors can take a class and get college and high school credit. I teach the college math class on Wednesday
and Friday mornings and James teaches the history class on Tuesday
and Thursday mornings. At the end of first period today, James came
to me and expressed his discouragement. He was very frustrated at his
performance in teaching the college class this morning and he was not
sure what the problem was. James is a master teacher and he really cares
about academics and instruction. He is young and very talented. We
only had moments to talk before the next class came in so I did not
have much time to encourage him. I gave him the old "we all have off
days-you will do better next time" speech but I could tell that he was
out of sorts for the rest of the day. At the end of the day I went over
to encourage him again, letting him know that I thought he was a great
teacher. He said that the topic that he had taught was not one of his favorites and he was not totally confident with the material. He also admitted that he was mildly threatened by some of the students in the
class that felt that they were intellectually superior.

After listening carefully, I advised James to really prepare for Thurs-
day's lecture and try to find some really interesting stuff about the topic.
(When math gets boring, I like to try to throw in some sex or something.
For instance, when teaching exponential functions, I always refer to the

reproductive talents of rabbits!) I also assured him that there would always be students in his class who thought that they were smarter than him, but that he would always be older and wiser! He agreed to think more about what he could do.

At the end of class on Thursday, I checked on him and he was elated. After much thought, he decided to share his concerns with his class and created a flow chart (see next page) for what had happened on Tuesday and shared it with his students. They had a lively discussion and then he began his lesson, for which he was fully prepared. I really salute his creativity and willingness to be so forthright with the class. It had never occurred to me to create a flow chart when I had a problem. Following James's example I have done so on two occasions and have found it a valuable self-evaluation tool.

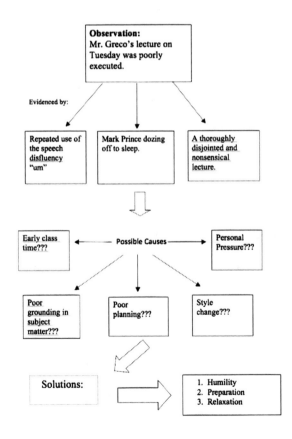

THE ANGEL IN THE YELLOW SLICKER

We have all heard that it is important to be in "good" with the school secretary, because she is the one who really runs the school. There is some truth in this, but I believe that the statement goes a little farther. No school can operate without support staff. If the school treats all employees equally, then it has made a major step towards improving the moral of everyone on campus. If the school does not, then it is the responsibility of the individual teachers to go out of their way to show gratitude and cooperation to every member of the staff. These folks are very under-paid and under-appreciated. I have found that when I am careful of any of my work that affects them, whether it is a grade report for the secretary or the cleanliness of my room for the cleaning staff, I make a very important friend.

Treating everyone on staff as if they have a college degree models compassionate behavior for your students, and makes everyone feel as if their job is crucial to the overall school operation. I don't know how you feel about it, but if the principal was gone for a week, I probably would not notice it, but if the secretary or maintenance man was gone that long, I would be dialing 911!

One of the most important things a faculty member can do for the school staff is to make their jobs as easy as possible. Paperwork should be complete and on time. It always amazes me that the teacher who complains at the lunch table about the student who never turns anything in on time, is the one who always has to be reminded by the secretary about her own delinquent reports. Making other peoples jobs easier will gain you a great deal of respect that will naturally filter down to the students.

Probably the most thankless job on campus belongs to the person that I used to call the janitor. Today he is known as the maintenance man. At the school I am teaching at now, he is a man with a great deal of responsibility and way too much do. He doesn't actually clean rooms anymore; that is contracted out to a cleaning company. Nevertheless, his responsibility is great and he takes his job very seriously. He has to be up at the school continuously to lock and un-lock the buildings and when the security alarm goes off at three in the morning, it is Mitch who has to "check-it-out." Rain or shine, he is setting out traffic cones, putting white lines on the soccer field, and setting up chairs in the mezzanine. On rainy days, I call him my angel in the yellow slicker, as he dons his school bus yellow overalls and raincoat. Nothing deters him from his responsibilities. As the campus has grown, so has his work load. We often talk in the mornings and we have become friends. I respect his time and talents by doing what I can to help him with his responsibilities. I have the students pick up paper and I keep my classroom neat. I pick up paper myself that is cluttering the hall and I make sure that he knows well in advance if I need to use any of the facilities for my extra-curricular activities. I then make sure that he has a list of what I will need done. I know that he is putting in extra hours and effort for me and I also know that he will not be compensated for all of his hard work. I do not take advantage of him or take him for granted!

He looks out for me and if there is some reason that I am not going to be at school, I make sure that Mitch knows it or he will call the highway patrol. When I moved he spent a Saturday at my new house hanging towel bars and curtain rods. He is just like that. In my opinion, he is the one person at the school who works the hardest and deserves the most respect!

I have not felt that way about all of the maintenance people that I have worked with over the years, but I have treated them all like I felt that way. Even if they did a terrible job, I never felt like it was my place to try to correct them. In every case, I found that the nicer I was to them, the nicer they were to me.

I also think that it is very important to model this type of accepting behavior for the students. I have been at some public schools where the maintenance staff included some mentally challenged people as well as those who would not be considered socially acceptable in the circles that the students and their parents frequent. If we are to teach love and tolerance to our students it is best taught through modeling respect for everyone who works on the campus.

THE MISSING LINK

Over the years I have seen many teachers that did a great job, lots of teachers that did an average job and a few teachers that did a bad job. Great teachers need to be cloned. Average teachers need to be inspired and motivated. Bad teachers need to be encouraged to look for employment elsewhere.

I have always dreaded having a bad teacher in my department because it makes everyone's work so much harder. I think that this is especially true in a subject like math. Math is so sequential that if a teacher does not do their job at a lower level they have created a "missing link" that is hard to overcome. This affects the student, the other teachers in the department, and the reputation of the department as well as the school. In every school that I have taught in there have been missing links. Some stay because they have been there forever and everyone is just waiting until they retire. Some stay because they are great coaches so they are forgiven for their lack of prowess in the classroom. Some stay because the administration has not been diligent in documenting their poor instruction. Some stay because they are related to the superintendent. I have even seen some stay because the other teachers protect them.

There will always be ineffective teachers that are doing their best, but are just not cut out to be teachers. Some people were just not meant to be in the classroom. They need to be worked with, mentored, and if they do not improve, thanked for their service at the end of the year and lovingly sent to another career. When offered help, they often become defensive and they continually deny that there is a problem. They are usually smart enough to keep the grades high enough so that students and parents do not complain too much. Students often love these teachers because they give lots of free time, are easily distracted into telling stories, and spend a lot of time behind their desks, leaving the students alone.

If you are a missing link, I am sure that you are not reading this book, but if you are, get help now and bind that chain! You are not being fair to the students or your fellow teachers. Re-think your priorities and give it all you have. Even a bad teacher can get better if they are willing to work at it. Find a mentor. Seek help from those who have taught your class before. Prove that a leopard can change their spots. I truly believe that if a teacher follows the basics, they will become better teachers. Start with bell to bell instruction. Vary instruction and engage the students. Don't sit down except at lunch. Plan more than the time allows. Let them know that you care, but that you are in charge. All of these things are doable and measurable. For the sake of the kids…TEACH.

DINOSAURS ARE NOT EXTINCT

I can tell any archeologist living or dead that I have proof that dinosaurs are not extinct! I know from very personal experience, because I am "one". I discovered I was "one" on the day that I had a discussion with a young teacher down the hall from me. Jerry is an excellent teacher and he provides endless short, entertaining conversations in-between classes. I respect him as a teacher and value him as a friend. Jerry and I however, have many philosophical differences about how a teacher should act! We have discussed these on many occasions and have basically agreed that we are just going to have to agree to disagree. Some of these differences are so fundamental to my teaching philosophy, that I just cannot let them go.

In every generation there are exceptional, good, mediocre, and bad teachers. I have even seen a few terrible ones. But most of the teachers I have taught with followed certain basic rules that are not necessarily adhered to now and their loss drives me crazy (the rules, not the teachers)! Jerry has me convinced that it was the switch from one generation to another but that does not make it any easier to live with. I guess that is what makes me a dinosaur. Here are few of my basic "teacher nonnegotiables" and how Jerry fossilized them.

I think that a teacher should be early or at least on time to school and should stay at school all day and never leave early. The obvious exception to my rule is any type of "real' emergency. Please note that I do not count picking up your dry cleaning a real emergency. I am amazed at the number of teachers who leave campus during their planning periods, leave for lunch, take off early, and come in late. Often times they underestimate the time it is going to take them to do something and end up leaving classes unsupervised. Jerry and I discussed this and he explained that his generation believes that as long as you get your work done, it does not matter when you do it. If a teacher can be excellent in the classroom and be late, leave early, and pick up their dry cleaning at lunch, he sees no problem. If he gets his work done during post planning, he has been known to use the last day to play golf with some of the other male teachers. He explained to me that my generation spends too much time worrying about time clocks while his generation only worries about the end product.

I think that a teacher should follow the same rules as the students with the possible exception of standing in the lunch line. The teacher should not chew gum, drink coffee, talk on their cell phone, text, or use the computer for personal business during class. Jerry disagrees. He says we are the adults. Chewing gum keeps his breath from being offensive; drinking coffee makes him less irritable, and if he needs to use his cell phone, he is mature enough to know when it is appropriate. He went to college for six years and he is a professional and therefore has the right to certain privileges. He thinks it should not bother me that another one of our young teachers locked his class out of the room for at least ten minutes into a class period because he was on his cell phone and was not ready for them to come in.

I think that teachers should turn things in on time. If a report is due to the office or a lesson plan is due to the principal, it should be done well and on time. Papers should be graded and returned to students as quickly as possible. Jerry believes in the better late than never philosophy, and his method of grading an essay is a little more like the hunt and peck method rather than a thorough reading and correction. He looks for key words and phrases and sees no reason to read the whole essay.

I think that a teacher should be at school unless they are feverish, have a broken bone, or are severely bleeding. Jerry believes that we all deserve 'mental health days".

I think that a teacher should be very conscientious about serving any assigned duty and if they are unable to fulfill their obligations, it is their responsibility to get the position covered. Jerry believed in the more laid back "que sera sera" philosophy until he took an administrative role and was in charge of the faculty duty roster. He is now in charge of seeing that the duty positions are covered and he has moved over to my way of thinking!

Now I know that I am a "pain-in-the-buttasaurous" and way too uptight about all of the above. I am a rule follower and it drives me crazy when others aren't. But in my defense, I truly believe that if I want my students to exhibit good responsible behavior I must model it for them. I want them to follow the rules and turn things in on time and show up when they have a commitment to do so. I want them to know when to talk and when to be quiet.

I know that my extinction is imminent and that I am outnumbered, but I must continue to try to save the dinosaurs because I know that there is no more valuable tool for instruction than to model proper behavior. I will never be able to convince Jerry of this because he wants to disappear into that classroom that is Walden Pond and drink his coffee with his feet propped on his desk as he discusses the classics with a small group of well behaved, enamored students.

My Cheese Got Moved!

There is a wonderful little book entitled *Who Moved My Cheese?* It is a very good read for any of us that have a tendency to get stuck in our ways, and especially for those of us who are convinced that our way is the best way. The whole premise of the book is that it is the nature of a human being to get in a rut and want to stay there. I would like to add the older the "mouse", the deeper the rut, and the more traumatic the moving of the cheese becomes. With that said, I admit I am an 'old mouse" and I like my cheese to stay exactly where I am used to it being, especially in my classroom.

My cheese got moved in a big way near the end of the year and I am afraid that I "squeaked" a great deal, to the point of mental anguish (mine and the unfortunate souls around me). My principal announced that finals would be administered differently this year. Instead of each teacher giving their own final, finals would be departmentalized. He stated that several schools had done this successfully and it cut down a great deal on cheating because all of the math finals would be given at the same time and students could not share what was on the final before another class took it. I saw the logic in this, but logic is not what I was interested in. I wanted to give my own finals and I quickly sent the principal a very tactfully worded letter letting him know all of the reasons why I did not want to go to his new plan. He respectfully replied in an email that I was a sweet lady and that we were going to give it a try. I was despondent, which I guess is a little hard for normal people to understand, but I am very picky about finals and testing in general and I did not want someone else testing my kids. I want to be in the room to answer questions and wipe tears and generally encourage and pray over them.

I also did not want to test another teacher's students. I would not even know all of their names and I certainly did not know who to watch for the straying eye! I was also concerned that the other teachers would create a final that did not last the entire period and I would be stuck supervising a class with nothing to do. On a selfish level, I teach three senior classes and two junior classes, and since seniors do not have to take finals second semester, I usually have a lot of free time during finals to finish out my work for the year and start on some projects for the next year. With the new system I would be proctoring three finals as well as floating during the math final. I was livid about the whole situation and although I was careful who I expressed my true feelings to, I did not hesitate to express them. Some of my close friends began to worry about my mental and emotional well being because the situation was stressing me out so much. I tried to not let it get to me but I was irrational! This often happens to me at the end of the school year. I am like a toddler; if I get tired or hungry, everything gets out of proportion and I become the center of the universe. At the end of the year I am exhausted and I get cranky.

Teachers were given instructions and a schedule. We explained it to our classes and it was all I could do to keep my mouth shut, but I refrained from whining to the students and told them that I was just sorry that I would not be able to be in the room with them because I wanted to be there to encourage them. We were all instructed to be sure that our finals lasted the entire 90 minutes and to be sure that we got the finals and instructions to the proctoring teacher two days before the finals were to be administered. Taking up textbooks was a challenge because the kids needed them to study for the test and yet they were taking finals in other teacher's rooms. I carefully typed out my instructions and delivered my two finals to the proper teachers two days in advance. Unfortunately the three tests that I would be proctoring did not arrive until the afternoon before I was to give them. In fact, I had to go after all three! The three days of finals were a disaster from my viewpoint. Kids had questions that I could not answer and the teacher was not floating by the room very often to help them. One of the finals that I proctored only lasted 40 minutes and on the day that I was floating to make sure that my kids had availability to me while they were taking my final, my proctor got sick and I ended up stuck in one room so I was not available if questions came up in the others. The whole process was a rotten experience for me and I complained to any adult who would listen. I was glad when it was over.

All of that being said; I am sure that we will continue to deliver finals in this manner and what I think is irrelevant. The parents like the new plan because scheduling drop offs and pickups is easier for them. There is less sharing of what is on the test, and cheating is down. So why am I still whining? Because the whole process, as painful as it was to me, was made worse by teachers not following instructions. Two of the three teachers, whose tests I administered are great teachers whom I respect and admire greatly. Yet, they could not get the tests and instructions to me on time. I heard many other complaints and most of them centered around teachers not doing what they were supposed to do. If you are going to "move my cheese", please do it efficiently! We "type A" folks need the comfort of structure and rules being followed in a new situation. We know that we are pains in the "tails", but we make up for it in being cute and dependable.

SHARPENING THE SAW

I am back from a wild weekend that has recharged my batteries! I spent a lot of time with friends and went to a college football game on Saturday and then on Sunday I went to a spiritual retreat after church. It was one of those things that I did not have time to do since I am moving in two weeks, but it was already planned and I desperately needed it. If I am going to be an affective teacher I have to sharpen the saw! Well this old saw got sharpened, polished, and painted with smiley faces.

Unfortunately I was bombarded as soon as I got in the door by faculty members concerned about the meeting that we had on Thursday afternoon about block scheduling and liberal education. They came up with concerns that were never even implied in the meeting. It is amazing how communication breaks down so easily. It is like that gossip game. There were rumors that we were going to a Greek liberal education and that we were going to leave our Biblical World View. Nothing could be farther from the truth! I was a little astounded at this and spent a good part of the day trying to calm down folks. I personally do not like block scheduling but I know that it is good for other teachers and I will deal with whatever is handed to me. Now don't get me wrong. I am no little miss merry sunshine but I know after so many years that it is probably going to happen with or without my support so I might as well make the best of it and keep my job. I love what I do and I have found that when something new is coming down the tube it is always better than it seems at first, and if it isn't, it doesn't last very long.

Because I "sharpened the saw", kept a positive attitude, and did not let the "nay-sayers" get me down I was better able to handle any and all classroom situations that arose. For instance, in honor's calculus today, I saw that several of the boys had rubber bands. I also saw one young man folding a small piece of paper in a manner that appeared to me to result in ammunition formation. Now there were probably several ways to handle this situation, but I chose to do it with humor. I walked over and took the "ammo" from the kid and went to another kid and asked for the rubber band. Then I proceeded to try to make a slingshot out of the rubber band and shoot the ammo. My problem was that I did not know how to do it and I knew that if I let go, I would just shoot myself. The guys started giving me instructions on how to shoot properly and I aimed high and let it rip. Unfortunately it did not go where planned and hit a kid on the thumb. Fortunately, I knew this kid's mom very well and had no fears of being sued! ! ! I then explained to the class the folly of shooting ammo off in the classroom. This entire scenario took approximately 3 minutes, we had fun and the point was made. I have not seen any more weapons in class.

Having "sharpened the saw", I was able to handle the situation in a fun yet firm manner. We have to take care of ourselves if we want to take care of others.

NCIS: GIBBS RULES TO BE OBEYED AT ALL TIMES. CONSEQUENCE IS A SLAP TO THE BACK OF THE HEAD

I love NCIS. As usual, it took me until about the fifth season to become a fan because I had to wait until it went into reruns on a channel where it was played back to back and I could view it before nine PM. I am not much into all of that blood, bodies and violence, what I am into is Gibbs. First let me say as a widow of 24 years that I find him very handsome, but that is not the attraction. I hear that Mark Harmon is a happily married man and I am way too old and too insignificant to ever appear in his social circles even if it were geographically possible. The attraction is to Gibbs' character. He is a man of few words, great expectations, and consistent actions. I think that is a great description of a school teacher. He does not nag, he expects. When I was looking up his full name for the dedication, I found his list of rules. If you are a fan of the show, you already know some of the more famous ones. Gibbs makes these up as he goes along so you will find two rule "ones" and two rule "threes". He also forgets what he has numbered to, so you will find lots of gaps. I thought it would be fun to see if I could adapt his rules to teaching. Some of them were a real challenge.

Rule 1: Never let suspects stay together. When trying to get to the bottom of a "situation" talk to the students privately and if you must talk to them at the same time be sure and let one of them say everything they want to say before letting the other one say whatever they want to say. Don't let them interrupt each other!

Rule 1: Never be disloyal to your partner. (I slightly re-worded this one to keep this book "G Rated".) Never talk bad about the other people that you work with in front of students. Never allow students to discuss bad things about other teachers in front of you unless you are needed as a counselor and it is done privately.

Rule 2: Always wear gloves at a crime scene. Be sure you have latex gloves in your classroom. If there is blood, put on a glove!

Rule 3: Don't believe what you are told. Double check. Be sure that you have the facts before you start handing out consequences. Never jump to conclusions without knowing the whole story and listening to both sides.

Rule 3: Never be unreachable. Make sure that the students always feel that they can talk to you and come to you with any problem. Be available to them in more ways than your subject area.

Rule 4: If you have a secret, the best thing is to keep it to yourself. The second-best thing is to tell one other person if you must. There is no third best. Keep your confidences with co-workers and with students. If you have to repeat personal information, tell your dog or your cat. If you lose the trust of students or other teachers it is hard to earn it back. Also know when a secret should not be kept.

Rule 5: You don't waste good. There is no act of kindness that is ever wasted. You may be the only act of kindness that a student sees all day.

Rule 6: Never say you are sorry. It is a sign of weakness. Sorry, Jethro, you are wrong on this one. Never be afraid to say you are sorry to a student. It is a very fast way to earn their respect.

Rule 7: Always be specific when you lie. I would like to tell you that I have never lied to a student, but that would not be true. I am not sure exactly what Gibbs means here, but my best guess is don't lie and if you feel you have to, be sure and remember what you lied about. Occasionally, I find myself not telling the truth when I am trying not to hurt a student's feelings. Each year I write over fifty senior letters and tell them all how wonderful they are and that I know they are going to make a positive difference in the world. I believe that to be the truth for at least 48 of them!

Rule 8: Never take anything for granted. It is a privilege being a teacher and having the responsibility of teaching young people. The subject we teach is only a part of the message we are sending to future generations. We should never take our influence for granted.

Rule 9: Never go anywhere without a knife. Once again we need to modify this. Never go anywhere with a knife!

Rule 10: Never get personally involved in a case. Even Gibbs admits that this is the one he has the most trouble with. I can see where this is a good rule to keep in general but sometimes you have to follow your heart.

Rule 11: When the job is done walk away. At the end of each year, do something just for fun to re-charge your batteries. Do something for yourself. Don't dwell on the last year, but plan for next year knowing that you will have another chance to do it better!

Rule 12: Never date a coworker. Let your conscience and school policy be your guide!

Rule 13: Never, ever involve lawyers. When I first started teaching, I would have said that this was a silly rule for teachers, but not anymore. There are so many things that I used to do that I cannot do now for fear of a lawsuit. There can be no more hugs unless they are sideways. I can't drive a student in my car without a release form. Heaven forbid if I post a grade or even call out the good grades in class. I know that most lawyers can be avoided with some common sense, but the problem is there are a few parents out there who are looking for someone to mess up so they can get rich quick!

Rule 14: Always work as a team. Teaching would be a lot more successful if a three pronged team approach was used on the education of every child. If teachers, parents, and the child worked together, can you imagine what could be accomplished? I find, especially at the high school level, that students do not want their parents to know what is going on at school and most parents don't get involved as long as the grades are acceptable to them. I try as much as I can to treat the parents as a valuable team member.

Rule 16: If someone thinks they have the upper hand, break it. This rule applies in two areas in the classroom. The first is in attitude and discipline. It is critical that any student who enters my classroom know that I am in charge. No student gets the "upper hand. " How I handle this is very important and should always be handled privately, but it must be handled swiftly and firmly. The second area is intellectually. Throughout my teaching career, I have always had students who are intellectually superior to me and there always will be. Since I teach upper level mathematics classes like calculus, not many of my students challenge me intel-lectually but a few do. My response to them is simple and usually public, depending on the circumstances. Sometimes I even start out at the be-ginning of the year with this comment. "I am sure that there are several of you in this room that are smarter than I. There is no one in this room, however, that is wiser than I. Please do not forget that fact. "

Rule 18: It's better to ask forgiveness than ask permission. I have heard this more than once when a teacher wanted to do something a little "outside the box. " The key thing here is that you have to know your administration. I have always been into seeking permission and I do very little that requires me to ask forgiveness because basically I am a chicken and live in a very small, comfortable box. I have seen other teacher's get seriously burned by the administration and parents because they decided to go for it and deal with the consequences later. That phi-losophy may work for inventors and NCIS field agents, but I think teachers should play it safe.

Rule 22: Never, ever interrupt Gibbs in interrogation I have a rep-utation at my school and at every school that I have ever taught at of being very serious about my teaching. I do not like to be interrupted when I am teaching. The secretaries in the front office are always very aware of this and only interrupt when necessary. Students know better than to interrupt my teaching, looking for a lost book, needing to talk to a friend, or checking on a grade or assignment. They know they are welcome in-between classes, but not during. I have had student aides beg not to have to interrupt my class, when given an errand to run by another teacher or administrator. I know that this makes me sound like a troll, but it is not like that. I have created an "aura' of healthy fear and respect that has reflected off my passion for what I do. I value what happens in my classroom and others quickly begin to respect that.

Rule 23: Never mess with a Marine's coffee if you want to live. I do not drink coffee. I however, have a lot of other things that I do not want messed with. I send out a strong message at the beginning of the year that I do not want the things in my room touched. I am not one of those touchy, feely, teachers who lets kids sit at my desk, stand behind my podium, or look in my desk drawers. My students know not to mess with my stuff. There are parts of my room that are student friendly where I supply pencils, paper, calculators, pencil sharpener, Kleenex, hand sanitizer, and band aids. Otherwise I dust for fingerprints!

Rule 27: There are two ways to follow someone. 1st way- they never notice you; 2nd way-they only notice you. As teachers we better always use the second way. Our presence is critical at all times if we want to avoid rule number thirteen. Omnipresence should be a skill that we all possess. If our presence is felt throughout the room, management is easier. The term "bigger than life" applies here.

Rule 35: Always watch the watchers: As a teacher, you are being watched constantly. Take cues from your "watchers". I can look out at a class and know it is time to stop talking and involve them in an activity. I can look at them and know when I have gone over their heads and need to back up. Learn to read your audience.

Rule 38:Your case, your lead. This is a very important rule if you want to be respected by your fellow teachers. Sometimes, as a young teacher I overstepped my bounds and tried to discipline students when I was visiting in other teachers' classes. If the teacher is present in the room, I need to respect their domain.

Rule 39: There is no such thing as coincidence. I have had more than one student tell me that it was just a coincidence that they missed exactly the same problems with the same wrong answers on a math test or homework assignment as the guy sitting next to them. I would imagine that English teacher's get a lot of this on essays or term papers that have been pirated off the internet. If I do not see them cheating on a test, I can only look at them and tell them that I do not believe in coincidences and that I will be watching them very carefully.

Rule 40: If it seems like someone's out to get you, they are. I taught thirty years in public schools and was amazed how hard it was to get rid of a bad teacher. I have taught eight years in a private school and I am amazed how easy it is to get rid of any teacher. Over the last four years, I have seen several teachers whose contracts were not renewed. It is a painful process because I believed some of them to be good teachers. I hope when I become an ineffective teacher, I will have the wisdom to move on. Once you are not wanted on a campus, it is probably time to go.

Rule 44:First things first, hide the women and children. This one has me stumped. I guess that if a gunman enters the classroom, it would be inappropriate to hide behind a student.

Rule 45: Clean up your messes. Sometimes I make a mess of my lesson. Sometimes I make a mess of a conversation with a student. Sometimes I make a mess with a fellow teacher. Sometimes I make a mess with a parent. See rule 51…

Rule 51: Sometimes-you're wrong. The easiest way to clean up messes that deal with people is to admit that you are wrong, try to make it better, and move on. If you don't try to clean them up, they will get nastier and the stain may never go away

Season Three, Episode Five, "Switch"
   Ziva: Just to be clear, are there any more of these rules I should be aware of?
   Gibbs: About 50 of them
   Ziva: And I don't suppose they're written down anywhere that I could
——
   Gibbs: NO!
   Ziva: Then how am I supposed to ——
   Gibbs: My job is to teach them to you.

THE NEXT RIGHT THING

Today is the first day of a two day spiritual retreat that our school participates in every fall. In the past it has been at the school and it has been a series of worship sessions, guest speakers, and break-out sessions led by the faculty. This year it was held at a very large church, five schools participated, and it was run by a professional conference group. Everyone was a little on edge because we had never done it like this before, but at the end of the day we all came away thinking that it had been a marvelous experience. The students had a little more freedom, yet they did very well. The leaders of the retreat kept them engaged and on task. Mark Hall the lead singer for Casting Crowns was the main speaker and he was marvelous.

I was mostly playing follow the leader through the day and taking lots of notes. I would just like to share a few of those notes that fall under the category of encouragement for teachers. This was admittedly a Christian Conference but the "nuggets" gained should be practiced by any teacher who cares about his/her students.

The first speaker talked about seeing people through the eyes of Jesus. WOW, how simple, profound, and difficult! I need that statement tattooed on the back of my hand. If I could constantly do that, I would be such a better teacher. I try, but I fall so short. The speaker then went on to say that "this day is bigger than you". That is exactly what I am trying to say in the way too many pages of this book! As a teacher, everyday is about what we can do to help improve our students' characters and lives.

We then went to a breakout session just for teachers and the speaker started getting real personal about us as teachers. He used First Thessalonians 5:14 to instruct us to be patient toward all men. Obviously he does not teach Missy and Joey. He then went on to encourage us to seek peace over preference, which is a sneaky way of saying that we should not always demand our own way and strive to get along with each other. He then stuck the knife in deeper when he said we should respect position not personality. I am sure that has something to do with respecting those who are in authority over us.

He really started stepping on toes when he instructed us to help the weak and not just talk about them. That is going to cut down on half of the conversation at the lunch table. If that was not hard enough we were then encouraged to maintain a joyful spirit and not let our attitude be responsible for bringing others down. As to being role models for the students he admonished us to exemplify thankfulness even in times of despair. By then I was thinking that he had too high an opinion of our abilities.

The afternoon session was great and the best reminder for me was that walking with Jesus was just doing the next right thing. Sometimes when a student or situation has gotten on my last nerve all I can do is the next right thing!

SELF IMPROVEMENT BY SELF ANALYSIS

This is a very long quote from a book entitled *Present Day Standards for Teaching*. It was written in 1926 by F. Burke Fitzpatrick. I think it is an excellent measuring stick as we seek to improve and become the teacher that we want to be. This excerpt comes from the chapter titled: Self-Improvement by Self-analysis. Some of the "new-fangled" educational ideas that we throw around are not that "new-fangled" after all. As we evaluate our own performance and seek to improve, we will find that someone else's check list can be very helpful. You may find the language a little "antiquated" but the ideas are not.

Practices of Superior Teachers

1   They emphasize a few important issues during each recitation. Do not try to teach too much. Sometimes good practice places emphasis on a single big idea or issue.

2   Superior teachers avoid talking too much. They get the pupils to talk; they know that their success depends upon pupil-performance more than upon teacher-performance.

3   Superior teachers make each child a special problem for study and give the proper regard to individual differences.

4   They plan for each recitation, select appropriate subject matter, determine the aims for presenting it, and use approved methods in all their work.

5 Superior teachers secure discipline without noise, or bluster, or scoldings, or threatenings. In a well-ordered schoolroom there is no evidence of discipline.

6 Superior teachers organize their subject-matter in terms of problems, projects, types, and comprehensive, thought-provoking questions.

7 Superior teachers use their classrooms as laboratories. Here they study in their regular work individual differences, try out different methods, experiment with mental and achievement tests, solve difficult problems, develop interesting projects, and so on.

8 Superior teachers take time to make definite and reasonable assignments with effective motivation.

9 They look beyond the mere giving of knowledge and its interpretation to the development of initiative, right attitudes, wholesome interests, and American ideals, together with correct habits of thinking.

10 Superior teachers subscribe to educational magazines.

11 Superior teachers give standardized tests early in the term, report the use of them often, and use the results as a basis for placing emphasis.

12 They often overlook minor faults, wisely stressing what is commendable.

13 They make themselves independent of textbooks.

14 Superior teachers make large use of supplementary material.

15 They provide interesting seat work.

16 They give an adequate setting for recitation.

17 They provide for systematic reviews, distribute their questions over the whole class, and keep all the class busy.

18 They work at times with open books.

19 They require neat notebooks.

20 They make large use of correlation.

21 Superior teachers require from their pupils complete sentences and consecutive discourse.

22 They use the whole method in memorizing.

23 They make large use of blackboards, charts, outlines, and summaries.

24 They hold pupils responsible for assignments.

25 Superior teachers not only rate themselves but seek rating by others.

Things to Avoid in Teaching

1 Avoid calling the name of the pupil before stating the question. Put the question to the whole class and then call on some particular pupil.

2 Avoid repeating the answer of a pupil.

3 Avoid the "and" habit yourself and have your pupils avoid it.

4 Avoid talking too much. Let the pupils talk.

5 Avoid questioning only a few pupils. Distribute your questions over the whole class.

6 Avoid disputing with pupils.

7 Avoid wandering from the main issue of the recitation.

8 Avoid assigning too much homework or assigning too much written work.

9 Avoid making homework too difficult.

10 Avoid indefinite assignments and assignments beyond the abilities of the pupils.

11 Avoid worrying over mistakes that cannot be remedied.

12 Avoid punishing the whole class for the offense of one or a few.

13 Avoid the use of corporal punishment.

14 Avoid asking too many small questions. Use a few well-thought-out, thought-provoking questions.

15 Avoid being late in the morning or leaving too soon in the afternoon.

16 Avoid indefiniteness in teaching.

17 Avoid questioning only bright pupils.

18 Avoid the use of sarcasm or ridicule. Courtesy and gentleness are always desirable.

19 Avoid letting all of the students speak at once.

BITS OF GLASS
It's All About Us

***If everyone was just like me the world would be a mess.
***Respect the kids and laugh.
***When I'm the Teacher Everywhere is a wonderful book of poetry by Elspeth Campbell Murphy. It is very practical and fun. Every teacher should own a copy.

***As a coach of the quizbowl team for 26 years, I have spent a lot of time in other schools and other teachers' classrooms. I have seen a lot of bulletin boards, posters and sayings. My favorite was a hand lettered sign that said the following:

WELCOME TO MY CLASSROOM

Now that you are here, don't think for one minute of trying to get away. You are all mine.

I am the teacher others have warned you about.

In my classes thinking is mandatory.

Do not attempt to escape.

All exits have been blocked. There is no backing out now. In spite of your every effort, there is simply no way of getting around it.

You are here.

I am in control.

I am your teacher.

There is only one way through.

You are going to have to think your way out.

***When I got out of college, I was going to save the world. Now I know that I can only save the world one student at a time.

***She was a teacher and she showed up! I read that somewhere and I think it speaks volumes about us just being there for our students on a day to day basis. Mental health days are called Sundays.

***Teaching is the hardest thing you will ever do except parenting but it is worth it!

***I know what I have given you. I do not know what you have received. *Chicken Soup for the Gardner's Soul*

***What is the nicest thing a student can say to you? My favorite thing is when they say that the time went so fast, they can't believe the class is over.

***Practice your best teacher "looks" and your best teacher "voices".

***The two most important words a teacher can use are "please" and "thank you".

***I get to play school all my life!

***Be authentic. Be gracious. Be relevant.

***One teacher in front of the class is better than three teachers sitting on their "behinds".

***Don't take everything personally.

***Stay away from the teachers' lounge. I have never been in one that is not a negative place.

***You need to be so passionate about what you do as a teacher that you truly believe that no one can do it as well as you.

***Hallmark Teacher: A teacher who cares enough to give the very best.

***How can we see the "butterfly" in others when we do not see the "Butterfly" in ourselves?

***If you are not feeling creative and need some ideas just window shop through a school supply store.

***Definition of meglamania: A mental disorder characterized by delusions of power. I confess, I am a meglamaniac in my classroom and I believe every teacher should have a touch of it without moving into cruel dictator mode.

***You must find that balance between being liked and being respected. Too much "like" and you are not respected. Too much "respect" and you become feared.

***There is no such thing as an expert and when you think you are one, God sends you a kid to prove that you aren't.

*** Max Lucado, in his book *The Great House of God*, told the story of his call to preaching. "As a young man I felt the call to preach. Unsure if I was correct in my reading of God's will for me, I sought counsel of a minister I admired. His counsel still rings true. "Don't preach," he said, "unless you have to. " As I pondered his words, I found my answer. "I have to. If I don't, the fire will consume me. " Is teaching the fire that consumes you?

Chapter Three
IT'S ALL
ABOUT THEM

Dedication

This section of my book is dedicated to my beloved husband Bob. He was the kind of wonderful teacher whose focus was always on "them" with no thought to "us". He was well loved because he loved well. His legacy is immeasurable.

DIVERSITY 101

EVERY STUDENT THAT WALKS through your classroom door is a unique individual with a DNA profile like none other. If television is to be believed, twins have identical DNA, yet any teacher or parent can tell you that even they are different. If you want to wax a little more poetic, they are like little snowflakes, each beautiful in their own unique way. Now I have had a few football players that I have trouble visualizing as "little snowflakes" but their uniqueness is still unquestionable. Wouldn't it be easy if they were all little clones and what worked for one, worked for all? Easy maybe, but consider two very important factors to think about, if that were true. First of all, heaven forbid, we might get a classroom full of the "evil" clones. Secondly, how boring it would be! We must celebrate their differences. The diversity that we are faced with every day is part of what creates our classroom dynamics and managed well, gives our teaching a dimension of expertise that enhances our professionalism.

I have found that most of that diversity can usually be grouped into some "student behavioral patterns" that recur on a very regular basis. Developing strategies to deal with these types of patterns often helps solve a lot of problems before they occur. Let me begin by saying that there are plenty of positive patterns as well as negative ones. We don't need to discuss the positive ones because they need no strategies. They take care of themselves! Below I have addressed those patterns which I see most. They are in no particular order and I can only offer what has worked for me. Your strategies may be better than my strategies. The important thing is to realize that we are "THE TEACHER" and any student behavior or attitude that hampers an individual student's progress or learning in the classroom, must be dealt with in a calm and immediate manner. Please note that every student you work with will be a long term project. There are no quick fixes for many of our challenges.

THE KNOW IT ALL

I have this one figured out because I used to be one! (Some of my friends will tell you that I still am.) There are two general categories of "know it alls". The first is the no-holes barred, obnoxious, pushy type. They always have a comment or opinion and they are sure that they are right. Some of them may be. The problem is that they don't give other students a chance to answer a question and they usually spend a good bit of time interrupting the teacher. If they just think they are right and aren't, they are also damaging their own standing in the class and possibly their own self esteem. This is definitely an attention seeking behavior. I start by trying to manage it with one of my best classroom management tools, not the individual student. By using chips to call on students to volunteer answers, my "too eager" child knows that raising their hand will not get them anywhere. If they blurt out an answer when I have called on another student, I just warn them kindly at first. If that does not work, I warn them unkindly. I may have to talk to them privately and develop a signal with them. I let them know that if I "scratch my eyebrow', I am telling them that I know they are the smartest person in the universe but they need to let someone else speak. I try to be very subtle at first, but if they won't calm down, I will start using their name and let them know if no one else can answer the question, they will be given a chance. A little private counseling is helpful here. They need to see how they look to their peers. Some of them will not care, but some will.

I was the second type. I was confident that I knew it all and sometimes I was actually right. I felt like my opinion always needed to be expressed and no matter what topic someone came up with, I knew something about it. I think part of this mentality came from my only child status. To my credit, I was shy around my peers and was usually subtle in "spouting off" in front of the classroom. My problem arose when I was in any kind of small discussion or conversation. My shyness disappeared in small groups and group projects found me bossing the other students, because I was so sure my idea was the best. My creativity flowed, but it drowned out everyone else's. Teacher monitoring helped manage my behavior, but what really helped start the path to my cure was a private conversation with a caring teacher.

THE MONOPOLIZER

This student is first cousin to the "Know It All", except his attention seeking behavior has nothing to do with his real or perceived intelligence. There is nothing subtle about him. To put it simply, he wants your attention and is usually clueless that he is taking up a lions' share of the classroom time. He is using up too much of your time, be it in a positive or a negative manner. She can be the kid who is very needy and not a self-starter, as well as the kid who is so proud of her work that she has to show you everything she does before she can move on. He can be a constant minor discipline problem, knowing just how far to go to stay out of trouble. She can be a young lady who cries at the drop of a hat and expects you to stop the class and deal with her ever present "life crisis". He can be the child prodigy with no social skills, who needs to be redirected as he blurts out abstract statements in class. Monopolizers come in all sorts of packages.

Once I identify a "monopolizer", I always start with a phone call home to speak to the student. Before I even dial the number, I make sure that I have a positive story ready in case I get a parent on the phone before I get the child. I do not want to talk to the parent at this point. I save that for later. If the child is not home, I just leave a message that I will call back the next evening. After about three attempts, I will give up on the phone call and tell the student that we need a little "chat" during lunch. It is important not to let them have any class time. Using their lunch time is not fun for most of them because they would rather talk to their friends than you. Once in a while you get the rare kid who would rather talk to you, but that is o. k. The point is that you are talking outside of the classroom environment. Be kind, especially to the boy with no social skills or the daily crisis girl, but be firm. Let them know exactly what they are doing wrong and how it is impacting the classroom. Tell them that you need to see some real improvement in their classroom behavior and that you will work with them to help them accomplish it, but you will not allow them to take up so much time. Give them the facts simply and let them know that their time consuming behavior cannot continue. Give them their choices. They can either learn to "lay low" or you will have to take more action. Tell them what "more action" looks like. If the chat does not work you will correct them in class, call their parents, and if all else fails, you will have to start assigning detention and use other disciplinary measures. What you do with each case depends on the child. Sometimes just ignoring them when they raise their hand or seek your attention will work, but that should only happen after you have tried other tactics. As you go through the process with the student you are trying to be patient and kind and re-directing their habits, not ignoring them and wishing they would go away.

THE QUESTIONER

This is a very specific case of the "monopolizer". I usually have about one of these a year. This is the student whose hand is always in the air. Sometimes they really need to ask a lot of questions about the material and sometimes they just like to hear the sound of their voice. I had one home schooled student who was just used to blurting out questions whenever he liked and he was having a hard time breaking the habit. My remedy for this issue is simple. Once I have identified the "Questioner", I find a convenient time in class and ask them to step out in the hall. I then kindly explain that they are asking too many questions and taking up too much time. If it is a student who is not struggling with the material, I tell them that they will have three questions a period and instruct them to choose them wisely. If it is a student who struggles, I give them five questions and make sure that they understand that I want to help them more but they are going to have to come before or after school to get extra help. All of these students quickly learn to hesitate and see if another student is going to ask their question before they raise their hand. I make myself perfectly clear that questions are good. I want my students to feel free to ask questions. I want my class to be a safe place to ask questions. Nevertheless, my students need to understand that sometimes you can have too much of a good thing!

THE CHIPPER

This kid comes into your class with a chip on their shoulder sometimes the size of a boulder. Whether you call it a chip problem or an attitude problem, it still smells the same. Sometimes their attitude is just directed at you, but most of the time it is directed at your subject, your school, and even the entire world. Whether it is personally directed at you or not, the first step in this situation is not to take it personally. No matter how much you would like to smack them on the side of the head, you are the adult and they are the kid; you are the professional and they are the piece of clay to be molded! My strategy on this one is to "out nice them". Don't overdo it at first. Smile at them if they will ever bless you with eye contact. Say "good morning" or "good afternoon" at least once a day. Don't be obvious and don't try too hard, but don't give up. Don't expect a reply. Chisel that chip down slowly, and do as many little acts of kindness as you feel are appropriate. If their "chip" publicly challenges your authority, deal with it decisively and then continue on your "niceness plan. " Never let them see any evidence that they are getting to you. That is exactly what they want. After you are able to gain their trust, you may be able to talk to them and identify if the problem is you or your subject, but I have found that given enough time, I can usually break through and make some progress by just ignoring the attitude and being nice. I have had some students that I was never able to reach. All you can do is try and never give up. I would really like to give them my "you owe the world, not the world owes you" lecture, but it is usually just like "spitting in the wind". All we can do is plant the seed and hope that someday it will sprout. If it doesn't these kids are going to have rough lives.

THE CHARMER

As a female teacher, once in a while you get a male student who has managed to charm his way through life. He begins working his charms on you the first day he walks in your class and he expects lots of special favors because he is so cute and wonderful. Evidently he has succeeded with this technique with the other women in his life and has found it highly effective. He may be a six year old or a sixteen year old, but his strategies are the same. He has moved mountains with his smile and those little dimples have saved him from a lot of harsh words. Those long eyelashes, blinked just right, have kept him out of many a detention. He is usually a sweet kid who is just a little mischievous but is able to get away with a little bit more because he is so personable and cute. He is always extremely polite and usually very sorry for whatever he did to irritate you. When you begin to correct him, he looks at you with those big beautiful eyes and you are a goner. This year I have a charmer named Eli. He is very personable and likeable, but he feels like he is too cute to keep his shirt tucked in and be quiet in class. He acts hurt when corrected like I have offended his sensibilities!

Watch out for this one. He is sneaky and manipulative. His counterpart is a girl in a male teacher's classroom. They pop up year after year, and they challenge our discipline strategies because they are so sweet that we want to lower our standards for them. This is dangerous on two counts. First of all, the more that you let them get away with, the more they will try to do. Nothing major, they know where the line is, just enough to be irritating to you and other students. The second and biggest problem in my opinion is that the other students are watching. They have seen this happen repeatedly and they are waiting for the time to come when "the charmer" meets his match and does not get away with more than the other students.

My most effective defense here is a very brief sentence that works wonders. The problem is in the timing. It takes a while to identify the charmer. Once they are identified, you have to be careful. You want them to understand that they will be treated like everbody else. Be careful not to crush their self-esteem, because even if it might not seem like it, they may be fragile. If you decide they are fragile, the sentence should be said in private. If they are not, it is best said in front of the class. Once this is determined, the next time the student is out of line, is corrected, and then gives you his best charmer look, you simply say: "Sorry buddy, that charm won't work on me anymore, so straighten up. ", or something very similar in your best teacher voice. Then make sure that you treat him like you would every other student; no extra chances! Once I had figured Eli out, I had no problem using my sentence in front of the class. The other students had watched Eli charm the teachers over the years and I gained a lot of respect when I did not allow him to charm me.

THE WHINERS

Watch out for these kids; some of them are professionals and some are very sneaky! Ninety-nine percent of whiners do it to get something that they want and have a high success rate because whining is so annoying. They end up getting what they want so that they will "shut up". If allowed by their parents, children master this at a young age and use it to their advantage for the rest of their lives. I am sure you know some adult whiners. In the classroom, whiners use their skills to get out of homework, work in general, extend project due dates, and postpone tests. As the teacher, you must be diligent in discerning whether whining is legitimate. If it is not legitimate, I have found that it can be nipped in the bud rather quickly by giving the student the opposite of what they want. If I start to make a homework assignment and I hear a whine that they already have too much homework or there is a basketball game tonight, I will comment that if they are not happy with what I assign, I will assign more. This quiets them quickly. If they try to talk me out of working and giving them free time, which happens rarely because most of them know better, I tell them that if they have time to complain about it, that means we can work a little faster and get more done.

The tricky one is the postponement of a test or a project due date. Sometimes the whines are legitimate on this and you have to use wisdom to make the call. If you are "whined" into too many postponements they have your "number" and you are a goner. I rarely announce a test more than a week before I plan to give it. Too much can change in a week and in a mathematics class, the coverage time line is not predictable even if there are no interruptions. We have a test calendar at my school and no more than two tests can be scheduled on a day in any grade level, so I check the calendar before I schedule a test. When I announce the test in class, I can usually tell by their body language if the date I have chosen is a problem. If I sense a rumble, I ask them if there is a conflict and then I listen respectfully. If their problem is real, and it is feasible, I re-schedule the test, if not I don't. Real problems are field trips and assemblies, not too much homework, or a game the night before the test. If they have a major project due for another class, they have probably known about it for a long time. If they have a game the night before the test, that happens too much to move a test. If, however, half of the class is going to be gone due to an anatomy field trip that I did not know about, I will re-schedule. I try to be reasonable about this and if they can convince me that moving a test is critical, I will agree, on the condition that we start new material on the day the test was originally scheduled. They do not like this and sometimes they will want to go back to the original test day. Beware of whining that would move a Friday test to a Monday. They beg for more time to study over the weekend. This almost always backfires on them. They have good intentions but they are too busy on the weekend and end up more exhausted from the weekend activities and now they are two days further away from the test review. They rarely do better.

I never postpone a long term project date for an entire class. If I have a student who has special circumstances, I may give private extensions, but never to the group. If I find out that the anatomy field trip is on my due date, those students may turn their project in early or before they leave school on that day, but they must turn it in.

THE CLASS CLOWN

This particular category does not need to be described because every teacher knows how to spot "one" and every new teacher has been in class with several over their educational career. First let me divide these clowns in two groups. The first group is the class clown that is annoying but is not really a discipline problem. Those are the ones that we will be talking about here. The second type is those who have crossed the line and have become a disruption to the classroom. Those will be dealt with in the discipline section.

The first thing to remember is that you will never get rid of the class clown. If you get rid of one, another is waiting in the wings to pop up. You may have more than one, but there is usually a dominant one. This student's motivation for comedy may be attention seeking behavior, but it is most often designed to seek peer acceptance. This is the young man who lacks height, but is always ready with a quick quip, or the chubby boy who tries to cover his self-consciousness with witty banter. It is the young person who knows that he is intellectually behind his classmates and uses self-effacing humor to insult himself before someone else can insult him. He is the hormone raging, teenage, male who does not know what to do with his sexuality so he tries to blend in with clever comments. It is any combination of motivations. It can also simply be environmental or cultural, depending on a student's home environment.

You cannot "cure" a class clown and if you try you will probably just crush him. Notice that I have used the male gender in my examples. In most of my experience class clowns are males, but I have had a few females and they were usually "doozies. " Class clowns who are not discipline problems need to be counseled and re-directed in a private manner. You do more harm than good if you try to correct them in class. Private phone calls, brief reminders after class, a gentle hand on the shoulder in class, and close proximity to you will help. They need kindness, not harshness until they move into the discipline category. They need someone to tell them the truth about how they are perceived by others and if you are not the one to do it, speak to the school counselor. Try to come up with positive ways to channel their energy. Assign them to find a "clean joke of the week" which must be preapproved by you before they tell it to the class. Give them positive reinforcement and praise in front of their peers and do not let their peers laugh at them in an un-kind manner. They often need protection from ridicule.

THE SLEEPERS

The sleepers also come in two groups. You have your professional sleepers and your situational sleepers. The professional sleepers want to sleep practically every day. Some of them are not getting enough sleep at home because they are studying too much, playing video games too much, working too much, or in rare cases, they simply can't sleep at night. Some of these sleepers are simply bored because they know it all, they don't know anything, or they simply don't care. It takes a little time to spot your professionals, but you catch on after a couple of weeks. I start out with kind words and the firm admonition that no one sleeps in my class. I invite them to stand in the back of the room if they have trouble staying awake. I make sure that everyone understands that this is not a punishment; it is just a way to stay awake. Standing is voluntary until I have to keep them from nodding about three times in a class period and then I make them stand. If the pattern continues, I talk to the student to see if I can find out what is going on. If this does not improve the situation, I call home and talk to the parents. I make it clear to everyone that sleeping in class is not an option. I have never had to go any further than a parent call and usually the threat of talking to parents cures the problem. My professional sleepers often become situational sleepers and we deal with it one day at a time.

Situational sleepers are those students who are usually very attentive and want to stay awake, but circumstances are working against them. They stayed up too late working on a project or studying for a test. They were at the hospital all night with a family member or didn't get home until two in the morning from an "away" game or a rock concert. Once again, I always start with an effort to keep them awake. If I realize that a student is sick or something is seriously wrong, I usually call them out in the hall and talk to them for a minute and tell them they may put their head down, but they are responsible for the work and this can only be a one-time occurrence. When we re-enter the room I announce to the class that Suzy is ill and is being allowed to sleep, but nobody else better try it! I cannot let the class think it is okay to sleep. The only time I allow sleeping in my class is if a student finishes a test early or if the circumstances are very unusual.

THE LANDFILL

Once in a while, you will get a student who I label "the landfill.' They will come to you with so much garbage, that you fear they will always "stink". This garbage can be emotional, physical, or educational. These are the kids who cannot see the light at the end of the tunnel. The emotional garbage has usually accumulated over their lifetime, the physical may be a fresh diagnosis of type-one diabetes, and the academic encompasses a prior history of just barely getting by. Once I identify one of my "landfill" kids, there is not much I can do for the emotionally and physically challenged except to be there for them and be kind and understanding. I do make an effort, once I feel that they are comfortable with me, to give them my landfill speech (described below). The educationally challenged, however, I can do more to help. Students who come to me with very weak backgrounds in mathematics are that way because they just do not have "math brains" or they have goofed off to this point. Either way there is help for them. The students who have goofed off just get the landfill speech and careful monitoring until we can get them back on track. If they choose to ignore my wisdom to start taking their work seriously, they will not make much progress, but I never give up monitoring. Sometimes they start doing better because they are tired of me and want me to go away. I am like a little aggravating gnat!

Those students who are educationally challenged because they cannot handle the material intellectually need the landfill speech, monitoring, encouragement, and an educational catch-up plan. Skills such as math, science, and reading are so sequential that missing something basic at the beginning can come back to haunt the student again and again. Students who did not successfully learn their multiplication tables, fractions, or how to problem solve will find that these topics never go away. Students who never conquered the art of reading with comprehension, will be penalized in every subject. There is a sequence in most subjects that require prior knowledge. When students cannot master the basics, they become overwhelmed as new material is added. These students need a lot more than the "landfill speech". I always start with the speech, followed by a conference where the student, parent and I develop a special plan for that student. The plan includes diagnostic tools, before and after school tutoring sessions, peer tutors, and any other methods that we feel would be helpful to the student. I like to create a contract that the student and parent sign, but this is not always necessary. Some of these students do not want to improve and will not make a lot of progress, but those who want to improve are usually willing to do what it takes. If they want it bad enough they will stick with the plan long enough to start seeing success.

So what is the landfill speech? The landfill speech is very simple. I ask the student to visualize a landfill. Every day more garbage is dumped in and when it reaches a certain level it is covered up and more garbage is put on top. The layers get deeper and deeper until it is impossible to imagine that it could ever be cleaned up. Yet, it can. Slowly, but surely, that garbage can be removed until the ground is clean again. It takes a lot of patience and a lot of time, but it can be done. There is no landfill so deep that hard work and time can't clean it up. I try to explain to them that their problem did not happen overnight. It accumulated over a long period of time and it is going to take a long period of time to correct it. They can start cleaning now and the layers will be easier to get through if they are patient, or they can keep adding on more garbage and it will get harder and harder to clean up.

SID

It is seventh period at the end of week two. Sid and I are walking over to the Sonic across the street from the school. He has an on-line class that is not meeting on Friday and I have a planning period. Sid has the reputation of being very bright and having dealt with him in quizbowl, I knew that he had lots of brain power. Nevertheless I have been disappointed in his performance. Before I decided what to do I talked to his other teachers and found out that he was un-motivated in all of his classes. I knew that I had to tread lightly. He showed no interest in class and I thought he was just bored until he made an 80 on his first test. Not only is he in my honors advanced math class, he is also in my SAT Prep class. We did a practice essay yesterday and in 25 minutes he wrote two sentences. It was the worst essay in the class. I needed to know what was going on before I decided what action to take. I knew that I needed to talk to him in a relaxed setting and do something a little different to get his attention. I emailed his Mom and asked permission to take him to the Sonic. We had a good talk. I told him that I had some alternate things we could do if he really was bored in math but not until he was showing me that he grasped the material and was making high nineties on his tests. I recommended a wonderful math book to him and loaned him a copy. We talked about his future and if he thought math would be part of it. We then moved on to the essay and he admitted that he was just being lazy. We talked some more and parted with a little better understanding of each other's expectations.

Today was writing workshop in SAT prep and once again "Sonic Sid" sat there and did not write a word. He was the only one. All of the students wrote one paragraph "essays" on a topic that the students had created. We would rate the results as a class and those that were voted most interesting would get candy. I randomly read all of the paragraphs to the class without anyone knowing who had written which ones. I made it clear that no one was to reveal that the paragraph being read was theirs or they would lose their prize if theirs was picked as one of the top ten. When I got to Sid's it was blank so I just kept going and did not say a word to him. During my planning period, I went through the essays and made comments on them and corrected the spelling and grammar. I was not at all sure what I was going to do with Sid. He is the kind of student that if he is pushed he will do less. His mom is at her wits end because he is so bright but he has been under-achieving his entire school career. He wants his grade to stay high enough to be respectable, which for him is anything in the low "A" range, but he does not want to put in any effort. He is very bright and his standardized test scores are off the charts! I decided to handle the situation with a sense of humor and a few points off of his participation grade. I cannot let him refuse to work without some penalty, but I can't push too hard either. The sense of humor part came in when I decided to write him a poem on his paper before I returned it to him.

There was a young man at Hebron
And no amount of pleadin
Seemed to motivate him to write
It was a very subtle fight.
The teacher wanted to see
Where lay his ability
But she couldn't get thru the fog
To get his brain unclogged
He resisted her every plea
And from reality he could not flee
To write an essay as a fairy tale
Made his countenance turn pale.
At her wits end as to what to do
She lowered his participation grade a point or two
Which is unfortunate indeed
Because his average it would impede.
So she decided to write him this poem
So she could really show him
You don't have to be good to write
You just need to do it with all of your might!

Sid reminds me of a student named Ben that I had about twenty years ago. Ben was exceptionally bright but he hated school and everything about it. He saw it as dull, drudgery and let everyone know how he felt. If he deemed that something was "busywork" by his standards he would refuse to do it. He constantly tried to sleep in class. I constantly tried to keep him awake. I never gave up on him and he and I went round and round with no clear winner in the battle. He was so smart that his test grades always kept him in the "B" range even if he never did his homework. His SAT scores were so high that he did not have any trouble getting accepted by a prestigious college. By graduation he was very glad to be escaping and I was glad to see him going. My prediction for him was that he would be kicked out of college by the end of the first semester or at least be placed on academic probation. I did not keep up with him, but to my surprise, five years later there was a Christmas card in my mailbox with his return address on it. I opened it up with a little trepidation as if there were a pipe bomb attached. To my amazement it contained the words: "Keep up the good teaching. It makes a difference. " You could have knocked me over with a feather. I can tell you in 40 years of teaching there are two pieces of paper that mean the world to me and that Christmas card is one of them. I contacted his mom to see what he was up to. He was in residency as a brain surgeon! She gave me his number and I called him to thank him for his kind words. We had a great conversation! Several years later I learned that he had a brain tumor and had surgery. He was no longer able to be a nuero-surgeon but he was teaching it in medical school.

Two years after the Sonic trip, Sid graduated and is now attending Georgia Tech. He never went into the high achiever range for me, but with my little poem, I was able to gain his respect and he started doing what I asked him to, even if it was not his best work. He scored a five on the Advanced Placement BC Calculus test and distinguished himself in many other ways. As I write this he is doing well at Tech.

P. S. Sid's mom said he hung my poem on the refrigerator.

THE POWER OF A PEPPERMINT

There is a great quote by the great football coach Tom Landry that I would like to apply to teaching. He stated: "My job is to get men to do what they don't want to do in order to achieve what they've always wanted to achieve. " His quote defines coaching as making players do what they don't want to do (practice and drill) in order to get what they really want (to win). Teaching is making students do what most of them do not want to do, to get something that most of them do *not* want. Ask one hundred seventh graders if they want to "get an education" and I bet that 80 of them will tell you no! It is one thing to work hard, sweat, and get banged up if you know that it will help win the game on

Friday night. It is another thing to work hard, sweat, and get banged up if you know that the game is not over for twelve years. Most of the students I know are into quick results and instant gratification (like most of the adults I know). So how do you motivate them to "get an education" when the rewards are not quite so immediate?

TO BRIBE OR NOT TO BRIBE, THAT IS THE QUESTION.

Any discussion on motivation usually brings up the time-honored debate as to whether students should be bribed or not. Let me lay my cards on the table early in this section and say unequivocally that bribes have been working for me for a very long time and I believe in them strongly. I will resist the urge to give you all of the reasons why I think bribery is a good thing, but suffice it to say that I am very guilty of working harder and longer when I see more immediate results. Bribery works! (If the word bribery is offensive, call it reinforcement.) That is not to say, however, that students should receive a reward every time they do something good.

Children learn early in life that sometimes you have to do something unpleasant to get something pleasant. Take vegetables for instance. My grandson Noah had not eaten very well and was allowed to leave the table, but he could not have dessert. His sister Emma had eaten her vegetables and was allowed to have ice cream. When Noah saw Emma with the ice cream he was outraged and let us know it in his usual two year old manner. His daddy calmly reminded him that he had not eaten his black-eyed-peas and Emma had. If he wanted ice cream, he had to eat the peas. All of a sudden Noah dried up, came back to the table, and ate his peas. The ice-cream followed and everyone was content again. Noah will repeat this scenario many times before he finally realizes that dessert is a reward for eating healthy and a treat, not an integral part of the meal. His parents have also trained Noah and Emma that every meal does not come with a dessert and not to expect one every time. It is a balancing act. More often than not, dessert is offered, but with the stipulation that it must be earned by eating what is healthy first and that it is a privilege, not an entitlement. Two and three year olds don't have a clue what privilege and entitlement mean but they know how it operates!

The distinction between tangible rewards and non-tangible rewards is an important balancing act for the classroom also. It is important to teach the studentsthat sometimes you do something just because it is the right thing to do without compensation. Although I admit that I am heavy on the bribery side, I do try to maintain that balance. There are many ways to motivate students and only some of them are considered bribes, so as usual, pick and choose what works for you and fits into your value system.

THEY ARE ALL UNIQUE AND WONDERFULLY MADE

I have often had the experience of being able to motivate one student and not another when I did exactly the same thing for both. This is not surprising in the light that every student is so unique and they all come from such different life experiences. Some incentives that would seem to be universal motivators do not appeal at all to some students. Take chocolate for instance, most students would pawn their I Pod to get some chocolate just before lunch, but what about the kid whose Dad owns a chocolate factory? I know that is a little far fetched, but I think it makes the point. It is our job as teachers to try to find what tactics motivate our students and then use them. Assuming they are legal and ethical of course! Because no one tactic works for everyone it is critical that you have a vast collection of motivational options. With some students it is difficult to find what will motivate them, but you have to keep trying. Never give up. In this section we will discuss a few general motivational tactics. There are a great deal more! Some can be found categorized in the instructional, management, and discipline sections found later in this book. Others can be discovered by talking to experienced teachers and exploring the internet.

TWO, FOUR, SIX, EIGHT...
WHO SHOULD WE TRY TO MOTIVATE?

Now that we have gotten the debate on bribery out of the way and the fact that different students are motivated in different ways, the most important thing to remember is that motivation comes in many forms and is critical to the learning and classroom management process. Some students will come to you with built in motivation. They will enjoy your "motivators" but they would have done great without them. Other students are motivated by their parents. Some of this motivation is because they want to please their parents and some of it is because they fear their parents. Either way they also will usually succeed. The trick is to aim our motivation at those who come without much of their own. Anything we can do to help a student want to succeed, for whatever the reason, is critical for some and the "icing on the cake" for others. Motivation dished out to the already motivated is still valuable. In other words, what ever you do to motivate your students is never wasted and for some, it will be the difference between success and failure.

MOTIVATIONAL TIMING

No matter how hard you try to motivate students, if you break any of the four basic "rules" of positive reinforcement, your efforts will backfire on you. Rule number one is that rewards, whatever the type, should be given as soon as possible. This quickly reinforces desired behavior. If you wait too long, the reward may not be associated with the positive behavior and even more likely, if you wait, you might forget. The students will usually remind you, but you build more trust if they don't have to. They need to be able to count on you. Keeping your promises quickly is a good way to build trust. The second rule is to be fair and consistent. If you show favoritism in any way you will quickly lose the respect of the students. The third rule is to find a way to reward effort, not just ability. Be careful with this one. The student should have actually earned the reward. Don't give out un-deserved rewards. You will lose your credibility. The fourth rule is not to "over do" any of the motivational tools. Use your choices and mix them up.

A MOTIVATIONAL TAXONOMY

Doesn't that section title sound educational? What it really means is that we are going to sort the positive motivators that I want to share with you into types. (We will be looking at the not-so-positive motivators in the section on discipline.) Some of them I will address in this section, and those with double asterisks will be explained more fully later in a more appropriate section. You should have your own collection of motivators. You need a long list so you can try different ones on different students and classes and you need to switch often to keep them on their toes! I mentioned in my first chapter that I categorize and sort all of my earrings into little containers. As I do this, I am always troubled by that pair of earrings that defies description and won't fit into one of my categories. Should the red and white polka-dot balls go in the red container, the white container, or the cute little ball container? Alas, so it is with motivators! They can, and often do, go under more than one classification, so you will just have to trust my judgment and know that I really agonized over where to put some of these. If you don't like my arrangement feel free to move some of them to another category so you won't have to lose any sleep over it.

MOTIVATORS BY CLASSIFICATION:
ABSTRACT:
*HIGH EXPECTATIONS-Over and over again studies have shown that high expectations make a world of difference in student performance. In most cases, you get what you expect, so shoot for the moon!
**MUSIC –(Lots more on this later)
*CONFIDENCE-Let your students know that you have confidence in them and then show it.

ACKNOWLEDGEMENT:
*HAND SHAKE-When a student does a good job, call them to the front of the room and give them a handshake. Don't do it all the time. It is more of a reward if it is saved for a special effort or performance.
*PAT ON THE BACK-I know that this might be illegal in some states, but a pat on the top of the shoulder means a lot to many of the students. It may be one of the few signs of affection they get all day. If you are not comfortable touching their back, try gently touching the back of their hand. If your school has a no touching at all rule, cut out some hand prints, write "pat on the back" on them and give them out instead of actually touching the student.
*NECKRUBS-This is a great stress reliever for you and the students.

Line up in a single file line around the room. Each student "massages" the shoulders and neck of the person in front of them. At a signal from the teacher, everyone turns around and repeats the favor. If you have room in your classroom, it is even better done when everyone can get in a circle. That way the people on the end do not get left out. Common sense needs to reign on this activity. If your class is not mature enough to handle this, do not do it. It works great with high school students who are facing a big exam or project. It should be about a two minute activity.

*THE BIG SCREAM-A couple of days before finals, I take my senior Advanced Placement Class outside for a loud scream. They are very stressed out and enjoy it very much.

*SMILE-Eye contact and a smile go a long way to encourage a student. It is also hard to misbehave for a teacher who is smiling at you.

*WINK-I guess in this day and time you have to be careful with this one too, but I find it an effective way to let the students know that I care about them when they pass me in the hall.

*COMMENTS-Be very specific in giving out praise, naming what they did right. You cannot "over do" this one as long as your praise and interest is genuine.

COMMUNICATION:
**GOOD PARENT PHONE CALLS-The value of the time spent here cannot be underestimated. (more later)
**GOOD STUDENT PHONE CALLS-Call the student at home and let them know how well they are doing. This is one of my favorite techniques. Students do not expect this and it means a lot to them. (more later)

CLASSROOM MANAGEMENT:
**SHAZAAMS-My best positive reinforcer. (lots more later)
**FREE TIME-Rare, but effective. (more later)

GRADES:
*MRS. SUTTON'S REFRIGERATOR-I made a "refrigerator" door

out of some silver Christmas wrapping paper and put it on the wall outside my classroom door. Every time a student made an "A" on a test or raised their test score ten points from the previous test, I put their name on the "refrigerator".

*GRAPES VINE-This is the same idea as the refrigerator door, but I put a big vine outside my door and then write their name on a leaf every time they scored well on the test. If they made a 100 they got a grape cluster.

*96 PLUS CLUB-Another idea for posting the names of students who score 96 or better on a test.

*CLASSROOM DOOR-My classroom door has a large window and I use glass paint to post the high scorer on each test for each class on the door.

*MY FAVORITE GRADES-To motivate students who rarely make "A's", I have a spot in the room where I post "my favorite grades". I continue to post the names of the students who do well, but I also post the names of those who have improved or who have studied hard, despite the test score.

INSTRUCTIONAL:
**MAGIC CAPE-Every teacher needs one! (more later)
**MATH MAGIC-Every subject needs some! (more later)
*MAGIC PENCILS-I pass these out for the final and tell them that it has magic powers to work problems correctly. In my present position in a Christian School I let them know that they have been prayed over and then I do just that. It really helps with test anxiety.
*SMARTIES-Give each student a roll of Smarties when you pass out a difficult test and tell them the green ones are to be used for the most difficult parts of the test!
*NO HOMEWORK-Sometimes these two magic words will keep a class attentive to the last minute of a class. For example if they start getting antsy in the last ten minutes, I just say: "If everybody stays focused to the end of the period and really participates, no homework tonight. " It usually works like and charm and I was probably not going to assign homework anyway.

*POETRY-You have already had a sample of my bad poetry and I will never win any awards, but the kids think it is funny and love it when I come up with some silly rhymes.

*BUBBLES-Blowing bubbles in class once in a while, can put some serendipity into the classroom. There are many times when this is appropriate, but it should be used rarely so it will not lose its effectiveness.

**CHIPS-Couldn't teach without them. (more later)

PEER COMPETITION:

**"MAGNET" COMPETITION-Another item I do not want to teach without. (much more later)

*SUPER SOAKERS-I have a year long competition in my AP Calculus class called Dragon Slaying. After the AP Exam, we have a water gun fight and the team that won the Dragon Slaying competition gets to have the biggest water guns!

TANGIBLE REWARDS:(Caution! These rewards cost money!)

**CANDY-I use candy constantly and I will be talking about it in several sections of the book. Individual students usually do not get candy. Candy is usually given out for many of the various team activities. Nevertheless, I always keep some handy. Once in a while a student will do something so phenomenal that I want to do something very special for them so I grab a Payday or a $100,000 Dollar Bar.

*GUM-Every school I have worked at has had a no gum rule. That is why gum is such a good reward. Normally I enforce the gum rule, but if a class has been very good, or done exceptionally well on a test I might get out the bubble gum. They can chew it until the end of the period, and on the way out the door, they have to wrap it up in its original paper and place it in the trash can that I am holding as they leave. That way there is no gum paper on the floor, no gum under the desks, and no students chewing my gum in another class.

**COKES AND LITTLE DEBBIES-I use these as rewards for my SHAZAAM drawing. (more later)

*WARM FUZZIES-Warm Fuzzies are those cute little fuzzy balls that you can buy in craft stores. You can get a lot of them for very little money. Any time you catch a student doing something nice like picking up trash without being asked or being particularly nice to another student. Give them a warm fuzzy. If a student is having a very bad day, give them a warm fuzzy. If a student is having problems at home, give them a warm fuzzy. You get the picture... Amazingly enough, this works at the high school level too.

In fewer words:

1   Bribes work, but should not be expected by the students all of the time.

2   Different things motivate different students. It is your job to find out what works for each one.

3   Some kids come with built in motivation, some come with none. Motivate everyone!

4   There are a whole lot of motivators. Use them to your advantage and switch often. The element of surprise is also a motivator!

SAM MADE A 100 TODAY

To say that Sam is not a mathematician would be a kind way to say that Sam stinks at math. The longer I teach, the more I am convinced that there are three kinds of people mathematically, the challenged, the chillers, and the challengers. Sam is challenged. He is just not good at math. He is a great writer and is an excellent student in history, and language arts. He just has a hard time with math. He is frustrated by the challengers, which are the students that have a "bring it on attitude" when it comes to math and problem solving. You can't challenge them enough. They love to solve problems and mentally wrestle with numbers. Sam, therefore, usually hangs around with the "chillers". Those are the students who do not particularly like math, but they make acceptable grades and "just do it", so they can get their credit and move on to more interesting things in their lives. They are often excellent students who do very well in math, they just don't love it so they just "chill" their way through the year. Sam hates it! He tries very hard to stay awake in class but it is a struggle. Math is such a foreign language to him that it would be like trying to be attentive for an hour of listening to a lecture on the habits of a slug, spoken in Swahili. His eyelids do not waver because he is willfully trying to be inattentive; they waver because there is only so much boredom the human soul can take.

He takes notes, studies, and does his homework. He does not perform well on tests. He works with other students outside of class. In Algebra I, he could make a low "A" or a high "B" with sheer determination, but as the subjects got harder and he got into advanced trigonometry, his efforts usually resulted in lower grades. He has lost some of his motivation to do well because he has worked hard and not been rewarded with a good grade on so many occasions. He continues to take honor's courses because of parental expectations. His dad wanted Sam to go to Georgia Tech, but has kindly seen that is not what is best for his son. When Sam signed up for Honors Advanced Math in his junior year, I was concerned that he would not be able to handle the pace. By the end of the first month, despite his coming in for extra tutoring, he was one of five students failing the class. He was still working at it and had not given up, but he just couldn't pass a test. With the approval and blessing of the administration, I created a contract with the five failing students. If they would continue to work hard and not give up, I would add ten points to their average with the understanding that their transcript would just say Advanced Math and not Honors Advanced Math. Sam and his parents agreed to this change and he began making low "B's". Sam is now a senior taking Calculus. It is not the Honor's Calculus class, but it is still challenging. He is still having trouble staying awake, doing his homework, and performs poorly on tests. Until last Tuesday that is; last Tuesday something miraculous happened. Sam made a 100 on his test! ! ! I was surprised, and boy was he surprised. He had even gotten part of the bonus correct and would have made a 102, but I do not give grades over 100. How do I explain this miracle? I cannot, but I know one thing for sure, it was very important to milk it for all it was worth! The next time I saw Sam, after grading his paper, I gave him a big hug, and told him that he had made a 100. I let him know how proud of him I was. I called home. I wrote his name on my classroom door and I made a big deal out of it when I gave the papers back in class. I wanted Sam to remember that all of his work had finally been rewarded after a very long time. Will Sam ever make another hundred? I hope so. Nothing succeeds like success and I will do everything I can to encourage him.

MAKING A DEAL WITH THE DEVIL

I have been in teaching situations before where football was king and you did not dare fail a football player or your career was over. Now this might be a slight exaggeration but we all know that "sports" is a serious business. I have had a few students who could not play because they were failing in my class but in every case, they were not willing to work and in my opinion deserved the consequences. Once in a while, however, I get a good athlete who works very hard and just does not do well in math, and I try to do everything I can to help them get their grade up so they can play. Phillip is such a student. I had taught Phillip three years ago and he was pretty good at math, but that was in a lower level class that was taught at a slow speed. He is now a senior and he is in a class that moves fast and assumes that a student has a basic knowledge of Algebra II. Phillip is not a "natural" and he has to work at math. Evidently he is a "natural" at football, because he was in a panic on Friday because if he did not make a 72 on the test, he would not have the grade he needs to play. He assured me that he had really worked hard Thursday night and I believed him. His problem was that he had not started working hard until Thursday night and the test covered lots of material. He had not been doing his homework. In his defense, it was not mandatory, but he had already failed one test and he should have figured out that he needed to do the work. Well, Phillip made a 68 on the test. That is exactly what he had made on the first test. His average is 68 and his football career appears to be over.

I know that it would be a very good lesson for Phillip to be pulled from the team. But is there a gentler way that would be just as effective? Is there room here for mercy? I think so, as long as it does not interfere with the role that Phillip must learn to take to be responsible for his grades.

I have done this before and usually with good results. I called Phillip's home and talked to his mother. We discussed what Phillip needed to do to improve his grade. His mother was very supportive and said that this was a good lesson for him. I agree, but I offered to "loan" Phillip four points so that he can play football. These four points will be taken off of his next test grade. I am really not giving him anything; I am just loaning some points so that he is passing now.

It is a little like selling your soul to the devil. You get what you so desperately need now, but you have to pay it back in the future. Phillip's mom was going to talk to her husband and Phillip about my offer and call me back later. I do not make a habit of this, but I have found it to be an effective tool. Not only does it give the student a chance to hang on to what they love, it gives them another reason to work hard for you because you have let them know that you care and you believe in them.

I got the call later that evening and it was Phillip on the phone. He was very grateful for my proposal and was willing to do most anything to pass at this point. We worked out a plan for him which included mandatory homework and before school tutoring. Another condition of my loan was that he and his parents not tell anyone what I had done. We also talked about how he could manage his time a little better to bring up his grade. I know that he is sincere and will start working. He understands that if he does not do well on the next test, he will not be passing and I will not help him again. Phillip never failed a test again.

PERSEVERANCE

One of the hardest things to help a student learn is perseverance. It is a character trait that a lot of adults do not possess and even fewer teenagers. In this age of immediate gratification, working hard for something, when it takes a long time to succeed, is rare. Encouragement is important, but even more, I believe that students need to hear success stories. Thomas Edison and the light bulb is a good starter, but it would be better if you could pull out a few from your own experiences and share them with the students. Here are two of mine.

When Jeremy was in the 8th grade I taught him Pre-Algebra II, which is a nice way to say that he is not a good math student and had to take Pre-Algebra twice. That was five years ago and I did not hold out much hope for his ability to excel as a mathematics student. Jeremy is a very polite young man with a great personality. I was always convinced that he would do fine in life but not in math. He had a special learning disability and his mother was diligent in getting him tested and getting him to special help. In his 9th grade year, I taught him Algebra 1. He had not made much progress and again struggled with the concepts. Nevertheless he continued to be conscientious about his work and tried hard. He had real organizational issues that drove his mother and me crazy but he was always sincere. During his 10th grade year he took Geometry. I was not his teacher and did not keep track of his progress but I saw him often in the hall and he told me that things were going fine. During his 11th grade year he took Algebra II and once again I was not his math teacher, but I did have him in an SAT Preparation class for the entire year and I was impressed by his progress. He amazed me at his sincere questions and the quality of his work. He proved that he really cared about learning. On several occasions he found a shorter way to work a math problem than I did! I could not believe that this was the same kid who had struggled so in the 8th grade. Jeremy had grown into a confident, capable young man. I give much of the credit to his mom who never gave up on him and his organizationally challenged ways! I was so impressed that I often emailed his mother. I believe that it is very important to let parents know when their kids are doing great. At the end of his junior year, Jeremy attended a summer camp that was engineering based!

When scheduling for his senior year, Jeremy came to me with an unusual request. He wanted to take College Algebra and Calculus in his senior year. This would mean skipping Advanced Math which is very necessary to succeed at Calculus. He was so determined that we worked out a deal where he would come in an hour a week before school and let me teach him the basic trigonometric material that he would be missing so he could succeed at Calculus. At the end of his senior year he had a "B" in College Algebra and Statistics which gave him two college credits and a "B" in Calculus. Jeremy is a prime example of motivation and determination overcoming a lack of natural ability.

Jeremy reminds me of a young man I taught many years ago named Walt. Walt came to me in Algebra I in the middle of the year and consistently failed all of his tests. He always did his homework and class work. His test grades, although failing, were high enough that he was able to barely pass the first six weeks. He started coming for extra help and slowly began to pass tests. By the end of the year he had gone from a very low "C" to a strong "C". He continued to come in for help as I taught him geometry and his grades progressed from strong "C's" to high "C's" and low "B's". The same pattern continued thru Algebra II and Trigonometry until he was making high "B's" and an occasional low "A". At the time, I was the only math teacher in a very small school and I taught Walt in every math course. It was such a privilege to watch him mature mathematically and never give up. What most impressed me about Walt was his determination. He never stopped showing up for help even when he worked so hard and still did not do well on the test. Walt ended up going to the University of Georgia and becoming a veterinarian. His determination was rewarded.

NO PERSERVERANCE

Keith was the opposite of Walt. He was loaded with brains and had a great mathematical mind. Unfortunately, he had the motivation of a sloth. He loved to work on cars, hunt, and other "red neck" type activities, but schoolwork was not on his agenda. He just did enough to keep out of too much trouble with his parents and he was happy with B's and an occasional C. I let him sign up for AP Calculus because he was so smart and I pushed him all year to do his work and stay engaged. He rarely did and had a C average two weeks before the AP Exam. I could not get him to tune in on the exam review and he was great at distracting the other students. I tried to think of what would motivate him and the only thing I could think of that I could afford was food so I emailed his mom and asked her if she would help me with a little contract that I would come up with. She agreed, and knowing that I had to do something very creative to get Keith to buy in, I wrote another one of my awful poems and used it as his contract:

KEITH'S AP CONTRACT:
*There was an old teacher
Who lived in her room,

With 13 AP students,
Only one completely out of tune.
*He was one of the brightest
Of that there was no doubt,
But as hard as she tried,
She couldn't figure him out.
*To have so many smarts,
And be so un-motivated,
To be so loving and kind,
Yet work ethically discombobulated!
*Determined she was
To help him be his best,
Even though he wanted mediocrity
And never studied for a test.
*She loved him enough
To keep her love tough,
She nagged and begged
But it was never enough!
*So one day she decided to
Try something new on the dude,
The boy liked to eat so she would
Tempt him with food.
*If Keith would just study
And stay engaged in class,
She was sure the AP Exam
He could pass.
*So for every ten minutes he studied
His mom logged in his time
And the teacher added more
When in class he was engaged just fine.
If he could make it to five hours
Before the exam
A large plate of brownies,
The teacher would put in his hand.
*His Mom was even willing
To treat him to a large meal

If he would only keep
His end of the deal!
*So that old teacher
Prayed as she presented her plan
Would Keith put in some effort
And show his real worth as a man?
*Only time will tell
The decision is his.
If he will not accept the challenge
His AP Score will hit the skids.

I am proud to say that Keith accepted the challenge and his mom kept him to task. He became engaged in class and came to two voluntary, after school, review sessions and one two hour Saturday session. He took a practice test at home. Keith really stepped up to the plate and I was proud of him and let everyone who would listen know that I was proud of him. He still grumbled all of the way but he showed up and was truly engaged. Mom's can make a child show up, but they cannot make them focus, and to his credit, Keith did. He came out of the exam feeling good. On his return to class I had a batch of homemade brownies just for him and his parents took him to Longhorn's for dinner. I pray that Keith did well. There is so much that he can learn from this lesson that has nothing to do with Calculus. Keith would persevere at what he liked, but I hope he learnes that to persevere at what he doesn't like is also very valuable.

THEY EAT THEIR YOUNG
TEACHING YOUR OWN CHILD

One of the most challenging students that I have ever had to teach was my own child. That is not to say that he was academically challenged or a psycho discipline issue, he was just mine. As he started kindergarten and worked his way up through middle school we had the usual "school stuff" to deal with like not doing his homework and throwing a stick and hitting another kid in the eye. But generally, life was good. Our biggest issue in middle school was that every time I tried to sit down and help him with his algebra homework he told me "the teacher did not do it that way. " We survived these murky waters and entered the new phase of "high school". At the time, I taught at a large comprehensive high school where there were plenty of math teachers. There were two of us who taught Geometry and normally I would advise anyone else to not teach your own child if another teacher is available. The other teacher was available, however, I did not have a high opinion of his teaching skills or of his dedication to his profession. Therefore I went to the registrar and asked that Scotty be placed in my class.

Since this was new territory for both of us, before school started we sat down to talk about how we would handle an awkward situation. I told him that I would treat him like everyone else and that he needed to call me Mrs. Sutton and treat me like I was just his teacher and not his mom. It took a little retraining, but he did a pretty good job going from "Mom" to "Mrs. Sutton" and we made it through that first year with few problems. The school was big enough that I rarely saw him during the day and he felt that he had a "life of his own. " It always amazed me that he still "forgot that we had homework" when I was right there to ask, but I like to attribute that more to the male, teenage "thing" than stupidity.

At this point in his academic career, the county was opening a magnet school in a very old elementary facility out in the country. The Ware Magnet School of Agricultural, Forestry, and Environmental Sciences opened that year with a federal grant and a wing and a prayer. Scotty wanted to go and he wanted me to go with him. Since the death of his father, we had grown closer and I was really touched that he still wanted to be in the same school with me. We went. I can never adequately describe what was so special about that school. When we started, the facilities were awful and it was all touch and go. The faculty, staff, and students bonded in a way that is rarely seen, and we all knew that we were at the beginning of something special. It was a very small school. Scotty's grade only had 19 students in it. I was the only math teacher!

We did fine in Algebra II. He stopped calling me Mrs. Sutton and went back to Mom. I would like to say that I did not treat him any differently than the others, but I had a tendency to be harder on him so that it would not look like I was playing favorites. I do not think that he was any worse for the wear. He continued to do well in trigonometry. I am sure that he got tired of my knowing all of his business in such a small school, but he rarely complained and when I heard "stuff", I tried to pick my battles to be fair to him. By the time Scotty was a senior we had found our "rhythm" and things started out well. As we went through this mother/teacher, son/pupil relationship, I developed a few basic rules that I went by which I believe are important, whether you teach your own child or they are just at the same school where you work. First of all I tried to be very careful what I said in front of my son about other teachers, students, and the politics of school. Secondly, I tried very hard not to show any favoritism and even more important, I did not request any from anyone else at the school. Scotty had to accept whatever consequences his actions brought. Rescuing him would do him no favors and put a big "chink" in my credibility. Last, but not least, I did not let Scotty run to me and interrupt a class whenever he had a problem. If he had forgotten to get a paper signed, field trip money, or a folder for a project, he had to get it between classes. This seems like a little thing, but it is not.

As I look back, I can see that the problem began with my own in-security. I was a pro at Algebra, Geometry, and Trigonometry, but not so at Calculus. I had four calculus classes in college and did well in the first three and survived the last one. After graduating, I had no exposure to calculus for 22 years. I suddenly found myself teaching a difficult subject that I remembered very little about. I studied diligently and let the kids know that we were "doing" this together. I traveled a lot slower than usual, but we managed to get through derivatives and the first semester without too much pain. The kids had really bonded by now and were feeling that pesky itch of senioritis that grows exponentially as the senior year progresses. They were becoming feisty and once in a while I had to come down on them because they were beginning to test their "adult-hood". In addition, the calculus was getting harder and I was getting more frustrated with my inability to figure out many of the problems. A teacher who is not confident with their material is like a swimmer with a bloody cut on their knee in a pool of sharks. My "sharks" were circling and it was not a pretty sight. To make it worse, my son was one of the sharks.

When I get mad, I cry. I hate that. It is one of my least endearing qualities. Most of the time I control it well and I wait until I get home or at least in the ladies room before I cut loose. I could count on one hand the number of times I have cried in front of a class in all my years, and those were usually because of a death or serious illness of a student or a colleague. I am not ashamed of those tears. One day in calculus, however, I got so mad at myself and the sharks that I was about to lose it. I was mad at myself because I was letting this calculus get to me and I was weary from all of the effort I was putting into it. I felt like my brain was being deep fried and laid out on a paper towel to drain. I cannot remember why I was mad with them but I think it had something to do with breaking pencils in class and generally not paying attention and helping me work through the problems. What hurt the most however is that my golden son who I loved so much was part of the pencil breaking patrol. It was a little thing, I know, but it meant so much to me. I read somewhere that polar bears eat their young and at that moment I understood why.

I gave the class a problem to do and excused myself and went to the ladies room and cried. When I pulled myself together, I went by the room and asked Scotty to step outside. I took him behind the school and we had a "little" talk. (This is one of those times that I should never have left a class un-supervised that long, but frankly at that point, I did not care if I got in trouble, got sued, and spent the rest of my life in Sing-Sing. There is no calculus in Sing-Sing.) The jist of our talk was how hard it was for me when my own son was being disrespectful to me. I let him know that what he did was not that big a crime and that he was no worse than the other students, it just hurt more because he was mine. He apologized and since my face was red and my nose was swollen we came up with a good lie to tell the class about why I was upset. I can't remember that one either, but it must have been a good one because the class seemed to buy it and was a lot better when I began teaching again. Scotty was never disrespectful in class again.

Looking back, I would not change a thing. Teaching my son was a privilege and joy for me and bearable for him. We shared many wonderful memories at the magnet school. I salute him because since I was the prom sponsor, he never got to go to a prom without his mother being there; and since I was very close with the faculty he never got to go on a field trip without my knowing what was going on in the back seat of the bus. He was a good sport about it all and the look he gave me going across the stage at graduation made me very happy that I had not eaten him in February.

THE ONLY ONE

In all of my teaching years, I have only "failed" a very few students. I know that I never "failed" them, they "failed" themselves, but it still wasn't any easier to take, knowing that the choice was theirs. I have always believed that a student who does their best should not fail. If their effort is consistent and they seek help, it is unlikely that they will fail, but on rare occasions they do. In those few instances, consultation with parents and administration usually resulted in a minimum passing grade. I know that there are different philosophies and policies on this and I understand both sides of the debate. I also know that there are some students that just can't get math and do not need to have their lives drastically changed because they gave something their best and could not make the mark. These students do not pick careers that are going to require upper level math courses and if they can make it out of high school, they will do fine. Most of the students that did fail, were in lower level classes and could make it up in summer school. I have had one other senior fail calculus but it did not affect his graduation. I worked with him all second semester and gave him many chances, but much to his mother and my frustration, he just gave up. Carl was the only student that ever had his graduation jeopardized by failing my class, and the anguish that I felt was unbelievable!

Carl missed too many classes. He was failing because he had made some very bad choices. He was absent on the day of the first test. There were several students out that day because we were going through a flu epidemic. Carl, however, came to school an hour late. This class uses the college syllabus and therefore the rules are a little tougher. There are five tests during the semester and if you miss a test for any reason you get a zero. The saving grace is that you get to drop one test grade. Due to so many flu cases, I decided to suspend the rule and let those who were sick make up the test with no penalty. Carl's situation however, was a little harder to determine. His Spanish teacher told me that he had overslept. So I decided to give him a zero. Two days later, the guidance counselor told me that he was having family problems and that he had been talking to his mother. Being the wimp that I am, I asked Carl to come by and talk to me. First I scolded him for not coming by and talking to me immediately. Then I asked him why he was out; he did not want to give me any details but he did tell me that what he needed to talk to his mom about was more important than the test. I gave him a copy of the test and told him to do it over the weekend and I would give him some credit. Anything is better than a zero. After a long weekend, I asked him for the test on Tuesday morning and he gave it to me with seven out of 28 problems done. I graded it and he made a 14. I put a 30 in the grade book. I tried to talk to him all week but I did not have a chance before the principal came by to see me. He told me that he had spent a lot of time with Carl on the senior retreat, and I told him what had happened with Carl's first test. He explained to me a little bit about Carl's home situation and I found myself going into wimp mode again. It is unbelievable to me what these students have to deal with at home. I changed his 30 to a 50. I talked to Carl and let him know that he needs to step up to the plate, but that I was going to show him a little compassion.

Carl did not heed my warning. He failed the second test. He was not doing any homework and not paying attention well in class. Once again I talked to him and he assured me that he would do better. He is a senior and if he fails the class he will not graduate. He soon had four absences and would not be able to get college credit, but he still had hope of passing. When he was absent again, I couldn't believe it. I had just gotten thru talking to him. I told him that I had never been the teacher who was the cause of a senior not graduating. I love Carl. He is a good kid, he is just self-destructing right now, and I do not know how to help him. I got a message after class to call his mom. She is out of town so she left me her cell phone number and I called her as soon as possible. She was not aware that he had been absent so much and was not aware that he was not at school that day. We talked for a while about what we could do to help him. I sent home an extra copy of the book and she got him a tutor. She is eager to do what it takes to turn him around. Carl would not focus in class and never really gave it his best. He rarely came before or after school for help.

Carl, his Mom, and I spent the first semester playing "Let's Make A Deal". I could not stand the thought of failing a senior. I ended up giving Carl many points and he passed with the minimum grade. He and I had several chats and he promised that he would be a new man second semester.

At the dawn of second semester, Carl seemed to be grateful for his mercy first semester and turned over a new leaf. He seemed to be very interested in the statistics that was being taught and was even eager to hear about the mis-use of statistics to win a debate, especially in the global warming issue. I really worked hard preparing that lesson to keep him enthusiastic and he did not show up for class. He had overslept. Before the semester was over he had several more absences and he kept shooting himself in the foot. His Mom and I had several conferences with him. He was failing, even with a tutor. He would not take notes in class and the tutor had no way of knowing what I thought to be important in the sections. Carl would rarely come in for help. It is amazing to me that students will not seek help from the person that knows what is going to be on the test. Just before the end of the semester, Carl's mom called me and asked me if Carl had a chance of passing if he took a day off to go out of town with his Dad. I told her that I did not know if Carl would pass, but I was sure he would not if he went, because he was already over his limit of absences to get credit. Carl stayed but made his displeasure known to me by pouting all period and not taking a single note. This was very sad, as it was on that day that I went over what would be on the exam. We had another conference and I told his mother that if Carl passed the exam, I would pass him, but if he did not, I could not. He failed the exam miserably. Carl was not going to graduate.

At this point his Dad entered the picture and a conference was scheduled with the counselor, the principal, myself and both parents. Nobody blamed me and everyone agreed that I had been most generous and patient with Carl. They did however want him to "walk" across that stage with his class and were willing to do most anything to see that happen. It was agreed that he would not get a diploma, but he could walk if he would agree to get a private tutor and work 30 hours with her and retake the final. The parents would pay for the tutor. Hopefully he would get this done in time to convince the admission office at his college of choice that he had graduated. Carl passed the final with the tutoring. I do not know if Carl will continue to lack the self-discipline to succeed at college. Maybe we should not have let him get bailed out at the end. I did not have it in me to refuse him that last rope. I hope it was the right thing to do... I do know that I am glad that I have had the privilege of teaching in schools where "the whole child" is considered but I always wonder if we are really helping in situations like Carl's. (Carl came by to see me today. He dropped out of college and is working for his dad.)

CRUSHING VERSUS CODDLING

Claire is a quiet little girl who does well most of the time. One of her friends died in a car wreck last week and she has missed six days of school. I am one of those "suck it up" kind of people, and I have to be careful to make sure that I do not expect too much. I do not want to sound harsh here but life has to go on and it is time for Claire to get back to school. We discussed this at the teacher's lunch table today and there is real concern that Claire is getting so far behind in all of her classes that she is going to have trouble catching up. Some of the teachers felt that we should cut her some slack and not make her make up everything, just the critical assignments and tests. I am somewhat OK with that and I surely did not want to sound like the "Grinch", but I have two problems with that suggestion. First of all, it is all of those little assignments that help her understand the math she has missed. Secondly, I am a great believer in responsibility. I am all for giving Claire extended time, but I believe that she needs to do the work. The funeral was four days ago and she has still not returned. I believe that we need to be there for her and support her, but coddling her will not help her in the long run. I don't want her to turn into a Joseph. . .

Many years ago, I was teaching in a comprehensive high school. I was also involved with a lot of extra-curricular activities, one of which was being the quiz bowl coach. For those of you who are not familiar with that activity, it is a fast paced academic competition using electronic buzzers and to be good at it you have to have good reflexes and a broad knowledge base. I had several excellent players. Quiz bowl players are usually good students but once in a while a good player is just not "school" motivated and struggles in school. Joseph was one of those kids. He was very bright but he would be the first to tell you that he was not into "busy work" or "homework". Joseph was on my team for four years and he managed to keep his GPA up high enough to keep off of academic probation so he could play. He loved quiz bowl! He was personable and fun to be around. I was extremely concerned when his grades plummeted during the second semester of his senior year. He was so close to graduation and he just quit working. He was failing three courses and his teachers and parents had tried everything they could do to motivate him. There was no way he was going to graduate. About a month before graduation, his family checked him into a mental health facility. I never knew what the diagnosis was, but I think it was some kind of depression. He was in the facility a little more than three weeks and was released just before graduation. It was the first time I had ever gone to visit a student under those circumstances and I just kept my visit light and airy. Joseph seemed very upbeat to me and I left feeling that he was saner than me! Now I know that depression is very real, and very scary, and I do not want to make light of it, but when lockers were cleaned out at the end of the year, I began to wonder if Joseph had played the system.

As a result of his situation, the administrators and teachers agreed to greatly minimize his work load and allow Joseph to graduate. He did not have to make up the tests he had missed and he was not required to turn in his senior English paper. All pressure was taken off and only basic assignments were required. His averages were adjusted so that he would pass. If Joseph was truly clinically depressed and possibly suicidal, I agree that this was the right thing to do. I wish that I had not had to clean out his locker. When I did, I found several books on mental health that were very detailed in giving symptoms and information. Now I knew Joseph very well and he was not the type of person that would borrow these books from the public library as self-help guides. He was the type of person who would read them to mimic symptoms to allow him to get out of the impossible situation that he had created for himself.

Now sometimes I think I am guilty of watching too much TV and being too suspicious of other peoples' motives and actions. Joseph may have been completely legitimate and needed coddling at that point in his life. I do not know and I never shared my suspicions with anyone because I had no real proof and I did not want to accuse anyone of something so serious. Nevertheless, I am always cautious of students who take "situations' and milk them for all that they are worth. I have learned, however, that if I "ere" it has to be on the side of compassion. That is what I chose to do with Claire.

MY FAVORITE STUDENT

I like all my students, and try hard to be fair,
But it has come the time to confess.
No matter how hard I try not to show it,
There is a certain type I have to like best.

My favorite students are the quiet ones,
Who make it so easy to teach.
They pay attention, and do their work,
And use their brains as far as they will reach.

My favorite students are the class clowns,
Who do anything to attract attention.
They keep my days from dying of boredom
With antics too horrible to mention.

My favorite students are the ones who don't care,
They really need my love and concern.
If I could just let them know, that in search of themselves,
There is so much worth their while to learn.

My favorite students are the whiners and fussers,
Who argue and grumble and groan.
I spend every day, waiting to hear what they'll say,
Wishing they were in the twilight zone.

My favorite students are the "V. I. P. 's",
Who think they are God's gift to the human race.
One day they will see, what the rest of us think,
And their perspective will painfully fall back in place.

My favorite students are the scatterbrains,
Who frustrate me so with their ways.
They search, they hunt, they drop, they lose,
They walk around in an endless maze.

My favorite students are the ones so full of hate,
Who fight any authority they meet.
Dear Lord please help them adjust, like the rest of us
Or they face a life full of pain and defeat.

My favorite students are all of you,
Who have filled my year with such pleasure.
Thank you for touching my life, and adding your share,
I love you in a way no one can measure! !
~ Lizzy Sutton

THE WHOLE CHILD

I remember sitting at a lunch table with a bunch of high school teachers many, many years ago who were engaged in a very lively debate concerning teaching the "whole child. " When you think about it, that discussion sounds silly. Is anybody really going to teach part of a child? Back then I was a young idealistic "whipper snapper" surrounded by veteran teachers. I was confident in my position but I had learned very early in my career to listen more and talk less. Therefore I just soaked it all in as several great veteran teachers declared that it was their job to teach a subject and not "babysit". The table was split and the dialog was lively. Eventually I could be quiet no longer and put my vote in with the "whole child" faction. I was amazed at how dogmatic the "not whole child" contingent was, especially since I respected some of them for their great teaching style.

That had to be 29 years ago and a lot has changed since then. I cannot even imagine that discussion going on with much debate in this age and time. When I first started teaching my only experience with what goes on in a student's home was what went on in my home as I grew up. I had a desk and a study lamp and parents who made sure that I had whatever I needed to succeed in school. Sports were great but they were not such high stress events that consumed such a high percentage of the student's time. I was pretty much clueless as to the situations that many of my students came from, but I quickly learned that teaching a subject was not enough. At one time or another every student comes to school with some "baggage" and we have to constantly be vigilant.

One of the first things we should do is quickly learn their names. This should be a top priority. There are several good "name games" that you can play and all sorts of memory tricks. Knowing a child's name quickly is an easy way to validate their existence and lets them know that you think they are worth the effort. This can be difficult if you have six different classes full of new faces, but it can be woven into the lessons and activities during the first week and it is the first step in letting them know how much you care.

Every child should feel that they are treated fairly and there should be no perception of "teacher's pets". If you practice enough and are sneaky enough they should all feel like they are your favorites. Be sure at least once a year that you privately tell every one of your students that they are special and that you believe in them and what they can accomplish. Be sure the quiet ones get as much positive attention as possible and don't let the more aggressive ones dominate your time.

If behavior patterns change, investigate and find out what is going on. Do not jump to conclusions if a child is absent too much, starts sleeping in class, or becomes surly. I have had to remove my foot from my mouth so many times because I did not check out the background before I began to deal with a situation. If you are in a public school pray for them in private. If you are in a setting where public prayer is welcome, let them know that you are praying for them and ask them if they would like for the class to pray with them. I take the time to let them know that even though I teach upper level math, I am empathetic to their problems and want to be there for them. I want to find out what is going on in every child's life and do what I can to make it better in my classroom. I cannot fix all of their problems and I will not lower my academic expectations. Nevertheless, I will help them manage their way through difficult times and help them see that I am on "their side. "

CINDY

Jerry, the young teacher across the hall was very distraught at lunch today and he could not even eat. I left the table early to see if he was O. K. He was very upset over Cindy. He had taught Cindy two years earlier and even though he did not teach her this year, she had taken a comment he had made when she was previously in his class out of context and was making inappropriate comments about him to the other students. Her statements were very damaging to his reputation and very unfair to him. To complicate things, she was also his teacher's assistant and was causing all sorts of problems with the students in that class. Every time he tried to talk to her she started crying. She was making his life miserable. I advised him to go talk to the guidance counselor and remove her as his assistant. In my opinion, she did not need to be in his classroom in any capacity. I also told him that I had my concerns about Cindy and that he needed to nip her comments in the bud, because she could do some real damage to his reputation. He needs to gently confront her, tears or no tears. I offered to sit in if he wanted to have a conference with her. He is thinking about it. We both believe that there is something going on in Cindy's life that we do not know about. It seems that the only attention she knows how to get is negative.

I have taught Cindy in three math classes and understood Jerry's frustrations. Cindy is a little hard to describe but here goes… For starters, Cindy loves and is good at sports. She is a very pleasant and respectful young lady with a bubbly personality. She, however, hates math and is not very strong in any of her academic subjects. She is a very social creature and a roller coaster of emotions. Watching her in the classroom, I believe that she really has a hard time focusing. To complicate matters she does not always think before she speaks. Her older sister graduated from our school two years ago and was an excellent student, excellent athlete, and is very much missed by Cindy. She was a tough act to follow, but Cindy never showed any resentment. Two years ago Cindy's parents got a divorce. All of this put together, it seems that Cindy is not only having a difficult time with Jerry, but she is also a problem in my classroom. Her math teacher last year was not anywhere as strict as I, and it seems that Cindy is "sticking her foot in her mouth" almost daily. A couple of days she tried to fall asleep in class and she was crying twice. She had three days to get her syllabus signed and it took her a week. Today was the deadline for everyone to bring one pack of three by five note cards and she did not have hers. I had assigned this as homework on the first day of school and told them that it counted as a homework assignment. Five students in the class did not have theirs, Cindy included. I told them I was taking one point off of their homework average. Cindy raised her hand, and when recognized, informed me that I cannot do that because I am punishing a non-academic assignment with an academic grade. Her tone, albeit polite, was a slight challenge to my authority. The problem was that she was right. My response was to tell her that she was absolutely correct and that I thought they would rather lose a point than have 15 minutes of detention for not doing as instructed. I then gave her the choice and not surprisingly she chose to lose the point. I gave the same choice to the other four and they all chose the point.

Cindy does not understand the material because she does not pay attention in class. She asks a few questions, but they are not very good ones. I asked her about coming before or after school for tutoring but she plays softball and works at Starbucks which might explain why she tries to fall asleep in class. I taught Cindy five years ago when she was in Algebra I. She has not matured. I know that it is going to be a battle all year because there are several other students in the room that encourage her comments and reinforce her bad behavior. When corrected, she either becomes defensive or cries. She is also usually careful not to go too far. She knows how to be highly irritating, but she doesn't want to get into big trouble so she never goes very far over the line.

Cindy came up to me one day in class and told me that she had met with the guidance counselor and that if she was going to get the HOPE scholarship she had to have an "A" in my class. Now I am not saying that won't happen but in my opinion it is not likely. I do not tell Cindy that. I told her that if she starts focusing all of the time it is possible.

Cindy has goofed around for three years and in her senior year, she wants a miracle. I did what I could to help her find her miracle but even with a lot of prayer she barely scraped by with a low B. Cindy is the type of student that it is very difficult to manage. She is a high mainte-nance drama queen that loves to entertain the class. She has to be kept under a tight rein, yet she is very fragile and breaks easily. She and I struggle because I am so into order and she is so into freedom. I don't think either one of us will change, but Cindy will find her place where her energy and enthusiasm can be put to good use.

Cindy graduated two or three years ago and I have not heard from her since she left. I always thought that she did not like me because I was so tough on her. I was amazed when one of our teachers left last year and when cleaning out her stuff, found a song that Cindy wrote. She shared it with me and I could not believe that Cindy thought so highly of me! I hope to catch up with her in the future and let her know how much the poem below means to me. It is a parody of "The Devil Went Down to Georgia" and a little hard to follow but here goes:

MS. REEMS WENT DOWN TO GEORGIA
Ms. Reems went down to Georgia
She was lookin' for some trig to steal.
She was in a bind, she couldn't find out sine
She was willin' to make a deal.
She came across Mrs. Sutton on a white board and writtin' it HOT.
She grabbed a marker, went up beside 'er and said:
"Girl, lemme tell you what…"
"I bet you didn't know, but I'm a math teacher too, and if you care to take a dare
I'll make a bet with you.
You solve a pretty good problem girl,
But give Mr. Starner his dues.
I bet an overhead of gold against your soul that I'm better at math than you. "
The lady said "my name's Lizzy, and it might be a sin, but I'll take your bet

You're gonna regret, I'm the best at math there's ever been. "
Ms. Sutton get your pencil and your calculator too.
Ms. Reems is gonna use trig functions and she's gonna get you.
If you solve cotangent you'll get an overhead of gold.
But if you lose, Ms. Reems will get your soul.
Run to the whiteboard write, write, write
Your math skills are outta sight.
If you beat Ms. Reems then everyone will see
How well you can solve a trig identity.
Ms. Reems sharpened her pencil and put her hand on her hip.
Then she checked the eraser and fire flew from the tip.
She went to the board and drew a thin line
She quickly began drawing the parent graph for sine.
2 Pi and Pi the lines will go through
But with the rest of the graph she did not know what to do.
And through the proper points SHE drew the lines through.
Ms. Reems threw down the marker cause she knew she'd been beat.
And she laid the overhead of gold down at Mrs. Sutton's feet.
Ms. Sutton said: "Come on back if you ever want to try again. "
I told you once you son of a gun, I'm the best math teacher there's ever been.

(It is amazing that Cindy would let me win at anything!)

WEENIE TEACHER

One of the things that I have always struggled with is what to do with students who really cannot do math. I am sure that this is a common plight in every subject as teachers try to deal with students that simply do not have the skills to succeed in a given subject. There are so many factors to consider here that it would take another book to be thorough on the subject, so I will stick to the math realm, the only realm with which I feel qualified to address. I think my position is best explained by an illustration.

I scheduled a parent conference with a senior and her mother because she was failing my college math class. I had participated in many phone calls with her mother all six weeks, but Stephanie was still failing.

Stephanie was a very sweet young lady who paid attention in class and did all of her homework. She showed up for tutoring sessions, but mostly because her mom made her. She had just failed another test and was in danger of failing the class. Immediately after the test I talked to her about what I observed as she was taking the test. She spent a lot of time staring at the clock, twirling her hair and looking around the room. This resulted in her running out of time. She knows that I never let them have more time than is allotted, yet from my perspective; she was daydreaming and not concentrating on the test.

Before the parent conference, I received this email from Stephanie: (Her punctuation and sentence structure!)

> Dear Mrs. Sutton,
> I really am confused now. Honestly, I'll say I struggled with making the decision of even taking college math, but I felt that if I took it now with a teacher I was comfortable with then maybe I would do better. Truth be told I am NOT good at math and I never have been: I just can't study well for math. . I can't memorize changing problems and formulas. I really try to do everything I can to help myself: I buy self-help teaching books, I have hired an extra tutor, and I do work nightly on the chapters. I could understand not passing if I did not apply myself but now I just don't know what to do? On the matter of my test. I thought I could come back to finish it after school because I did not have time to go back and finish certain problems. I do know that I looked up at the clock and looked around the room as well, I have problems focusing on one thing for too long and it begins to give me headaches. I have to take a moment where I clear my head and try to re-focus myself. I am sorry, I have been trying to fix it...trust me. It happens too often and it really affects my grades. I really need to pass this class, do I even have a chance anymore? I will do anything it takes! I guess right now I just need advice and my options. I really hope this does not make you angry, that's not my intention

AT ALL...I just wanted to let you know how serious I am about trying to pass your class. I do look forward to having that conference so we can talk in person. This is just to let you know ahead of time, I'm sorry it's so long. Thank you for everything you have done for me.

- Stephanie

Stephaine is not the only desperate student that I have had over my teaching career and I am sure that she will not be the last. I have faced many "ethical delimmas" concerning grades over the years and have finally come to the conclusion that is right for me. I think that math is different from most other subjects in the fact that once a student who is "bad" at math is through with their education, they do not need any of the high school or college math to flourish as a contributing member of society. I think it is good that they have taken all the math they can because I firmly believe that it strengthens their reasoning skills and thought processes. Nevertheless, I am fully aware that some of my students will never use the actual math that I teach them. Therefore if a student is willing to show me how hard they are trying, I will materialize the magic grading fairy and help them out under the following conditions:

They must come in for tutoring with me at least two times a week.

They must come in and work with me to correct every test on which they have scored below an 80.

They must do study problems for every test.

They must do all of their homework.

They must be very attentive in class.

They will arrange a student led parent/teacher conference once a six weeks to evaluate progress.

They will sign a written contract attesting to the above requirements. If they do not sign the contract or they break the contract, I send the grading fairy back to "Neverland"!

At the first parent conference, I make sure that the parent and the student understand that if the student passes, it will be on effort and not math skills. It is very important for the parents to know that the mathematical ability is weak so they will not be surprised at low SAT and achievement test scores. It is also important to the parents and students to know that MIT and Georgia Tech are probably not good choices and that engineering is out as a career option.

Amazingly enough, if the student sticks to the plan, grades come up without any help and the student learns that a lot of hard work can overcome lack of natural ability and the grading fairy was not needed! I have been accused of being a "weenie" for being so soft, but failing a student in a subject they can't do and won't directly need, when they are working very hard is something I cannot do. A contract was signed by Stephanie and her mom and Stephanie held up her end of the contract and passed with a 70, with a little help from the grading fairy.

THE FIFTH CLASS

I have a teacher in my department who is a veteran teacher. She does an excellent job with four of her classes. She teaches bell to bell and has a good rapport with her students. She has a fifth class, however, that is giving her a problem. This class is a group of low level seniors, many of whom were ready to be finished with math and graduate on the first day of their senior year. There are about 22 students in the class. About a third of them are respectful and work well but the rest of them are disruptive and whine constantly. When instruction is being provided they do not listen and then when they cannot do the work, they ask for the instruction to be repeated. When the teacher will not repeat the lesson, they say that the teacher does not teach the material. To make the class real, the teacher has gone to a lot of trouble to arrange guest speakers to prepare the students for the type of consumer mathematics that they will need after graduation. The students complain that they will never need to figure their taxes because H&R Block can do it for them. No matter how hard she works, they are unappreciative and unruly.

Everybody faces a class like this once in a while and the year seems longer because the teacher is just as ready to bid them farewell as they are to "get otta here". The key to making it through the year as their teacher is to view them as a challenge and not a problem. These students are not going to be neurologists or mechanical engineers. They have probably had a rocky path through high school and they are just waiting on some freedom and a change. Most of them are going to find the skills that they need to succeed in life and do just fine as soon as they survive school. Some of them will go to college and be teachers and social workers and businessmen and wish they had applied themselves more in high school. Nevertheless, your goal as a teacher is to guide them successfully through their senior year with as little trauma as possible.

My first advice for this teacher is to not to take it personally. We have all had classes like this. I told her to summon all of her professionalism and experience, and no matter how hard they tried, not to let them see that they were getting to her. She needed to hang a punching bag in the garage and take out her angst on it every night and face the class cool calm and collected. It was a game for them to try to push her buttons and upset her and she needed to make sure they lost at that game. Students will never respect a teacher that cannot control their own emotions. There have been many times when I wanted to get out my "ray gun" and zap an entire class into some parallel universe, but they never knew it.

My second piece of advice was to get control of the unruly students. She needed to stop trying to correct them as a class, but to deal with individual students. If a student talked while she was teaching, she needed to correct that student with a warning and if it happened again she needed to take disciplinary action. I suggested talking to the administrator in charge of discipline and letting them know what she was experiencing and that she needed help getting the students in line. I advocated starting with an individual warning and then assigning a detention followed by a phone call home. If none of these efforts worked, I would fill out a discipline form and let the administrator deal with the problem. It might take a month or two to let the students know that you are serious, but you need to spend the time that it takes to get the class under control before you can hope to teach them. The bottom line for me is that I will not teach until I have the attention of the class.

As she works to get the class under control, she needs to begin to be an encourager. Negative comments directed at the entire class must be eliminated. Search and find positive things to say. If the class does bad on a test, find something to say to give them hope. I have a calculus class that does great on the problems that only require mechanics but they do terrible on the application problems. Nevertheless I keep giving them application problems and tell them each time that they are doing better and how proud I am of their improvement. Compliment everything that is positive and do not linger on the negatives.

As teachers we tend to treat lower level classes differently. We need to let them know that our expectations are high and we know they can do it. They know it if they are treated as "not as capable" and we have to be careful not to send subtle signals that we are treating them as intellectually inferior. Do we offer fewer opportunities for them to try higher level thinking and keep everything on the knowledge comprehension level? Are we as patient on "wait time" when we ask a question and give them time to think about it before answering? Do we call on everyone equally and do we give them prompts to help them answer successfully?

Every class deserves our best, even the "fifth" class. They challenge our professionalism and aggravate us into early retirement, but they are no less worthy of our efforts than our accelerated classes.

THE PERFECT JOB FOR YOU

(You can tell how old this is by the references to some of the people! I don't remember writing this or why I wrote it but it is obvious that I was frustrated with the students. I probably Xeroxed copies and handed them out. Since I do not believe in nagging, sometimes my poetry is a not so subtle way of "getting something off of my chest".)

Are the odds in your favor,
To be what you want to be?
What are the chances of being the real you?
Let's take a look and see!

If you are the class clown type,
And are always looking for a chuckle…
There can only be one Bill Cosby,
So buy a red suit with a big black buckle!

If you have a rotten attitude,
And grump around like the grim reaper,
There can only be one Grumpy Smurf.
So do the world a favor, and be a light house keeper.

If you don't care about your work,
And sleep in class each day.
Rip Van Winkle already has your job,
So see how well a mattress factory will pay!

If you think that you are always right,
And everyone else's opinions are wrong,
Kaddafi has your job taken for now,
But according to Mr. Reagan, not for long.

If you always say you can't,
Before you know if you "could",
Pee Wee Herman already has his application in.
So you had better start chopping "would".

If you are in the habit of making excuses,
And putting everything off until later,
Scarlett O'Hara does it a whole lot better,
Why don't you learn to operate an elevator?

If you think you are really hot stuff,
And the world would burn without your charm
Don Johnston and Christy Brinkley have that all wrapped up,
Maybe you can invent a better smoke alarm.

If just getting by is your game,
Instead of always doing your best.
Than almost everyone qualifies for your job,
So stand in line with the rest!
~ Lizzy Sutton

THAT SPECIAL DAY

It is just a little thing but on every student's birthday I give them a fun size Snicker with a bow tied on it with a "Shazaam" attached. (Shazaams will be explained in the next chapter.) As I present it, the whole class sings happy birthday. If a student has a birthday in July we celebrate it on the appropriate day in August and we celebrate June birthdays in May. I am very careful not to miss anybody's birthday. Some of the students blush and some of them bask in the glow of attention. It is amazing how much such a little gesture shows how much you care.

I read an article in the AARP magazine about a teacher who sends a birthday card to every student past and present. Each student receives a personal, handwritten birthday letter from him every year. He figures that he has penned about 33,000 letters to 2,500 students over 25 years. WOW! ! ! I did that once for about three years and stamps got so expensive that I had to quit.

PANTY HOSE AND PEP RALLIES

It has been a very interesting day. It started out with panty hose and more underwear than I am accustomed to suffering through. All staff and seniors were expected to dress as for a wedding, graduation, or a funeral, depending on your mindset. (Anytime I have to wear panty hose it puts me in a funeral mindset.) I had thoroughly explained the dress code to all of my seniors and the minute my college class walked in, I spotted three violations. Ginger had on leggings, Hannah's top was too low and Amy had on three inch heels. Now granted these three girls have never had me before and therefore, I guess they haven't learned to take me seriously, but they sure did this morning. Ginger has to roll up her leggings so that no one could see them. (That made them about as comfortable as my pantyhose!) Hannah's front got the safety pin treatment. Amy just happened to have another pair of shoes in the car. The fun never stops.

The class was dismissed thirty minutes early so that we could report for the senior convocation. Thus the reason for my discomfort! This was the first time that we had this particular activity at our school and no one knew what to expect. The high school faculty sat on the stage, all of the senior parents sat in chairs on the gym floor, all of the seniors sat between the faculty and the parents and all of the underclassmen sat in the bleachers to the left of the stage. It was a very solemn and touching ceremony. The seniors were prayed over, challenged, and dedicated. There were many tears and we all knew that a wonderful thing had just happened. There was only one fly in the ointment. With all of the teachers on the stage, no one was supervising the underclassmen. Most of them were respectful but some of them were acting like it was a pep rally, talking, punching, etc. If looks could kill, many of them would be dead as a doornail, as the faculty tried to control them with their eye movements.

After the assembly was over, I cornered three of the worst on the bleachers and had a little talk with them while their peers exited. They were all apologies and promises that it would never happen again. I let them know that if it did there would be serious consequences. The assistant principal did not take too kindly to all of their behavior and lunchtime became a prayer meeting for one and all!

After lunch, I changed into more comfortable attire. I can only stand pantyhose so long. Things seemed to be going smoother until the fire drill bell went off in the middle of my calculus test. I guess if you are going to mess up a day, you might as well mess up the whole day. So out we go, and then in we come. On the way in, I saw a young lady whose shirt was un-buttoned where it should have been buttoned. Usually, I just warn the student about dress code violations; tell them to fix it; they say yes "mam"; and life goes on. This young lady and I had already gone through this ritual earlier this morning so it was time to give her a dress code cut which will result in her losing her casual day next week. I have never taught this young lady but we had gone round and round about dress code all last year. At the end of last year I tried to talk to her and can only describe her attitude as "surly" "disdainful" and "extremely annoying". This year I did not even try. When I saw her un-buttoned again, I had her step in my room and fill out a dress code form and gave her the top copy. I did not try to preach to her, I just made it a point to be very polite (when I would have liked to have smacked her), and stayed all business. She made it a point to be reticent but her body language and eye rolling spoke wonders. I am afraid she and I are in for a long year.

The grand finale on the day was no planning period because of a pep rally! I must admit that it was a good pep rally, but I had planned to grade my calculus test and it did not get done. The only way not to take them home was to stay after school. Since it was the Labor Day weekend, I decided it was worth it to stay and keep the weekend free. I got one test graded and then had an un-expected parent visitor. As much as I don't like being interrupted when I am grading calculus tests, I put on my "very glad to see you face' and welcomed my visibly upset mom.

Katie's mom and I have been trying to get Katie through math for five years now. Katie is a senior and is finally being evaluated for learning disabilities. She suffered a major blow to her ego last year when she realized that her dream of going to a major University would not be a possibility because of her grades. She had been told that more than once by her parents and teachers but it never sunk in. She was beginning to realize that it was going to be tough to get in at a lot of schools. Reality had hit Katie in the face and it was difficult!

So why the visit on a Friday afternoon? Katie was in class on Thursday and a teacher had made the comment that; "Most of you will be going off to the college of your choice, and those of you who have goofed off, have made your bed and now you have to lie in it! " This teacher was not thinking! That was a cruel thing to say, even if it was true in some cases. I know this teacher and if he realized what he had said, he would never have said it. It was the proverbial case of sticking your foot in your mouth.

Katie's mom came to me for advice. Should she go talk to the teacher and let him know how devastating that comment was to Katie and her fragile self esteem? Should she talk to the principal? She did not want to get the teacher in trouble but she was afraid that if she talked directly to him that he might take it out on Katie. We talked for a while and I tried to explain to her that he was young and simply lacked the wisdom to always run his words through a "proper teacher filter". I encouraged her to talk to the teacher first and then if she still felt that she should, talk to the principal. She did not like that idea because she was totally convinced that there would be repercussions for Katie and I could not convince her otherwise. I know this teacher fairly well and I offered to talk to him for her without revealing whom the offended student was.

She was very relieved. She only wanted to make sure that he knew that he needed to guard his words.

By the time she left, it was too late to grade papers. Oh well, what else would a teacher do on Labor Day?

Challenging Authority Properly

I think one of the most valuable things we can teach any student is how to disagree respectfully with an authority figure. Students who learn this skill will have an advantage throughout their lives and will be much happier and more successful. I have seen so many adults that were constantly sabotaging their own efforts by the way they related to people in authority over them. I was taught at a very young age that I was to respect my elders, bosses, and the President of the United States! I might add here that it did not matter if they earned my respect as a person, it was the position that I was to respect. Too many of today's young people are not being taught to respect and it is causing a world of trouble. Note that I did not say young people should always agree with people in authority, just that they ought to respect their position. Students need to be taught how to disagree respectfully because we do not want them to blindly follow authority figures and be bullied by them when they overstep their power.

In the classroom there are many opportunities to let the students know that it is OK to disagree with the teacher. It is like most everything else in human relationships; it is not what you say, it is how you say it. When I give back a test, I always call out the correct answers and then give the students an opportunity to come speak to me if they feel like their paper has not been graded correctly. At the beginning of the year, even before I have given the first test, I let them know that disagreeing with me is Ok as long as they do it with the right attitude. Therefore, they know if they approach me with concerns about their test, it better be in a respectful manner. If I have a kid approach me with a chip on his/her shoulder, I send the student back to their seat and tell them if they can get their heart in the right place, I will be glad to talk to them after school. The students find out quickly that I will not deal with them at all if they do not treat me with respect.

Students also learn that a sense of humor and humility goes a long way with me. Here are two letters from two young men who have learned to deal with authority respectfully. The first young man forgot to sign his honor statement on a project and is begging to get his points back. The second letter is from a young man who failed his final exam and is begging for mercy in a critique of the course.

Dear Mrs. Sutton,

I write this letter to recognize your teaching power, and not to challenge it. The purpose of this letter is to ask for your grace and mercy on my soul. I, Darren Wilson, forgot to write my honor statement on my work that you assigned for our probability project. I, by myself and with no help received or given from or to any classmates, worked these problems, numbers one through thirty, on Saturday, April 17, 2010, from about 8:00pm to about 11:00pm while watching movies with my family. John Wilson, Sue Wilson, and Dan Wilson are all witnesses of my work on these problems. Although, I forgot to turn in my honor statement, I would be very grateful and thankful if you would allow me to receive the five points, or even partial credit, given for the honor statement.

Thank you for your consideration,
Darren Wilson

Dear Mrs. Sutton:

I implore you to review my exam with a grain of salt. I have no reason for pity other than the fact it has been a hectic past few weeks. On the subject of class improvement, I see no need for change. You exemplify the image I conceive when thinking of the ideal math instructor. I learned a plethora of concepts taking your class and while my grade may have suffered because of opting for an honors course this year, the extra knowledge gained was well worth the lower numerical grade value. After all, is school not about

learning instead of the endless rat race towards the highest
GPA it seems to have become?

With the utmost respect,

Jack

These two young men have learned that often when you deal with
authority, a little "smoozing" and a lot of humor gets them a long way.
Darren got four of the five points on the honor code and Jack did not
get anything but I loved his letter! (Even though Jack failed the final, he
passed the class.) By the way, I responded to both of their letters with
a written letter. Dealing with authority is a valuable lesson and as teachers we have the perfect opportunity. The payoff is huge for us and the
student.

DID YOU GET THE DEER?

A month ago, I hit a deer. If the truth be known the deer hit me, but
no one seems to care which way it happened. I was alone. It was late at
night and I was scared and tired. I acted like a grown-up and did not
call my son until it was all over and I was on my way home. When he
answered I calmly told him that I had hit a deer. The first thing he said
to me was; "Did you get the deer? " He hesitated a minute after I did
not answer and asked: "Are you all right? " In the background I heard
his wife say: "That was the wrong order buddy! " Boy was she right...
He wanted deer meat and I wanted to kill him. I needed a little bit of
comfort and concern and all I got was an inquiry as to how I would be
able to lower his grocery bill.

Once I got over the urge to kill, it began to dawn on me that I was
just as guilty as he was of asking questions in the wrong order. So often
when a student has missed my class, I will ask them when they are going
to take care of their make-up work before I ask them how they are feeling or show concern over their absence. Even though I am all into responsibility, my first concern should be more personal and empathetic.
When I ask the questions in the wrong order, I am missing an opportunity to let the kids know how much I really care. It is impossible to
know what a child might be going through in other areas of their life.

Getting some background information before asking the questions is always a wise move!

GIRL SCOUT COOKIES

I have a young man, Tim, who likes to make comments under his breath. Since school started he has done it a couple of times and I have not been able to hear what he has said. The kids around him laugh and it disrupts class. I usually ask him to repeat what he said and he does so and it is usually benign. Another young lady in class, Lindy, seemed to be bothered by his comments, and not understanding their history, I did not know why. I talked to Lindy before school this morning and she said that he is always teasing her about selling Girl Scout Cookies. Lindy is very insistent in her yearly quest as a cookie salesperson, so I could see how this was possible. Evidently Tim had been teasing her for several years and although it bothered her, she never told him. After class, I asked Tim to stay and firmly explained to him that comments under his breath that entertained other students were not acceptable in class. I also let him know that it was time to stop teasing Lindy, not only in my class, but in all classes. I made it very clear to him that if he continued to torture her, I would torture him for the rest of his high school career. He responded graciously and there were no more issues.

SARCASM

One of the most difficult things to discern in the classroom is when teasing crosses the line to sarcasm. I wish I had the magic trick for figuring this one out because it has gotten me in trouble before and is a serious issue for many teachers. I think it is part of the human condition to have "foot in your mouth disease" on occasion and I do not think that this anatomical enigma will ever be obliterated from the planet, but as a teacher, we do not have the luxury of "inserting" too often.

In this day of "political correctness" it seems that it is easier to get in trouble. There are so many groups that you could possibly offend that careful choice of words is even more critical than in the past. I never set out to hurt anyone's feelings, but I still manage to do it on occasion. I have developed a few guidelines that I try to use to keep myself in check, and I try to run them quickly through my brain before I say something clever.

***Young teenage girls seem to be the most sensitive and I try to stay away from any teasing at all with this group. Their self-esteem is very vulnerable, especially from about 6th grade to 10th. Any references to the body should be avoided, unless you are sure that they will be viewed as positive. Some of these young ladies are what I call "drama queens" and even when you say something positive, they can turn it around and create a crisis with your statement.

***If you even suspect that you have said something that can be misconstrued, be proactive. If possible, find the student and apologize immediately. If not, call the student at home. If the student has already told the parents, it may be necessary to apologize to them too. The best fix for a "foot in mouth" mistake is a heartfelt apology and the assurance that it will not happen again.

***New teachers and teachers who are new to a school should hold off on teasing until they get to know the school environment, the parents, and the whole picture. Teachers who have not established their reputations should be very careful. Having been at my present school for ten years now, I will be forgiven much. The first few months however, I was very careful to keep my mouth in check. I am still careful now, but not as much as before.

***Get to know your students ASAP and find out about their home lives. You do not want to tease a student and find out that there is something in their situation that makes that a sensitive topic.

THE FEAR FACTOR

I had such a tough year trying to bond with my seniors last year that I was bound and determined to make every effort to endear myself to them this year. In the past I have had them as Juniors and Seniors but our school is getting bigger and I have lots of seniors that I have never taught before. I needed to "bond" as soon as possible if I was going to make a difference in their lives in the brief nine months that I had left with them. I have been asked to go on the senior retreat every year and I have refused every year. My idea of camping is a Hampton Inn. A weekend in a cabin with 12 girls and no sleep was not anywhere near the top of my wish list. I was promised if I went that I would have private sleeping accommodations in deference to my age and I agreed to go. Now I know that "just being there" is the best way to bond, but I was about to find out when "just being there" crosses the line into insanity.

I went out of my way to be pleasant and personable and try to ignore minor infractions that would have normally needed correcting. I went out of my way to try to participate in everything and be a real trouper as they hiked, did low ropes courses, and played volleyball and football. I tried to ignore the fact that everywhere we walked was uphill and the steps to the cabins were very steep. I even did everything I could to ignore the pounding of my heart and the pulse racing in my temples as I tried to prove that there was still something left in the old girl! What I could not ignore was that nagging in my soul that urged me to face my fears and try one of the high ropes course elements.

Now I could pretend that I was doing it for the seniors. I could pretend that I was not comfortable asking them to face their fears if I was not willing to face mine. I could even pretend that I was making this grand sacrifice so the other faculty members would feel comfortable following suit. But I knew that the real reason was my new found courage. I had gone para-sailing the summer before and now I wanted to prove that my quest for adventure was not a fluke. I have been somewhat of a chicken all of my life and I am enjoying shocking people with the new me! Therefore I did the unthinkable. I climbed a very long extension ladder all the way to the top rung, skirted around a big pine tree and stepped out on a telephone pole suspended between two trees. I walked the length of the pole and back and then I just sat back and let gravity pull me down. I was secured in a harness and there was never any danger or disaster, but that did not help my fear. I was genuinely terrified and was grateful to be back on the ground. In writing, it sounds like I did all of this quickly but it really took forever, or so it seemed.

Was it worth it? You bet! As I was trapeezing across that telephone pole, Drew was on the ground standing next to Mrs. Bernard. He looked up at me and told her that he had a "new respect for Mrs. Sutton. " It is important to know a little about Drew. He is a very bright young man with a cynical nature. He has a lot of talent but not a lot of motivation.

His mantra is pretty much to get as much as he can with as little effort as possible. He is a very natural mathematician but is not into what he refers to as "busy work". I had been working a long time to get him to respond well to me so that I could guide him along a more productive path. Ever since I walked that pole, he is a new student. I am not sure exactly why there was such a change in such a little amount of time and why it took an act of sheer terror on my part to get him to perform at his ability level, but I am sure of one thing. Drew sees me in a different light and it has made an impact on his performance in my classroom.

BIG GIRLS DON'T CRY

When the Four Seasons sang that song in the 50's, (or was it the 60's?), they obviously had no experience with middle and high school girls. Some of them cry at the drop of a hat and many of them have perfected their conjuring up of tears to an art. Now there are many directions I could go with this topic, but I am going to stay within my own experience so this offering is about what I call "grading tears".

I am referring to those delicate little girls who cry anytime they make a 93 instead of a 98 or 100. I do not find that trait admirable, and it irritates me to no end. If I give a young lady back a test with a 53 on it, I often wonder why they do not cry, and if they do, I am full of sympathy. I would probably cry too. My problem is with all my "perfect Pollies" who make a big show out of their intolerance for imperfection in themselves.

I have a small number of girls and even a few boys whose body language is so predictable when tests are returned that I can set my watch by it. The boys don't cry but they do their version of crying with what I call the male pout. I think some of their reactions are attention seeking maneuvers to let people know how well they did. For instance, comments like: "I can't believe that I made a 98. I should have made a 100. " Nevertheless there are a few that are truly devastated when their results are less than perfect and as much as that annoys me, they need help. I do not respond to them during class, but I always make it a point to talk to them outside of class or call them at home. I have found that my attempts to change their behavior are usually useless over the short term, because their problem goes so deep that my un-educated counseling falls short. I have to try, however, and I have found that I have never had a negative effect on them. If I have them long enough, I see a little improvement in their ability to keep a stiff upper lip on test return days. It is very difficult to convince a motivated teenager that what they are learning is more important than what their grade is. Parents and society send them the opposite message and those who are eager to achieve and please others can't see past the grade. They have been told most of their life that good grades mean a good college, which leads to a better job which means a better life.

STUDENT PROFILE: S. D. S.

Everybody teaches one. It is just a matter of degree. I teach several. I come in contact with ones I do not even teach. There are a couple of "these" at my church and I even teach with an adult one. They come in every shape, size, color, and age. So what does S. D. S. stand for? Surly, disdainful, and sour.

Often I find this type of student the most difficult to deal with. I have difficulty communicating with them because they won't talk back. Most of them will not look you in the eye and if they do it is with a level of contempt that makes you very uncomfortable. When I teach them and I know them a little better, I start working on them. Sometimes it is hard to distinguish between SDS and shyness. It is important to tread very slowly and carefully with SDS. We never know what the child is facing at home. If I came from some of the situations that these kids do, I would have SDS too!

So what is the best cure for SDS? I have found through experience that these kids are hard to crack and take a lot of patience. If I teach them, I find that just being in my classroom helps to break them out of their shell a lot. My reputation in the school is that I am tough. I feed this reputation by enforcing the rules between classes and at lunch, so many students that I do not teach only see me in my role as an "enforcer". Therefore, they have their defenses up the minute that they walk into my classroom. When they get me in class most of them find out that I am strict but that I care very much about them and that I know how to have fun. They begin to loosen up and I do not have to do much to get them to respond to me. Once in a while, however, I get a student that has SDS so bad that they become my challenge for the year. They often see my idea of "fun" as immature and silly and that just adds to their negative "attitude".

The "hardcore" SDS kids need to be spoken to in a "very mature" manner every day. A simple "good morning" or "good afternoon" is a good start. Whenever they do something well, they should be recognized and praised without being gushy. If they are disrespectful to me, I am always careful to deal with the problem in a swift, yet positive manner. It is critical to do this in private. If an SDS student makes a comment in class that challenges my authority, I simply ask them to step outside and I teach until I can come to a point where I can go outside and talk to them. I am then very careful to diffuse the situation. You cannot win the battle if you argue with them. I try to think of one positive thing to say and start with that. Calm them down and take the wind out of their sails. You must be the professional here. Let them know what they did wrong and why you do not wish it to occur again. If they won't speak to you, that is OK. If you feel like you need more time to talk to the student, tell them to see you before or after school or at lunch. When you do get together, give them the opportunity to tell you how you have offended them. Let them talk if they want to. Most of these kids came to you with SDS. They are not mad at you, they are mad at your subject, mad at the school, mad at their parents, or just mad at the world. You may be the only one that can break through to them because you are the only one with the patience to give it some time. Sometimes I never make that break, but most of the time by the end of the first semester I am making progress. The key thing here is to never give up.

Students that I do not teach are a little harder to "cure". Between classes I have to deal with dress code and "horsing" around issues. I see a lot of SDS! There was one girl in particular that had a case so bad that she might as well have had SDS tattooed to her forehead. I have been working on her for two years and the only progress that I have made is that when I ask her to tuck in her shirt, she will now say "yes, mam". Granted it is more like an implied growl, but at least she is talking instead of just glaring at me with that "look to kill". To be totally honest, I hope that I never get her in the classroom. I am not sure that my patience with her will hold out!

As to the adults with SDS, I have found that the strategies that I use on the kids work great for them. We are all just big kids!

THE GREAT CHEATING SCANDAL

If I tried to remember all of the details of this incident, I am sure that I would not be accurate and it would take a very long time to explain everything. There was a very complicated series of events that involved hours of talking with students, parents, and administrators. In a nutshell, a young lady took a test early one morning and did not finish it so I let her come back at lunch and work on it some more. During this time she shared information about the test with another young man by pointing out problems on classroom worksheets that she knew were the same ones as on the test. It was not just an issue of letting the make student know what topics were on the test, she gave the specific problems. Some accounts said that she asked him for help on the problems so that she could work the problems when she came back to finish the test. She swears that she did not seek help for herself. The young man that she showed the problems to, shared his information with several other students and by the time I found out about it there were six students identified as questionable. I am confident that there were others involved but I will never know who they were.

The original young lady involved is one of the kindest, sweetest, respectful students imaginable. She, however is not a natural mathematician and she struggles to keep a "B" in math. There is a lot of pressure from her parents to maintain her average. In addition, she has a grueling sports schedule. She is an excellent athlete and plays on the school team as well as a travel team. I think that the pressure was just too much for her and she made one wrong decision. The other five students involved, when confronted, lied about their involvement on the first go-round of questioning and then admitted their guilt when they realized that their peers were reporting otherwise.

I was devastated because these students were all "good kids. " I guess my ego got involved also because I could not believe that they had done this "to me. " I know that kids cheat and I am diligent to try to stop it, but I guess it was the magnitude of the "scandal" and the kids who were involved. These were honor students.

Each student had to appear before the honor board and most of them were given a zero on the test and one day of in-school suspension. A couple of them were just given the zero because they did not lie about their involvement in the beginning. I also requested that they be given two hours of detention with me. I used up a lot of time on this incident, and I felt that it was only fair that they pay "reparations" and help me clean my room and do other chores. I also wanted some "quality time" with them to talk about what occurred. Most of the parents were very disappointed in the students and accepted the consequences well. I talked to all of them personally and let them know that their child was forgiven and once the consequences were met the incident would be forgotten and we would move on like it had never happened.

One parent, however, insisted that what their child had done was not cheating and they refused to accept the consequences. The amazing thing to me was that these were the parents of the young lady that had started it all! If she had not discussed the test and sought help, none of this would have happened and no one else would have been in trouble. The parents appealed the decision of the honor board to the headmaster and insisted on a conference with me. The headmaster stood behind the decision of the honor board and supported me completely, but not before much damage had been done to the emotions of the young lady.

I will never understand why parents can't see that their reactions to situations involving their children may have a larger negative impact on the child than just letting the child face the consequences.

After the decision of the honor board, I went out of my way to be nice to these students. They had to know that they were forgiven and that I truly meant they could start over. They had a hard time looking me in the eye for a while, but they soon became comfortable with me again. They all showed up for a two hour detention and I gave them all tasks to do in the room. We joked around; I brought refreshments; and anyone observing would have thought that we were having a party. Nevertheless, they were working hard and a little hard work sooths the guilty conscience. I gave them a way to pay me back for the wrong that they had done to me and it had restored their dignity. It is not enough to give forgiveness, you have to model it.

A TEACHER'S GIFT
(I pass this out to all of my students at the end of the year…)

As our paths so quickly cross, and you go your way and I continue mine;
I would like to grant you each six gifts, something memorable and divine.
I do this with infinite gratitude, for all you have shared with me.
If I only had the power to really grant them, how content I would be.
I wouldn't give you instant happiness; it could just as easily be taken away.
I would grant you the ability to see the simplest joys in the everyday.
I wouldn't give you instant wealth; such luck often tends to turn sour.
I would grant you an occupation of love where benefits are not measured by the dollar or the hour.
I wouldn't give you instant wisdom. It's more than any mortal can bear.
I would grant you with an insatiable curiosity, a need to know what is going on "out there. "
I wouldn't give you instant love, if unearned; it can crush your soul.
I would however, grant you the art of caring, life-long friendships would be your goal.
I wouldn't give you the perfect attitude, perfection is hard to get.
I'd give you the gift of intelligent conversation;
And the blessing of knowing when to quit.
I wouldn't give you all the answers, even if I knew the missing link.
If I only had one gift to give you, it would be the desire and ability to think.
~ Lizzy Sutton

THE SELF FULFILLING PROPHECY

Teenagers are legendary for their self-fulfilling prophecies and it is our job as teachers to knock those prophecies right out from under them. The media is very guilty of sending messages that if you are a teenager you will be rebellious and have a bad attitude. I have taught a gazillion teenagers and I can assure you that rebellion and negative attitudes are not natural. So let me help you burst a couple of negative bubbles as we go through two misplaced classroom ideas held by young people today.

*If I were not so bored I could ——————! Whether you fill in the words behave, learn, make good grades, concentrate, etc. , the concept and cop out is still the same. I know that there are many bright students that truly are bored and we need to find them quickly and see what we can do to make our classroom a more enriching place for them. With all of the technology available today it is easier to challenge them than it ever has been. However, we should never allow students to blame their lack of whatever on boredom. Everyone deals with boredom and young people need to learn that boredom must be managed and not allowed to become a reason for lowered expectations. Boredom is a condition not an excuse. If I have a student that tells me their grades are low because they are bored, I tell them to show me. Start making an "A" on everything, show me you are just bored, and I will make some modifications for you that will challenge you. Amazingly enough they soon become satisfied with the level of work they are being given. To a student, enrichment usually means more work. When we assign enrichment it should be different, not more work, or it feels like a punishment. Students who use boredom as an excuse for misbehavior need to be privately conferenced with and redirected.

*I can't do math, science, English, history, you name it. I just can't understand this stuff. The problem is that most of these students have been lying to themselves so long that they honestly believe these statements. Teachers have had enough education courses to know all about right brain, left brain, and there is enough research to prove that some students are "naturals" at some subjects. Others have to struggle to understand the material. Parents do not help when they tell their children that "they did not inherit the math gene" or sympathize with them by telling them they could not do a certain subject when they were in school either. Students need to be taught that with enough focus, hard work, and motivation they can succeed academically at any subject. As the teacher we must monitor them carefully and help them accomplish small baby steps of success that will eventually build and accumulate. We must be patient and encourage them when the hard work does not pay off every time and we need to let them know that we believe in them. We need to make sure that they know that quitting is not an option and they can do what they set their minds to in the long term. We must help them find the motivation that will help them overcome their negative mind set.

GLOOM, DESPAIR, AND AGONY ON ME

If you are under the age of 50 this title probably does not mean a thing to you, but most of us "old timers" recognize it as a song that was sung every week on the television show HeeHaw. "Gloom, despair, and agony on me, deep dark depressions, excessive misery, if it weren't for bad luck, I'd have no luck at all, gloom, despair, and agony on me". It can be sung with much drama and for me it is a valuable tool in lightening the mood when I have a class that is under a great deal of stress.

Students need some guidance in managing stress and handling difficult situations. At the high school level, the stress in the classroom can be almost palpable when a big project is due, the state playoffs are in full swing, or a big drama production is about to open. Most students have not had a lot of experience in time management and prioritizing tasks. They need to be taught constructive ways to blow off steam and accomplish what is most important. The trick is that it must be done without preaching and nagging, and I find that humor is just the ticket.

When I feel that the stress level is high, I stop the lesson, sing the "gloom" song once and then have them sing it with me. (I have the words saved on my Promethian Board so I can get to them quickly.) I then go around the room and give each student 30 seconds to whine about whatever is causing them stress. There are no explanations, judgments, or efforts to fix the problem from me, just good old fashioned venting from them. We immediately go back to the lesson. At the end of the period I try to stop 5 minutes early and talk about how they could better use their time and how sometimes you have to "sharpen the saw" and get some rest so you can think clearer. We also talk about how to handle stress in general.

I only do this once or twice a year, but sometimes when something major is coming up and the stress can be cut with a knife, I just stop and sing the song. My hope is that this song will stay in their heads and when they get into a stressful situation in their lives they will be able to manage it better by singing the song and remembering to smile. Once is a while in my AP Calculus class we follow the song with a quick trip outside for a good loud scream…

I have been criticized by another teacher for allowing my students to vent. I, however, find it a very useful tool in depressurizing students in many situations. I have used my 30 second vent rule for dress code complaints, "senioritis" complaints, and unfair test complaints, among many others. I don't always sing "the song"; I just whip out my trusty stopwatch and go around the room. It does not take very long; it lets you know your students a little better; and it lets them know that they are listened to. If a student says something too inappropriate they can be stopped and talked to privately.

BITS OF GLASS
It's All About Them

***Being the world's future isn't easy.

***I refuse to have a battle of wits with an unarmed person.

***Civilized Zone: Come in as friends. Bring kindness and consideration. Build up a pleasant atmosphere. Be simple and sincere. Be patient and understanding. Be helpful and co-operative. Be positive in everything. Ask yourself: What kind of class would this be if every student were just like me?

***There is an opportunity hidden in every student.

***Compete with yourself and co-operate with others.

***You have a right to your own mind. I have a right to insist that you use it.

***Take a new twenty dollar bill, fold it, stamp on it, get it dirty, rip it. It is still worth twenty dollars. The value does not change.

***Remind them of their strengths not their weaknesses.

***True nobility is not being superior to any other man but being superior to your previous self.

***My mother used to say every kid should have someone who is irrationally committed to their future. If you are relentless from the first day, the kids will understand that education is important. Tony Danza

***Keep your expectations high for the students. It is better to lose in the Olympics than to win in Little League.

***PEER PRESSURE IS EVERYTHING!

***Thank you for always encouraging me and for rewarding the quiet kids.

Chapter Four
IT'S ALL ABOUT CLASSROOM MANAGEMENT

Dedication

This section of my book is dedicated to Dr. Spencer Silver, the guy who invented sticky notes. Thank you for making me look like I know what I am doing!

CLASSROOM MANAGEMENT 101

CLASSROOM MANAGEMENT IS WHAT "makes or breaks" classroom climate. Managing your classroom effectively is the oil that keeps everything else working smoothly. Notice I said "effectively", not "efficiently". I like both, but efficient management is not enough. If you rule your class well, but with an iron hand that allows for no interaction, humor, or relationship building, it might be efficient but it is not as effective as it could be. Good classroom management is like being able to take all of the individual steps in a dance and turning them into a smooth flowing routine. It is pulling instruction, discipline, and communication together into a well orchestrated thing of beauty. Classroom management is knowing when and how to turn the kaleidoscope so that all of the pieces fit.

I am not a fan of late night TV for several reasons. First of all I cannot stay up that late and secondly, I find them a little too dicey for my personal taste. I have however been exposed to David Letterman's "top ten lists" and I have found some of them humorous and insightful. Therefore, I have decided to introduce this section by creating a top ten list of classroom management essentials. The hard part for me is to rank them because I think they all should be number one, but I am going to try. A basic list of management tools can be invaluable to a new teacher or a teacher looking to improve their management strategies. I would not want to teach without them. It has been impossible to write this book without already introducing some of these to you so please forgive any repetition. Even though I have explained them briefly, I now want to explain them in more detail.

NUMBER ONE: **CHIPS**

At the beginning of the year, I write each student's name in permanent ink on a plastic chip. I used to use poker chips but they are kind of bumpy to write on so I use colorful counting chips from a school supply store, nevertheless, poker chips are cheaper and they do work. When I used an overhead projector, I used transparent chips so that I could put them on the overhead and they could see their names. It really does not make any difference as long as they are plastic and make lots of noise when you rattle them in a small glass fish bowl. I teach five classes so I took six water bottles, cut off the tops, took off the labels, and wrote on each one with a permanent marker which class it contained. For me it was "first", "second", "fourth", "fifth", and "sixth. " On the sixth water bottle I wrote "teams. " I placed the chips for each class in their respective bottle and placed all six bottles in a carrying case with a handle similar to an old fashioned bottled Coke case. Picnic silverware holders would also work to hold the bottles if you can find one with enough slots for your classes. In the sixth bottle I put chips with numbers on them. If the most teams that I have in any class is eight, I put eight chips numbered from one to eight. I then place the chip holder and the glass fish bowl in easy reach. I use these chips constantly and in so many situations that I am sure I will forget to list some of them but here are the most important ones.

* When I ask a question, I hesitate so that everyone in the class can form an answer and then I draw a chip and call out a name. There is no hand waving. Everyone has an equal chance of being called on and no one is favored. Most of the time I put the chip back in the bowl so that a student can immediately be called on again. This keeps the entire class attentive. Sometimes I keep the chips out that have been called until everyone has a chance to answer. Chips keep me from calling on a few students most of the time and allowing some students to dominate while others just fade into the background. If a student cannot answer my question, I either lead them to the answer or draw another chip and let another person help lead them to the answer. If I want to walk around the room, I have an apron with two pockets that I use. I put the chips in one pocket and as I call the names, I put the used ones in the other pocket.

*Using chips greatly cuts down on favoritism because if I need an errand run or help with something, I simply draw a chip and see if that person is willing to "volunteer".

*I often want to create temporary teams that will work together just for a short time and I use the chips to help me select the teams.

*If I am explaining something and the class seems to be losing their focus, all I have to do is rattle the chip bowl and everyone perks up because they know that someone is about to be called on to answer a question or discuss something.

* I usually draw two or three chips at the end of the class period and ask the students to tell me one new thing that we learned today.

*Sometimes when it is time to go over homework, instead of calling out the answers, I will draw five chips and ask those five students to put their answer to a particular homework problem on the board. I will number the board from one to five and they fill in their assigned answer. If someone in the class does not agree with them, they simply go to the board and write their answer next to the one they consider wrong. We then work together to discover the correct answer. Once in a while no one will get the correct answer and we really get into some good discussions.

NUMBER TWO: **MAGNETS**

I have a large magnetized board and a gazillions little magnet squares that used to be part of the scheduling system for a large high school. It is a great positive reinforcement tool. The board was already painted with horizontal and vertical lines that made a grid with a lot of little squares just the right size for the magnets. It was large and heavy duty and leaned well against a wall on a low bookcase or desk. I took thin pieces of colored tape and divided it horizontally into five sections, one for each class. Each section has 8 horizontal rows and each team is assigned a row. If a class has less than eight teams, all rows are not used. The first column has team numbers in it and the last three columns are separated by one piece of vertical tape. As the teams receive magnets, they place them on the row for their team and collect them horizontally until they fill up their row to the piece of vertical, colored tape. The first time they fill up their row everyone on the team gets a piece of peppermint and they take down all of their magnets and place a shiny silver magnet in the first column to the right of the vertical tape. They then try to fill up their row a second time. When they pass the vertical tape a second time they all get "smarties" and another silver magnet. They then try to fill their row a third time. Not many teams accomplish that third row because we start over every six weeks, but if they do they all get a canned drink in class. At the end of the six weeks if no one has crossed the vertical line three times the team in each class who is ahead will get the drinks. I never take magnets away. They work hard to get as many magnets as they can, not so much for the candy, but for the competition. I keep the actual magnets in a small drawer next to where I check homework so I can get to them quickly. Here are some ways I use the magnets to motivate.

*Every time a student does their homework they get one magnet. If I have unequal teams I have "two magnet" people. In other words if most of my teams have four students on them and I have a team that only has three people, I make one of those three the "two magnet" person so that every team can get the same number of magnets for a homework assignment. I usually let the teams pick who they want their "two magnet" person to be and they are wise enough to pick the person who always does their homework.

*I have a lot of "magnet problems". I will put a problem on the board and have the teams work it and put their answer on a note card and bring it to me. If they get it correct, they get a magnet. I will not help them do a magnet problem and some of the problems get very tough. If they are too tough, I will make them a two or three magnet problem. If I give a magnet problem and only one team gets it right, they get a bonus of four magnets for a total of five.

*I have magnet races. I will give the class five problems to do and say "go". The team that finishes first gets a bonus of three points. I will call time about one minute after the first set of answers is turned in. The teams get three points for every correct answer, minus two for every wrong answer, and minus one for every blank answer. The teams total their points and turn them into me on a note card. The team with the highest points gets five magnets, the next team gets four, the next three, the next two, and all the rest get one.

*I use magnets as all sorts of rewards and am very spontaneous and unpredictable as to how I give them out.

I have rarely had any trouble with students moving magnets or cheating but on occasion I have a student try to be clever and trick another team or me. If I catch the perpetrator, be it an individual or team, I punish them to the full extent of the law; they may not participate in the magnet competition. If I cannot catch anyone and there are no confessions, I suspend the magnet "race" for the entire class for six weeks and explain to them that we will try again next six weeks. This is one of those rare occasions that I have to use group consequences.

NUMBER THREE: **SHAZAAMS!**

My Shazaam! system is easy, cheap, and super effective. Shazaams! are simply tickets. Start with a large roll of tickets; I like yellow but any color will do. You can get them at Walmart or Oriental Trading Company for less than ten dollars and I find that one roll will last all year. I have a container labeled for each class and one container labeled blank Shazaams! . These can be placed anywhere in the room, I just make sure I keep them where I can keep an eye on them. When I tell a student "Shazaam! ," they immediately get up, write their name on the back of a blank ticket and put it in the container for their class. It takes no effort on my part.

At the end of every six weeks, I have a Shazaam! drawing. In each class I place four free homework tickets (red, also purchased), three individually wrapped snack cakes, and three cold, canned drinks on top of a student desk. I then empty the Shazaams out of the container for that class in my glass fish bowl and begin drawing the names. They pick their prize in the order they are drawn. After the drawing I throw away the remaining Shazaams! and start over for the new six weeks. If they pick a snack cake or a drink they may eat it in class. If they pick a free homework pass, they write their name on the back in ink, bring it to me to initial, and then they may use it for any future homework assignment. I will not take free homework passes for study problems or homework that they have already missed. At the end of the year if they have any free homework passes left, I allow them to exchange them for Shazaams! just before the last drawing. For the last drawing I have five drinks and five snack cakes and no homework passes. Here are a few ways to use Shazaams! .

*If a student catches me doing something wrong and brings it to my attention in a respectful manner I give them a Shazaam! . As a math teacher I make careless mistakes, and it seems that the older I get the more I make. I want to know as soon as I make a mistake because some of the problems I work get rather lengthy, and I do not want to spend time working them incorrectly. This is especially important because I have students that understand what I am teaching and get bored as I continue to develop the material for the class. Watching for my mistakes keeps them engaged. Students that are easily distracted also stay on task.

*If a student comes up with an "out of the box" idea or solution to a problem I give them a Shazaam! . If I have a student who rarely contributes, when they do, I give them a Shazaam! .

*If I want a positive reinforcement for all or part of the class, I will give them a Shazaam! . A good example of this might be when I ask everyone to turn to a certain page in their textbook and I find out that about half of the class does not have his/her books. I will tell everyone who has their book to fill out a Shazaam! . If a whole class does well on a test, I might give them all a Shazaam! . If It is an unofficial senior skip day, I give all of my seniors who show up for class a Shazaam! . You get the idea.

* If I see a student doing something very nice for someone else, I often give them a Shazaam! to reinforce and reward their behavior.

*The bottom line is that getting a Shazaam! is a good thing and I can give one out for anything that I want.

NUMBER FOUR: **BLOOPERS**

I will discuss bloopers in the discipline section. They are an easy way to manage minor discipline issues that do not disrupt the classroom. They are very important to my classroom management system!

NUMBER FIVE: **QUIZLET BOARDS AND PLASTIC BOXES**

Under each student desk is a "quizlet" board and plastic "cigar" box. Each board is a tri-fold dry erase board that is connected with duct tape. I bought a large sheet of reasonably priced dry erase board at Home Depot and they cut it into 9 inch by 16 inch rectangles. Because I was a teacher they cut it for me for free. I then just duct taped three of the pieces together to create the tri-fold. On top of each tri-fold is a cheap plastic school supply box like the old fashioned cigar boxes. You can get these super cheap at the back to school sales. They contain several items that are used on various occasions: dry erase markers and a paper towel to be used on the quizlet boards, notecards, protractors, six inch rulers, and cricket clickers. The boxes contain the things that the students are going to need at their fingertips. Here are some uses for the quizlet boards and the box contents. At the beginning of the year I require all of my students to bring in one package of three by five notecards and I am able to keep the boxes filled all year. We use a lot of notecards.

*The main use of the quizlet boards is to help students stay honest during a test. Any time I give a test or a quiz I have the students put up their quizlet boards. I also give a lot of quizlets which are one question pop tests. When the students hear the signal they clear off their desks except for a notecard, writing instrument, and their quizlet board. When they are finished with whatever the assessment is they fold their quizlet board up and lay it flat on their desk on top of their notecard or paper. I can then look around the room and see when most of the students are finished.

*I use the dry erase feature for many activities. The students like to use the dry erase markers on the board since it is something different. I have several activities where the students use the dry erase boards for instructional purposes. We use them often but not for long periods of time because the odor of the dry erase markers can become over-whelming.

*I use the boards for activities such as think-pair-share and as quizlet forts when the students are trying to discuss problem solving strategies. They can pull their desks together and face each other and set up two or three quizlet boards around them and have some privacy as they com-pete with the other teams.

*The cricket clickers are used when we want to make some noise! I learned about making noise at the Ron Clark Academy, and I try to use the clickers in the instances when I might want a drum roll. I also try to use them in instructional ways. I will put a problem on the board and as each student solves the problem they click their cricket. There are all sorts of variations and most of what I do with the clickers is pretty spontaneous!

At times it is necessary to remind the students that the quizlet boards and plastic boxes belong to me. I ask them not to doodle on the quizlet boards with anything including the markers since it wastes marker ink and stinks up the room. If I catch students doodling on the non-dry-erase side of the board they get some serious detention time. I also ask them to keep trash out of their boxes and do not take anything out of their boxes unless they are told by me to do so. If you let them know that you are serious about "your stuff" they will learn to respect it and use it for its intended purposes.

NUMBER SIX: <u>**QUIZMOO AND ASSORTED TIMERS**</u>

I have several timers in my classroom. I believe that maintaining con-trol of the clock makes your classroom more effective, therefore, if I say you have three minutes to work five problems, that is exactly what

I mean. I use a basic electronic kitchen timer to time assignments, team activities, and sometimes even my activities. If I have given out the correct answers to a test and want to spend ten minutes going over problems, I set the timer. If I want to lecture for ten minutes and then switch to something different, I set the timer. I also keep a stop watch very handy if I want to time things in smaller increments. I also have some timers in my room that do not look like timers but are very useful in time management:

*Quizmoo is an animated cow that has been with me for eighteen years. She is battery operated and when her teet is squeezed she does the chicken dance to the catchy little chicken dance tune. It takes her about 80 seconds to complete her dance. I found her in a drug store and pray that she does not retire before I do because I will never be able to replace her. She has become a legend! When I want to give a quizlet, which is a one question pop test, I squeeze her and she starts dancing. The students have until she finishes her dance to get ready for the quizlet. It is a very effective and fun way to get the kids ready!

*My I-Pod serves as a timer also. When I am ready to check homework at the beginning of the period, I turn on a song and the students scramble to get to me and get it checked before the song is finished. The length of an average song is three minutes and it is another fun way to time something.

NUMBER SEVEN: **THE ORANGE BAT**

Once again this management tool will be discussed in the discipline section. It is just an illusion, but used properly it is very effective.

NUMBER EIGHT: **DOORBELL**

I have a cheap electronic door bell that plugs in the wall and is activated by a remote control button. It is a wonderful prop and discipline tool. When I want the classes attention immediately because they have been doing group work or because they are too noisy, I push the button and the doorbell chimes. That is a signal to them that they need to "freeze" immediately with their mouths and their bodies. It is a very effective tool if it is not used too often!

NUMBER NINE: **HALL PASS AND TARDY LOG**

In the back of my classroom, right beside the door, I have two clipboards. One is a hall pass log. The second is a tardy log. Both of these logs save me a great deal of time and allow me to manage hall pass requests and tardies. I used to have students fill out their own hall passes and hand them to me with a writing instrument for me to use for signing. They used notecards for this purpose and when they returned they put their notecards in a box on my desk. Periodically I would check the box to see if anyone was abusing the privilege. I trained the class not to interrupt me when I was really into instruction unless it was a real emergency. I have enough transitions every day that the wait was not long if they needed my signature. This worked great for me for years until I got careless one day and did not read carefully what a student had written on a pass and this is when I moved to the hall pass log. (explanation on that little snafu later)The hall pass log simply asks the students to sign their name, the date, and where they are going. It requires no effort on my part and no disruption of the class. If a student is tardy to class, they simply sign the tardy log with the date, their name, and the reason they were tardy. Every three weeks I check the logs and if a student has been tardy or used the hall pass more than three times, I give them a warning and tell them that they only have one tardy or one hall pass privilege the next three weeks and if they abuse either, they will be serving a short detention. If I have a student who is chronic at being tardy, I will not wait three weeks to deal with the situation. I always read the reasons and try to be reasonable. Having these two logs in the back of the room allows me to deal with frequent tardies and frequent "room leavers" when it is convenient for me, and not disrupt class time.

NUMBER TEN: **DOODADS**

I have saved doodads for last because they did not work for me this past year. They worked great for the past eight years so I really do not understand what happened, but I am going to try them again because when they work, they are a competitive motivator that accomplishes many goals for me. I have five wooden, eight inch spindles on a base, one for each class and I took some "treasure chest", cardboard jewels and gold coins and punched holes in the middle of them and called them "doodads". It would work just as effectively to have a cut-off water bottle for each class and use beans or marbles. What you call them is up to you. The classes compete for six weeks trying to get more "doodads" than the other classes. The class with the most "doodads" at the end of the semester gets to walk across the street and buy a treat, missing almost the entire class period. Now this is a great reward for two reasons. I never give them free time and to have almost a whole class period where they are not doing math is a great reward. The second reason is that they love to leave campus and buy food (everyone has to buy their own). I know that this reward will not work for all schools and all teachers but you could come up with your own great reward.

Classes may earn up to five "doodads" in a day. They are given one for each of the following: 1) 100 percent attendance with no checkouts2) No tardies 3) 100 percent homework for those present 4) No bloopers5) No one signed the hall pass log and left the room.

In each class I ask for a volunteer to be my "doodad" person. It is his/her responsibility to keep track of how many "doodads" the class has earned and place them on the peg at the end of the period. The "doodader" can easily check the tardy and hall pass log and I always congratulate the class if they have 100% homework or attendance. By paying attention it is known whether or not any bloopers were given. This student counts the doodads at the end of the semester for that class and one other class and records these numbers on a notecard and hands it to me. Having them count one other class keeps them honest on counting their own because they know that I will be double checking. If the two counts do not agree, I average them.

In the past the classes were very excited about this and the peer pressure was enormous for students to do their homework, be on time, stay in class and not get a blooper. The system took no effort on my part. It was positive reinforcement. I even enjoyed the bonding days of walking across the street! This year's group however, never got excited about the system, and the students who volunteered would forget to put the "doodads" on the spindle. I think it is a good system, but if it is not motivating to the students it is just another one of those good ideas that did not work! You decide.

FIRE ALARM ANTICS

Today we had a fire drill in 5th period. The students were not at all concerned about missing my stimulating lecture on position, velocity, and acceleration. Fortunately, it was a very sunny day in November and we actually enjoyed being outside. Even I was not ready to go back in when the "all clear" was sounded. As soon as we got back in the room, one of my boys filled out a hall pass, put it under my noise to be signed and then left the room. When he came back in, he was snickering a little, and his friends were snickering even more. He came up to me and showed me the hall pass. Instead of writing down that the restroom was his destination, he had written in that he was leaving class to pull the fire alarm. I usually am very careful about looking at these but I sure missed it that time. The class had already been interrupted so many times that stopping for a laugh did not seem to be a bad idea. I let the kids laugh at me about this and then we moved on.

This little incident immediately changed my method of handling hall passes. I was tired of being interrupted during class to sign something and I obviously was not doing a good job of paying attention to what I was signing. That is when I put a clipboard in the back of the room marked hall pass. Since they could not carry the clip board to the restroom, I created my own personal hall pass which is a large blue swim flipper hanging next to the clipboard with my name on it. Only one student may leave the room at a time so if the fin is gone, the student knows they have to wait. I let them know in no uncertain terms that they better be careful what they put in for the destination. Some of the guys were getting grossly creative with the bathroom description and had to be given a short course in etiquette.

BEGINNING OF THE YEAR POEM

(On the second day of school, as the students walk in, this poem is on the Promethian board.)

Students are unusually lucky,
Like a cat who has nine lives.
They get to start completely over,
As the month of August arrives.

Old problems with teachers behind them,
Old failures over and done.
When you get to meet a new teacher,
You have really just begun.

Work hard from the very beginning,
Don't waste a minute of your day.
Learn as much as I can teach you,
In the long run it will pay.

If you start to have a problem,
Don't let it get out of hand,
Come talk to me about it,
We'll come up with a plan.

I'm looking forward to working with you,
And accomplishing great things this year.
Please come by and see me,
When I'm needed, I'll always be here!
~ Lizzy Sutton

CLASSROOM CLIMATE

There are a lot of things in the world that we cannot control. There are a lot of things at school that we cannot control. But there is one thing that we can control and that is our classroom climate. I am not naïve enough to believe that it will be utopia, but we do have control over the tone; how we respond to students and their behavior goes a long way to set that tone. When students walk in our door on the first day they should feel "it" and "it" should permeate the room like a cheap air freshener. If you can accomplish a proper classroom climate, discipline, management and instruction flow more evenly.

*Immediately, without directly saying so, let the students know who is in charge. Do this in subtle ways that convey the message that you are "running the show".

*Make everyone "response-able" and help them understand the concept of reciprocity. Let them know it is a fancy word for "even-Steven". If you behave and concentrate on your learning in the classroom, I will be nice to you as we learn together and have fun in the process. If you misbehave and disrupt your learning or someone else's, I will turn into your worst nightmare and the fun will be sucked right out of the room.

*Define the values that you want to prevail, then set the standards for proper behavior based on those values. Do not just post a list of rules; create an atmosphere where students want to do "right" because they understand why the rules are important and they want to be positive members of the micro-cosmos called your classroom.

*Make it a safe place for everyone to learn. Make sure that everyone feels protected when they answer a question. It has to be o. k. to be wrong and all opinions are valued. Use your speech and encouragement to set a positive tone for dialog.

*Do not let any students dominate and do not let any students hide. Everyone answers questions and is involved in the learning process.

* If possible, announce a common enemy. For me it is the SAT or the AP Calculus Exam. I call them the "Evil Testing Serpent", and I have a very ugly dragon in my classroom that we refer to often. We try to outsmart the dragon and he, not I, becomes the object of the students ire and frustration.

*Be sure that they have a goal to work for. I heard in a workshop once that "the ultimate goal of a 3rd grader is to make it to 4th grade and not feel dumb when they get there. " Always talk to students about where they are going and how they are going to get there and do your best to instill the love of learning into them. In my opinion that is always the ultimate goal for them even if they do not agree.

*Make your room user friendly. Have hand sanitizer, tissues, and Band-Aids. These items say: "I care about you as a person. " Have pencils and paper where they can easily get to it. These items say: "I am serious about what I teach, and I do not want small, cheap things to get in the way. " (I buy in bulk at WalMart at the beginning of the year when they are so cheap they almost give them away.) I used to loan them out and try to get the pencils back and even tried the shoe exchange once but it was too much effort on my part. Have a pencil sharpener, a hole punch, tape, scissors, and extra calculators easily available. These items say: I care about you as a student and I want your life to be as easy and organized as possible. " (Not really, I just get tired of their asking so I put them out so they won't interrupt me.)

*Arrange your room carefully because teacher and student desk placement affects your control. Every room is different and every situation is different but my number one rule is that I be able to walk around and get to each of my students. I got away from straight rows a long time ago, but if that is necessary I am sure that I can circle all away around the rows. I like to teach from the back of the room as well as the front. My desk is placed so that I can see the door and the students. I rarely sit at my desk but when I do, I want to be fully aware of what is going on inside my classroom and who is coming and going.

*Sometimes I have had control of the temperature in the room and sometimes I have not. For a couple of years I shared a thermostat with a basketball coach who was a very big man. The thermostat was in his room, and my room was always too cold no matter what the season. The only thing I could do was wear a sweater all year and encourage my students to bring in a jacket in August. When at all possible, however, worry more about keeping the kids comfortable than your personal comfort.

*A very simple, effective change in seating can have a big impact on student performance. At the end of every six weeks I move my teams so that the ones sitting in the back move to the front and vice versa. No student sits in the back or front all year and sometimes I find that when they are moved up they do a whole lot better. There are obvious exceptions to this rule if students have physical limitations or they just "have" to sit close to the teacher so their behavior can be monitored. I try to rotate the others as much as I can.

*The appearance of the classroom should be clean, bright, and appealing. Your own style is very important here. I have been accused of decorating my room like an elementary classroom because there are bright things all over the walls, curtains in the windows, and animated cows. Colorful and bright is the environment I like to work in but some of the best teachers I know have very simply decorated classrooms that still feel inviting and safe. The point is that your room should reflect the fact that you care about the kids and are glad they are there. Bulletin boards do not have to be fancy but they should be changed once in a while. In my opinion, one tired bulletin board used all year sends the wrong message to the students.

*I ask my students to practice the three "P's"-patience, peace, and perspective. I let them know that in this classroom we will create peace by being patient with each other and trying to see each other's perspective. I have to remind them quite often at first but they catch on eventually. They also know that every day is a new day and that no matter how rotten they were yesterday, it is forgiven and forgotten. I hope that as I model this for them, they will apply the lesson to their own relationships.

*Create a classroom that is off the wall fun once in a while. I have what I call my "happy stick" that I pull out once in a while when the mood is getting too serious. It is a long green fluorescent looking tube that makes an obnoxious sliding, whine noise when you turn it over. I bought it at the dollar store and the kids love it. Use lots of props and be silly. I do not care how old the students are they love anything serendipity and the more of it you weave into your classroom, the more positive climate you will create.

GUYS JUST GOTTA HAVE FUN

When I walked in the door, I found Eli Manning's stats for last Sunday's game on my board. Only one person would leave them there and that was James, the history teacher across the hall. He loves to walk into my math classes and give them what he considers "pertinent math facts' that I have neglected. Last year he came into my advanced math class and showed them the formula for determining a quarterback's rating. So when I saw the stats on the board, I knew where they came from. James was at it again. Keith, who was really into the formula last year, copied down the stats so I could have my board space and then he tried to find the formula. Naturally, he had not saved the formula from last year and neither had James. I headed to my black basket. There it was next to the bottom. Keith copied it down and made the calculations. He was now ready to go on with Calculus because he knew Manning's rating! So what is the point of this story? Well there are two. First of all, it is always good to interject fun into the classroom. James and I are great at playing good cop, bad cop. He is the good cop and I am the bad cop. He interrupts class and I pretend like I am appalled. He adds a little spice and I pretend like he is an intruder. I drag him out the door and he just opens it back up. It is fun for the kids, and as long as it doesn't happen too often, I think it is a harmless distraction. Secondly, Keith had a primal male urge to figure out that quarterback rating! As soon as he had it, he happily rejoined the calculus discussion. If I had insisted that he wait, he would have been distracted the entire period. Sometimes you just have to go with the flow.

THE PURPLE PEOPLE EATER

One of the major positive climate techniques that I use is the constant use of music. Music is a very important part of almost everything I do. It keeps my classroom un-predictable and interesting. It keeps the mood light and I enjoy it. It keeps me cheered up and lively and that transfers to the kids. They are rarely surprised when I break out into some karaoke! I am not a good singer but that does not stop me. I started this musical approach to mathematics education when I cleaned out some stuff of my Moms and found a large collection of eight tracks and an eight track player. The collection was full of Elvis, Johnny Mathis, and show tunes with Frank Sinatra and Barbara Streisand thrown in for a little variety. This was in the days when CD's were still relatively young and cassettes were on the way out and the students were fascinated by the system, if not the songs. I did not use the music for instruction at that point but I did use the songs as timers and to liven up the mood. There is nothing like a little Elvis to stir things up. It broke my heart when that eight track player died but not to be outdone, I brought in a CD player and continued the music. I could never replace all of those eight tracks so the music became a little more contemporary with Elton John, The Beatles, and Simon and Garfunkle. Note that when I say contemporary, I mean for me, not for them. I continued with the CDs for many years and my collection of songs expanded to include many that I could use for instruction as well as classroom management. Recently I was given a used I-Pod by one of my students. It took me a while to learn how to use the thing and even longer to learn how to use I-Tunes so that I could load specific songs off my computer, but I am so glad that I took the time. I now have a limitless supply of cheap music at my fingertips that I can navigate quickly and efficiently. I also have to say that it enhances my "aura" as the students are impressed that I even know how to use an I-Pod at my age! Fortunately for me, my Promethian Board came with "sound wired in" so all I have to do is plug my I-Pod into the "box thingy" and I can blast them out of the room. If I did not have the built in sound, I would get some BIG speakers...

It is very important to be sure that you are playing appropriate music for your situation. When I taught in public schools I could not have played a lot of what I play in a Christian School simply because of the religious content. There are a million songs out there which obviously should not be played in any school because of the language or content. What I have to be careful of is songs that have things in them that I do not understand and may be sexual or controversial in nature and I do not even know it. When in doubt, I check with a young teacher and have them listen to it for me. I do take requests from students and check the lyrics on the computer, but I still do not trust myself so if I am not sure, I check with someone else. One of my favorite songs was "Another One Bites the Dust". It was perfect for an elimination activity that I do in class. All I was familiar with was the chorus, which was perfect for what I wanted, but another verse in the lyrics was un-acceptable. I had listened to the song more than once but sometimes the lyrics go so fast or so garbled that I did not understand them. When a student brought it to my attention that I might want to check the lyrics I was mortified at one section of the lyrics and the song had to go. (One day I am going to take the time to learn how to just get "snippets" of songs but that is a long way down on my perpetual "to do" list.) Just be very careful what you use. There are plenty of great songs out there. Also, do not assume that the kids will not enjoy the "oldies" and a wide variety of songs. One of my favorite songs is the oldie "Build Me Up Buttercup" and the kids love it too!

I have already shared some of the songs that I use to help me teach in the instruction section so I will not reiterate those but I will just say again that songs make wonderful "hooks" to help student remember things. I play every kind of music imaginable when I am checking homework. Here are some of my other favorites:

*When I want to lighten the mood, I will play "Buttercup", "The Purple People Eater", "Don't Worry-Be Happy", "Feelin Groovy", "Dancing Queen", "Calendar Girl"...

*When they are about to take a difficult test I will play the theme from "Jaws", "The Impossible Dream" from the Man of LaMancha, "Help! " by The Beatles, or "The Good, The Bad, and the Ugly". . .

*When I am giving back a test that they have done well on, I play "We Are The Champions of the World", "It Is Well With My Soul", "The Star War Theme"....

*When I give back a test that they have done poorly on, I play "Big Girls Don't Cry", or "It's My Party and I'll Cry if I Want To".

*When I just need to break up the monotony on a day when I am having trouble keeping students awake I play "Dynamite" by Taio Cruz or one of my many television theme songs like the theme from "Andy Griffith" or "The Flintstones".

*If I am having a hard time learning names at the beginning of the year we play the name game using the song by the same name.

Music adds a dimension to my classroom atmosphere that is hard to describe in words but easy to feel. My mission statement is to "dilute the misery",and music is an integral part of my mission!

HOMEWORK PROCEDURE

Checking homework comes in almost as many forms as there are teachers. There is no right way or wrong way; I am in favor of mixing it up and using several methods during the year. The main issue is not how you do it, but is it really an efficient method. My definition of an efficient method is one that fits these criteria:

1   LOW GRADING TIME: I love to plan, research, create, organize, and imagine. I spend countless hours on what I call "my schoolwork" and grading quiz and test papers. I do not want to invest hours in grading homework.

2   IMMEDIATE FEEDBACK: Students need their papers under their noses when the homework is discussed and they need im-

mediate feedback.

3   ACCOUNTABILITY: I have to do some kind of check or most of my students will stop doing homework. Sometimes I check for accuracy, but most of the time I just check for effort. It is important that they never know when the homework will actually be graded.

4   LOW CLASS TIME: Whatever system I use, it should take minimum class time. I want to teach!

Different subject areas need different systems and once again flexibility is the key. I have created a system that works great in a math classroom but it may not work great anywhere else. It takes about a week to train the students, but once they are trained it meets all of the criteria above and makes my life easier. On the first day of school as my students exit the classroom, I give them a handout with the following instructions:

HOW TO SUCCEED AT HOMEWORK:

1   When an assignment is given, place it in your agenda.

2   When you are working your assignment, be sure to show work, circle your final answers, and check your work. If you miss a problem, try it again in another color. If you miss it a second time, be sure and put a big question mark by it so that you can ask about it in class. Be sure that your homework is in the proper section of your notebook.

3   On the day that your homework is due hang on to it until the music begins, then bring it to me, still in your notebook. You do not have to line up, just approach me calmly. If you did not do your homework, fill out a note card with your name, the date, and the reason that you did not do your homework and get in line with the card. (Note cards are located under your desks in the plastic box.) If you were absent just write absent

as the reason on your card. If you only did part of your homework, get in line with what you did and a note card explaining how much you have, why you did not finish, your name, and the date.

4   When you get to me, I will stamp your homework and give you a magnet if it is satisfactory. If you do not have your homework at all, hand me your note card. If you have part of it, show it to me and hand me the note card. I will tell you how many points to take off. Go finish filling out the card and bring it back to me with the appropriate number of points marked off.

5   If you have a make-up assignment to show me, go to the homework box and pull your absence card, and bring that and your assignment to me with your regular assignment.

6   If someone on your team is absent, fill out a card for them, including the assignment and hand it to me when you are getting your homework checked.

7   If your homework was satisfactory, place your magnet on the magnet board and return to your seat.

8   When I begin going over homework, ask questions about the ones that you had trouble with.

FROM THE TEACHER'S POINT OF VIEW:

1   When you are ready to check homework, start the music. I try to pick popular, yet motivational songs. Silly songs are good too. Seasonal songs are used where appropriate. Once in a while I throw in a "golden oldie" for me. If music is not appropriatin your classroom, have some other type of homework cue.

2   As the students approach, (I make my younger students line up), get out your rubber stamp and open your magnet drawer. Any rubber stamp will do. I have one with my name on it. The

purpose of the stamp is to keep another student from getting in line with a paper that has already been checked.

3   As each student comes by, you should have a comment for them: "nice job", "how's your mom? ", "you look great today", "how was the game last night? ", "glad to see that you figured these out", "you'll get more right next time,"etc. It is very important that you make eye contact with every student individually and it takes very little time.

4   If they have followed directions and the assignment is complete, give them a rubber stamp and a magnet.

5   If the assignment is not satisfactory, but something is on the paper, give them a rubber stamp and tell them how many points to take off. Each assignment is worth three points. So if they worked most of it successfully, you may want to just say: "minus one". If it is barely there, give them a "minus two". Send them to fill out a card and get at the end of the line to return it to you. If they have at least earned two out of three points, give them a magnet. Once I get the students trained to this process, I can check all homework within three minutes which is the average length of one song.

6   If they have no homework and just hand you a note card, be sure and comment and then take their card. They get no magnet.

7   When the line is finished, take the note cards and stack them on your desk for later recording. Turn off the music.

8   Go over homework. If you see a problem that had a lot of question marks by it as you glanced at papers, start with that one. Never assign more homework problems than you have time to go over. If you assign it, you need to answer any questions that the students might have about it. Allow students to ask   questions   until   all   problems   are   addressed.

GRADING HOMEWORK:

1 At the beginning of each grading period, go into your grading program and give each student a 100 for their homework average.

2 During your planning period or at the end of the day, take the note cards for those who lost homework points and go into the program and subtract the appropriate number of points from their average. (This way a parent or student can always look up to see what the homework average is at any time.) For example if you are going to use six weeks as your grading period, and you estimated you will have 20 assignments during that six weeks, each homework assignment is worth a total of 5 points. I use a semester as my grading period so I count each assignment three points. It is very important to put this information in the syllabus so the parents understand why there is only one homework grade. This system works great at the high school level. I am not sure that it would work for middle school. Middle school parents like to see lots of grades. If I taught middle school I would do it my way; I would just be sure that my parents were educated on my system.

3 Create two note card boxes with alphabetical dividers. After you have recorded the cards place them in alphabetical order in the first box. I keep this box on the corner of my desk and I keep these cards all year for "evidence". Nothing is better at a parent conference than being able to pull out cards in the students own handwriting as to why they did not have their homework. In the second box, a smaller version, you will file the cards of those students who were absent and may make-up the work. Put this box where they can have easy access to it. When they bring in a make-up assignment, they pull this card out and you tear it up as you stamp their homework and give them a

magnet. At the end of the grading period, pull all absent cards that are left and were not made up and subtract the appropriate points from the grading program and move them to the "evidence" box. You want to keep the evidence box all year for three reasons: 1) If a student questions their homework grade, you can pull their cards and in their own handwriting, they can see what points they missed. 2) At a parent conference you have, in the student's own handwriting, what was missed and why. 3) If you notice a pattern of note cards showing up on one student you can pull all of the reasons and have a little chat with the student. It is very "eye catching" to see all of those cards spread out in their own handwriting when they "can't remember not doing their homework that many times."

MANAGING ABSENCES:

1   If a student is absent from class on the day an assignment is made they should be encouraged to check the computer homework program and have it ready on their return. They are not required to have it, however, so if they don't, they fill out a note card with their name, date, and the word "absent" written on it. Officially they have two days to make up the work, but I usually give them a week.

2   If a student is absent from class on the day an assignment is due, a member of their team fills out a note card for them, placing their name, date, the assignment and "absent" on the card. This team member hands the absentee's card to the teacher when they go through the line and show their own work. It is easy for the teams to forget to do this so I try to remind them when I check attendance to fill out a note card on those absent. To further help them, remember, I will not give the absent student a magnet if their team forgets to fill out a card on them. Therefore, they get full credit on their homework but no magnet.

3   When a student has a make-up assignment to show me, they simply go to the homework card box, pull their notecard, get in line with it, and I stamp their work, give them a magnet, and tear up the card in front of them. This way if they make up all of their work, nothing was subtracted from their grade.

VARIATIONS:

1   Once in a while I want to collect homework and grade it myself. I never do this on the first day that they have had to do a concept on their own. Instead of turning on the music, I just tell them they have one minute to put their name on their homework and get it in the metal basket on my desk. If they do not have it for any reason, they fill out a note card and put it with the other papers. I then go over all of the problems in class, encouraging them to take notes. When I have graded the papers, I assign each a point value from zero to five based on correct answers, not effort. The next day, in order to have the note cards I need, I have every student who turned in a homework paper fill out a card, write their name, date, and how many points they earned. The reason I have every student turn in a card is that so no one will get embarrassed. I throw away the cards for the perfect papers and deduct the rest from their homework grade on the computer. I then file them in the box. I do not do this very often, just enough to keep them on their toes.

2   On other occasions, when I want to give an "accuracy" grade instead of an "effort" grade, I let the students grade it themselves and fill out the note card as to how many points they missed.

3   Sometimes, I am in a hurry. I have a lot to cover and I do not even want to spend three minutes checking homework. I will then ask one member from each team to come to me and get a magnet for every person that has all of their homework done.

LIZZY SUTTON

> They should also bring me a note card for anyone who does
> not have their homework or anyone who is absent.

As I try to break it down to explain this system, I know that it sounds very complicated but it is not. It is very easy and lowers the teacher's work considerably. It also gives you a record of exactly how many points were missed on homework and why.

THE POT CALLING THE KETTLE BLACK

It has always been a little ironic to me that the very teachers who complain about the kids talking too much are the ones that will not be quiet at faculty meetings. At the lunch table, teachers complain about the kids turning things in late and yet they never get a report to the office on time. We as adults are no different than the kids we teach and I think it is very important to remember that. Let me give you a case in point.

I was teaching a staff development class on differentiating instruction for the teachers at my school. There were a total of four sessions, one a month. The sessions were in the afternoons and most of the teachers were tired and had a million other places to be. They were about as interested in my instruction as most of the kids that sit in their classes and we made this issue one of our topics of discussion. I think some of them got greatly enlightened!

At the end of the second session I assigned homework. At the beginning of the third session, I took up the homework and had each participant that did not do theirs fill out a card stating the date, their name, and why they did not do their homework. I was modeling one of my techniques and trying to continue to make my point to them that we are really no different than the kids, even when we "grow-up". I think the statistics that follow make the point much better than I can:

91% of the faculty was present at the session when the homework was assigned.

9% of the faculty was absent when the homework was assigned and 80% of those did not request make-up work.

6% of the faculty that turned in their homework forgot to put their name on it.

17% of those who were present when the homework was assigned did not do it.

2% of those who were asked to fill out the note card did not do it.

4% did the homework during the session and tried to turn it in at the end.

19% of those completing the homework did not follow directions.

2% of those who had to fill out the card because they did not do their homework made fun of my system.

One teacher wrote as her excuse on her card:

I did not do the homework because a mind-altering alien visited me during my slumber and took all the knowledge I had acquired in my 37 years, so how on earth can I be expected to remember my name, much less my homework.

Needless to say this made for great discussion at our fourth workshop!

NOTEBOOKS
MY WAY OR THE HIGHWAY

I love notebooks! I love notebook checks. I thrive on organization and I love the smell and look of a new notebook with lots of brightly colored dividers. I want all of my students to have perfect notebooks. I want nothing in the pockets, I want nothing hanging out the edges, and I do not want any "ratty" pages in there. I want it to be visually appealing and organizationally correct. I also want world peace and I am confident that I will not be getting either one in my lifetime.

For years, I was very strict on notebooks. Every student had to keep one and they had to do it my way. Early in my career, I took up notebooks, created a grading rubric, and spent many fun filled hours checking them. It didn't take me long to figure out that I was spending a lot of my time in an activity that wasn't improving my student's organizational skills. I was punishing them for not being organized, but I wasn't helping them.

My next approach was an improvement over the first method. Somewhere in some book that I read many years ago, I discovered an ingen-

ious system to quickly check notebooks in class! This meant no wasted
time for me, but I was still punishing the kids who I deemed "unorga-
nized". I would ask the students to clear off their desks of everything
except one clean sheet of notebook paper, a writing instrument, and
their notebook. I would then ask them to place their name on the paper
and number from 1 to 10. I would then proceed to ask 10 yes or no
questions for them to answer:

1   Do you have the proper number of dividers in your notebook?
    (yes)

2   Is your name on the cover of your notebook? (yes)

3   Are there any papers in the pocket of your notebook? (no)

4   Do you have your dividers properly labeled? (yes)

5   Do you have the worksheet on dividing integers in the notes
    section? (Yes)

6   Do you have the homework for August 28th in your homework
    section? (yes)

7   Do you have the skills for September 4th in your skills section?
    (yes)

8   Do you have papers from any other subjects in your notebook?
    (no)

9   Do you have your copy of the class syllabus in the "stuff" sec-
    tion on your notebook? (yes)

10 If you hold your notebook upside down and shake it, will any-
    thing fall out? (no)

I would then take up their papers and give them minus ten for every
wrong answer. This was great for me and all of my "type A" students.
It is the kind of structure for which we live. I was convinced that I was
improving their organizational skills by teaching them that "there is a

place for everything and everything should be in its place. "It took me several years and a tape by Kathy Tobias to realize that what I was doing was punishing many of my students because their organizational systems did not match up with mine.

In a lecture entitled "No Two Alike", Kathy Tobias shifted my paradigm on organization. Her point was simple. If a student, or anyone for that matter, can find a piece of information in a timely matter, does it matter how they store it? Is my goal to have them hang on to things "my way", or hang on to things "any way", and be able to find information quickly? I still believe that organization needs to be taught and stressed. I think we should start with elementary students and teach them how to set up notebooks properly, and how to work with assignment notebooks and agendas. I think that we should have lots of notebook checks in the lower grades and decrease them gradually to none by the time they are in high school. The way we grade "notebooks", however, should evaluate a student's ability to access information, not how they hang on to it.

Although my attitude towards grading notebooks has changed, my idea of how notebooks "should be" has not. At the beginning of the year, I set out very clear expectations of how I would like them to be. I give the students a handout that I expect them to keep in their notebooks. It gives them very clear details of what I expect. (I will never get over the need to try to organize them, just the need to punish them with a grade.) It is important for my smooth classroom flow that the majority of the students have properly maintained notebooks the majority of the time. I simply require them to keep a one-inch, three ring binder with five dividers and clean notebook paper. The first divider is marked HOMEWORK and it holds all of their homework for a six weeks. The second divider is marked SKILLS and it is where the students keep the skills that they do at the beginning of each period. The third divider is marked NOTES and it is where they keep their daily notes, work, and handouts. The fourth divider is marked KEEPERS. This is where they keep all of the important math rules. The fifth divider is marked STUFF. This is where we keep anything that won't fit in one of the other categories like the course syllabus.

So how do I grade "notebooks" now? In Algebra I and Geometry I have the students get out a clean sheet of paper, a writing instrument, their "math notebook" and the kitchen sink if they like. One boy just sets his book bag, which we both fondly refer to as "the black hole", on top of his desk. I then ask ten questions similar to the following:

1   What is the first word in the third paragraph on the class syllabus?

2   On the homework assignment on page 238, what was the correct answer to number 14?

3   On March 12th, what was the answer to skill number 4?

4   In the class notes that we took on April 2nd what was the title of the only keeper on that day?

5   On quiz 4, what was problem number 6?

6   On March 15th, I told you what three things were going to be on the next test. What was the second thing?

7   On the homework assignment on page 265, what was the correct answer to problem number 6?

8   On the worksheet on dividing polynomials, which I gave you on March 9th, what was the answer to problem number 5?

9   What is keeper 24 about in three words or less?

10 On April 1st what was the answer to skill number 3?

The key is to be able to find the answers in the given span of time. Those who have neat notebooks, can easily answer the questions in the given amount of time. Those who are still digging in book bags, etc. can not find their stuff fast enough! I try to be very reasonable on my timing, so that a student who has papers in "other" places, besides their notebooks, have time to find them if they are not too far away. As Kathy Tobias says, as long as they can locate what they need in a reasonable amount of time, what's the problem?

In my junior and senior classes, I do not grade notebooks at all. If they have not learned to hang on to papers and find them by the time that they are juniors and seniors, I am not sure that anything that I do will help. I still give them my expectations; I just don't ever assign a grade for a notebook check. If they go to a rigorous college where organization is necessary for survival they will figure it out. If not they will do just fine and their spouses can "fix" them when they have to start sharing a closet!

MASTER NOTEBOOK

Have you ever watched one of those movies where everywhere the President of the United States goes, he is followed by a scary looking fellow with a briefcase containing all of the national security codes? If I remember it correctly, I think they call it the "football" because the guy holds it so close to his body and hangs on to it so tightly. As silly as it seems, I feel the same way about my master notebook as the President feels about his security codes. Since I can't afford armed protection for my important papers, I have at least placed them in a notebook that is by its nature marked "very important stuff in here". My one splurge, and it is not really a splurge because it will last forever, is a real leather bound three ring binder in which to keep my essentials. This is the notebook that I will grab in case of a fire drill or a bomb threat. If I could only have one book on a desert island, this would be the one! (Not really, if I were stranded on a desert island, I wouldn't give a rip about rolls, grades, or seating charts.) This notebook is like my master control center and I keep it underneath my podium and out of sight except at the beginning of the class. My notebook has a clear cover that allows you to slide in a sheet of paper and I have a Bible verse printed on that sheet that helps to keep me centered on why I am in the classroom.

I have eight dividers in the notebook. I buy the kind of plastic dividers that have pockets in them. The contents of the notebook are as follows:

* The first thing in the notebook is a very brief overview of the week's lesson plan for each class on a one page grid. I can open the notebook and know what I am doing in every class on any given day.

We have already discussed this in detail in the lesson planning section.

* Then I place the first divider, labeled "schedules. " Behind this divider I put any alternate schedules, lists of students that are going to be out for a field trip, sporting event, or memos concerning interruptions to the regular school day. At our school we have several alternate schedules for special events and it is hard for me to keep up with them if I do not have a special place to put them.

* The next five dividers are labeled for each class that I teach. Behind each one of these dividers I place five things:

- First is a seating chart. After the first day, I never call roll so I use this seating chart every day to take attendance. I also place textbooks numbers in the slot with their name. I also have a tiny copy of the official roll with first and last names taped to the bottom of the seating chart.

- Second is the check off sheet for the present unit that we are on so I can tell immediately where I have left off. If we have any worksheets that we are working on I place them immediately behind the check off sheet with the problems crossed off that we have already done.

- Thirdly is a full sized roll with test grades and study problems on it. (Having used a grade book for 39 years, I find that I cannot let it go completely and trust the computerized program. You never know when there will be a nuclear attack on some server in Omaha!)

- Fourth, is the most recent Renweb print out. (RenWeb is that computerized grading system I mentioned.) This contains the class averages so far so I can keep track of who I need to keep an eye on. I update my print out for every class every three weeks and replace the old one with the new one.

- The last item in the section is the class syllabus. I pass these out at the beginning of the year, and I like to keep it handy so that if there are ever any questions about class rules, grading procedures, or supplies, I can quickly find the answers.

- The reason that I want plastic dividers with pockets is

because those pockets are great organizers. When I pass out a worksheet or test and a student is not present, I put their name on the paper and place it in the pocket. If I am returning papers and they are absent, I put it in the pocket. Since this pocket is right to the left of the seating chart, I always have the papers handy when the student returns.

* The next divider is one that contains information on any other classes that I have to supervise. I teach a discipleship class about once a month and I keep the roll and pertinent information here.

* The last divider is not used until second semester. It is my "storage" divider for final Renweb printouts for first semester as well as my lesson plan overview sheets from first semester.

This notebook saves me so much time and energy!

NOTHING NEW UNDER THE SUN

Once again I have discovered that no matter how long you teach there are still some surprises left. I gave a quiz in advanced math Friday and when I recorded the scores in the grade book, I had one paper that did not have a name. This is not unusual. All I had to do was look for the blank space and I knew who the paper belonged to. I looked and there was no blank space! I had 24 students and 25 papers. Now that had never happened before. So I passed back the quizzes except for the one without a name. I had everyone hold up their quizzes to make sure that I had a one-to-one correspondence. I did. I then expressed my amazement that there was something "new under the sun" in my classroom. I then walked around the room comparing handwriting and looking for the right "fit", a little like Cinderella and the glass slipper. When the match was made, I asked the culprit to explain why he had turned in two quizzes. (The quiz in question was a drill quiz that I administer on more than one occasion.) Dusty reported that he had gotten out an old quiz to check and see how he had done on his new quiz and accidentally turned in both of them. We all had a good laugh and I gave him the lower of the two grades!

MOOD METERS

I forgot my Dove Dark Chocolate today. I always put two pieces in
my lunch box in the mornings. It is the act of kindness that I do for
myself. I eat one at lunch and one at the end of the day. Today I forgot
my chocolate. The little green flag that I made out of a small wood
dowel and some yarn became my little yellow flag. If my cat had died
that morning, when I got to school it would have become my little red
flag. These flags are my mood meters. They let the class know where I
stand on that day. The first time I have to switch from green to yellow,
I explain to the class what it is all about. For example, today was the
first day all year that I changed it from green to yellow. I explained to
them about the loss of my chocolate treat and they seemed very sympathetic. Some of them even volunteered some chocolate. I told them
I was grateful but if it wasn't DOVE DARK, it just wasn't the same. I
then gave them an example. If the green flag is up and I see you doing
homework from another class, I will probably just take it up and hand
it back to you at the end of class with a sad smile and a kind word not
to do it again. If the yellow flag is up, I would take it away and not give
it back until the end of the day with a strong scowl and a harsh reprimand. If the red flag is up, I would take it away, have a public tearing
up (the paper not the student), stomp on it, fling it into the shredder,
(not really) and make sure that it was gone forever. They get the point
quickly. The flags are a great way of letting them know ahead of time
when to tread lightly. It is healthy for both of us. I find this especially
helpful since my hitting "the change. "

It is also very important that the flags are not overused or they will
defeat their purpose. My flag stays green 98% of the time. When it
changes to yellow or red the students know that I am serious and they
are so well behaved it is amazing.

CAN YOU HEAR ME NOW? ? ?

As a young teacher my hearing was great. I could hear a pin drop and
I was always catching students saying inappropriate things because they
were so sure that I could not hear them at a distance. Well there has
been a lot of water under the bridge since then! My hearing is not what
it used to be, but my desire to hear when my students speak has not de-

creased. I do not like it when I am addressing students and they mumble or talk so quietly that I can not understand them. It is not only annoying to me; it annoys the rest of the class if they need to hear what is being said. I think speaking clearly and audibly is an important skill that will help the student in every area of their lives. Getting all of the students to speak up with confidence can be an especially sensitive topic. Often the ones that speak so quietly are the shy ones that do not wish to have any attention drawn to them. In my opinion, the problem must be solved, yet it needs to be solved in a delicate manner.

A few years ago, in an Algebra I class, I had a young lady who spoke so softly that I could never hear her. Since it was the beginning of the year, I did not know her very well and I did not know if she was shy or was not confident in her answer. She did not seem shy when she was speaking to her peers. In fact, her decibel level was more than adequate. When I called on her in class, however, I could never hear her answer because she spoke so softly. Several times I kindly asked her to repeat herself and talk louder. I joked around about being hard of hearing. She still would not speak up. When she got an answer right, I really praised her so that she would be more confident. After the first six weeks there was no improvement in her responses to me. I then talked to her privately and explained my dilemma and asked her why she talked loudly in social situations but not when answering my questions in class. I got the usual answer: "I don't know". I explained to her that I needed her to speak up and if she could not do so, I would ask her to stand when she was called on in hopes that this would help her remember to speak audibly and clearly. We did this a couple of times in class and miraculously her speaking improved! I never had to ask her to stand up again. I am aware that this technique would not work all of the time. If this young lady had been shy around her peers, or if she had "teared up", I would have backed down and not made her stand. I now teach her in a higher level class and she has no problem speaking up.

I use this technique with the whole class on occasion just to put some variety into their responses. I think it is good for them to stand and address the entire class when they are answering a question or giving an explanation. I always make it very clear that my class is a safe place to do this and that they will not be laughed at. If they cannot answer the question, I help them and do it in a way that they can maintain their dignity.

Running a classroom like this is a little antiquated like playing Little House on the Prairie, but I have found it to be effective at times.

I HATE PROJECTS

I love to do projects and often times I find myself miserable if I am not in the middle of several of them. They allow me to express my creative side. I like to assign projects to my classes to be used as alternate assessments so that those students who are not great test takers have the opportunity to show me that they understand the material in a different way. I love discussing projects with the class and creating detailed rubrics so that they know exactly what is expected of them, and I know exactly how to grade them fairly and consistently. I love to show them a model of a good project. I love grading their projects and seeing what my students are capable of doing and laughing and marveling at their creativity.

I love everything about projects except returning them to students after they are graded. I hate to argue about project grades. No matter how much time and effort I put into it, I always have some students argue about their grade. Now don't get me wrong. I do not mind discussing the final project grade with a student, but I am not into confrontation and I avoid it at all costs. I have a procedure for giving back projects that I use to allow the students to question their grade, in a respectful manner and it usually works. Before I give back projects, I give them my "respectfully disagreeing with authority" speech. I let them know that it is alright to disagree with me, and talk to me about their concerns, as long as they are respectful and non-emotional. I also let them know that if I have graded their project wrong, I will be glad to change their grade. I then pass out the projects and set my timer for five or ten minutes depending on the size of the class. I then invite the class to look over the grading rubric and come to my desk if they need to discuss their grade. Thorough grading rubric construction keeps me consistent, but there are always a few students that show me where I missed something. Most of the time I missed "it" because "it" was out of order or I could not read the handwriting, but once in a while I did miss "it" and I change the grade with a happy heart.

Once in a while, however, a student loses their composure during the discussion and this is when I really hate projects! In fact, it happened twice during this last grading period. The first incident was the result of a student being absent. He was a senior that went on a college visit that lasted four days! We were doing a unit on probability, and instead of a test, I assigned a project that required the students to write each rule, followed by a worked out example, in a portfolio. I encouraged them to be creative and illustrate their examples. This portfolio would count as their test grade for the unit, and give them something to take with them to college in case they ran into another math class requiring probability knowledge. John was not at school on the day that the project was discussed. On his return, he was given a grading rubric and told if he had any questions he could see me before or after school and I would go over the rubric with him. He never came to talk to me and when I graded his project, he had an 84. He had left out two of the rules and examples and, although he had drawn some pictures, there was no color, so he got no points for creativity. He was upset because he said that he had copied someone's notes and that they did not have those two rules in their notes. I let him know that I was sorry, but that he was responsible for getting all the notes. He could have come to me and I would have been sure that he had them all. When I did not agree to change his grade, he raised his voice and started arguing with me in a very disrespectful manner. I told him that I would not discuss it with him anymore until he could calm down. I invited him to come in after school and warned him not to say another word or this could become a disciplinary issue. Fortunately, he backed down and returned to his seat. He never came to talk to me privately. If he had, we might have been able to reach a happy medium. My concern for this young man is that he is going into the military. If there is anyone who needs to know how to deal with authority in a respectful manner, it is John. If he had come in after school and apologized for the way he acted, I probably would have given him an opportunity to fix the two rules he missed and bring up his grade. He chose to pout instead. When I tried to talk to him the next day, he still reeked with attitude and I decided not to try anymore. He kept his 84 and I lost a great deal of respect for him.

The other type of scenario that comes up when I return a graded project is the plea from someone who simply cannot "make that grade. " I had a project in my SAT Preparation class that involved filling out the FAFSA form required to receive any form of financial aid. I had specifically told the class that I did not want any private information such as social security numbers or actual incomes on the form. I instructed them to sit down with their parents and fill out the form using the parents 2008 tax forms, but modifying the actual numbers. Carol, a very creative young lady with good grades, was mortified when she made a 68 on the project. She came to me with tears in her eyes. She could not make that kind of grade on the project; she had never made a grade that low and her mother would kill her. We looked at the rubric together and I asked her why she left so many spaces blank on the form. She told me that her mother would not let her use their personal information and told her to leave it blank. (Ironically, on the day that I assigned the project, I emailed the parents to let them know that I did not want any personal information, I just wanted my students to have the experience of filling out the form with their parents before they had to do the real thing. I made it clear to the parents that when sensitive questions were asked they should just make up something close. Obviously, Mom did not get the correct message either.) I reminded Carol of what I told them to do and she went into dramatics stating she had to do what her mother told her to do. I then told her that if she would get a note from her mother stating that she had instructed Carol to leave blank spaces instead of filling in "dummy" numbers that I would let her correct her work and earn some points back. She gave me one of those "you have to be kidding" looks, and I repeated my instructions. At this point I suspected that Mom had probably never seen the project, but I couldn't prove a thing. Carol never brought back the note and never said another word about the project. Evidently her mother did not kill her after-all!

These are just two examples of the trauma I experience when I assign and return projects. Nevertheless, I continue to do so, knowing that they are a wonderful form of alternate assessment and very good for the students.

Substitute Assignments

I used to assign lots of work for the kids when I had a substitute. As we all know, idle time is the devil's workshop. I did not want them to run out of work. I made sure that the material was doable and that it was current. I did not assign busy work. The work assigned was pertinent to what we were doing in class. I expected the students to work together and to help each other. If I knew ahead of time that I was going to be out, I warned the kids about their behavior. Misbehavior for a substitute is an automatic phone call home and detention. I let the kids know that I wanted them helping each other and that they were allowed to talk quietly as long as it was math. I instructed the substitute to allow talking as long as it was on topic and at an acceptable level. If it became unacceptable, one warning should be given and if it happened again, the class had to work silently for the rest of the period. I asked the substitute to leave me the names of the students who misbehaved or did not work. I had the students hold on to the work that they did and bring it back to class the next day. I instructed the substitute that this work was not to be finished for homework. Often a substitute forgot and assigned the work anyway. I instructed my classes that if that happens, they were to say "yes mam" and then just don't do the work. Never argue with a substitute!

This approach worked well but it created problems for me because when I returned I had a lot of work to go over. It is my policy to never assign work that students do not have an opportunity to ask questions about. Since my faster students were able to work a lot of problems, I had to be willing to go over a lot of problems and the class died of boredom before we were finished with the process. To solve this problem I started having a "substitute drill" at the beginning of the school year. I let the students in each class know how important to me it is for them not to miss any instructional time and I gave them very specific instructions as to what to do if I had to be out. I tell them that if I faint in class I would appreciate it if someone would call the office, but please step over my body and keep learning math.

During a substitute drill I show them how I want them to carry on if I am not there. One student should take the lead and pull a chip out of the bowl and that student should go to the board and work an assigned problem. The whole class should help and encourage until the problem is worked. If a problem cannot be worked or anyone does not understand, a list is kept and I will work it when I return. Chips are pulled all period and everyone encourages and helps everyone. I still ask the substitute to write down the names of students not engaged in the process. I even instruct my students that if I have an emergency and cannot send lesson plans in time, they should start where we left off and find problems in the book and continue on. If we have just taken a test or they can find no good problems, they know to review for their final by going back and working old stuff. A few days after going over this with my classes, I walk in and say "substitute drill" and sit in the back of the room and see what happens. I knew this approach was working when I got this note from a substitute:

> Mrs. Sutton,
> It was a very good day! You really do have some terrific students and it's obvious that they really respect you because they were so respectful toward one another and toward me as well today. It doesn't always work that way when classes are primarily student led so today's exceptional efforts are a real testimony to what you're doing in here. As a parent as well as a sub, thank you for all your doing to create such a great learning environment for our kids. You are a blessing.
> Substitute and Parent

Taking the time to prepare the students for a substitute makes life easier on everyone. Class time is too valuable to waste and a well trained class can learn for a short time without the teacher standing in front of the room.

MY FIRST BLOCK DAY EXPERIENCE

It is the third day of school and since we are on modified block, it is the first day of block. I have avoided block scheduling like the plague for many years and did not have a good attitude about it, but it had caught up with me and I had to deal with it. After taking roll by seating chart, and making those tardy sign the clipboard; I checked homework with a very perky song. I sang a little as I checked off their homework and danced with a couple of them much to their surprise. I want them to know that when I am serious, I am serious, but I can have fun!

I then introduced the class to magnet problems and quizlets. I divided the class time up so that when I felt that I had talked enough, they had to get active. In trig, I was drilling them on the six trig functions and I got out my red rubber ball. They loved it! I only taught two classes today, but I am exhausted. It is tough keeping students entertained for 90 minutes. I had a lab and did the red ball thing and tried to really vary instruction and make sure that they got up out of their seats. No one fell asleep but it sure wore me out.

If you are a science teacher, you love the block because you need that extra time to do labs. I understand that completely. I am a math teacher. I do not like block! Kids skip semesters of math and break the continuity and then when they try to pick math back up it is harder. Ninety minute math classes are torture for students who are not fond of the subject. There is less teaching time when you are on block. I have a bad attitude about block. Nevertheless we are on modified block, and I "do it" two days a week. I guess I should be praising the Lord that we are not on full block. What I see in other classes around me is sixty minutes of teaching and thirty minutes of doing homework in class. If you are going to teach block, do it right. Break the class up into activities and lecture. Use it for discovery. My block day does not always fall at the appropriate time to do a math lab, but I can always find an activity or game that will break the monotony of my talking. It has always been a puzzle to me that the students do not enjoy the sound of my voice as much as I do! Even in the highest level classes with the most rigorous curriculum, a good teacher will vary instruction using things that are more interactive.

Let me demonstrate this concept with one of my small yearly challenges. About half way through the year we have seniors who are about to leave for college come back to visit. They like to show up out of uniform and "strut" around campus. I welcome them, give them a hug, and they usually go away. This is good because I do not want to stop class to visit and they know that. They know that I love them and I enjoy visiting before or after school but not during class time. Today

Steve came in my Honor's Calculus class and he did not want to go away. Being the first block day, we were in discovery mode, and I invited him to join a group and told him that he could participate. I thought it would be good for him to help the group discover because he should have remembered the material. If you can't get rid of them, suck them into the lesson! This is a great tactic on most occasions but it did not work this time. I let him stay for a few minutes and he became disruptive to the group. He did not remember the math and he had his I-Phone out and was impressing the team members by his ability to scroll between screens. I politely thanked him for participating and asked him to move on with my blessing for a wonderful life! He knew it was time to leave and he did.

Later in the day in my biggest class, I had assigned a timed activity that the teams had to do without me. I sat in the front of the room with a steno pad and as I kept looking over the room, I jotted a few words every once in a while. I accidentally found this to be a very effective tool. I was actually writing notes to myself to help me remember their names, but they did not know that. They thought that they were being observed and that I was taking names. The technique would have been just as effective if I were making out a grocery list. The students really stayed on task! I love sneaky. It is amazing that after so many years of teaching a teacher can inadvertently stumble on a new discipline strategy!

TESTING LOGISTICS

Administering a test well not only verifies who is in charge in the classroom, it also creates an environment for success. Testing rituals give the students a sense of security because they know what to expect. As usual, every teacher must develop his/her own plan based on the subject and the general school climate. What works best is what works for you. Here is what works for me:

BEFORE THE TEST

As much as I would like to create a semester syllabus and give the students the test dates for 18 weeks, I have never succeeded at that. I find that the pace in mathematics class is controlled by the comprehension of the students, not my plan book, and I am always adjusting my time frame as I teach. The other reason a semester syllabus won't work for me is because of constant teaching interruptions like junior class meetings, pep rallies, and bad weather. Nevertheless, I make a point of announcing a test at least one week in advance. I always build in at least one review day, once the material is covered. This day is an activity oriented day where I use rotation cards, magnet problems, or any number of activities that are found elsewhere in this management section. I also have the students write down what will be on the test so there is no question as to what I am testing them over. I remind them to look over their keepers and work on their study problems. The only homework assignment I give the night before a test is study problems. I also remind them of how many before and after school tutoring sessions are available to them prior to the test.

ENTERING THE ROOM ON TEST DAY

As the students enter, I have projected on the board, what equipment they will need for the test and a sweet little reminder that the time they waste is their own. They know that I will not begin the test until everyone is ready and quiet. They turn in their study problems in a box on my desk; and then return to their seats and get ready per the instructions on the board. When they have followed all of the instructions on the board they put their quizlet boards up, which is their signal to me that they are ready for the test. Peer pressure motivates them to hurry because even if they don't care about wasting test time, some of their friends do. When everyone is ready I pass out the test and give any instructions as needed.

DURING THE TEST

Once the test is started, I take roll by the seating chart and put the names of those not in class on top of blank tests and file them in my master notebook. Next, I record the study problems in my grade book and throw them away. I then monitor the test. How much time I spend looking for dishonest behavior depends on the class. Some classes, I feel comfortable sitting at my podium and doing my work, only looking up occasionally, but some classes I have to watch like a hawk. No matter what, I do not sit at my desk; I sit on a tall stool behind the podium. I want them to be able to easily see my looking at them. Students that have a history of "wandering eye" are watched more carefully, and I make sure that I make eye contact often. I let them know that if they need to take their eyes off the test, they better be looking up counting the dots in the ceiling tiles. Students who are caught cheating are given a zero on the test and brought before the school honor board. There is no mercy.

Not only do I watch for dishonesty, I watch for anxiety. I often move to a student and just put my hand on their shoulder or give them a sticky note that I have written an encouraging note on. If I see that they are really struggling I will give them one of my pencils and tell them that it is magic or I will put a package of "Smarties" on their desk and tell them the green ones have super powers. I am Mother Teresa when it comes to compassion and encouragement, but I go back into my Attila the Hun mode if they ask for help on the test. I will not help a student with a question on a test. If they have trouble reading my writing, I will read it to them but I will not help them come up with an answer.

When a student is finished with a test, I have them fold their quizlet board on top of it and they may get out work from another class, read a book, or take a nap. Once the board is folded down they may not touch the test again until it is time to turn it in. There may be no communication with another student. Ten minutes before the test is over I start giving them time warnings in three minute increments. I do not give extended time on a test. When the bell rings they must turn the test in. One minute before the bell, I ask those finished to bring me their tests and tell the others that they have one minute to finish. They know from training to fold their papers like a hotdog and put their name on the outside. When the bell rings, I take up the remaining papers, finished or not. There are usually some frantic students, but I make no exceptions. I will not make them late to another teacher's class and if they are allowed to leave the room and come back later they will probably seek help on the test. (As always there are rare exceptions. I had a young man who had an IEP with adaptations, and I allowed him to turn in his paper, and come back after school as long as he did not tell anyone that I was letting him break my rule.)

GRADING THE TEST

I desperately try to get a test graded and back to the students on the following school day. This is not always possible but I do my best; the fresher the feedback, the better. The first thing I do is check my answer key. I pull about five papers of students who have historically scored very high on my tests and I grade them. If several of them are wrong according to my key and yet agree with each other, I rework the test questions and then if necessary change my key. Once I am satisfied my key is correct, I put it in a page protector because I am notorious for marking my answer key instead of a student's paper. I then grade the tests. In a difficult class like calculus I find it helpful to grade them one problem at a time so that I can be consistent with partial credit. I go through the entire set and grade all number ones and then number twos, etc. As a math teacher I feel very strongly that partial credit is a good thing, and I usually am very generous in giving it. On occasion, however, I make part of the test partial credit and part not. The real world does not always allow partial credit and as the students get older, they need to face the reality of a right or wrong answer especially if they will be attending a rigorous college or university. If a student's paper is so messy that I cannot follow their work, I will not give partial credit. Life is too short. If a student has left a question blank I always write "NA" in the space so that they will not fill in answers when I hand back the test and go over it and then tell me that I graded it wrong. Once the papers are graded I place the raw score at the top of the page and record it in my grade book next to the number of study problems that they attempted. Even though we have a computer grading system, I always put test scores in a grade book so I can record raw scores and see what type of adjustments I have had to make.

It is now time to get out my 'pyramid of mercy" or as I am fond of calling it, "the magic grading fairy". I go through the papers and add points for study problems. I put these new grades in the third column for the test and I look to see if the grades are acceptable; acceptable to me is when almost everyone has passed. If I like what I see these become the final grade. If I do not like what I see I ask myself why. If I feel that I have taught the material well and the students did not apply themselves, I do nothing. If I feel that the test was exceptionally difficult and the highest grade with study problems is an 82, I might add 8 points to everyone's score and record it in the fourth column. If I feel that my instruction was lacking or did not address the questions on the test well, I add points. If not many people finish the test, I may add more points. By this time it is very judgmental and only my experience guides me. The point is that I am the teacher and I can raise the grades however I wish as long as I am fair and consistent. I refuse to fall into the student "mentality" that they have to have an "A", but I also protect my professional right to adjust grades up.

Once the final grade is established and recorded on the paper, in the grade book, and on the computer, I put the papers in my return sorter. I then post some results on my "test motivator". I have used several "test motivators' over the years. When I have had space on a wall outside my classroom I have created a large refrigerator out of silver wrapping paper and labeled it "Mrs. Sutton's Refrigerator" and posted all the "A" names on the door of the refrigerator. I have also put up a large vine and each student who made an "A" got to write their name on a grape and put it on the vine. I have had a "96 Club" where students who made a 96 or above got a magnet for their team. When I did not have wall space outside, I have posted the highest score from each class with a glass marker on my classroom door. The students like to see their names posted. On the doors to my supply cabinet I place "My Favorite Grades" by taking a digital picture of the students that I want to honor. The thing I like about this particular one is that if I have a kid who always makes a low "C" and they make a low "B", they become my favorite grade. It is not all about the highest grade and it gives everyone a chance to be recognized. I would also like to add that high school students are not too grown up for stickers. I love to put gold stars and funny stickers on their papers.

RETURNING THE TEST

My students learn very quickly not to come by and ask me if I have a test graded. I will not give them back or announce a grade until I have an entire class graded and it annoys me that they ask. When they come in class the day after a test, they start on skills and follow their usual routine. Often, just for fun, I pick music that gives them a hint as to how they did on the test. If the grades were generally low I usually play "Big Girls Don't Cry" or "It's my Party and I Will Cry if I Want To" and if they are unusually high I will play "The Halleluiah Chorus" or "We Are the Champions of the World". If the grades are very bad, I have a large black hat with a long black veil that I wear and I pass out tissues as they enter the room. When I am finished with attendance we go over skills and then I pass back the tests. I pass them back upside down so that the students can have privacy if they want it. They quickly learn that I am not going to discuss individual test scores until I call out the answers so they settle in to record correct answers. I call out the correct answers in a totally quiet room, slow enough for them to write the correct answer by the ones that they have missed. If the answers are too complicated, I write them on the board. I then explain how much each question was worth and encourage them to make sure I added up their points correctly. I then ask any student who believes that I have made a mistake grading their paper to come to the front. I usually do not have many of these and I deal with them one at a time while the others begin reworking all of the problems that they missed on a clean sheet of paper. If I have graded a paper wrong, I apologize and have them fill out a notecard with their name and the correct grade. I use these to help me remember to change the grade. If I miss a wrong answer and give a higher grade than the student deserved, I praise the student for their honesty and leave the grade the same. I never lower a grade once a student has seen it. I also bend over backwards to be fair. Once all questions about grading have been answered, I have the students put up the test and we start our lesson. They know that they are to correct the test for homework. I will not spend more than ten minutes in a day going over a test because those who did well are bored and those who did not do well usually won't pay attention more than ten minutes anyway. The day after I give the test back, I set my timer for ten minutes and answer questions. If I do not get all of the questions answered I let them keep the test another day. If after two days, I cannot answer all of the questions, I either decide to let them keep the papers another day or I take the tests up and tell them if they have any questions left they will have to see me before or after school. When I am through going over the test in class, I take up the test and the corrections and file them. I usually keep the tests until the end of the semester. If a student loses the test, their test grade drops two points. They know this ahead of time and do a good job hanging on to the test. It is important for me to get the test back. Once I develop a really good test, I like to keep using it.

The only thing that can mess up this process is if I have students absent on test day. Then I must decide if I am just going to show the students what they made and give the test back when they are all made up, or go ahead and give it back and just send the student(s) who were absent out in the hall as I call out answers. I usually like to hold the test until it has been taken by everyone because this puts peer pressure on the absentees to make it up quickly. However, I still believe that it needs to be returned quickly, so, I once again make a judgment call based on the number of students who were absent and the situation.

FAILING A TEST

I do not give blanket retakes. If most of the class fails a test after the curve, I allow them to earn a few points back on their corrections. If there is a very unusual circumstance with a student, I may allow an individual re-take, but it is very rare. If a student fails a test, I contact the parent immediately by email. I include my home phone number and invite them to call me in the evenings if they would like to talk. If I do not get a reply to my email, I then call home. I always recommend that the failing student start coming in for my tutoring sessions. If a student makes a terribly low grade, I have been known to play "Let's Make a Deal". If you will come in for tutoring three times and let me help you work on these skills, I will change that 22 to a 60. Note, it is still failing, but at least it is a grade that can be rescued.

MISSING A TEST

I do everything I can to encourage my students to be present on test days. If they miss a test they have to make it up before or after school. If transportation, work, or extra-curricular schedules interfere and they have another class during the day that the teacher does not care if they miss, I will let them come in then, but I will not let them use my class time for make-up tests. It is their responsibility to get the test made up in a timely manner. Most schools that I have taught at give students two days for every day they are absent to make up their work. I follow this rule and sometimes stretch it, but I let the students know that the longer they wait, the more they will forget the material. How helpful I am to the student in preparing for a make-up test is directly proportional to the reason they were absent. If they went on a cruise, they are pretty much on their own, but if they had the flu, I do everything I can to catch them up. *This is an area where a teacher has to use a lot of common sense.* Especially if a student is present on test day, but was absent prior to the test. My usual rule is that if they knew when the test was going to be and they only missed the review day, they are still expected to take the test. If they were absent enough to have missed new material I never expect them to take the test. If they are present on test day and are not taking it, I ask them to work quietly in the room and when the first student is finished with the test, I send both of them to the media center so the absent student can get help from the finished student. I realize that I am taking a risk of the student telling what is on the test, but I ask them to be honest and hope for the best.

THE CRICKET IN THE BASKET

A new math teacher came to me to look over his first major test. He wanted to know what I thought about the length and difficulty of it. It was obvious that he had spent a great deal of time and thought putting it together, but he was concerned about the level of difficulty and the timing. The test had a broad range of thinking levels on it and was beautifully designed. Nevertheless, no matter how much forethought goes into a test, if it the first time you have ever administered it to a class, you may have to make adjustments. I explained to him that if I give a test and the majority of the class does not finish it, I do not let them finish it, I just pick that point where most of the class got to and grade up to there. I have often given a bonus point for every problem past the grading point that was correct. I feel very strongly that a student should finish a test within the allotted amount of time. There are two reasons for this and they are both very important to me. Reason number one is simply that I am preparing them for standardized tests and college and they need to learn to manage their time. I train them to go through and do all of the easy ones and then come back, but some of them are hard to train. It is against their nature to go to the next problem until they have finished the one before it. This is a very dangerous way of thinking on a math test. The second reason is that I do not feel like I have any right to infringe on another teacher's time. When you have one or more of your students remaining past your class time, you are making the job of their next teacher harder. I get a little irritated when I have taken roll and checked homework and am starting to teach my lesson and have to stop as tardy students come in the room and take care of all that business over again. If I do not want that done to me, I should not do it to anyone else!

The second concern that this teacher had was that the test was too hard. Again, I told him that he had the "power of the pen". Grade the test as it is and see what the range of grades is. If the highest grade was a 72, then the test was too hard and I would probably add at least twenty points to all tests. This is a case however, where professional judgment, based on the ability of the class and the situation has to be used. When you give the test back, be honest with the class and admit that the test was too hard. If they start whining when they are taking it, just tell them to do their best and if you determine that it was too hard, you will help them out. Be careful not to let them whine your expectations down. Find the proper balance.

Finding that balance can be hard; sometimes it is too easy to cave in to parental and student pressure to make sure grades are "good", especially if the student has "always had an "A". Our job is to prepare them for their future and teach them well, not to make sure that they have an "A". What a joy it would be to teach and not assign grades.

I have a basket of artificial, silk greenery just outside my classroom door. This morning there was a cricket in the greenery making a loud chirping noise. I thought how sad. The plant looks real and in fact is quite attractive, but it has nothing to offer the cricket but protection. If the cricket continues to hide there it will die of thirst and mal-nutrition. It reminded me of some of my students and their parents, finding protection in good grades, while they are dying of educational mal-nutrition.

THE LIST

I think every person on the planet has some kind of addiction. I have three, food, sleep and lists. I just love to make out lists. I am such a list maker that if I have a list and do something that is not on the list, I will write it on the list after I have done it so I can cross it off. I have a list at school, a list at home, and several other lists for special projects. I have perpetual lists and short term lists. If that is not an addiction, I do not know what is. In my defense, I think lists make me more efficient, better at handling details and less likely to forget something. I do not suggest that everyone become an obsessive list maker like me, but I would like to recommend that you create two types of classroom lists.

SPECIAL PROJECT LIST:

Every time I have a special activity that will occur again, I create a list the first time I do it and then after the event I edit and improve the list based on what I learned. The next time I have to do the activity, I have an accurate list and I do not have to reinvent the wheel. Major projects like planning proms, graduations, banquets, and honor programs become more manageable with lists that can constantly be revised and updated.

REGULAR CLASSROOM LISTS:

I have several types of regular classroom lists that help me stay on task and make my life easier.

*My first week of school list looks like this:

Day One:
Textbooks1234567
Name Game1234567
Announce Tomorrow's Syllabus Quiz1234567
Announce Seating Chart Will Be Made Out Tomorrow1234567
Mrs. Sutton Must Have Fun1234567
Teach Something New1234567
Assign Homework1234567

Day Two:
Seating Chart/Name Game1234567
Homework Checking System1234567
Go Over Homework1234567
Syllabus Quiz1234567
Discuss Skills Procedure1234567
Teach1234567
Assign Homework1234567

When It Comes Up:
Skills1234567
Brainplex (Free Tutoring)1234567
Keepers1234567
Shazaam1234567
Blooper1234567
Study Problems1234567
Cell Phones1234567
Dismissal1234567
Book Bags Blocking Aisles1234567
Dress Code1234567
Magnets1234567

This list is very important to me because I can never remember what I have said in what class. I simply circle the class number when I have done the thing on the list. I do not like to go over all of those rules or systems on the first day because they would never remember all of them, and I want to actually teach something, so I discuss a rule the first time it is broken. Since I can never remember in which class I have discussed what with, my "When It Comes Up" list is very important. For some classes it takes me a month to finish this list!

*My lesson plan list looks like this:

PLANNING CHECKLIST
_____ Big idea
_____ Essential questions

_____ Motivation
_____ Hands on
_____ "Blooming" is evident
_____ Assessments varied and "Blooming"
_____ Writing Across the Curriculum
_____ Math Vocabulary
_____ Summarization/Keepers
_____ SAT type questions
_____ Biblical World View
_____ Retention checklist
* All tests at least 20% cumulative
* Beginning class skills cumulative
* Utilize textbook review problems
* Keepers Algebra I thru Calculus
* Mini pop tests old important concepts
* Foldables
* Departmental atmosphere of expectation that old material will be retained.

This lesson plan checklist was developed by the entire math department, and I refer to it whenever I am creating or editing a unit. It helps me make sure that I have as many of the important components in my lesson plan as possible.

*My perpetual list is like a "to do" list that never gets completely done. I keep it in a steno notebook that lasts all year. On the cardboard back, I record all of my passwords, usernames, copier codes, etc. On the back of the cardboard front I put a few inspirational sayings that are important to me. The first and largest section is my regular list. I write down everything that I need to do and cross it off as it gets done. On Friday, I tear the page out and create a cleaned up list for the next week. This keeps things on my mind and I rarely forget to do anything. By Thursday my list is a mess where I have crossed off and added on but I never forget what remains to be done. Each morning I take a highlighter and highlight what needs to be done that day so I can focus on priorities.

Near the back of the steno book, I put three little plastic tabs with "save", "department" and "borrowed" on them. I dedicate about five pages to "save" and "department" and only two to "borrowed". The "save" tab is for stuff that I want to remember which does not require any action on my part. I am head of the math department and the "department" tab is for things that I want to remember to put on our next meeting agenda or information that I need to keep that requires no action on my part. The "borrowed" tab is so that when I loan something out I can find it if I need it. Over the years I have loaned out so much and not been able to remember who borrowed it, so now when someone borrows something, I write it down.

This steno book lasts all year and works great for me. Over the years I have tried all of the fancy planners and day books, but this is the simplest solution for me. Now, I am going to end where I started. I know that I am obsessive about my lists and that it is really weird how much I enjoy them, but they make me a more efficient teacher, and I recommend that you give them a try. Find a happy medium that works for you so you do not have to join my chapter of "Overlisters" Anonymous!

THE BEST LAID PLANS...

No matter how hard you try, sometimes you have to decide if what you are doing is effective and accomplishing its objective. I have to constantly re-evaluate my systems, because what worked for one class may not work for another and what works at one school won't work at all schools. Some of my best critiquing comes from students so I often ask them to evaluate my class at the end of the year. These evaluations are always anonymous. I often find that I am clueless about some things when I read their thoughts. Here is an evaluation that I got from a student in my College Algebra class.

"The class has been good, especially first semester. Would it be possible to not have so many flipcharts for statistics? I think it made it harder to pay attention and understand. Working problems would be better too. And keep on not punishing people for not paying attention. It's their problem and their loss. Like you said, they need to be better prepared for college and being spoon fed in every class is going to cause a problem once they get to college. Also, I wonder if you should stop using quizlet boards... it provides a great opportunity for certain people to cheat on tests/exams. I know it keeps people from cheating off of others, but it can hide notes or make it not as obvious as people look down in their book bag at strategically placed notes to cheat with. Anyway, just a suggestion. Thanks for all you do. "

I was very concerned when I read this evaluation because there were so many places where I was clueless. I had spent so many hours creating flipcharts for my Promethian Board that it never occurred to me that the students did not like them. I was trying to make the material more fun and real with fancy graphics and lots of websites. After reading the above comments, I was reminded of the old adage that "you can get too much of a good thing. " I had taught the entire semester off of flipcharts when I should have been mixing up my instructional techniques.

This class is a joint enrollment class with a local college, and I wanted to treat them like college students, so first semester if they did not pay attention or did work for another class while I was teaching, I did not say a word to them. It went against every grain of my being but these were seniors and they needed to take responsibility for their own learning. I managed to keep my mouth shut first semester but second semester I required them to pay attention to me because it was obvious to me that their choices to be inattentive first semester were not successful for them. I still do not know what is the right thing to do. This is a joint enrollment class where students who make a "B" get high school and college credit and I should be treating them like college students but it is hard to watch some of them orchestrate their own failure. I finally compromised by leaving them alone as long as they have an "A" or a "B" but I will stay on them if their grade drops below a "B".

My greatest shock in this evaluation was the cheating. When I taught in public schools the cheating was so bad that I stayed on guard all of the time. When I moved to Christian education, I knew that I was still working with teenagers and cheating would still occur. I found it less rampant, but it still exists. After several years in this new environment, I had let my guard down and had no idea that the kids were using the quizlet boards to hide cheat sheets. If I take the quizlet boards away from them they will look on their neighbor's papers. I decided to make them put their book bags in the front of the room on test days and clear off their desks except for a writing instrument and a calculator. I told them to take the covers off of their calculators and keep them in their book bags. I provided them with paper. If the class is small enough to put an empty row between all students, we do not even use quizlet boards.

I will continue to adapt even my best strategies and continue to seek student evaluations.

STICKY NOTES AND MICROWAVES

Heloise's Helpful Household Hint's is such a catchy name. I would like to come up with something like that to categorize the tricks in the classroom that save time and stress. How about Lizzy's Luscious Lassroom (no that is not a typo, I needed it to start with a "L".)? Lizzy's Lupine Lifts? ? ? OK, I will work on the perfect name for them but what I am really talking about are ways to make your classroom more efficient. In my opinion the two greatest inventions in my lifetime have not been the cell phone and the computer. The two greatest inventions are the sticky note and the microwave. The microwave does not apply to my classroom so I will stick with the sticky note and how it can be used in so many ways to simplify my classroom life. I am confident that if all the teachers got together and shared, we could come up with one million and one ways to use a sticky note, but time and space allows me to share only a few.

***For every class have a sticky note that says "start here". Place it in your teaching notebook so that you can remember exactly where you left off. The kids are amazed that I always know exactly where to start. Even if I am in the middle of a math problem, I put the sticky note under the last line that I did in my notes and boy does that degree of "remembrance" impress the kids. This little tidbit seems even more critical when you are on block scheduling, since I do not always see a class on two consecutive days.

***As a math teacher, I used to spend a lot of time hunting for answers in the back of the book. I now put a sticky note in the spot. I give one to each of the students so they may do the same. Even if you do not need to refer to answers, there might be a chart, table, index or something that you need to refer to often.

***I will write questions on the back of sticky notes and put them on the classroom walls so that the questions do not show. I then call a students' name after drawing their chip and they go to the wall, choose any question and answer it. This is a great review!

***As the students walk in the door, I hand them a sticky note. Some of them have questions and some of them have answers. When class "beginning business" is finished I give them 3 minutes to find their match. They know from the beginning not to start looking until I say "GO".

***During the first week of school, I give the students a sticky note and ask them to write their name on it and wear it until I can get all of the names memorized.

***When I plan a lesson I put correlating textbook numbers on sticky notes instead of on my papers so when the book changes, I can just change the sticky note.

***I have the students create study sheets by layering out sticky notes on a piece of notebook size tagboard. They overlap so you can see the question at the very bottom and when you lift the sticky note above, the answer is revealed. They can punch holes in the tagboard and keep a running "study sheet".

***Any time I make a promise to anyone about something that I need to do for them, I write it on a sticky note before I let them get out of my presence so that I won't forget my promise.

***I keep sticky notes by every place that I work on school stuff. I write myself notes constantly and stick them to something in my book bag so I can remember what I need to do or an idea I have.

***Layering sticky notes makes a great "to do list". Space them far enough apart and write on the bottoms so you can see everything on your list and then tear one up when you are finished. It is very easy to add to and delete without having to write over!

BITS OF GLASS
Classroom Management

***Some things you change and some things you manage.

***Your ability to achieve your goals is directly related to your willingness to use the waste basket. Throw it away if: it is for your information and you know it; it exists elsewhere; or it is too old to be useful. Ask yourself what is the worst thing that can happen if you throw it away.

***When you send papers home to be signed be sure that they have the student's names on them and then if you cannot read the parent's signature or the last name is different, you will still know whose paper it is.

***If it only takes a minute, do it now.

***If something needs filing, do it now. Do not start a filing box! Go through your files once a year and purge.

***We all have the same amount of time. Rushing around "ain't gonna" catch a bit more of it.

***Put your desk in a prominent place and then only sit at it during your planning period.

***Even if you are not OCD, you need to keep an accurate calendar and check it regularly. Be sure to put your responsibilities such as lunch or car pool duty on it so that you will not forget.

***Sometimes I want the students to fold papers that they are to turn in horizontally and sometimes vertically so all I have to do is say "hotdog" or "hamburger" and they know exactly what to do.

Chapter Five
IT'S ALL ABOUT DISCIPLINE

Dedication

This section of my book is dedicated to Attila the Hun. He has been my inspiration in disciplining my students over the years. He reminds me daily that my classroom is my empire and I am the conqueror! Megalomaniacs of the world unite!

DISCIPLINE 101

WHETHER AN EXPERIENCED TEACHER or a first year novice, almost every teacher at one time or another, feels that training as a referee might have been more helpful than education 101. It seems that a whip and a chair would be much more effective teaching tools than an intricate lesson plan. If it is any comfort, there is no such thing as an expert on classroom discipline. The best disciplinarian in the world was not born that way. Trial and error is the process by which every teacher discovers successful techniques. As you decide what is right for you and your style, remember that nothing works for everybody. There are a few basics that always apply, but the variations are endless. The suggestions that I am about to make are grouped into three categories: prevention, reinforcement, and extinction. More attention is given to prevention since in the discipline business an ounce of prevention is worth a ton of cure.

PREVENTION

Prevention has been divided into four main categories: the teacher, the environment, the lesson plan, and the rituals.

The Teacher: There are many ways to prevent discipline problems before they begin. The most obvious place to start is with you, the teacher. Does your very presence emit authority or invite rebellion? There are a few basics that will help you develop a command presence:

1   Speak in short sentences with emphasis on verbs when you issue commands, being sure to say please.

2   Stand your full height. (This one is particularly important for us short people.)

3   Become as omnipresent as any mortal can. Make the students feel like you are everywhere.

4   Use your eyes more than your voice. Make sure that you have clear eye contact.

5   Use the "Tower of Pisa" approach. When talking to a student about misbehavior, lean very slightly toward him/her.

6   Don't turn your back too soon.

7   Don't ever lose control of yourself. One of the fastest ways to lose that command presence is to lose your cool. It can be fun to see a teacher blow up, and for many students that is reinforcement for bad behavior. Don't be a button waiting to be pushed.

8   Never argue with a student. Teachers do not need to win arguments to make their point. If you refuse to argue, you can't lose. At the same time, don't be afraid to admit you made a mistake and apologize. All kids know that no one is perfect. If you try to act like you are, it will only make you appear foolish.

9   Do not continually repeat what you are saying. They must learn to listen. Be reasonable about this, but keep your expectations

high on their listening skills.

10 Conduct smooth transitions.

11 Be sure that any chaos, and there will be some, is controlled chaos and that you can pull your class back together when it is appropriate.

12 Be a benevolent dictator. Share something about yourself once in a while but don't try to be everybody's pal. You are not trying to win a popularity contest. Firmly rule your "kingdom", caring about each student while demanding good behavior. Your room becomes a safe place for everyone when you are totally in control. If you can't make the class behave, you can't prevent a bully from doing his thing. You will gain much more respect by consistently enforcing your rules than by trying to make friends.

13 Don't be a blowfish. Nagging at the students is the most ineffective way to get results and the students get so used to it that they tune it out. Say it once, twice, and maybe three times, but after that, stop nagging and start letting the students experience the consequences of not listening. Several years ago, I caught myself almost begging a class to improve their work ethic and I decided that I needed to have a visual reminder to keep me from nagging them. I went to a souvenir shop and bought one of those dried out "blowfish" and hung it from the ceiling over my overhead. Having it in my line of sight helped me remember that "blowing" a lot of hot air was not nearly as effective as telling the students once or twice and then just expecting it to happen. I kept it up there for about a year, until I learned to expect, not expound.

The Room: Environment can go a long way in determining your class's behavior. We are often restricted by room size, furniture, and class size, nevertheless, we should do all we can to make the physical environment conducive to learning.

1   Place your desk in a prominent place.

2   Leave room between student desks for you to circulate. The more you walk around the room, the more on task behavior you will have.

3   Post your most basic rules in a prominent place where the students can see them.

4   If controllable, keep temperature levels comfortable. Tempers fly in a hot classroom.

5   If you use the board regularly, make sure that students can easily see it. Students with vision and hearing problems should be identified and seated as near to the front as possible.

The Lesson: It is easy to say "Make lessons interesting to students and they will work happily and not misbehave. " Unfortunately, how things are and how things should be are not always the same. Much of our curriculum is less than palatable and making every objective exciting is impossible. There are however, a few things that can be done in planning lessons and activities that will help control discipline. First of all, over prepare all lessons. Know your material well and have more prepared than you can possibly use. Demand certain standards for work and stress quality, not quantity. Keeping expectations high and letting students know you mean business improves your classroom control. Begin each lesson with directions that save you time, effort, and much frustration by following a few simple guidelines.

1   Make sure you understand what to do.

2   Don't speak until everyone is listening. This cannot be emphasized enough.

3   Speak clearly and loudly.

4   Use understandable language.

5   Show the finished product if possible.

6   Don't try to cover too much with one set of directions.

7   Invite questions, but not until you have given all directions.

8   When preparing a lesson, incorporate student interests if possible and try to teach more than facts, changing teaching styles whenever possible.

The Rituals: Your rituals or habits in the classroom set the mood. Train the students from the first day of school and be consistent.

1   Establish a classroom starter that gets students quickly settled down and keeps them busy while you are doing your "beginning of the period" administrative work.

2   Calling roll is a waste of time and a great place for trouble to brew. Always check roll quickly with a seating chart.

3   When calling on students to answer questions a lot of embarrassment and hard feelings can be saved with one simple rule. While a student is struggling with an answer, don't allow the others to wiggle their hands in the air or convey their desire to answer. Every student should sit quietly while that student tries to answer and assist only if requested by the teacher. Usually it is not best to keep one student on the hot seat too long. I use a "chip" system so there is never any hand waving.

4   Develop "cues" to help the students make smooth transitions between activities and have consistent systems to take care of homework, testing, and make up work.

5   Beware of negative rituals that the kids quickly spot. They will spend most of the year looking for your Achilles heel. Make it a hopeless search. Do you come back from lunch full and happy and let that class get away with a little? Is Friday a sure sign to the kids that they can talk you into anything? Are there

a few pets that can give you their winning smile and get a test moved or a homework assignment changed? Do they know that they can get you off track if they start asking questions about your children or grandchildren?

6　　Never, ever, except in case of nuclear attack, allow the whole class to have free time for more than two minutes. Idle time is the devil's workshop!

REINFORCEMENT

When prevention does not handle the situation, our second phase of classroom control is the ever popular reinforcement theory. Reinforcement has taken much abuse from classroom teachers, mostly because it has been seen as an entity in itself. The more reinforcement a teacher hands out the less extinction techniques she will need, but reinforcement was never meant to stand alone in the average classroom. The first step towards reinforcement is letting the kids know what is expected of them. Explain rules in simple terms and post the most important of them in a prominent place in the classroom. When rules are followed and positive things happen, reward the students. There are many alternatives available. The least expensive choices are non-material. A pat on the back, a smile, a wink, a comment, or a good note home can make a child's day. A class reward might be a shortened homework assignment, two point bonuses on the next quiz, or bragging about them to the next class. Many other options can be offered depending on the classroom routines and set up.

I like to give inexpensive material positive reinforcements such as candy, and drinks. Many teachers feel that material awards are nothing but bribery and we should not have to bribe kids to behave. You have to follow your heart on this, but I have been doing this for years and it works. When handing out reinforcement, be it material or not, there are a few guidelines which yield maximum benefit:

1　　Give the reward as quickly as possible after the desired behavior.

2　　Be as fair and consistent in handing out rewards as you are in handing out punishments.

3   Reward effort, not just ability or end products.

4   Be specific in your praise. Let students know what they are being awarded for.

5   Do not reward too much.

EXTINCTION

The third and final stage of classroom control is extinction. On some days it is tempting to visualize extinction as lining a bunch of difficult students against a wall and shooting them at dawn! Extinction, however, refers not to the students but to their undesirable behaviors. To extinguish bad behavior the punishment must be swift and just. Sometimes it can be very difficult to be consistent when the circumstances differ with different students. If two students commit the same "crime" and you choose to give them different consequences based on their past record or special circumstances, tactfully explain why the punishments are different and accept no arguments.

A very important factor in extinguishing behavior is to make sure that the student knows it is their action that you disapprove of and not them. If appropriate, also let them know that even though you may understand why they did what they did, they made the wrong choice and they must accept the consequences. Be very careful, however, and never give a student an excuse for misbehavior. If we continue to make excuses for them because they have come from a troubled family, they are on medication, or they have lost a loved one, they begin to believe that unacceptable behavior becomes acceptable under certain conditions.

In determining what consequences are appropriate, several factors must be considered. Probably the most important is whether a behavior is a direct challenge to authority or just mischief. If the behavior is a challenge, it is critical that you act firmly and decisively and get the upper hand quickly. It is important to know the difference. If a student is involved in horseplay and gets in trouble, that is just mischief. If, on the other hand, they stomp in the room, slam the door, and slam their books on the desk while you are trying to teach, that is a challenge to your authority and must be dealt with immediately, and privately. The consequences for these two students must be different.

It is also important to know when to ignore and when not to ignore certain behaviors. This is one talent that comes with experience. There is no magic formula for knowing "when to and when not to" ignore, but there are a few questions that we can ask ourselves as we decide. Will your attention to a minor rule infraction cause much more interruption to the class than the misbehavior itself? In the case of a minor infraction, will correcting a student, who has previously made much progress in controlling their behavior, do more harm than good? If ignored will the behavior quickly go away on its own? Is it a challenge to your authority? Ignoring bad behavior should be the exception, not the rule, but it does have its place in good discipline management.

Once you have decide the behavior is a challenge and you decide not to ignore it, it is time to think about what options are available. When at all possible these options should be exercised on individual students and not on the entire group. You should not use group punishment except as a very last resort. (I try to avoid it all together.) There are as many consequences for poor behavior as there are students. What works for one, may not work for another and it is the teacher's job to find out what will work. Remember your basic guidelines: quick, fair, fits the crime.

My usual first step is my "evil eye". I have spent many years developing my best "teacher glare". I have even learned to make my glasses slide down to the end of my nose so I can look over them! One good look is worth 50 words and it let's my students know that I mean business. It is easy and quick and although directed at one or two students it is as effective as bird shot in letting all the students "in range" know that it is time to straighten up. It does not disrupt the class and I can do it without missing a beat.

If the "stare' is not enough, I will ask the student to stop doing the particular behavior. I always call them by name to make it personal. If more than a simple statement is needed or the student begins to argue, I will either ask them to step outside, if I want to deal with the issue during class, or I ask them to stay after class. I find it very effective to let students stew in their own juices. If I send a student out in the hall, I am in no hurry to get out there. I make them wait at least 2 or 3 minutes. It is not wise to leave them out there too long. If I cannot trust them, I tell them to stay after class and then I talk to them. Never argue with them in front of the class!

I need to add a statement here about the word "outside". I have a collection of "one-worders" that are "non-negotiables" with my students. They are direct commands that say a lot with no effort on my part, except for my tone and facial expression which can give a clue as to how much the word should be dreaded. If I am really mad, I just grit my teeth and say "outside". If I am not mad, I will say "outside please". If I am livid and about to have an internal meltdown, (Remember that you can never have an external one.) I will say "out" and point with my most menacing stare. "Outside" is a mystery. Outside should be inpredictable for them. They never know if they are going to be talking to Dr. Jekyl or Mr. Hyde. When I get them out in the hall, I am always respectful, but firm. If I am angry or feel that we need more time than I am willing to give at the moment, I will let them know that they are in trouble and that they should see me after class, after school, or call me at home before 9:00pm that evening. It gives me time to calm down and them time to worry. I find this postponement very effective. Sometimes I need to talk to a student privately about a poor grade or a dress code issue and do not want to call attention to them personally. If the class is involved in an activity, I will call three or four students out in the hall one at a time, including the individual I really want to talk to. The random ones that I did not need to talk to will be complimented on their work ethic or just thanked for being such a great student. I love to scare them a little when I say "outside please" and then get them out there and tell them how wonderful I think they are and how I am glad to have them in my class. No one knows that one of the students that I talked to had a problem except me and that particular student.

Often more than one student is involved in an altercation and I am not sure exactly what happened, however I know that a disturbance has resulted and I need to get to the bottom of the situation. I ask the suspected perpetrators to step "outside" while I give the class a task. (If it is unwise to put some of them outside together, leave some in and some out until you can get in the hall.) I then ask one of the students to tell me exactly what happened and tell the other(s) to be very quiet. I listen attentively and when he/she is finished I ask him/her if there is anything else they want to say before I give the other student(s) a chance to speak. When I am sure that they are done, I turn to the other student and give him/her a chance to tell his/her side. I never let one student interrupt another. If I need to allow them to talk one more time, it is done it turn, with no interruptions. After everyone involved has a chance to speak un-interrupted, I make my decision as to the proper consequences. Most of the time, a verbal warning is enough. I always make sure that I can see in the classroom door window when I have students out in the hall so that I can maintain order with my eyes. I make it very clear from the beginning of the year that if I am dealing with a discipline issue in the hall and anyone misbehaves in the room there will be double trouble.

Often a student will deny his guilt. If you actually saw the offense, don't back down and don't argue. Just let the student know you do not believe him and that he can accept the punishment or discuss his innocence with an administrator. If you are not sure of a student's guilt, let him know that you strongly suspect him and that if that behavior occurs again it will be considered his second offense and dealt with appropriately. If the accused will not admit his guilt and you have no other clues, it is rarely wise to act too strongly on just the word of another student. Also make sure the accuser did not do something to provoke the other student. It might not change the seriousness of the crime but it may determine the tone of the punishment.

Two consequences that deal with a classroom situation very quickly are "bloopers" and a discipline log. Bloopers are so important to me now that they are discussed fully later in this section. Before I started doing bloopers, however, I used a discipline log and found it very effective in deterring minor disruptions and rule violations. The log also helped me determine conduct grades at the end of a grading period, since I had a dated list of infractions. I also found it helpful during parent conferences. I created a discipline log with a funny Dennis the Menace cartoon on the front. In it I had pages with four columns marked off: name, date, crime, and signature. The crime column was the widest so they could be specific. There was also room to write "not guilty" if they wanted to discuss their "crime" with me. At the end of every day, I checked the log to make sure the students were filling it in properly and to see if I needed to discuss any "not guilty" statements with any students. If a student wrote not guilty, I either called them at home that night or talked to them at the beginning of class the next day. It is critical that you follow up quickly. If the student convinces me that I was wrong, I apologize and void their name in the log, otherwise it stands. When a student breaks a rule or disrupts the class, I ask them to sign the "log". I do not miss a beat and they know not to argue with me or make a joke out of it with a big sigh, rolling their eyes, or disrupting the class on the way to the "log". If they do, the minor infraction became serious and they step "outside. " Sometimes signing the book is enough and no other action is necessary. Be sure the students know that every time they sign the book, they are affecting their conduct grade. Come up with a scale that fits your grading system and announce it and post it in the front of the notebook so that the students know what the results of signing the book will be. If any student fails to sign the log when asked or writes something incorrect in the log, that is a direct challenge to your authority and it is time to bring out the big guns! This is one of the times to let the other students know what has happened so they will benefit from the mistakes of their classmates. As usual this should be done in a kind manner and the perpetrator should remain anonymous.

Another alternative form of consequence is the written assignment. You have to be careful with this one because you do not want to turn the students off to writing and sometimes it is more trouble than it is worth because if you assign it, you have to read it. But short, "fit the crime" assignments can be very effective. Written assignments are useful when students call each other names or poke fun at one another. If Johnny calls Sam stupid, I will have Johnny write 10 times that Sam is not stupid. It does not make any difference if Sam is stupid, Johnny is still going to write. If a student cannot stop leaning back in his chair, let him look up head trauma on the internet and write a paragraph on what a sharp blow to the head can cause. If a student talks during a test, let them write "I will not talk. " 25 times. If they talk again, have them write again. At least it keeps them busy until the test is over. If I assign a student a writing assignment and they do not complete it in the allotted amount of time, I do not double it or triple it, I simply give a "bigger" consequence. If they cannot do something simple on time, I will assign detention, call home, or if they are really being stubborn to challenge my authority, fill out a school discipline slip.

Staying after class is a good tool, but you should be taking away the student's locker and bathroom time, not interfering with another teacher's class time. I am a real stickler on students being on time to my class, and it is a very rare occasion when I keep a student so long after class that they need to be tardy to another class. If they are going to be tardy, I write them a pass and make it a point to apologize to the teacher later.

Isolation is another good discipline tool. I always thought that every school should have a room with a retired Marine drill sergeant in it that could be used to house students who needed some "alone" time; or at least a sound proof isolation booth in every classroom. Since neither one of these suggestions is fiscally possible and fertile ground for an American Civil Liberties Union lawsuit, teachers have to be a little more creative. If you have a corner; a desk in front; or a desk next to yours, use them to your advantage. When you have to put a student in the "time out" desk, make sure that they have their back facing the class, and that they are staying on task. They need to be watched, especially if the desk is close to yours or they will get creative with your desk top objects. Students who talk too much should be near the front.

Your seating chart is a critical factor in handling discipline. I remember an activity once that I used in a gifted class where we studied the character traits of some of the great figures in history and then the students were asked to pretend that they were a teacher and all of these people were in their classroom. They were asked to make out a seating chart for 30 people like Mother Teresa, Adolf Hitler, Winston Churchill, Queen Victoria, Jesus, Bill Gates, Charlemagne, Henry VIII, Aristotle, etc. It was a wonderful activity because one of the students made the statement: "There are not enough corners in the room. " How true that is when you are trying to make out a seating chart! What I always do is let them sit where they want on the first day of school as they choose their own teams and then move them as problems arise. As we change teams each six weeks, I may have to make slight adjustments to make sure that those students who need to be near the front are. Seating charts are critical to me because I believe that calling roll is fertile ground for discipline problems at the beginning of the period.

Depending on your school situation, I have found detention a great discipline tool. Unless a student has committed a serious classroom "crime"; I usually hand out detention in 15 minute blocks. If a "blooper" is drawn the student gets 15 minutes. If the "crime" required more than a blooper, than I might go straight to detention. There are some infractions that are so serious that I give out an hour of detention. An example of this is misbehavior when a substitute is present or activities that challenge my authority. I teach mostly Juniors and Seniors and transportation is not usually a problem because most of them drive. Detention does interfere with sports, drama, jobs, and their personal lives in general so I try to be flexible as long as they have a good attitude and are respectful. I give them two weeks to serve in the morning or afternoons. If they convince me that before or after school is impossible, I tell them that I am going to talk to their parents and if this is true I will work out lunch detention with them. Once I say that I am going to call their parents, it is amazing how they are able to free up some time before or after school. If, however, I do need to make the call and the parents agree that before or after school would be a hardship, I arrange for lunch detention, being sure that they have time to eat. No matter when the detention is scheduled, it is a work detail. They clean boards, dust shelves, and my personal favorite is the cleaning of leaves on my silk plants. I do ask if they have allergies, before I ask them to dust, and if this is a problem, I have them sort my paper clips into colors or some other mindless task. I do not want them to come back. If a student does not serve their detention in the allotted time, I double it and give them two more weeks to take care of it. Once their detention time reaches two hours, I call home and if they still do not serve, I fill out a discipline slip and send them to an administrator. What usually happens at this point is that the administrator adds another hour and sends them back to me to serve three hours. The kids know this and rarely let it go this far.

I firmly believe that an important discipline tool is the parents. Although there are a few parents that believe their child is perfect and should not be reprimanded, the majority of parents expect their children to behave and will back the teacher. A simple phone call may solve many recurring discipline problems. When my basic techniques are not working on a student, I call them first and talk to them at home. They are usually shocked that I want to talk to them and not their parents and are very relieved that I have given them the chance to deal with whatever the situation is. Sometimes it is hard to get to talk to the student if a parent answers the phone. They immediately want to know if there is a problem and I tell them that I just need to talk to "Suzy" about what is going on in class and if a problem develops I will let them know. This usually works, but if you have a particularly "control freak" parent, you may have to tell them what is going on. Nevertheless, the student will be grateful that you tried to talk to them before you talked to the parent. If, after my call to the student, the problem is not solved, my next phone call is to the parent. I find that notes and email are good, but personal contact on the phone is better.

One of the basic keys to individual discipline is the "forgive and forget" rule. Once a child has been punished, teachers do not have the luxury of holding grudges or staying mad. Start over with each student. Treat the student like nothing bad happened and give them a chance every day to succeed. This one tactic will go a long way to gaining their respect and showing them how much you care about them. Sometimes this takes super human effort and an Oscar winning performance, but it is worth every painful second of forgiveness that is required.

Let the kids know from the beginning that you do not like group punishment, but that they will have to learn as a class when to talk and when to listen and if they do not learn this quickly, there will be consequences. If several students or the entire class are engaged in conversation or are not ready to listen it is important to have in place signals that warn the class that group action is about to take place. Some teachers flip the light switch, start whispering, or write a message on the board. I have a remote control door bell that I use. The bell unit plugs into a standard electrical outlet and I have a small remote control button that I keep on my podium. When the bell goes off, the class knows that they have 15 seconds to get absolutely quiet and be prepared to listen. It works wonders and can be found in any home improvement store. Any student, who is still talking or out of their seat when the time is up, is immediately given a blooper.

When the class is working on an activity and I just want them to quiet down a little, I find it effective to stand in front of the class and start making out my grocery list or my "to do" list. I look up every once in a while and then write something. They think I am taking names and start talking in whispers again. I am also fond of the "strike three rule". If I have asked a class to work quietly and they start getting a little noisy, I just say strike one. They settle down for a while and if they get loud again I say strike two. If I have to say strike three, the activity goes to a solo activity and they cannot work together anymore. If these tactics do not work, start picking out individual students and ask them to correct their behavior by name. Always be specific. Do not continually say "now class, settle down". You are not going to beg. Be assertive and demand their attention. Do not start instructing until you have the attention of everyone and if someone can not conform, pull out your best "outside"! On very rare occasions, I may give the entire class a short writing assignment. If, after a couple of warnings, the whole class is still antsy, I may assign them a 100 word essay on "How Mrs. Sutton Could Ruin Our Christmas Break If We Do Not Calm Down And Start Focusing". It is very important when this assignment is made to allow those who feel that they are being treated unjustly because they were paying attention to defend themselves. They still have to write the essay but they get to vent at the unfairness of it and declare their innocence. It makes them feel better. I might add that when these are turned in the next day, I usually give them a small award for the most creative one and share some of the best in class. This is the kind of foolishness that wastes about five minutes of class time but breaks the monotony and is a lot of fun! Loss of class privileges is another way to discipline a group, but remember that group punishment should be very rare.

There are a lot more tactics to extinguish bad behavior, and as you teach you begin to develop your own "arsenal" of defense tools. The important issue is to start small and save your "big guns" for when you have done everything you can to diffuse the situation. If you use your strongest forms of discipline first you will have nothing to fall back on when real trouble occurs. Your best defense is what the kids think you are capable of doing, so save the big guns until the war breaks out. For me the 'biggest gun" is the administration. Because I rarely send a discipline issue to the office, I know that it will be dealt with decisively. I cannot emphasize this enough so let me say it in a different way. If you send students to the office too much for discipline issues, you will not be taken as seriously and the administration will begin to wonder about the abilities of the teacher instead of the conduct of the students. It is so rare for me that there are some years when I do not refer a single student to the office for a discipline issue. Do everything you can to handle it yourself, but if the situation does not correct itself, a referral should be made. Ignoring a major discipline issue is not good for the student or the class.

In closing there are a few very important points that should be made:

1   One of the major mistakes that most teachers make with discipline problems make is that they are like the dog who is all bark and no bite. Don't continually threaten without carrying through. Never make a threat which you are not prepared to carry out. Once a class figures out that you are all mouth and no action, you can just go ahead and throw in the towel.

2   It is very important to maintain a sense of humor.

3   Be prepared to roll with the various changes that affect the school. Don't keep thinking about the way it used to be. When I started teaching we just spanked them. I was never very good at that because I was too short and weak, so I was kind of glad to see it go. Complaining to students, parents, and teachers about how students' behavior is getting worse is counter-productive.

4   Give the students the opportunity to disagree with authority in a courteous manner. I believe that this is a very important skill that should be taught to the students.

5   Help students realize that with freedom comes responsibility.

Give them freedom to make some mistakes but also hold them accountable for the decisions they make. Show them that they cannot blame their parents or teachers for their classroom behavior. They have to realize that it is their own responsibility.

6 Do not try to punish bad attitudes. You can document comments and body language for future reference, but trying to discipline a "shoulder shrug" makes you look silly and lets the student know that they are "getting to you". The best way to handle a bad attitude is to "out-nice" them.

AN INTERRUPTED ATTENDANCE CHECK

The class settles in and as they do skills, I am checking my seating chart and writing the names of those missing. Before I write down a name, I generically ask the class if they know where the absent student is. This keeps me from writing their name down if they have been called to the office, etc. When I ask where Mary is, Joe calls out that she has been in a terrible wreck and is hanging on to life by a thread. Knowing Joe, and that this is just his mouth engaging before his brain, I very sternly told him to please step out in the hall. When I got him out there I asked him how he would feel if Mary did end up in a bad accident. He said that he would feel real bad and what he said was stupid. I agreed. I then asked him how the class would feel about him if what he said came true. He said that they would hate him. I agreed again, letting him know that hate was too strong a word but they wouldn't feel warm and fuzzy about him. I then told him to be sure that he checked with his brain before he let his mouth speak.

I know that Joe was just trying to be clever and did not think before he spoke. This was not a premeditated comment to put Mary in critical condition or a deliberate challenge to my classroom management. So why come down so hard on him? It is the little things that I do to control my classroom that send a message. This message is very important because then I do not have to deal with so many big things. There were three things wrong with what Joe did. Number one is that you never say something like that jokingly about anybody because if it had really

happened, Joe would have had to live with the shadow of that comment
for the rest of his life. Number two is that kids who need attention in
my class do not get it by blurting out inappropriate things at inappropriate times. I make that known and nip it in the bud very quickly at the
beginning of the year. Joe did not want the kind of attention that he
got. A private conversation outside the door is not what the students
want . The third problem here is that Joe messed with one of my systems! I do not want any goofing around when I am taking attendance.
My procedure is simple and it is not the time to be clever. Interrupting
an attendance check is serious business!

RULES

I tell the students in my classes that I only have one rule and that rule
is "Mrs. Sutton must have fun". We discuss the fact that if they do not
do what they should in my classroom, I am not having fun and therefore
they have broken the rule. I am sure that the students feel tricked because for a room with only one rule, there sure are a lot of things that
they should do and not do. They find out very quickly what they are,
without my having to go thru a long list on the first day of school.

As a rule is broken, I discuss it and then move on. The first person
to break the rule, rarely gets any consequences, unless it was so serious
a breakage that I cannot ignore the punishment phase. For example one
day I had three people simultaneously lay their heads down in Advanced
Math and try to go to sleep. Now there is nothing more irritating to me
than someone sleeping in class. It becomes triple irritating when there
are three of them. I like to think that my classes are so interesting that
no one would want to fall asleep, but alas it is not so. I cannot have fun
when students are sleeping. Therefore, I have a zero-tolerance, no-sleep
rule. Since this rule had never been mentioned, I kindly called out the
names of the three offenders and told them that they would not sleep
in class. I then invited them to stand in the back of the room at any
time that they felt that they could not stay awake. I explained to the
class, that this was not to be a thing of shame, but an act of courage. I
have been places where it was not the speakers fault, but due to personal
circumstances, I could barely stay awake, and I wish that I had been of-

fered the option of standing. I also asked them to tell me if they were really ill. Even my zero tolerance rule, has exceptions.

On another occasion one of the students new to the school pushed the button on my "quizmoo" and the creature, not the kid, started dancing and singing. In a kind but firm voice I told the class it was time for the next rule announcement and proceeded to give them a lecture on not touching anything in my room that is not for the express use of the students. I have plenty of student friendly areas that they are encouraged to use. In the back of the room there is a counter with pencils, calculators, notebook paper, stapler, tape, pencil sharpener, tissue, and the magnet board. In the front of the room there is a lost and found box, the box with homework cards, the blooper box, and the shazaam box. They may also have access to the quizlet boards and boxes under their desks. Everything else is pretty much off limits. I give them a lecture on respecting my stuff that makes it pretty clear how I feel. I then end the lecture with my usual: "Today's perpetrator will not be punished because he/she did not know the rule. You all now know the rule now; future violators will be punished to the full extent of the law. "

Thus it goes with the first unfortunate student in a class whose cell phone goes off or tries to talk when I am talking. By about the end of the first six-weeks, all "rules" have been broken and discussed.

BLOOPERS

It took me thirty years to find it, but I finally discovered a discipline tool that has worked wonders for me. I always resented the amount of time that it took away from instruction when I had to deal with minor discipline infractions. A teacher gets enough distractions from students coming in late and announcements over the intercom, without having to deal with talkers, punchers, spit ballers, etc. Now when I have a minor disciplinary infraction, I do not even break my stride, I simply say, "Johnny – blooper warning. " And keep right on teaching like nothing ever happened. If Johnny straightens up for the rest of the period, no more is said and nothing is done. If Johnny does not straighten up, on the second infraction, I say, "Johnny – blooper. " If it is convenient for me, I walk over to him and hand him a blue ticket. If it is not convenient for me, I make him come get it. He writes his name on the back and puts it in the blooper jar. At the end of the six week grading period, I draw 10 bloopers from all of my classes. Those ten students have to serve 15 minutes of detention for every blooper with their name on it that I have drawn out of the jar. I had one senior who never served and owed my two and half hours. I would not sign off on his graduation form and he spent the last day of school with me for three hours, while the other seniors were dismissed after graduation practice. It was a great bonding time for us and a great help to me as I was taking down bulletin boards and washing baseboards!

I must be careful that bloopers do not become a joke. Any student that laughs or makes fun of Johnny ends up with a blooper also. As long as I stay very serious about them, the students do. Bloopers are not a joke and should not be treated like one. If a student makes a mockery of this "system", I simply go ahead and sign him/her an hour of detention. Only one student per class ever has to serve that hour, because the rest of the students are quick learners! Students are usually grateful that they have an opportunity of not being punished when only ten bloopers are drawn. This becomes a good lesson in probability, odds, and mercy. (Teaching in a Christian school also gives me an opportunity to talk about grace on blooper drawing day.)

Bloopers are great for so many minor discipline issues, such as gum chewing, that I am not going to try to list them all. The important thing is to use them consistently and fairly and to keep teaching. When I issue a blooper, I am sure that the student is guilty. If I am not sure, I have them step in the hall and give them a chance to defend themselves. This takes more time but it does not happen often and if they were guilty, they get their blooper.

If an infraction is a little more serious sometimes I give them more than one blooper. The point is that bloopers take very little class time and are a great discipline tool. At the end of each six weeks, I throw out the old bloopers and start over. I buy rolls of tickets from Oriental Trading Company. They are cheap and they have lots of colors. The first year that I started doing this, I decided if I was going to use tickets for a punishment, I also needed to use tickets for rewards so I began using "shazaams". I also was using tickets for free homework passes.

Therefore, I needed three colors. I use blue for "bloopers"; yellow for "shazaams"; and red for free homework passes.

Before I started using the bloopers, I had a chat with my principal to let him know what I was doing. I was not sure what kind of reaction I would get from parents if two students did the same "crime" and one of them had their name drawn and got detention and the other did not. I explained my philosophy to him and he was willing to support my efforts to try this new system. I have been doing it for over ten years now and I have not gotten a single complaint from a parent.

FIVE BIRDS WITH ONE STONE

I called on Sam to answer a skill. He hesitated and then started off wrong. Several of his buddies laughed at him. I wasn't sure exactly who the offenders were, but I do not want anyone laughing at anyone else. In a very normal, but firm tone, I asked everyone who had laughed at Sam to come get a blooper. Five boys came to the front of the room as I continued to help Sam work the skill. Every one who laughed may not have been honest, but I had made my point with little effort and class time.

I have found this technique to come in handy on several occasions throughout my career. It is amazing how honest the students will be when given the chance. It is a great way to get students to spit out their gum. I will teach a while and then say that I see three students chewing gum and I will generally ask all who are chewing gum to spit it out. I usually get more than three who head to the trash can. No penalty is assigned to these honest souls but if I catch another student with gum during the same class period, I call out their name and have them fill out a blooper.

CRIME AND PUNISHMENT

There is no "best" method to handle any given situation because even if the "crimes" are the same, the students and the circumstances are not. Nevertheless, I would like to give you some possible solutions to some common classroom disruptions. As usual, just add these to your tool kits and see if they are helpful for you.

INAPPROPRIATE LANGUAGE

The punishment here depends on the severity of the language. If it is totally unacceptable, I would start with a phone call home and an hour of detention. If it occurs again, I would refer the student to the administration. Bad language in the classroom should not be tolerated. If it is of a milder version, the teacher's approach can be much more creative. My experience has been with the milder version and I have several techniques that I use.

If it is an uncharacteristic outburst of frustration and a first time offense, stepping out in the hall is usually enough. Most of the time, I find that the student is horrified that they let it slip and are very apologetic. If this is the case a warning is enough. If the student is not remorseful, I will attach a brief detention. If it was a mild infraction, but the student does not seem to regret it, I usually discuss the need for a phone call home and a longer detention. Once I say "phone call home", most students change their attitude quickly and become very "sorry". At times, I have made the student write a short essay explaining why "the word" is not appropriate in my classroom and then just had the parent sign the essay. All of the above get a "blooper" no matter what category they fall into.

On a personal note, there is one word that is socially acceptable, yet I will not allow it in my classroom. I guess it is a product of my old age but I do not like the word that rhymes with "ducks" but starts with an "s". See, I can't even type it. The first time it is used in my classroom each year, I simply ask the students not to use that word and I tell them that it offends me. I do not punish anyone. If it happens again, I give a few warnings before I start handing out bloopers. It is such a common word with young people that I try to give them several chances not to use it in my presence. I kindly remind them that I am a sensitive old lady and just do not want to hear "that word".

SOUND EFFECTS

Often, especially in middle school classrooms, you will have to deal with "ball point pen clickers", "little drummer boys", and "diver Dans". These are the students who are clicking their pens, beating on their desks, or making those annoying little bubble noises that underwater divers make. Sometimes students are doing it unconsciously and sometimes on purpose just to annoy you. Sometimes you know who is doing it and sometimes they are playing a game with you and you cannot catch them. No matter the cause or source, they are very annoying and distract you and the other students and it must be stopped. If I know who the culprit is and believe that it is unintentional, I simply ask them to "please stop' and they usually do. If it repeats or I believe that it is intentional, I give them a "blooper warning" and keep teaching and if it happens again I give them a blooper. If it continues, I slowly go up the scale of possible consequences until I break them of the habit. If a student is ADD and really needs to move his or her hands, I encourage that student to bring a rubber ball to class to squeeze with the understanding that it must stay in his/her hand and not be used for "evil".

If I do not know who is making a distracting sound, I simply announce to the class that someone is making an annoying sound and would they please stop. If it stops, I never try to find the source. If it continues, I then ask someone to confess. If no one confesses, I let the class know that if the noises continue, I will work diligently to find out who the culprit is and if I catch them there will be serious consequences, but I will not continually stop the class. It is important to keep your cool and sense of humor in this type of situation. If you can catch the correct student, make sure that the punishment is harsh enough to let them, and the class, know that you will not tolerate this type of challenge to your authority. They had a chance to confess, and did not; so show no mercy.

A rather delicate category of sound effects is the ever popular passing of gas in the classroom. This is most often performed with gusto by a male adolescent. The immediate response is usually widespread laughter. The first time this happens in the classroom, I make sure to put on my most serious teacher face and in a very no-nonsense voice, I let the class in general know that there will be no laughing or disruption in class due to a digestive problem. I also let them know that if this occurs too often, some phone calls will be made home, requesting some medical procedures be conducted to identify the source of the problem. This usually solves the problem. No child who has real medical issues should be allowed to be laughed at and once this situation is realized you should work with the student, parents, and peers to deal with the situation. Students should be taught to ignore mishaps.

EXCESSIVE TALKING

If your problem is only a few students talking when they should not, simply go through your discipline ladder, starting low and gradually moving up. Start with warnings and trips outside the door to see if you can identify the problem. Rearrange seats and if that does not work give them bloopers. If that does not work, and it won't on some, start assigning detention and calling home. The first time I call home, I would talk to the student, not the parent. The second time I call home, I would talk to the parent. If the student is still talking out of turn I would request a parent conference. If none of that works, it is time to get out the big guns and refer them to the administration. I think it is important to try everything you can before the referral. The student has to learn when to talk and when to be quiet and if they cannot do that, they need to be disciplined.

If you have an entire class that is talkative or disruptive in any way and you want to modify their behavior I think you should tackle the problem with positive reinforcement. Discuss the problem with them and let them know what they are doing incorrectly and what your expectations are. Let them know that you believe in them and that they can meet your expectations. If it is appropriate, take suggestions from them as to how the problem can be solved. Come up with creative rewards and start with small "behavior intervals" and then increase them. Let them know that if they make it through a class without a discipline infraction the class will get a treat the next day. On the following day give them all a cookie or a piece of gum depending on your budget, and let them know how proud of them you are. Then tell them to get the treat, they have to go five days without an infraction. They will protest that they cannot go that long, but you will assure them that you believe in them. If they mess up, let them try again until they get the five days. If they decide that they just can't do it and give up, go to negative reinforcement. When they finally succeed at five days, reward them and up it to ten. When they succeed at ten, reward them one more time and then it is time for a classroom discussion on "good behavior should not have to be rewarded" and the treats should stop. Once in a while, I will still give them unexpected treats if they have been especially good.

If positive reinforcement does not work, I get out my "terminator board'. When I used an overhead projector, it was a transparency sheet about three inches wide with each student's name written on it in permanent ink. I would place it on the overhead and work my math problems on the side of it. As a student talked or exhibited any other un-desirable behavior, I would cross out their name with a water based pen. I did not skip a beat in my teaching and I allowed no arguments. If a student wanted to protest, they would have to do it on their own time. The first time I did this in class there was no penalty for the student's whose names were crossed off, we just had a brief discussion on what would happen if I had to get out the terminator board again. I usually told them that if they got their names crossed off they would get a 15 minute detention. If you do not mind the record keeping, you could keep track of the number of times they were "terminated" and have different levels of consequences, but I usually just like to have simple immediate punishment. You can also give a reward to those whose names are not crossed off, mostly to irritate those who did get crossed off! Once I switched to my Promethean Board, I could not use the transparencies as easily, but a little creativity with a laminated poster board list will work just as well.

NOTE PASSING

If I see a student passing a note in class, I do not say a word to them, I just simply walk over, intercept the note, place it on my desk, and keep right on teaching. I read the note to myself after class and if the contents are not inappropriate, I forget the incident. This is usually enough to stop the behavior. If it continues, I will speak to the student outside of class and start dealing with it as a discipline issue. I believe that one of the worst mistakes a teacher can make is to read these notes out loud in class.

BREAKING RULES OF ENGAGNEMENT

It is my desire that my students remain "engaged" at all times. When they do any activity that breaks that engagement, I do my best to swiftly "re-direct" them. If I catch them doodling on my desks or quizlet boards, they become part of an after school clean up detail. If you mess it up, you clean it up! Not only do these activities distract them from the lesson, they are also destructive to my property. My biggest problem in this area, however, is when students try to do work for another class in my room. I make it clear from the beginning that every class is important, but this is my class time and I do not want to see them working on anything else. I usually just take the work up and keep it until the end of class and give it back to them with a stern warning. If it happens again, I take it up and give it back to the appropriate teacher and have the student retrieve it from them. If it continues, it is time for a phone call home to the student first and then to the parent. I make no exception to this rule. Even if a student has a good grade in my class, I want their full attention!

As a math teacher I also have a problem with students playing games on their calculators when they should be doing math on them. As tablets come into the classrooms, I believe that this will become a problem for most teachers. The first time I catch a student I simply give them a warning. After that I take their calculators away from them for very brief spans of time. If it becomes a real problem, I will contact the parents and let them know that the student will not be able to use the calculator on a test. This can be a serious problem in a calculus class. It is very hard to catch students using their technology improperly, but when you do catch them, make the punishment severe enough that the student and their peers will think twice before doing it again.

If I catch a student listening to their I-Pods or texting or using any other various gadgets, I take them up and turn them in to the office and let the students or parents retrieve them. I have a low tolerance for anything that distracts my students.

FOOD AND DRINK INFRACTIONS

The only food or drink that I allow in the room is what I give them with the exception of water. Some of the students are experts at having snacks in the pouches of their book bags and sneaking them when I am not looking. If I catch them, I ask them if they have enough for everyone in the class. If they say yes, we pass it out. If they say no, it is a blooper warning. If the problem continues with that student we slowly go up the discipline ladder. If I have a student with a medical problem, exceptions are made.

Students chewing gum are generally shot at dawn. Not really, but I try to extinguish their behavior quickly. I have scraped too much gum off of shoes and desks to tolerate its existence in my classroom, not to mention the fact that it does not look good. These young people need to understand that they should not go to a job interview chewing like a cow. I think some of them are going to get married with gum in their mouths! When I see it, I immediately ask them to spit it out. No swallowing, please! If it happens again, they get a blooper and every time after that they get a blooper. If it becomes a daily problem with the same student, I start going straight to detention and phone calls home. Some of them will try to out stubborn you so remain strong.

MAKING THE PUNISHMENT FIT THE CRIME

Here is a beautiful example of how crime and punishment can be an effective learning tool.

Yesterday, I returned from a trip to the Xerox machine, and found another teacher reprimanding a student in my empty room. It was during my planning period and the teacher had commandeered my room to handle a discipline problem. I waited outside the door for a minute. The teacher soon stepped outside and asked if the student could sit with me for the rest of the period. I agreed. The young man just sat there for 40 minutes. The next morning, fifty-five minutes before the start of school, I saw that student sitting in that teacher's room copying notes from the overhead.

What a great idea! If you cannot sit in the teacher's class and behave, you can get out of bed early in the morning and make up the material on your own time. This kid was too young to drive. Can you imagine explaining to your parents that they have to get you to school early be-

LIZZY SUTTON

cause you cannot behave in class? I love this because it is such a good example of making the punishment fit the crime. I know that this is not an option for every student and every teacher. Some parents might not be able to provide transportation. Some teachers might not want to get to school early. The teacher did not teach the lesson again, he just made sure the student knew that he was responsible for the material and if he could not behave to get it in class, he would have to do it on his own time. The message was very clear; disruptive behavior is not appropriate in this teacher's classroom.

THE ORANGE BAT

I almost didn't put this discipline technique in the book because it can backfire so easily! Used improperly, this is material for a lawsuit, so please know that this one has to come with a warning: USE AT YOUR OWN RISK! Nevertheless, it had to go in the book because it has been such a great tool for me. To implement this method you need to go out and purchase a light, plastic, brightly colored, kids, oversized bat.

My orange bat did not start out orange and it did not start out light. It started out wooden and heavy. I would never have brought a bat into my classroom, even though there were many occasions that I could have found a very justified use for one. It appeared in my room as a gift from a parent who had given me very specific instructions to use it on her child whenever I thought it would do the most good. I was a little taken aback, since the bat that she sent was a regulation baseball bat that qualified as a lethal weapon in the wrong hands. I found it very effective however, since all I had to do was pick it up and her son, Jarad was good for at least ten minutes. One day Jarad had tested me to my limits, (he was hyperactive and very verbal), and I actually picked up the bat and touched him on the side of the head. I did not tap, I just touched and barely made contact at that. He was good for at least thirty minutes, and I began to see the possibilities in the bat.

I went looking for a bat that would be very symbolic, yet not as lethal, and found the perfect one in the dollar store. I took the wooden one home and started "applying" the orange bat to other students. Done with a sense of humor and no force, it became a very effective tool for me. Here are my "orange bat" rules:

- Only use it on students that will not be humiliated or take it the wrong way.

- Only use it on students whose parents you know very well and you are sure will not get offended when you use it on their child.

- Only use it as a threat, as a touch, or a very light tap. Never really hit a student.

- Use it infrequently so it will count for something when you use it.

- Use it with a sense of humor.

- No one touches the orange bat but Mrs. Sutton.

I like to use the bat when I want a quick fix to a student's action that does not interrupt my class, yet gets the message across that I mean business. Once I start walking to the orange bat, which lives by the front board, I have everyone's attention and with a quick bounce off of the offender's head, I can go back to teaching without a word. They know what they were doing; I know what they were doing, and they will stop doing what they were doing without my saying a word!

Sometimes the orange bat works great when a behavior needs correcting and I do not know who the student is that committed the crime. Let me explain with an illustration. My classroom is right next to an outside door and it is important in the winter to keep my door closed so we can keep the room warm. I do not lock my door at lunch, and I would often come back from lunch and the door would be open after I knew that I had shut it when I left. Several students drop off their books on the way to lunch and one of them had forgotten to shut it. I had no problem with the books being dropped off and I did not want to lock the door or tell them that they could not leave their stuff. I talked to the class about this and explained why it was important to keep the door shut. It was left open again. No one admitted to leaving it open. I talked about it a second time and reminded them of my general "three strikes and you are out" rule. It happened again. This was not an act of rebellion or a challenge to me, it was just forgetfulness. The next day I told the class that the next time the door was left open at lunch, I would draw a name and that person would get the "bat. " It happened again about a week later and I drew a name. It was one of the sweetest, quietest girls in the class. As I approached her with the bat, three young gentlemen jumped up and said "hit me", so I did. The young lady was off the hook! Now remember that I really don't "hit" them, it is just symbolic, but they wanted to spare her from even that. No one left the door open for the rest of the year. I will have to retrain next year. The point here is that the situation was handled with humor and something outrageous enough to help a hungry teenager remember to shut the door on the way to lunch. It was also handled with almost no class time involved. If I had been an English teacher I would have used this incident as a springboard for reading and discussing *The Lottery*.

I also find the orange bat effective when I want my students to stay on task when they are doing seat work. All I have to do is walk around the room with the bat, and everyone miraculously gets interested in what they are doing.

JIM SAYS "CLEAVAGE"

I am fondly referred to by students and staff alike as the campus "dress code Nazi". I am a careful "enforcer" of tucking in shirts and watching the length of skirts. When I taught in public schools, we were not worried so much about tucking in, just covering the territory and making sure that there were no "free advertisements" for "non-school like substances". It makes no difference if you are with or without uniforms, you still have to deal with the dress code. One of the touchiest issues anywhere, (excuse the pun) seems to be that of exposed cleavage. In today's fashion world, it seems that the more cleavage showing, the more fashionable an outfit is. This fashion comes in very definite conflict with my school's present dress code. I have found that my girls are very creative on casual dress days in interpreting the dress code, so that they can show as much of this "cleavage" as possible, without being sent home. Usually a kind reminder to button a couple more buttons helps, but I am often faced with a decision of what is acceptable and what is not when a button will not fix the problem.

So why am I talking about Jim and cleavage in the same sentence? Because even though I started out that way, this ramble is not about dress code. It is about another conduct tactic that I find most useful. I am walking out of the cafeteria one day and Jim is talking to a beautiful young lady that I do not know, who is showing an abundance of "cleavage". I say "excuse me" to Jim and motion for him to step back a moment and give the young lady and me some privacy. He does so, and I talk to her about the problem and ask her to button two more buttons. She complies and promises to do better in the future. As I begin to walk away, Jim, in a very loud voice, says: "CLEAVAGE", pointing at the young lady. I do not believe that this was particularly embarrassing to her, but I found it unacceptable behavior and told Jim to come with me. It was quite a walk back to my building and I put my arm under Jim's like he was escorting me down the aisle at a wedding. We walked that way for several minutes and I kindly explained to him why I thought what he had done was immature and inappropriate. Several people who passed us commented on what a gentleman Jim was! I did not try to correct them. If they only knew!

I could have given Jim detention, a phone call home, or a firm reprimand, but what I thought Jim needed was a little sensitivity training. Not necessarily towards the "young lady', but towards the "old lady". I was offended that he chose to say the "word" so loud in such a public place and he needed to understand that he should engage his brain before his mouth. This tactic continued to be useful for me. Whenever Jim even looks like he is thinking about mischief, which occurs quite often, I just crook my arm like I am looking for an escort and he settles down!

PRAYER AS A DISCIPLINE TOOL

Rick is a fine young man. He is very respectful and polite. He is the type of young man that I would be proud to have as my son. He has a great sense of humor and is always the life of the party. He likes to goof around with his friends and this often involves poking and pushing. He is a great athlete and a good student. Academics are not his first priority, but he does keep his grades acceptable so that life at home can be pleasant. He does not have a mean bone in his body. He is often the last one to start an academic task in class, as he has much socializing to do and schoolwork gets in the way of communication! He never does anything bad, or almost never, but he is a constant challenge to keep focused and on task. He is seldom concerned about being on time to class and is just a happy-go-lucky guy on the surface. He wouldn't hurt a fly unless it was in the football uniform of an opposing team and then he would block it into oblivion.

To understand my next discipline tactic, you have to understand that this only works on good kids like Rick and it rarely has long term effects, but it works for a season. We have just finished going over skills at the beginning of class and Rick is poking Lou, the young man next to him. Rick was slow in getting started because he was goofing off and Lou has difficulty with the work and needs to be left alone. Rick is always aggravating Lou and Lou enjoys being aggravated. I, however, feel that Rick should leave Lou alone so he can learn. They are not bothering anyone else, just each other. Did I mention that these young men are not in middle school, they are high school seniors? Normally I would just separate them, but the other teams are working great together and why should I punish other students because one or two of them are acting immature and can't get with the program?

After we go over skills, I always pull out one "chip" and that student prays for the class. It is usually a prayer for staying safe in sports, doing well on tests, world peace, etc. On this particular day, Rick's name was called and I asked him to pray for something that was on my heart. He agreed and I explained to him that I was having trouble making a very important decision. The teams in that class were perfect except for two individuals who could not stay on task and work without distracting themselves and those closest to them. I needed some guidance to know if I should split up the teams, which would punish everyone in the class, or should I just work with the two students involved and try to keep the team structure in tact. I also asked Rick to pray about what would be an appropriate punishment if the two students in question continued to act in this manner. As Rick prayed, he shortened my request to: "

Lord please don't let Mrs. Sutton break up the teams on our account, we will do better. "

As I said, the good behavior may only last for a week or two, but I gave them a chance to straighten it out before I went to another level of punishment. In a public school, you could modify this strategy and instead of asking Rick to pray for your concern, ask him to give you his advice on the proper decision. (Rick and Lou behaved for at least a month!)

YES MAM

I had watched Troy in the hall for the last couple of years and all I saw was a cocky young man who seemed to spend a lot of time outside of classroom doors chatting with teachers about his conduct. This year Troy was in my lower level calculus class and he was not a star student academically. I knew to treat him with kid gloves and I did my best to make sure that I went out of the way to be pleasant and earn his trust. He failed the first two tests but I played "Let's Make A Deal" with him and he started doing study problems. He made a 70 on the next test with a little help from his study problems.

As I got to know him better, I learned that he had always had a problem with authority. I know that he has a problem with his parents, but I really don't know what the problem is. I have had minor go-rounds with him but they have been simple things like no homework or dress code violations. He is passing right now, but it is by the skin of his teeth. We found a balance that is working for us, nevertheless we came close to a blow out.

I wish that I could remember our discussion word for word, but it started when he had on a non-dress code sweatshirt. I told him that I would have to take away one of his casual days. He responded with an attitude like he did not care. I reminded him that I had already warned him about this infraction and he replied "not really. " At this point I knew that I could escalate the situation or diffuse it. He was on the way to the rest room, and so was I, so I told him that I would meet him in the hall when we both were finished. I met him in the hall and asked him to step outside the building. I started talking to him about the dress code violation and as I was talking I could see the vein in his neck just throbbing. He was so angry at me and I was not sure why. I told him to calm down or he really would be in trouble and he made the statement that he was already in trouble so a little more would not hurt. I let him know that I was not trying to get him in trouble but that when I corrected him on dress code or any other rule infraction, all he had to do was to change his behavior and simply say "yes mam" to me and I would usually consider a warning enough. I tried to explain that it was his reaction to me that got the casual day loss. He shut his eyes and continued to get madder. I knew that something more was going on here when tears started running down his cheeks.

I told him that many times in my life, I have gotten mad or hurt at someone but I still apologized when I didn't mean it, just to keep peace in my life. I talked to him about being polite to authority even if he felt that he was being treated unfairly. I then asked him if he understood what I was saying. He opened his eyes and said "yes" but could not get out "yes mam". I then asked him if I had not earned his respect this year. He shook his head yes, and then when I asked him again if he understood what I was trying to say. He slowly said "yes mam. "

I told him that I would love to wipe away that tear, but it would not be appropriate so I wanted to give him some "motherly" advice. I told him that he only had about two-thirds of his senior year left and he could control himself for that long. When he got angry, he needed to find a punching bag or run a mile until he calmed down. I then asked him where he was going to school and he named a college several hours away from home.

I then told him that in about seven months there would be no dress code and no parents telling him what to do in every area of his life. He just needed to hang in there and learn how to deal with authority. He said "yes mam" without my asking him to and we hugged. He dried his eyes and I told him to pull himself together and I would let his teacher know that he would be a little late and to please admit him. He actually smiled at me! I am sure that Troy will have more problems this year, but I hope that something that I said can stick. De-escalating always gets better results than confrontation. There is a line that can be crossed, but there is no sense in pushing them over the line when they can be talked back off of it.

KICKED OUT OF TUTORING

Today I had a parent conference with a young man and his mother. It is another one of those boys who has a horrible time saying "yes mam". He and his brother had come in early for tutoring a couple of days ago as he often did because his mother made him. His shirt was un-tucked. I asked him to tuck it in with my usual "please' and he informed me that he did not have to because it was before school. Now this is a negotiable point. The problem is the way he said it. If it had been in a kind matter, I would have probably said: "You're right, just have it tucked in by the time first period starts. He did not say it in a kind matter. He was arrogant and a definite challenge to my authority. He made another smart comment but I did not hear it. I asked him to repeat it and he would not. He gave me a simple no. I told him that if he felt it was necessary to say "no" to me he had better be able to explain himself and it better be "no mam". I then told him that our conversation could end one of two ways and it was his choice. I asked him if he wanted a chance to de-escalate the situation. He said no. I told him that I would not be tutoring him that morning and would not do so until I had a conference with his mother. I also assigned him one hour of detention. Fortunately for me his brother was present. When Brady left, I asked Ben if he thought that I had over-reacted. He said definitely not and that Brady had a talent for letting his mouth get him in trouble. I had never kicked a student out of tutoring and it un-nerved me.

I have taught these boys for several years and their mother is the kind that is very involved in their education. The boys are usually kind and respectful. Ben is very docile and sweet. Brady has some attitudinal issues but is generally respectful. The mother is wonderful to the teachers and the school and spends many hours volunteering. I called her and let her know the situation and asked her to come in for a conference. I requested that Brady be present also. I had asked her to talk to Brady and Ben before she came in so that she could already have their side of the story. Today, Brady came in and apologized to me so I know that she had already gotten "hold" of him.

It wasn't necessary to recreate the crime scene since she had already talked to the boys and I did not feel it necessary to defend myself. I simply wanted to know why Brady was so disrespectful to me over such a silly issue and why he found it so hard to say "yes mam' to me. His mother told me that there were a few women in his life that he had trouble saying "yes mam" to, including his grandmother, who he loves dearly. He couldn't or wouldn't tell me why he had such a hard time saying it to me but promised to do better and even said "it" before the conference was over. He still must serve his detention, but he may now come back for tutoring. When he does, I will welcome him as if nothing has happened.

STOUT GIRLS DRESS CODE

It is very important that I be consistent in enforcing the dress code. I do not enjoy "zapping" a student for not having a shirt tucked in or having the wrong kind of jacket on, so I will usually warn them once before I give them a dress code infraction. Sometimes, however, this is a major ethical dilemma for me, even though it sounds like a trivial issue. I know that many parts of the dress code are just about neatness and not modesty, but I try to enforce them all to be fair. I also believe that the dress code is about obedience which is a character trait that is not in vogue much anymore, but needs to be taught.

So where is the ethical dilemma? When I was in school I was always overweight. I would have died before I tucked anything in! ! ! I always wore lose clothes and I was always mortified by my big stomach. Some of the students in my school that are overweight, boys and girls alike, are very self-conscious about their size and do not like to tuck in their shirts. It is so hard for me to tell them to do that when I know how mortifying it is for them to have to obey. This is why I have an ethical dilemma. I know what is right according to school rules and I know what is right according to teacher fairness guidelines, but I cannot seem to make myself ask these students to tuck in their shirts. Because I also know what is right in the realm of humanity and love.

At the other extreme, I had a young lady who refused to tuck her shirt in who was very thin. She simply hated the dress code and the school, and it was a minor source of rebellion for her. She was a very complicated young lady with lots of serious issues and she had to be dealt with very carefully. She was never disrespectful and I loved her very much, but she put me in quite a tight spot. Her father was an administrator at the school. For her sake, I wanted to be lenient, because any action on my part sent her closer to the "edge", however if I did not give her consequences, it would look like favoritism. I discussed this fact with her father and he deferred to my judgment. In the end, I decided it was not worth the battle and let it slide. Fortunately no other student ever made a comment about my lack of enforcement but if they had, I would have talked to them privately and tried to explain to them that there were certain circumstances that were not theirs' to understand, and that they would have to trust me on my decisions as to when to discipline and when not to.

I strongly believe in all of my statements about teacher consistency. Nevertheless, consistency should be trumped by compassion in special cases! With experience, I have learned "when to" and "when not to" when it comes to most discipline issues.

THE OLDEST PROFESSION

Well, Jack just can't seem to do anything right. He is my class clown and his bloopers seem to take up their share of space in the blooper box. One day in class I was introducing The Quotient Rule for finding the derivative. The fun and easy way to remember it is HO DEE HI MINUS HI DEE HO DIVIDED BY HO SQUARED. Now I know that if you are not a math person that makes no sense to you whatsoever, but you do not have to understand it to get my illustration. After I have played some seven dwarfs "hi-dee-ho, it's off to work we go" music I explain this formula with the statement "What do you think the HI stands for? " and they answer "THE NUMERATOR" and then I ask "What does the HO stand for? " and they laughingly answer the "THE DENOMINATOR". This is a group of seniors and they are mature enough to handle this. I would be more careful in the questions I ask in a lower level class. I then tell them to get their minds out of the gutter and think garden implement or LOW for denominator. Well before I could even mention the gutter and garden implement, and right after I asked "What does the HO stand for? " Jack deliberately points to the girl sitting next to him. I then told Jack to please step out in the hall. I was furious. I have been doing this for years and no one has ever been brave enough to make anything else out of it. I let Jack stay in the hall for about 5 minutes to stew in his own juices. I also waited five minutes so I could calm down or I would have pinched his head off. I then went out and told him how horrible I thought he had acted and what that could do to a girl's reputation. I used a lot of words like disappointed and egregious error; he knew that he had really crossed the line. I then told him that he would apologize to the young lady and he better make it good because if it was not from the heart, I would jerk it out and hand it to her! He knew he had used up any grace that I might be feeling. I called the young lady out in the hall and he performed an Oscar winning apology and she accepted it. I sent her back in, handed him three bloopers, and told him that the next time he sneezed too loud he would have a one hour detention and a phone call home.

DYING YOUNG OF INK POISONING

In SAT Prep today, I noticed that Sam had ink marks on his arm. I asked him if he had acquired them during my class period. He said yes. I then asked him if they were self-inflicted. He said no. I then asked him to identify the perpetrator. He asked me to define perpetrator and I did commenting that perpetrator was a great SAT word. He then said that he could not divulge the perpetrator. Due to the location of the marks, there was only one possible guilty party and I looked at Ian with a knowing smile. He immediately admitted his guilt. I remarked that his behavior was not acceptable and he replied that he had been provoked. Sam had stolen his pen. Alas the plot thickened! I now returned my attention to Sam, who with a sheepish grin said, "yes, I stole his pen, but I could die of ink poisoning. " Sam quickly replied that he could have failed a test without his pen and then his parents would have killed him and he would be dead too. This entire conversation, or shall I call it friendly banter took less than two minutes and did not disrupt class as they were working on an independent activity. In the end, I had them shake and agree to behave themselves in the future. I felt that the whole episode added to our student-teacher bonding experience, while correcting a minor behavior infraction. I also believed that both Sam and Ian were equally guilty and that no punishment was needed. If Sam died from ink poisoning or Ian flunked his test and was murdered by his parents, I would know who to go to for litigation purposes.

GROW UP

I have a group of ninth grade boys whom I do not teach, that are always horsing around in the hall. I usually just step into the hall and give them a warning to calm down and move on to class. I have noticed that there are two of them that seem to always be in the middle of the fray. I have taught both of their older siblings and they seem to be a little bit scared of me in a respectful sort of way. I have asked them to step into my room on several occasions and had a little chat with them about all of the reasons why they should not goof off in the hall. Well, today in the hall, I heard a ruckus and my two little "sweethearts" were having a scuffle in the hall that involved a "touching incident" and some kicked books. I once again invited them into my room. I knew from past experience that they were good friends and that they would not "rat" on each other, but I had not seen what had really occurred so it was hard for me to decide the direction I should go. I asked Billy to tell me what had happened. He said they were just kidding around. I then asked Mike and he agreed but I could tell by his facial expression that Billy had started it. I am afraid that my frustration showed and I came out with that old cliché "grow up. " Now I really hate it when I do that because there are two problems with that directive. Number one it is impossible to do on short notice, and number two it is a reflection of my frustration and not my wisdom! I tried to redeem myself with another brief lecture, and an admonition that the next time I could not decide what had happened, when I witnessed an incident, I would proclaim them both equally guilty and give both of them detention. I predict that they will last a week before that happens!

THE DOUBLE EDGED SWORD

I used to think that after you taught long enough, you had seen and experienced about everything there was to see. All you needed to do was "tweek" your response to match the varied situations and changes in culture over the years. For example, you used to paddle them, now you give them detention, but the crimes are basically the same. Well the crimes are still basically the same, but technology has created a whole new world of possibilities and after just three sentences, I am already ready to change my first statement. No matter, how long you teach, there is always the possibility of something new every day! One thing for sure, teaching is not boring.

I have a young man named Mitch, who likes to sit on the back row so he can be as un-obtrusive as possible; especially during baseball season when he needs some privacy to catch up on his sleep. Not being the kind of teacher that allows students to fall through the cracks, I find myself calling his name about once a day to wake him up and get him to pay attention. Mitch is a very respectful kid with a mother who is very motivated. The only reason he does "math" is about the same as most of the students, it keeps him in school, which allows him to play ball on the school team. Mitch is a good student but he is not a great student. I really have not gotten to know him very well because he does not contribute in class unless forced to. His grades fluctuate, depending on how attentive he was to the lesson.

On one of his downturns, Mitch made a 38 on a test. I immediately emailed his mother. The next day I gave the test back in class and we went over problems. I had graded Mitch's paper correctly, but I had given him the score of the points he had missed instead of subtracting them from 100 and giving him the correct grade. Mitch should have had a 62. This still was not a great grade but it was a whole lot better than a 38. Mitch was relieved and I was apologetic because I knew that his mother had given him a hard time about the 38. I immediately pulled out my cell phone in front of the entire class and asked Mitch for his mother's number. (This was extremely unusual as I never pull out my phone in class, so I had everyone's attention.) I dialed and she answered. I told her that I was calling her in front of the entire class because I felt that a public apology was in order. I never said the grade over the phone but I explained what I did and told her to add 24 points to his grade. She said that she was relieved that it was not so low. She also said that she already knew. When I asked her how, she said that Mitch had just "texted" her. When I repeated what she said, you never saw a student's face fall so fast. Mitch's moment of joy, quickly turned into a moment of panic. Our school has a very strict rule about calling or texting during school hours. I am very diligent to watch out for "texters", but obviously I am not diligent enough. I told Mitch's mom that I would be taking his phone away from him, but I would give it back to him at the end of the day since it was his first offense. She, the class, and I had a good laugh, but Mitch did not find the situation as humorous. It was one of those teaching moments that makes this job so much fun!

WHEN ARE YOU GOING TO TEACH THIS?

Stephanie is a young lady who is very bright. How do I know that? Because her mother told me so! I first had Stephanie in my SAT Prep class. She is very good on projects and she did well in class, but she was so surly and quiet that I never really saw any giftedness. She never smiled, and I was not sure if she was perpetually mad at me or just unhappy. We never bonded. Last year she was in my Honors Advanced Math class, and I still have not seen that "giftedness" that her Mom was talking about. I do think that she has a very good recall memory that may be bordering on "photographic". She is able to memorize lots of information. She, however does not seem to be a higher level thinker. She was not much of a problem solver. Her grades were good but I suspect that she had never been required to do a lot of thinking. She works hard, but she also has an attendance problem. She is sick quite a bit and she is a cheerleader so she misses some classes for extra-curricular activities. I have tried to be extra kind to her but she still never smiles.

This year I have her in my College Algebra class and nothing has changed. After three years, she has not warmed up to me so we just co-exist. She is such a benign student that I would never have thought that she could "get my goat", but she did. We were reviewing for a test. I had assigned a magnet problem that required them to use what they had learned. The issue arose because the problem that I assigned was not just like the ones we had done in class and it required the students to think instead of just spouting back information. When time was called, I called out the answer and asked if there were any questions. Stephanie raised her hand and asked me: "when was I going to teach this. " If I had been a cartoon character, you would have seen smoke coming out of my ears and my face turning crimson red. Please try to understand the power of a student who has never volunteered two words in class for three years, coming out with a statement like that! I pride myself in my ability to instruct and my ego and pride were being crushed by a female teenager with a chip on her shoulder. I am sure that I hesitated too long before I answered her because I was trying to make sure that I thought my reply through very carefully. The room had grown very quiet and the tension was palpable.

I did not dare say what I was thinking so I was trying to get my brain readjusted. What I ended up saying was; "Stephanie, I have already taught the concept and I expect you to be able to apply it. " There is so much more that I would have liked to have said. I wanted to lecture her on how it was going to be when she got to college. I wanted to expound the necessity of not only acquiring knowledge but being able to transfer it. Nevertheless, I knew it would do no good, so with that one comment we moved on. I might add that when I got home, my cat heard everything that I had wanted to say, just to make me feel better.

THAT'S RIDICULOUS

I never question whether God is out of the business of miracles when I deal with students. Taylor is a tow-headed blond with a likeable personality and just enough mischief to drive a teacher crazy, but he rarely cross the line. He has the kind of classroom behavior that is hard to describe to a parent. I had a conference with Taylor's mom and tried to let her know how he disrupts the class, but when I hear myself describe his behavior it even sounds "benign" to me. I tried to describe it as middle school behavior, but then I couldn't really define that outside of the usual comments, laughter, and not keeping your hands to yourself. All I know is that when he is not in class there is a remarkable difference in what I get accomplished and how little "managing" I have to do. The teacher next door came up with a great word for this. Taylor is a catalyst. He is not really at the class clown level, but he keeps the kids around him "churned up", and the class is a little more lively than I like. Taylor has a diagnosis of ADHD and he is on medication. Every time he has a bad day he tells me that he is working with the doctor to get his medication adjusted. He has a great deal of trouble focusing in class and he whines a lot. When he cannot answer a question he compensates by saying something clever. When he does not understand a concept that is being taught, he makes a public announcement as to the difficulty of the material. When I try to get him to come before or after school for help, he lets me know that he is getting "tutoring" elsewhere and will not be needing my services, or he is just too busy. That "tutoring" usually just means doing his homework with a friend. He is mostly talk and very little action when it comes to preparing for a test. He is not serious about his school work and his grades reflect it.

I have used minor disciplinary measures on Taylor because he never does anything really bad. Taylor, however, crossed the line from mischief to challenging my authority and made me angrier than I like to be. I had given a test in two parts. The take home part counted 50% and the in class part counted 50%. I had the in class part graded, but the take home part was very time extensive in grading and I decided to let the kids grade their own papers in class. I rarely do this because I know it has many pitfalls, but I wanted to get the tests back to the students and I was in one of those weeks where there were not enough hours to accomplish everything that I needed to do. Therefore, I had everyone clear off their desks of everything, passed out the papers, and distributed colored markers. I went over every problem as we went through the test and explained to the students how to score their papers. All was going much better than I expected through the first eight problems. We then got to a section where seven of the problems all depended on plugging a different constant into a trigonometric equation. The answer then included a unit of measure requiring the students to put dollars and millions. As we graded the first one, I told them that they got four points for the correct answer if it included the dollar and the million. If they forgot the unit designations they would lose two of their four points. Taylor knew that there were six more problems like this and he had left the units off all of them so he thought that he was going to lose two points on each one. His immediate response was "that's ridiculous" in a very loud voice. I could not believe that he had said it and the minute it was out of his mouth, he knew that he had made a serious mistake. There was absolute silence in the room for at least 20 seconds while the students waited to see what I would do and

I counted to ten so I would not do what I wanted to do, which was illegal in all 50 states. In a very firm and no nonsense voice, I told every student to fold their paper like a hot dog and pass it to the front of the room. I took up the papers and then had them put up their colored markers and get out their notes. No one argued, because the tension in the room was so strong it could be cut by a knife. I never addressed Taylor, and I never addressed the fact that I would be grading the tests. I never addressed the fact that I was only taking off 2 points for not having the unit of measure on the first problem and not all seven. I just continued to teach. In about five minutes I had my good mood back and the lesson went well for the rest of the period. Taylor did not make a squeak and everyone was on their best behavior. I think that this was the first time all year that I had shown any anger and how I handled it was important. I did not yell, I did not lecture, I did not immediately deal with Taylor, I just took about five minutes to calm down and moved onward. I think this is a priceless lesson in anger management for the students. I am sure that the students were upset that we did not get to finish grading their papers, so I am sure Taylor had to suffer a little grief from the others in the class. I however was preparing my "grief" for him.

I was definitely not through with Taylor. I planned to speak to him privately and let him know that his behavior was unacceptable. I was going to put him in his place and let him know that if he was ever disrespectful to me again that there would be serious consequences. The problem was that Taylor did not come to class for the next two days. We are on modified block so his class does not meet with me on Thursdays. On Friday he was out for a one act play competition. On Monday he was back and very subdued. I know that he was waiting for the other foot to drop, but he was so well behaved and attentive that I did not want to break the spell by having a negative discussion with him. Maybe it was good to keep him in this state of fearful anticipation of consequences. Or maybe he just thought that I was senile and forgot and didn't want to do anything to remind me. On Tuesday he was out again and on Wednesday he was so good and attentive that again I did not want to break the spell. I did take him out in the hall once during the period and compliment him on his improved behavior never mentioning the "ridiculous incident". Friday he was perfect again, and I decided that I was going to back off any repercussions because I liked the new Taylor and I wanted him to remain that way. I also decided to call Taylor's mom and let her know what a changed student he was, just to help reinforce his good behavior.

Friday night I attended the school production of Man of La Mancha. Taylor was running the sound board for the play and I talked to him for a minute before it began. Once again I congratulated him on his improved behavior and told him that I had decided not to deal with his "that's ridiculous" statement because I was so proud of his classroom behavior and attentiveness in the last two classes. I also told him that I was going to call his mom this weekend and let her know about the "new Taylor. " He was beaming and told me that after the "incident" he had gone to the guidance counselor to get out of my class for the next semester. He knew that I was not happy with him and he didn't have a grasp on the concepts and was fearful as to what the second semester would bring. He also told me that he was so good for the two days because he knew that I was mad at him and he was scared not to be good. He also found out in those two days that when he behaved and paid attention, he could understand the material. He stated that he knew he could do the material and he wanted to stay in my class and meet the challenge. Talk about a miracle! We hugged and there was a joy in my heart that winning the lottery cannot compare to. I wonder how it could have turned out differently if Taylor had come to school the next day and I had taken him out in the hall and given him a lecture on "that's ridiculous"...

EDUCATIONAL TERRORIST

Over the last few years, I have watched Justin come up through the grades. He is what I refer to as an "educational terrorist". An educational terrorist is the kind of student that disrupts the class at regular intervals and is a constant challenge to the teacher. His behavior will not change, it can only be managed. He uses up a lot of teacher energy. I use the male gender here because in my experience most of my little "terrorists" have been male, but I have had a few ladies to fit the category!) I have heard the other teachers talk about his behavior and I have seen his behavior in the hall. I have dealt with him in the past concerning dress code and various forms of horse-play when I was on some kind of supervisory duty. He is not a bad young man. When corrected, he respectfully complies and then when out of sight, continues to misbehave. He is characteristically un-organized, rarely has his materials, and cannot concentrate to study without one-on-one attention. He is always talking out in class and rarely on task. I believe that part of his problem is the fact that his mother is always "rescuing" him and he rarely has to face any consequences for his behavior and choices. In my personal opinion, he has gotten away with too much in the past. He is too much of a disruption to the other students, and he needs to be given a very short rein.

Every school has a few "educational terrorists". They disrupt almost every classroom and every program. They are irritating distractions in classrooms where the teachers have control and they are totally disruptive to the learning situation in classrooms where the teacher's are not in control. Everyone knows who they are. They stay in and out of trouble. I believe that students that fall into this category must be managed with a team effort, almost like an intervention. If you have one of these young people in your class, you need to talk to the administration about arranging a conference with all of the student's teachers. Options should be discussed and a plan or contract should be developed. The plan should then be introduced to the student and parents in a conference that includes the administration and all of the teachers. This may not be easy if the parents are in denial. It may be necessary to document behavior to give the parents an idea of what is going on at school. These students should not be allowed to "bully" the adults and other students. It will take a team effort based on consistency and determination to see improvement in behavior but it will be worth it to everyone.

BITS OF GLASS
It's All About Discipline

***Meglamania: A mental disorder characterized by delusions of power.

***What to ask if a kid gets in trouble: 1) What do you want? 2) Is what you are doing getting you what you want? 3) What can you do to get you what you want?

***Nothing will work until you get control. Train them well.

***I took a first responder class one summer where we were instructed to check the air way and breathing before we did anything else. One of the students asked if that might not make a neck injury worse and the instructor made the comment: "If they ain't breathing, what else matters? " Teaching is a little like that, if they ain't paying attention what else matters?

***Do not beg for their attention, demand it.

***Kids need boundaries. Start early and be consistent.

***You must always be aware of what is going on in your room.

***A gifted teacher can control behavior and not miss a beat in the teaching.

***Criticize the behavior, not the student.

***You probably lost control gradually. It will come back gradually with consistency.

***Use your voice to control. You need lots of inflection. Practice at home on the dog.

***Don't rush into a difficult decision unless absolutely necessary.

Chapter Six

IT'S ALL ABOUT INSTRUCTION

Dedication

This section of my book is dedicated to Leroy Jethro Gibbs, Senior Special Agent, NCIS. Gibbs instructs by setting a good example. His words are few, but his expectations are high. He believes in his people and they deliver.

INSTRUCTION - THE HEART OF TEACHING: IS YOUR CLASSROOM BUZZING OR BORING?

GOOD INSTRUCTION DRIVES LEARNING. It is that simple. So what is good instruction? Good instruction is a set of delivery methods designed to create a classroom atmosphere that engages all of the students and promotes thinking and the acquisition of knowledge. Instruction is not what you teach; it is how you teach it. If I give you a topic, for instance World War II, with a little preparation, anyone on the planet can deliver the information. How much learning actually takes place depends on several factors, some of which are inherent in the presenter, some in the actual delivery method, and some in the learner. There are a few students that will learn the material no matter how bad or boring our delivery. They don't really need us, the law just requires that they have us. The majority of students, however, need to be "instructed" in a way that will increase the probability that they will be able to actually internalize the information.

Now I am sure that if I had looked up "instruction" in Webster's Dictionary, I would have come up with a more concise definition, but I wanted one that came from my heart. I want us to look at instruction as how we present the material and how important our delivery is. Many teachers do a good job covering the material, but they are so un-imaginative and predictable that the students lose interest. In today's world of instant everything, students need lots of interaction and stimulation. With the ever changing challenge of keeping the students engaged, we have been given many technological tools and options for delivery, but what I am talking about is much larger than the new advances we have available today.

What makes our instruction good is the passion we put into it. It is our desire for the students to really see the forest for the trees. It is our willingness to appear a little foolish at times as we dress in costumes, break out in song, and do something totally unpredictable. Good instruction is being able to make smooth transitions, knowing when to be serious and when to be silly, and having the good sense to know when it is time to punt and start over. It is about the teacher being animated and interested. It is also about the teacher's ability to break the material into "digestible" chunks and to tie this material together into a big picture. It is about making the material real for the students, and helping them claim it as important for themselves.

You know good instruction when you see it because the classroom is buzzing, not boring. As you read through this section, I hope you will find some new ideas and strategies that will help your classroom "buzz" a little more. The real trick to good instruction, however, is to make sure that the activities and interaction are present, but do not become the focus. Good instructional practices are the "means to an end", which is always acquisition of knowledge and critical thinking skills.

PEANUT BUTTER AND JELLY

Throughout this chapter, as I try to write down all of the procedures that I use in the classroom, I find that what seems so easy and natural for me gets a little complicated when I try to explain it to other people. It is so much easier to demonstrate, than to give step by step written directions. When you read thru the detailed lists that I have had to use in this book to get my point across, I am sure that you are going to think that the procedure I am talking about is more trouble than it is worth! Let me assure you that it is not. With a little practice, these procedures will become second nature to you and the students. They will become great organizational tools and time savers once they are working properly. It is worth the patience and time investment it takes to train yourself and the students. Please remember not to try to do too much at once. Get one "system" running smoothly before you try another.

Let me give you an example of what I am talking about. If you had no idea what a peanut butter and jelly sandwich was and I asked you to make one, it would seem like a very complicated task. When I analyzed the process I came up with 17 distinct steps from the beginning to the end. I am sure that had I given it a great deal of thought; I could have come up with more. Think of all the variations! Maybe you put the jelly on the bread before the peanut butter. Maybe you, like most husbands, forget to close the bread or leave the peanut butter on the knife before you put it in the jelly. Maybe you like more jelly and less peanut butter. The point is that there are an almost infinite number of approaches to making a peanut butter and sandwich and they all have the same end result. Some are more efficient than others, and some are neater, but they all have the same end result.

Therefore, do not be discouraged by the lengthy descriptions of some of the procedures. Once you go through any given instructional process, I think you will find that it is not as complicated as it looks on paper. You will also want to modify many of them and use your own personal touches.

PLANNING TIME WELL SPENT

"Be prepared" is not only a great Boy Scout motto, it is crucial for the survival of a classroom teacher. An un-prepared teacher is easier to spot than a black cat in a marshmallow factory, and just as out-of-place. The students pick up very quickly, that you are a teacher without a plan, and they jump on you like sharks on a wounded manatee. So much for the metaphors and the similes, the point here is that preparation will solve a lot of problems and make your life easier. We are going to address three planning issues in this section. First we will look at what good lessons should include, then we will look at picking what to plan for, and finally we will look at some efficient ways to plan lessons.

A GOOD LESSON PLAN:

It does not matter what level or subject you teach, each lesson plan should contain a few basic ingredients that will help make it more successful. Depending on the length of a unit, every plan should contain all of these. Like a child that you would like to see eating their vegetables at every meal, it is not always possible to get them to do that, so you go for an overall balance in their eating habits. So it is with lesson plans. If you can not squeeze all of the essentials in every unit, aim for including everything over a period of time. Or, as in the case of eating your vegetables, shorter plans may not contain all of these elements, but over time, they should all be evident.

At this point I should remind you that I am not the definitive expert on lesson planning. There are a multitude of college texts and other resources that will give you excellent advice and all sorts of forms and structures. In some of these books, the effort required to put together one of their lesson plans is gargantuan, leaving very little time for actual teaching. I am convinced that building a structure that is practical and perpetually useful to you as a teacher is much more important that dotting every "I" and crossing every "T" in a lesson plan form. You must also conform to what is required of you in your school. I also urge you, before you even begin to plan the actual lesson, to use the backwards design model and create your summative assessment, so as you choose your activities and instructional strategies they are always geared to what you want the students to know. With that said, below are my essential elements to a good lesson plan.

1   Start each unit with a creative beginning. This should be an attention grabber. In mathematics it might be a moment of "math magic' that fits with the lesson. In history it might be a

fact in history that is so outrageous it is hardly believable. In science it might be a "neat" experiment that holds everyone's attention. In language arts, it might be a writing topic that is downright "shocking". Whatever it is, it should have the students wanting more. For some students "wanting" more may be pushing it, but at least they aren't dreading more! If it is a long unit, you may not only want to have a creative beginning, but a creative middle and end. Students need to feel some excitement in what they are learning!

2   Tie your beginning into a lesson that is well thought out and very sequential. Build on skills or knowledge that they already know and use as much review of what was important or pertinent in the old as is possible in the new. Make sure that your instruction is clear and that the body of your unit is not too complex. Break the complex down for the students into manageable learning "bites". Present with a clear voice and an obvious knowledge of the material.

3   Be sure that your instruction incorporates the three learning modalities, visual, auditory, and kinesthetic.

4   Fill your instruction with smooth transitions from teacher "centered" instruction to student "centered" instruction.

5   Provide real life applications whenever possible.

6   Provide purposeful seatwork to practice new skills, incorporating as much peer instruction and interaction as is appropriate for that unit.

7   Plan too much!

8   Include intermittent evaluations so both you and the student will know if they are making progress.

9   Summarize the key points and make sure the students know what is most important for them to remember.

PACING AND TIMING:

Knowing how to pace your instruction and how much time it will take on each lesson, is a skill that comes with practice. Most textbooks come with some type of suggested pacing guide, but the writers of the textbooks are not aware of your situation. New teachers should always seek the advice of seasoned teachers in timing their lessons. No matter how long you have been teaching, if you are required to stay at the same pace as the other teachers who teach your subject, you will not have a lot of choice in your pacing, and there should be a lot of collaborative planning. You will plan one way for block scheduling and another for traditional. Even if you do not have the pace determined for you, you must always be sure to cover enough material in your area to insure the success of the students in the future.

No matter what your situation, the key words here are preparation and flexibility. You should have enough material in each lesson to thoroughly cover the topic and reinforce the concepts. You should also have pertinent enrichment material waiting in the wings. If you run out of time and are not able to present everything that you had planned, be sure that you presented enough to ensure student success. My own philosophy on this is to teach the skills rather swiftly at the beginning of my time frame and then review, mix them up, and summarize them often in the remaining time. This way if I run out of time, I did not miss the proper instruction on any item that will be included on the test. If I get everything done and have time left, I pull out my enrichment activities.

The first year you teach any subject will be a learning year. Keep notes in your plan book to help you improve instruction in the future. Learn from your own mistakes. If you spent too much time on one topic and neglected another, just don't repeat the mistake the next time you teach it. The first year I taught Calculus, I spent 90% of my teaching time on the mechanics, and 10% on the concepts. I did not realize what a big mistake that was until I got the results back from my AP Exam scores. The AP Calculus exam was much more into concepts than mechanics. I adjusted my curriculum greatly during the next school year and I continue to adjust it.

Only experience allows you to accurately judge how long it will take to teach something. But don't get too comfortable with your experience, because as soon as you do, the fire drill alarm will go off. If it is not the fire drill, it will be a pep rally, a snow day, or an electrical power outage! Recently I had a very important Advanced Placement Calculus Test scheduled for a Friday afternoon. About an hour before the scheduled exam, the power in the entire school went off. It was literally 103 degrees outside and the room became increasingly warmer. When the calculus kids came in, the electricity had not come back on and the thermostat was up to 86. I could have given the test because there was enough light in the room, but I was more interested in the students doing their best, than staying on schedule. I was, however, not willing to get off my time schedule which is very tight in an honor's level class. The kids were elated when they came in and I announced that the test would be postponed until Monday. They were not at all surprised, however, when I told them that we would be doing Monday's work on Friday. I had planned an exploratory lab to introduce the next chapter. It was a paper and pencil lab and was very low stress and could be done in less-than-perfect circumstances. My kids know that there is no such thing as a free period.

As structured as I am, I do not pass up a teachable moment! Imagine a surprise snowstorm in late October in Georgia. Oh the possibilities! ! ! If I were an English teacher, we would throw out the plan for the day and after romping outside in the snow for a while we would discuss simile and metaphor, and how the snow on our faces was like..... . If I were a social studies teacher, after romping outside in the snow for a while, we would discuss how the first settlers to America must have really suffered in the winter and what really happened to the settlers at Roanoke. Was it the Indians or the weather? If I were a science teacher, after romping outside in the snow for a while, we would discuss why it was snowing in October and what kind of weather conditions create snow. As a math teacher, after romping in the snow for a while, we would discuss how no two snowflakes are alike and discuss pentagons, hexagons, and other regular polygons. I could go on, but you know more about your subject than I do. I do not care what age level you teach, go play in the snow for a few minutes and turn it into a lesson. You can get back on track the next day. Don't lose a situation that will make learning more fun and bring the joy and wonder back because it might mess up your lesson plan.

CHOOSING WHAT YOU TEACH

At first this section may seem useless to those of you who have a very structured curriculum handed to you, but it has been my experience that no matter how "tight' your curriculum, there are always choices to make. At some schools, I have been just one of many teachers who taught my subject and my choices were few. At another school, I was the only math teacher and I had more flexibility in selecting my topics within reason. Most of the time, I have been in the middle of those extremes. I have also found that in most situations the textbook is the curriculum. The objectives are retyped in a notebook to look official, but they pretty much follow the table of contents in the book. In all of my years of teaching I have never finished all of the objectives in the textbook, therefore at some point I had to pick and choose what was most important. I have always felt that there was too much material and too little time.

Sticking with my belief that we all have choices to make about what topics within the curriculum we should teach, whether we have a lot of freedom or a little, I have developed some guidelines that I use.

1   You need to do some research and get a feel for what will be most important to the students in the future. This is no simple task. No matter what subject you teach or at what grade level, your teaching should be geared to what will serve the student best. If you are teaching elementary school you should be talking to the teachers in the next grade. If you are teaching middle or high school you should be looking at the skills on standardized tests and what the curriculum in the future demands. (this requires a little crystal ball reading on your part)It you are teaching high school you should be looking at the SAT, and the ACT and talking to the teachers that will be teaching them in the next two grades. I also listen to what corporate America says they want in their future employees.

2   Be sure that you are careful about not letting your own preferences dictate what you teach. For instance, I did not like Physics in college. I think it might have had something to do with the fact that I fell in love at that point in my college career and my motivation for education went down the tube. Because I was distracted, I did not learn it well and when I get to a chapter on vectors, I would prefer to skip it. Vectors aren't hard, I am just not comfortable with them and they bring up bad memories for me. I could do without them. I am also not fond of matrices, but alas, they are in the curriculum and should be taught. Therefore I must overcome my personal biases and teach what is most important for my students.

3   Another area that we must be careful of when planning, is not to skip the higher level thinking skills because they take too much time. As a math teacher I have been very guilty of this in the past. It is very easy to teach the skills and not always as easy to teach the concepts. Concepts take more time and effort on the part of the teacher and the students. The one thing that is requested over and over by the employers of the future is that students be able to problem solve and think critically. The time spent on developing these skills is more than worth it.

PLANNING WITHOUT RE-INVENTING THE WHEEL

Over my teaching career, I have had to plan in so many ways that I cannot even begin to remember them all. Sometimes I have had to write formal educational objectives and sometimes none at all. Sometimes I had to match objectives with state standards and list SAT skills and ITBS skills and anything else that would validate the existence of the objectives. Some principals required a certain form or a certain plan book. I also found that as soon as I got organized with one way of doing lesson plans, it would change and I had to start from scratch again. If I put together all of the time I spent planning lessons to meet administrative expectations that did not help my classroom instruction, I could have probably have gotten another degree! One principal was into color coding and another insisted that they be updated daily so that when he walked in the door, we were teaching exactly what our lesson plan said. I have also had principals that never checked them and couldn't care less as long as we were effective in the classroom.

STEP ONE UNIT NOTEBOOKS

After all those years of every kind of lesson plan imaginable here is what I learned. No matter what you are teaching, start a loose leaf binder for every unit that you teach. How you organize the binder depends on what you teach. You can organize them by chapters, by topics, by units, etc... Include notes, work sheets, activities, and assessments. You can keep adding and subtracting from these notebooks over the years. You should make sticky notes to yourself to improve for the next year. I put page protectors on my notes and use them over and over with my modifications. If I create a Powerpoint or a flipchart, I print it out and include it in my notes, so I do not forget that I have it. If I find a joke that fits, I cut it out and tape it to my notes. Anything that is helpful to this lesson is included in my notes. If I get too much stuff and only use part of it, I create a folder for the extra stuff and put it in a file cabinet where I can find it if I need it, but it does not clutter my notebook. I clean out my notebooks every year as I teach the unit and put what is not necessary for that year in the folder, but I do not throw it away, because it may be necessary again. I try not to record textbook pages in my notes, since those will change, but I do put little sticky notes with references to pages in the book that can be easily replaced when new books are ordered. The idea here is that you are building a great unit that will last for years. If you are required to use SAT, ITBS objectives or state standards, write them on sticky notes and place behind the page protectors, but do not write them on the unit; they will change. I also list technology that I want to use so I can remember websites.

I am constantly upgrading my notebooks as I learn new ideas and new stuff. If I have a principal or a system that mandates a certain form for lesson plans, I create it and put it in the notebook and then just Xerox it every year and turn it in. If I have to post my lesson plans on the computer, I save those pages and put them in the notebooks. It helps me see how the time frame was in the past and I can easily type them back in for the future. I teach out of those notebooks and they are living breathing things. I do what I have to do to make my paper work fit the requirements of the powers that be, but my true planning is what is in those notebooks. At the beginning of the year, I explain to my parents that my plans may look a little puny on the computer screen, but I invite them to come into my classroom and view my real "planning books. "

When I am starting a new unit, I always read through the textbook and get my basics down on paper and in order. Next, I create my summative assessment to insure that what I am going to teach matches what I expect the students to learn. I then Google the topic and see what the internet has to offer and print out what is helpful. I investigate supplementary materials and am especially diligent in looking for life applications. In a subject like mathematics, I am always looking for some math history to make it more interesting. I find worksheets and adapt them to what I am trying to do and I create my formative assessments. This whole time, I am planning for classroom instruction without the burden of special requirements. This part is a joy and should be the major emphasis. When I find new, "neat", things about the topic, it is like finding a hidden treasure and I quickly add it to my treasure chest (unit notebook).

GOOGLE

Speaking of finding special treasure, I need to confess my tardiness at one of the most valuable places to dig. It never ceases to amaze me how I resist technology and then when I cave in, I can't believe that I waited so long! I am usually the last one to do anything concerning computers and electronics in general. I held out on the internet, caller I. D. , texting, and come to think of it, the microwave. I just never learn, because all of the above have made my life a lot easier. I do not understand why I am so resistant, since I was the first one to jump on the pantyhose, sticky note bandwagon. It may have something to do with all of that power, battery and electrical, and the fact that as soon as you learn it, it changes. Once you learn how to operate pantyhose and sticky notes, your training lasts forever.

Teaching today without technology is a little like a surgeon using leeches to heal a patient. It might work sometimes, but there sure are better ways. I could go on forever about how every time I get something figured out, "they" update it and I have to back up twenty steps, but this "ramble" is about Google so I better stick to the topic and stop whining.

Every teacher spends endless hours preparing lessons, searching for background material and creating demonstration tools like Power Point. We read "teacher" books and watch around us for anything that will make our instruction more relevant. As recently as two years ago this "old foggie" was still doing it the hard way because she was so late in discovering the power of Google. Whether you Google or Bing, don't miss out on the possibilities there are for saving you time and improving your instruction. I would also like to add that I have shared my Power Point search strategies with several of my younger co-workers and they were not using Google to their advantage either.

I am not going into all of the possibilities of the search engines here because there are too many of them and you probably know more about them than I. What I want to accomplish here is to be sure that you know how many "ready made" lesson plans and Power Points there are on the internet. Many of them are for sale and many of them are free. When I start planning a lesson, I simply go to Google and type in the topic such as "quadratic formula Power Point. I will be presented with several possibilities and all I have to do is pick and choose. There is no reason to re-invent the wheel and the folks who are sharing their Power Points are usually more talented at creating them than I am. I can also type in a topic like "quadratic formula lessons plans" and find more lesson plans than I can possibly use. I read through several and get some wonderful ideas, especially if I am looking for things like essential questions and big ideas.

I also encourage you to just browse the internet for good teaching strategies. You will find a lot more than can be put in any book. Having trouble with a kid who thinks he is "class clown". Google "teaching strategies to handle the class clown" and see what you get. Need help handling a difficult parent conference? Google: "difficult parent conference". Want to see how other teachers handle discipline issues? Google "discipline scenarios". The possibilities are endless.

STEP TWO CHECK OFF SHEETS

When I have my unit notebook like I want it, I go back and create a check list. This is just for me. I started doing these about three years ago to save my sanity and I wish that I had been doing them my whole teaching career. I started making out check off sheets because, teaching five different classes a day, I was losing too many brain cells to keep up with what I was doing when in each class. The best way to explain a check off sheet is to show you one:

TRIANGULAR AND CIRCULAR TRIG RADIANS CHECKOFF SHEET

_____Degrees, Minutes, Seconds/ Decimal Conversion

_____PAGE 238: 1-9

_____Celsius Kid Scan

_____Radian investigation and definition notes

_____unit circle scan z drive scan folder

_____blank unit circle scan z drive scan *folder worksheet 1*

_____*rotation cards*

_____PAGE 238: 10-17

_____WORKSHEET 2

_____Arclength notes

_____PAGE 238: 27-33 PAGE 239: 58-62

_____Area of a Sector notes

_____PAGE 238: 43-54

_____worksheet 3

_____Linear and Angular Speed notes

_____PAGE 238: 34-42

_____PAGE 251: 9-32, 43-58 radians

_____QUIZ

_____sine and cosine function graphs notes flipchart graphing template for sine and cosine on z drive

_____Basic trig graphs (favorites) www.purplemath. com/modules/triggrph.htm

_____Prepared hand out on trig function graphs
_____Basic trig graphs transformation flipchart z drive
_____transformation notes
_____PAGE 264: 1-22
_____Worksheet 4
_____Worksheet 6 accel. Only writing trig equations
_____inverse trig functions revisited, principal values
_____PAGE 288: 1-16, 29-40
_____Worksheet 5
_____*Quiz*
_____Test Review
_____*Test*

I know that all of this makes no sense to anybody but me, but remember this is for me and nobody else sees it. Since they are saved on my computer, I can easily modify them as my unit notebook changes. As I go through the lessons, I make notes on this sheet and check off what we have accomplished. It is a life saver for me. It helps me to remember when I have a good flipchart, a good website, or a good activity. It is ok to list book numbers here because they are easy to change if the books change.

STEP THREE WEEKLY TIME PLAN

Once the unit notebook and check off sheet are complete, I start thinking about my time line. I plan specific time strategies one week at a time. To plan farther out than that never works for me because I either move faster or slower than I had predicted. Remember, I have the whole unit planned already so if I move faster in a week than I predicted, I have plenty of material prepared for the students. Once again this framework is for me and helps me set up what I enter into the computer that is seen by the students, parents, and administrators. I start on this every Thursday, and have it in the computer before I leave on Friday. Like the check off sheets, it keeps me on track and lays out the week for me in a glance. Here is the template that I use:

	College Algebra and Statistics	Regular Calculus	AP Calculus	Accelerated Pre-Calculus	Honors Pre-Calculus
Monday					
Tuesday					
Wednesday					
Thursday					
Friday					

The blocks are bigger and it fills up a whole page so that I have about a square inch in each block to fill in a brief statement about what we will be doing each day in that class. Armed with my notebook, my check off sheets, and my calendar template, I have done everything I need to do to be prepared to teach. Now it is time to look at what my administration needs.

STEP FOUR FORMAL LESSON PLANS

The administration never sees my unit notebooks, check off sheets or calendar, unless they ask of course. They only see what I put on the computer and my formal lesson plans. Our school uses RenWeb for our management software and it is very easy to take out my weekly time calendar and put my basics on the computer. We are not required to put in formal objectives or correlations, just enough information to let everyone know what is being taught in the classroom on a daily basis. I have taught at many schools where we had to correlate to the SAT, ITBS, and state standards and I always thought this a colossal waste of time but you have to do what your administrators require. In the olden days when we had paper plan books that had to be turned in, the textbooks did not already have everything correlated for you and it was really a time consuming task.

All of this having been said, one more element is required, and that is a formal lesson plan for each unit. Each school system has different requirements for this. When I arrived at my present school these formal lesson plans were put in a big notebook and collected dust from neglect.

They were called "the curriculum" and all they really consisted of was a list of the table of contents of the textbook. About three years later we moved to unit plans, which were much better than a list from the book, but they lacked "energy" and were still more paper work and once again collected dust. In the past two years, based on the work of Grant Wiggins and backward design we have moved to what we call PLE's (Planned Learning Experiences). They are well thought out lesson plans that basically include big ideas, essential questions, objectives, formative assessments, summative assessments, student activities, and modifications. Each department was given the freedom to develop their own template for these and we have a goal of completion for the entire school by the end of the next school year. PLE's take time and thought but if well executed they will be a valuable source for all of the teachers at the school, especially to the new teachers joining the staff. They are living lesson plans that should be added to each year as teachers discover new activities to add to the lesson. Hopefully they will not collect dust. Here is an example:

PLE Math Department Template:

CLASS: Pre-Calculus **UNIT:** Triangular and Circular Trigonometry in Radians

STAGE ONE: DESIRED RESULTS
BIG IDEAS:

Degrees and Radians are both units of measure for angles.

Radians allow us to convert degrees into more "usable" numbers.

Radians allow us to measure arcs in linear terms.

The trigonometric basics stay the same whether you are working in radians or degrees.

Some trigonometric formulas only work when the angles are expressed in radians.

Trigonometric functions are periodic and can be represented graphically.

The basic transformations of any functions can be related to trigonometric functions.

Reading and graphing trigonometric functions by looking at their equations.

ESSENTIAL QUESTIONS:

Why are radians necessary and how are they expressed?

What is the relationship between a radian and a degree and why is it called a radian?

How is working in radians similar and not similar to working in degrees?

How do the transformations affect the trigonometric graphs?

STUDENTS WILL BE ABLE TO:

Convert from radians to degrees.

Find the value of trigonometric functions, given the angle in radians.

Find the area of a sector and the length of an arc using the radian formulas.

Find linear and angular speed.

Graph any of the three major trig functions without a calculator.

Write a trigonometric equation, given the transformation information.

CONTENT STANDARDS:

Meets all common core standards.

NCTM: 2,3,6,7,8,9,10

STAGE TWO: ASSESSMENT
FORMATIVE:

Quizzes

Quizlets

Magnet Problems

SUMMATIVE

Test

STAGE THREE: LEARNING PLAN
LEARNING ACTIVITIES:

We will begin with a brief discussion on units of measure and a little unit of measure of history. I will then show them the Celsius/Fahrenheit cartoon and we will discuss it.

I will introduce the radian concept with an activity where the students use different size circles to measure the arc when a radius is molded around the circle, thus the name radian. Each team will do their own investigation and report back to the class. If they have been accurate enough, the measures will be approximately the same. We will then use this activity to continue to explore the relationship between a degree and a radian.

We will then explore changing degrees to radians and vice versa with several practice opportunities including rotation cards.

I will then try to convince them that radians are important because you simply cannot go into a hardware store and ask for 42 degrees of fence for a part of a circular flower bed so you must have another unit that represents a linear amount. We will then dive into the arc length and area of a sector formulas and practice them.

We will then review everything we did in the previous unit, using radians and showing that it is just a different way of representing the same thing.

I will then introduce them to linear and angular speed as another application of radians. We will use practical applications to make it seem real. I will bring in a bicycle wheel and mark a spot on the tire and talk about the difference in angular and linear velocity.

They will take a quiz on everything they have learned about radians.

We will then explore trigonometric graphs by using the pre-set-up flip chart and graphing individual points. I will then give them a few minutes to explore the different trigonometric graphs on their calculators. We will sketch each one, emphasizing the proper scale in degrees and radians. Once we have established the basic parent functions, we will review algebraic transformations of the parabola and use the calculator to see if they still hold for the trigonometric functions. We will then pull it all together and summarize in their notes.

I will then pass out a worksheet that practices stating the transformations from looking at the equations, followed by a worksheet that gives the transformations and asks the students to write an equation.

We will then review all material and take a test.

MODIFICATIONS:

The Honor's class will skip linear and angular velocity as well as writing equations. More time will be devoted to the rest of the material.

BIG IDEAS AND ESSENTIAL QUESTIONS

When I began teaching math, I stuck to the book like glue. I dutifully taught starting at the beginning and taught until I ran out of time. I trusted the authors to deliver the material to me in the right order so I could deliver it to the students in just the right order. There were no "big ideas" or "essential questions" at that point; I just taught each section as the book introduced it. I did that for several years without giving a thought to tying it all together. I was teaching the "trees" with no thought to the "forest".

When I got my first exposure to big ideas and essential questions in a workshop, I experienced the usual over-zealous reaction and tried to come up with a different essential question for every day. I was driving myself crazy and the students could have cared less. Our principal at the time was big into essential questions, but she didn't even require a different one each day so I was torturing myself for no reason.

As I have attended more workshops and gone through more educational phases, a lot of new ideas have come and gone but the importance of these two concepts have never faded. Students need to know what the big idea is. It is possible to teach unit after unit on war after war without the kids being able to tell you why they are learning about so many wars. In math, we teach skill after skill with the students never seeing where we are going until we get there and then they often fail to make the connection. Big ideas help you plan your lessons and focus on what is fundamentally important. There is always too much to teach so pick "the big ideas" as your anchor points and try to sneak the other stuff around it. Give the students a framework with the big ideas in the center and help them organize all the other concepts around them.

Essential questions help the teacher get in their mind the usefulness of the material. They answer the "So what? " questions and allow the teacher to anticipate the "What is this stuff good for? " question. If teachers use essential questions as a guide, it helps to pick out the most important concepts in the unit and helps teachers keep their focus. The questions should be thought-provoking to the students. They are great to stimulate discussion, debate, dissent, and research. If you go to the internet and "Google" a topic you will find that most units already have a long list of essential questions. You do not have to reinvent the wheel.

Helping the students see the "forest for the trees" opens the door for higher level thinking skills, and helps encourage engaged learners.

PROBLEM SOLVING IN TRIGONOMETRY

This poem was written after a very frustrating day in which I had tried to problem solve with the students and all they wanted was for me to give them a rule and move on. Teaching kids to think is challenging. I shared this poem with the class on Wednesday and we had a good laugh.

I slammed the door and kicked the dog,
I yelled at the kid and fussed at the clog.
Why such a bad mood, on such a nice day?
My trig class wanted answers and my mind wanted to play!

Susy and Johnny and Festus are all real bright,
They memorize, study and do homework at night!
But what's gonna happen when it comes S. A. T. time,
And all they can do is mimic, memorize, and Mime?

They don't want to explore, it confuses their brain,
They don't want thinking problems, it sends them down the drain!
They want nice neat answers and all problems the same.
When their brains turn to mush, will I be to blame?

When I go thru the process of finding a clue,
They frown and complain that "I" don't know what to do!
When we try a certain way and hit a brick wall,
They give up and wonder if I have any brains at all.

Well, I'm gonna show them if it takes all year,
Problem solving is the answer, even if it's what they all fear!
So batten down the hatches and hold on to your G. P. A.
If you got lost on Tuesday, just wait until today!

WHERE DID ALL THAT MATH COME FROM? ? ?

It does not matter what subject you teach, you have to find ways to spice it up and make it come alive for the students. In social studies this is pretty easy because all you have to do is dig a little deeper and tell the kids what really happened. You won't find the good stuff in the history books. You have to make your revelations age appropriate, but there are all sorts of great books on blunders in history that can spice up a lesson. You can also have students write journals and letters, hold mock debates, answer "what if" questions, dress and perform as historical characters, and the list goes on forever. In science you get to do all of those neat experiments and blow things up! In languages you get to travel to other nations and explore other cultures. In physical education you get to play with balls, in art you get to play in the mud, and in music you get to play all of the time.

There are two subjects, however, that are rarely picked as the fun classes. It has always been amazing to me that "reading, writing, and arithmetic" are the core of education and yet the students see them as the most boring part of the day. I think that language arts teachers have done a better job of not putting the students to sleep than math teachers. There are all sorts of creative things to do with reading and writing. I am sure that grammar is just as dreaded as math, but at least that is only one-third of the curriculum!

So what is a math teacher to do? I think that most math teachers miss the boat by leaving out so much rich and wonderful math history. Sometimes it is very important to give the students the big picture in mathematics. What a majestic picture it is when you look at the history and development of mathematical symbols and systems.

If you study the history of mathematics you can help it come alive to the students with real people having real feuds and real mathematical breakthroughs. History humanizes math. Did you know that circle graphs were used extensively by Florence Nightingale? Thales was able to do the impossible and measure the height of the great pyramids using similar triangles. Improper fractions were once called vulgar fractions and that terminology survived into the 20th century. The history of Pi is fascinating! If you dig deep enough you will even find that Pythagoras was not the first to come up with the Pythagorean Theorem and the first female mathematician was tortured to death by being cut with oyster shells. No wonder guys are perceived as being better at math than girls.

The internet is rich with math history and I like it because I can just go straight to Google and type in "history of integers" and come up with what I need for what I am teaching. There are also a lot of great books that I use as resources. My three favorite are: *Mathematics Is God Silent?* , *The Math Book*, and *The Parrot's Theorem*. *The Parrot's Theorem* is written as a murder mystery and is a very easy read, weaving the history of mathematics into the story. There are a few words in there that I wish were not, but otherwise it is a marvelous little book and with parental permission, I like to share it with my gifted students who really seem interested in mathematics. *Mathematics Is God Silent?* is not always an easy read but it is a phenomenal source of information about the history of mathematics from a theological perspective. It is a great read for Christian school teachers. *The Math Book* is subtitled "From Pythagoras to the 57th Dimension, 250 Milestones in the History of Mathematics. " I like this book because it has a lot of great pictures and a lot of contemporary mathematics.

No matter what kind of teacher you are, your job is to breathe life into your curriculum in whatever is the best way to keep the students engaged. The bottom line is that no matter how well you "teach" the material, if the students are not involved and focused there will not be a lot of "learning" going on. If you are enthusiastic about what you teach, most of your students will be too!

DIFFERENTIATED INSTRUCTION
THE MYTHS

Differentiated Instruction is a combination of two scary words that cause a great deal of stress and eye rolling among most teachers. It is the kind of educational issue that we all know is good and necessary, but it is easier said than done. To begin with I will define differentiated instruction and then we will address some of the myths concerning differentiated instruction. I will be using the definition and myths presented in an article entitled Busting Myths about Differentiated instruction which appeared in the middle school edition of Principal Leadership, March 2005, pages 28-33, by Rick Wormeli.

I have seen a lot of definitions of differentiated instruction but I like this one best. Mr. Wormeli defines differentiated instruction as doing what is fair and developmentally appropriate for students. It's a collection of best practices strategically employed to maximize students' learning at every turn, including giving them the tools to handle anything that is undifferentiated. It requires us to do different things for different students some, or a lot, of the time. It's whatever works to advance the student. It's highly effective teaching. His bottom line is to teach in whatever way students best learn.

Now no reasonable teacher argues with the definition or the bottom line, but there is plenty of debate over the mechanics of delivering differentiated instruction. Wormeli presents these arguments in ten myths:

MYTH ONE: <u>Students will be unprepared for tests.</u> Some are concerned that differentiated instruction means differentiated assessment and that this will interfere with standardized test scores. Differentiated instruction does require differentiated assessment, but it does not necessitate throwing out standard testing practices either. It is good to vary assessments, but students must be taught to handle the format of standardized tests. There is room for both. The critical issue here is that students do well on standardized tests when they know the material well. When a teacher differentiates instruction, more students learn more and perform better.

MYTH TWO: <u>Differentiation equals individualization.</u> Individualized learning keeps students working in isolation. Differentiated learning moves students through whole class instruction, group work, and individualized work. With differentiated instruction teachers learn to find a balance, between the three categories of instruction, that makes the best fit for their students. There will be times for individualized instruction, but it is only a small percentage of the total instructional effort.

MYTH THREE: <u>Differentiation means unbalanced workloads.</u> Wormeli states that "what is fair is not always equal". If possible, the work load should be roughly the same for the students. Gifted students should not be given more work; they should be given a more rigorous quality of work. Struggling students may be given essential "subsets" of the work, since it will take them longer to complete the assignments. Once again balance is the key. There will be times when every student is expected to do the same thing. But there must also be times when students have options. I think the biggest problem here is creating the type of classroom community where the students are accepting of their differences and do not challenge the teacher when the assignments are not the same.

MYTH FOUR: <u>Lack of mastery at the same time as classmates means lack of credit.</u> Wormeli states that "it doesn't matter when students demonstrate mastery. If they give a sincere effort all along, let them retake tests and assignments for full credit when they are ready. " This is a very controversial issue and I have participated in my share of discussions on this at the lunch table. I admit to being rather hard-nosed on this issue. I am reminded however that most adults have more than one opportunity to take certification tests, driver license tests, etc. The key word for me here is "sincere effort all along. " I employ several adaptations at test taking time that I feel are adequate in most situations. I do this on an individual basis and it has worked well for me. I have been known to give re-takes if I felt like there were special circumstances. I also have given points back to students who come before or after school and work with me on what they missed on the test. I will not, however, allow every student who fails a test to retake it.

MYTH FIVE: <u>I taught it. It is up to students to learn it.</u> Our job as teachers is not just to tell the students the information. Accomplished teachers not only deliver the information but they do it in such a manner that students find meaningful. Wormeli encourages us not to concentrate on what we are teaching but on what the students are learning. Delivery is everything and must be differentiated not only for the sake of learning but also for the sake of staying awake. Using all modalities and shaking up instruction every fifteen minutes is very important.

MYTH SIX: <u>Lesson plans must be turned in.</u> What does a perfect planbook indicate? Could it possibly indicate a lack of differentiation? Sometimes differentiated instruction looks a little messy on paper. I could go on about this for hours without any help from Mr. Wormeli. Some of the worst teachers have the best planbooks and some of the best teachers have the worst planbooks. A lot of differentiated instruction can go on without a lot of extra notation in the planbook.

MYTH SEVEN: <u>Summative assessment leads to learning.</u> This myth really misses the mark. Research report after research report as well as good old fashioned experience has shown that formative assessments do more to enhance learning. Formative assessments are those numerous and varied checkpoints along the way that let the teacher and students know how they are doing before they get to the "big test. "

MYTH EIGHT: <u>Students won't be able to compete in the real world.</u> Differentiation is not about "dumbing down" instruction or providing crutches so that students cannot help themselves. Differentiation is giving students tools and choices so that they can learn in the way that is best for them. It is teaching them to adapt to the circumstances and to problem solve their way through situations. Differentiation maximizes instruction and allows the students to learn more. What better way to equip them for the real world?

MYTH NINE: <u>If we don't differentiate, students will toughen up.</u> I am sure that this is true in some cases but the general rule is that students who do not succeed at learning either barely survive or simply quit. Most adult jobs allow workers to seek help when they do not know how to do something by looking in a manual or asking a supervisor. The real world is differentiated, why should we insist on everyone learning exactly the same things in the same way?

MYTH TEN: <u>There is only one way to differentiate.</u> Whoever came up with that statement is about as flexible and compassionate as a Marine drill sergeant. There are as many creative ways to differentiate as there are teachers. Don't forget the definition. It is a collection of best practices strategically employed to maximize students' learning. It is like having a tool kit and knowing when to use the wrench and when to use the hammer. Most woodworkers I know have a lot of tools in their shop and know just which ones to pull out to do any given task. That is the way a good teacher is with differentiated instruction. In fact, I think almost all teachers use differentiated instruction they just don't all call it that! What they do is try to treat each student as a unique individual while instructing them as if they were identical! They believe in their students, even when the students don't believe in themselves.

DIFFERENTIATED INSTRUCTION
HOW HARD CAN IT BE?

In Differentiated Instruction, The Myths, we looked at a good definition of differentiated instruction and some myths concerning it. In How Hard Can It Be? , we are going to look at "student types" and what we are dealing with when we try to meet the individual needs of the students. As we all know, students come in every shape, color, intellect, disposition, and background. I think we will also agree that no matter how diversified they are, if we can keep them engaged we will stimulate learning. Keeping them engaged requires different tactics for different students. There have been literally tons of pages of educational research on learning styles, personalities and intelligence levels. Below I have listed a few that I found listed in *Differentiating Instruction with Style* by Gayle H. Gregory :

5 learning styles
7 common brain principals
2 brain hemispheres
3 basic learning styles
4 Gregorc learning styles
4 Kolbs experiential learning profiles
4 Lowry's color inventory
4 McCarthys 4MAT model
4 personality types learning style profiles
4 Silver and Hanson
12 Costa and Kallick intelligent behaviors
8 Gardners multiple intelligences

6 Blooms thinking levels

5 Krathwohl's levels of affective domain

8 Williams level of creative thinking process

Now if I have done the math correctly, that's 2,477,260,800 possibilities for differentiation, assuming the independence of the categories. That doesn't even count physical limitations, linguistic differences, or cultural differences. Talk about overwhelming! How in the world are we to teach to all of the possibilities when most of us could not list Krathwohl's levels of affective domain, much less spell the guy's name. Differentiating for the diversity of learning styles, intelligences, and thinking in your classroom does not mean that you have to know every detail of every theory and individualize for every student. Simply becoming conscious of the collective needs of students is a way to get to know them better and make the right choices for your classroom. Don't get overwhelmed with the literature and the vastness of the task.

I would like to suggest a neat tool to use with your students which is fun and not only helps you learn their styles, but helps them understand themselves and their differences a little better. It is also contained in *Differentiating Structure with Style*. Gregory takes several of the learning styles off of the list above and turns them into four categories, beach balls, clipboards, puppies, and microscopes. She then creates a matrix of learning styles and a synthesis of learning styles theories. She gives learning attributes matched up with learning activities. It is very user friendly for students of all ages and I have found this to be a wonderful tool to help me increase the selection of tools in my differentiation box.

Most important, remember not to get bogged down in too much research and expert advice. Get to know your kids and increase the size of your toolbox. Be flexible and keep them engaged as long as possible before you switch tools.

DIFFERENTIATED INSTRUCTION DISCIPLINE AND ASSESSMENT

Our next look at differentiation will be concerning discipline and assessment. Both of these topics will be discussed elsewhere in the book, but here they are discussed as tools to differentiate. We begin with discipline and a personal anecdote. I have four grandchildren between the ages of one and nine. If I wish to discipline the nine year old, I give the usual amount of warnings, but it usually leads to a pop on the back of the leg with a wooden spoon. She is very strong willed but responds well to pain. (We will not get into a discussion here on the advantages or disadvantages of corporal punishment. You do what is best for your grandkids!) The six year old is a very social creature and I find after a few warnings that a time-out is very effective. My eight year old grandson has a very tender heart, and I have to be careful that I do not even given him a stern look or he goes ballistic. I find that he responds well to a gentle request with no need for warnings. Now remember that all three of these "younguns" were "hatched" in the same nest, and yet their response to discipline is greatly varied.

How much more varied will be the responses of a classroom of 25 students? It is to your advantage as a teacher to get to know your students as soon as possible and figure out what motivates them in terms of discipline. Your bag of tricks for these issues should be just as varied as for instruction. You need to be totally unpredictable and yet totally safe. The students always need to worry a little about what you might do. You always need to switch around your techniques and apply the best discipline practice for the circumstances. Let the punishment fit the child as well as the crime. Do not over use any technique, and try to maintain a sense of humor. One of the quickest ways to lose the respect of your students is to discipline with too much severity. I like to think of myself as Attila the Hun with a sense of humor. When I say "out in the hall" they never know if they are going to get Mother Theresa or Simon Legree. Once again it all depends on what they did and what form they "need" to curb their negative behavior. I need to also emphatically state that I never lose my temper. No matter what they have done and how angry they make me, I never lose control. This is critical!

Differentiated assessment, like discipline, utilizes all sorts of evaluation tools. It helps the student retain the information better by purposely helping them "not to forget. " Using techniques that help the students tie the knowledge to what they already know, apply it to their own experiences, or just create mnemonics or other "hooks" will help them retain the material. Most critical, however is the fact that assessment is ongoing throughout the lesson and not something that pops up at the end. Often a pre-test lets the students know how much they already know about a topic and lets the teacher know where to start and how much time is needed. In my opinion, as important as a pretest is, giving students opportunities throughout the unit to show what they know without having to wait for the traditional "test" at the end is even more critical. These formative assessments allow the students to get a taste of whether or not they really understand the material. There are many techniques that can be used throughout the lesson to check on a student's progress that do not use up a lot of class time and are easy to implement. Small white boards and dry erase markers are a great tool to check student responses. Gestures as simple as thumbs-up, thumbs-down, and thumbs-sideways, tell a teacher a lot. Response cards are a wonderful tool and the book *Differentiated Assessment Strategies: One Tool Does Not Fit All* by Carolyn Chapman and Rita King (Corwin Press) gives several specific examples of how these can be used. There are several other ideas in this book. Better yet, come up with some of your own. Let the students help you come up with ideas. It gives them ownership!

Possible summative assessments (the big evaluation at the end of the unit) might include audio recordings, brief reports, speeches, debates, essays, interviews, posters, riddles, songs, poetry, commercials, outlines, demonstrations, graphic organizers, timelines, displays, brochures, cartoons, inventions, collections, journal entries, portfolios, literary circles, reenactments… The options and creativity are endless. Teachers should also provide opportunities for all students to use higher order thinking skills. Too often, those who excel are the only students given these alternate tasks. Those who have difficulty learning are too often given basic, rote assignments and assessments. All students benefit when they are challenged with essential skills, questions, processes, and ideas to learn within their personal levels of understanding. It is also well to remember that the real world rarely requires a written test. Some students who excel on standard written tests might develop a false sense of security and confidence, failing to realize that many careers require many abilities which are difficult to measure. Students need to be exposed to alternate assessments.

As we think about differentiated assessment we need to create a climate that does not separate the students into "smarties" and "dumdums". We need to build a classroom community of acceptance. Negative feelings create barriers to success. It is imperative for teachers to maintain a positive, comfortable, and inviting assessment environment. Teachers' voice tone, high expectations, energy, enthusiasm, and genuine interest are key elements in the classroom assessment atmosphere. We should make students feel good about guessing in class so that they will feel comfortable doing it on the test. We need to be sure to send the right messages. Wrong Message: We have to do this, we don't have a choice. I don't want to do this either. We can have fun as soon as we finish. Right Message: I can hardly wait for you to show me how much you have learned. I am anxious to see your answers. Show me your best work!

We also need to create a climate of "no assessment". This usually happens in one of two ways. Sometimes we teach a concept that is so embedded in other material that it is critical for understanding future concepts, but it is going to show up so much in the future that a summative assessment is not necessary. There will be future opportunities to check for mastery. Formative assessments are rarely optional, but summative ones are. Once in a while blow the class away with teaching a lesson and then letting them know that there will be no test. The second "no assessment" opportunity comes when we need to expose students to information that we do not need them to master. This occurs quite often and should be a time of learning and exploring with no pressure or stress about a test. This is the kind of experience that sets the students up to be life-long learners. There is not always a test.

Now we are to the most controversial part of differentiated assessment. Grading adaptations are a sensitive area and must be used in the most judicious manner possible. One of my favorite quotes that I try to keep in mind when I am grading is: "Ask yourself, is your assessment tool a physical exam or an autopsy." My apologies to the originator of that quote; I cannot credit them because I do not remember where I heard it, but it is too good not to use. If our purpose in assessment is to punish them for not doing well and prove to them that they did not master the material and it is too late to fix it, we have just performed an autopsy. If our purpose it to reward them for what they can do well and show them what they have not mastered, giving them another chance to "fix it", then we have performed a physical. I like that and I try to keep it in mind. As a high school teacher, it is necessary for me to walk a tightrope of grace and accountability. I am extremely aware of the rigors of some colleges and universities and that there will be no "molly-coddling" at most institutions of higher learning. Therefore, I must admit I go back and forth from "physical" to "autopsy" so that I am dealing out grace, while holding my students accountable to reality. I would think that the younger a student is the more grace should be ad-ministered. No matter where you stand on this issue, I am sure that at one time or another you have exhibited grace and therefore you have already used grading adaptations. Here are a few that I have seen or used over the years: (Once again my apologies to original authors!)

GRADING ADAPTATIONS THAT WORK:

Base part of the grade on the processes that the student used to com-plete the work, or the effort that the student put forth.

Base part of the grade for an essay on how well the student com-pleted the planning, organizing, and editing of the first draft.

Base 15 of the 100 points for a research paper on how proficiently the student used the editing functions in the word processing program, such as the spelling and grammar checker, thesaurus, and tools for mak-ing charts and graphics.

Assign 10 of 100 points for a math word problem worksheet to the number of problems that the student attempted with a criterion of 10 completed to earn 10 points.

Make an agreement that if Mary can raise her average quiz score from 60 to 75 percent you will add 5 percent to allow her quiz average to be a B. This will not affect her overall average that much since I only count her quiz average as 10% of her overall grade, but it will be a good mo-tivator.

Give five bonus points for each correct paragraph that the student writes beyond the three paragraphs required.

Assign "study problems" before a test and if the student turns them in they may use them for point insurance if they fail the test. If they have done enough good quality study problems, they may earn from one to three points on the test and if they failed the test, even more.

Once again there are so many options and the creative teacher will vary her choices with the student and the circumstances. I have to add in one word of caution based on my experience with grading adaptations. I am always willing to make reasonable adjustments when a student has consistently put forth effort, but if it is necessary to do this on a regular basis, the parents must be aware of the adaptations. If a student's grade is a reflection of effort and not mastery, the parents as well as the school administration must be made aware of the situation. Have I ever passed a student with a "C" who I did not feel had mastered the material? Yes I have and I do not regret it. If that student worked hard all year and came in for extra help on a consistent basis, I let them pass. My rationale is simple. Students mature intellectually at different times and over the years I have had many late bloomers who have barely survived my class and did very well down the road. I keep the parents very informed throughout the year and keep the administration up to date. I did have an interesting situation once where the father wanted the grade based on mastery and the mother wanted it based on effort. We had an interesting parent conference and compromised on mastery on quizzes and other assignments and effort on major tests. Now that was differentiated assessment!

The last comment I want to make on differentiated assessment is the problem of students sharing grades. Once in a while I get a "that's not fair" comment from another student in the classroom when tests are not graded identically. This comment also happens when the assignments are slightly varied per student. If I have created a "caring community" in my classroom, these types of comments should be very isolated, but they will still occur. The best way to handle them is to privately talk to the student making the comment in a gentle but firm manner. If you can get away with it, refer them to Matthew 20:1-16 and the parable of the workers in the field. If not, talk to them about mercy and compassion in general terms, without explicitly talking about the "other student". Talk about your professional judgment and the fact that nothing was taken away from them. Leave them feeling that you care just as much about them and if they ever need a break, you have enough mercy to go around.

DIFFERENTIATED INSTRUCTION PLANNING IDEAS AND RANDOM THOUGHTS

Hopefully at this point we all agree that we need to differentiate instruction, discipline, and assessment. The question is how do we do it without driving ourselves and the students crazy? Will planning become such a nightmare that it sucks the joy right out of teaching? Will classroom time become such a delicate juggling act that the stress to succeed with every student overwhelms the beauty of a well orchestrated classroom ballet? If it does, then we are not doing it right. As with everything flexibility and the willingness to back pedal are essential. There are a gazillion options for differentiation. Use trial and error to see what works for you. Innovate and experiment. Keep an open mind and over time you will find the perfect combination that works for you.

Now we are ready to talk about planning for differentiation. My first caution here is that if you create a monster, you are going to have to feed it. Keep it simple. Begin with your basic unit notebook. Once your unit is in place; continue pulling varied instructional strategies from as many sources as you can. I strongly encourage you to create a checklist of instructional strategies so you will remember them. We too easily fall into the habit of using a few good ones and forget that we have a large range of possibilities. I have one that I keep in the front of my plan book and I refer to it all of the time. Although I created my own list, a great way to start with a prepared list is Gayle H. Gregory's list in her book *Differentiating Instruction With Style.* She carries through with her clipboard, beach ball, puppy, and microscope analogy and suggests all sorts of activities and strategies for each type. As you make your plans, remember we can't possibly do everything in each unit, but over a semester we should have balanced out the instruction to have included every learning style

As you develop your game plan begin to develop instructional tools that can be used over and over again. Do not try to re-invent the wheel. I am sure that you already have some excellent instructional tools that are great for differentiation just as they are, or with a little "tweaking". Here are a few examples:

*The entire class studies the same content, but individual students are allowed to choose assignments at different levels of complexity.

*Multi-level learning stations where each student receives an assignment sheet as to what numbered activities they are to complete.

*The teacher creates flexible groups of students according to strength, need, or interest and the groups change frequently.

*Students who are struggling should be encouraged to create their own attempts at graphic organizers and study sheets which they may trade in for ones the teacher has created. As the year progresses, the students will get better at developing their own.

*Create innovative and attractive handouts that can be used in several ways.

Remember that it is not what we teach that changes, it is how we teach. If the final product is required then the product is not negotiable. If the curriculum mandates that a student can write a three point essay you don't say it is ok to do a diorama instead. If however, learning Kreb's Cycle in biology is a required skill, it doesn't matter how they learn it. Set expectations and work from a perspective of optimism and possibilities rather than one of pessimism and difficulties. BELIEVE.

UNEQUALLY YOKED

It is now time to take the leap from planning to instruction. A very large part of my instructional philosophy is based on the students working in teams and "instructing" each other. The success of students working in teams has a lot to do with the make-up of the teams and team dynamics. Therefore, before I get into specific instructional teaming techniques, I want to discuss teams in general. Do you remember doing group projects or being assigned to a team in school? It was a horrible experience for me. If it was a sports activity, I was always chosen last because I was a hopeless athlete. If it was an in-class assignment group, I was always chosen early because they knew I was a perfectionist and would help the team get a good grade. If it was a long term project, the other students were actually fighting over me because they knew I would do most of the work and they could do as little as possible. Kids who normally would not give me the time of day became my "best friends". When I was put on a team, I never felt "equally yoked". It was always obvious to me that I was never chosen for my sparkling personality. I resented doing more than my share of the work and everyone getting credit. Knowing my dislike of teaming and group work, you would think that as a teacher, I would avoid those situations like the plague. Not so! Now I love group work and putting students in teams is one of the first things I do. So what caused this monumental shift in my way of thinking?

COMPETITION

Competition is one of the most motivating factors in society. Always has been, always will be. It is the most dominant characteristic of sports, and the American economy thrives on it. Kids learn about it very young as they learn when you play a game, you either win or lose. Heaven forbid if they ever had a tie and ended up with two winners. No, now you must go to "sudden death"! That's a pleasant thought. Competition does indeed have its virtues and vices. Healthy competition is good. Too much competition causes a great deal of stress and anxiety. I also need to say here that if we are to prepare our students for the working world, we have to teach them to be team players. Most businesses will tell you that they are willing to train a new employee to do their job, so prior skills are not as important as work ethic and the ability to work well with other people. Synergy is alive and well in the work place and we need to prepare our students to be a contributing member of a team.

The trick for the good teacher is to find that level of competition and co-operation that is healthy in the classroom. Finding the level that motivates students to work harder, without creating stress or feelings of low self-esteem, is a balancing act that takes practice. In my teaching career, I soon learned that as a student, I had been one of the weird quiet ones, and that most kids loved and thrived on some level of team competition. As a teacher, teams could accomplish for me, what I was never interested in as a student. At the same time, my own experiences helped me structure my "teaming" approach to make it more palpable to those few students, like me, who would rather work alone. I can't make everyone happy all of the time, but I choose to go for the "common good"!

SELECTING THE TEAMS

At the beginning of the year, I put each one of my classes in teams. The size of the teams depends on the size of the class. If it is a very small class, I usually have teams of two or three. If it is a large class, I have teams of four. I have several ways that I have students assigned to teams and I always reserve the right to re-assign a person if the team dynamics are not working. Every six weeks I change team membership. (In AP Calculus, I select the teams very carefully at the beginning of the year and they stay in the same team all year.) This is very important because it allows them to experience different people. Here are some of the ways that I pick teams:

*** First six weeks, I usually let them pick their own teams, with the understanding that if their choices do not work, I will rearrange them.

***Second six weeks, I ask them to line up according to height from shortest to tallest and then count off in twos, threes, or fours to form the teams. The first four students in the line will be team one, the second four will be team two, etc.

***Third six weeks, I ask them to line up according to their date of birth and then I count off as above.

***Fourth six weeks, I have every student select a playing card as they enter the door. I have pre-selected the cards so that I will get the number on each team that I want. For instance if I have a class with 22 students, I might want 6 three man teams and one four man team. I would then pre-select 3 aces, 3 kings, 3 queens, 3 jacks, 3 tens, 3 nines, and 4 eights. The students with the matching cards would be on the same team. (With this method, I warn them as they pick a card that there will be no switching.)

***Fifth six weeks, the students are matched up according to their hobbies. The day before I am to select teams, I have each student write on a notecard what their favorite hobby is. They have no idea what I am going to use this information for. That night, I group them by hobby. I cannot match them with exactly the same hobbies but I get them as close as I can.

***Sixth six weeks, just when they think they have me figured out, I line them up alphabetically by their last names. Instead of the usual counting off, where the first four in line are team one, I have them count off from one to seven and then all of the "ones" are team one and all of the "twos" are team two and so on...

BUILDING THAT TEAM SPIRIT

How much time I spend on team building depends on the age level of the class and how tight the curriculum is. For instance in an Algebra I class, I would spend more time on the team building process, than I would in a Calculus class. As you read the following sections, please pick and choose the activities that seem appropriate for your time frame and age level, but remember, don't get so caught up in the team building, that you forget the curriculum. Also remember, that there are many fine books full of activities for team building available out there and the internet is "teaming" with ideas.

***Once teams are selected, give the teams a few minutes to come up with a team name. Be sure that they understand what is "school appropriate". It must be a positive name.

***Have each team design a team flag. Give them a 3in by 5in notecard and a few markers and let them design their own. Then have them tape it to the end of a pencil as a flagpole and use it to signal when they are through with an assigned activity. I had one group take their pencil home and with a push pin and some kite string, they created a little pulley and were able to raise and lower their flag on the pencil! Playdoh also makes a great stand for a pencil flag.

***If I have the money, I order enough white cotton baseball caps from The Oriental Trading Company for each team to have one. I give them fabric paint and let them decorate it with team name, colors, motto, etc. These caps are very useful in letting me know when a team is finished, especially when we are competing to see who can finish first. As soon as a team is finished, someone on the team puts on the cap and I point to them and say first, second, third, etc...until each team has finished or time is called.

***Each time a new team is formed, a new captain is picked. I let each team member pick a number from one to four. If they are a three man team they pick from one to three and so on... Before any of this is done I write a number from one to four on a note card and put it in a sealed envelope. Before we start picking numbers, I show them that the "captain" number has already been decided and is safely tucked in the envelope. Once everyone on a team has a number they write it on their notebook paper and circle it. (No switching numbers!) I then call out the number in the envelope and that person will be captain until I decide to change again. If a team only has two or three members and I call out four, the highest number on the team is captain. I usually leave team captains all six weeks, but if I sense a change is necessary, I go through the process again and pray that the "offending" captain does not get selected again. (If they do, I might have to pull my Atilla the Hun card and go into dictator mode and appoint a captain myself.)

MANAGING TEAMS

Having had so many bad experiences on teams in my youth, I was determined that I would make it as pleasant an experience as possible for my students by trying to solve some of the objections that my former self had to "teaming." I developed a set of team rules that I use religiously

1   I do not give team grades on anything. There are no team projects that are graded. If I assign projects, they are always individual projects. I know from experience on both sides of the fence that it is very rare for all of the members of the team to do an equal amount of work. All of my team activities are part of a competition that leads to rewards like candy, cokes, etc., not grades.

2   I constantly monitor my teams during class. I never just sit at my desk or do other work while they are working. My involvement is critical to the teaming and teaching process. I do not allow students to just sit back and let the others do the work.

If a student will not work with their team after a couple of warnings, I separate them for that activity and make them do the work by themselves.

3 When I hear any whining about team work, I stop and explain that in the real world you will be placed on teams all the time, and usually you do not get to choose who you work with. It is important that you be able to work with anyone. If that does not satisfy them, I give them my best "life is not fair" speech, and tell them to do it because "Atilla" said so.

4 As I monitor to make sure everyone is working, I also monitor for "bossy, controlling" behavior. If a student is constantly dominating the group, I will walk over and set a piece of duct tape next to them. They know that the tape means that they must go mute, until I pick it back up. It usually manages to slow them down so that others may contribute. It is mostly symbolic, but it usually does the trick. On rare occasions, if I know the parents well enough, I will apply the duct tape to their mouth. I also make a deliberate effort to get the "mousy" student involved. As I monitor, I ask them what they think and refuse to take an answer from anyone but them.

5 I never allow anyone to put another team member down in any way. If they do, I remove them from the team and make them work alone.

6 I do not allow the teams to talk to other teams. They may only talk to members of their own team.

THE GREAT MAGNET, CHIP, PEBBLE, BEAN… RACE

Twenty-six years ago, I had the best "teaming" tool of all time dumped in my lap. Well to be totally honest, I rescued it from the "dipsey dumpster"! I was teaching at a large comprehensive high school with a large student population. The registrar had just been trained to do scheduling with a computer program. Gone were the days of scheduling by hand! The large magnet scheduling board and all of the trillion little magnets that had been used for years to visually arrange the schedule and adjust it, were going to be thrown away. Knowing my habit of dumpster diving, the registrar asked me if I would like to have this marvelous board before she threw it away. Of course I said yes. I was not at all sure what I was going to do with it, but it had to be good for something! It measures about two and half feet wide and about four feet tall. It looked like a chalkboard, but it was magnetic. It was so heavy that I could not pick it up. It came with a large collection of little one inch square magnets in different colors and some vary narrow tape, to mark off grids.

After much thought, I decided it would be a great tool for using competition and peer pressure to get more kids to do their homework. I divided the board into my five sections, one for each class. I then divided each section into teams for each class. I used the red magnets for class markers and team numbers. I put the rest of the magnets in a container that I kept near my overhead. Every time a student had their complete homework assignment they received a magnet. I will explain how the rewards worked in the management section but the most important point here is that I used a piece of trash and came up with a system that was easy for me to manage and the students love it. I have been using that same board for 27 years! As ideas begin to form for me on teaming, there are now other ways to earn magnets besides doing homework. If something unfortunate were to happen to my magnet board I would be devastated, because I do not think that you can buy them that large anymore. I did see some smaller ones that were magnetic white boards, but I am not sure where you could get the small square magnets. I have shared this idea with other teachers and they have found innovative ways to do this without the board. They have used cups and beans, jars and poker chips, laminated poster board and dry erase markers, etc...

GENERIC TEAM BUILDING ACTIVITIES

On the next few pages you will find a collection of possible team building activities. Whether any of these activities will be useful to you depends on how much time you have to spend building your teams. In my upper level math classes, I have very little and do not use any of these, but in my lower level classes, I use any of these that seem appropriate. Some are not original ideas and I have credited the author when I had the information.

TEAM STUDYING

This one is great when you are trying to get a team to work together to study something. First, I took a math worksheet out of an old activity book and modified it greatly by adding a lot of random, useless, information and pictures. The purpose is not to do what the worksheet says, but to try to memorize as much of the information on the worksheet as possible. You can use any fact or picture sheet in any subject because the material is not the point. I give one copy of this sheet to every team and tell them they have three minutes to study it and then I will be asking questions. I do not offer any strategies. I start the clock and observe how the teams go about memorizing as much of the sheet as they can. When three minutes are up, I have every team number a sheet of notebook paper from one to ten and as a group, I let them confer and answer the questions together. A few example questions might be:

1   What word was in jug ?

2   How many eyes were in jug 7?

3   What was Sammy's last name?

They usually do well as a team and I give prizes for the team which did the best. We discuss possible team strategies such as assigning everyone on the team a section of the worksheet to concentrate on, making up questions of their own, etc. I then give them three more minutes to study the same worksheet and see if you can do better. When the three minutes are up, I have each member of the team number a piece of notebook paper from one to ten. I then ask ten questions and this time they may not help each other. Again, they are all just nonsense questions.

1   What color was the first jug on the paper?

2   What was the page number at the bottom of the page?

3   Complete the statement on the page. Fractions are _____.

At this point grade the papers and give the team score based on the total correct from each student. They feel like they have been tricked because they were not allowed to work together! If it had been a real study session for a real test, they would have had to go solo, so they need to learn to study as teams and test alone! They should then discuss team study strategies that expedite individual success. This activity should then be applied to subject appropriate material to be studied instead of nonsense sheets.

COOPERATIVE LEARNING ACTIVITIES

Cooperative learning is a very old concept that has been instrumental in turning the classroom from teacher centered to student centered. There are lots of definitions, books, workshops, and websites on cooperative learning. I consider cooperative learning as any activity that involves the students in the learning and allows them to be instructors as well as students. As the teacher, I become more of a facilitator and a monitor. Sometimes the cooperation is formal, and sometimes it is not. There are so many good activities to suggest that I only offer a few. I suggest you research and find more and better yet, come up with your own. Some of these activities require pre-made note cards. In the classroom management section, I will give you some ways to create and store these sets that takes some of the work off of you.

GREMLINS

Have the teams arrange their desks in as much of a circle as possible. Each team is given a set of three by five note cards on the topic. All sets are the same but in different colors. Twenty cards per team is a good number of cards. On the front of the cards is a question or problem and on the back, very tiny, in the bottom corner, is the answer. The students count off and are assigned a number. Player one takes the first card off of the stack and reads the question to player two. Player two answers and player one checks the answer. If player two is correct, he/she gets to keep the card. If they are wrong player three answers. If player three is correct, he/she keeps the card, if not, the card goes around the circle until someone gets it right. If no one gets it right, it goes in the middle of the circle to the "gremlin" pile. If anyone on the team, needs to see how a problem is worked or does not understand the answer to the question, they may challenge the student who got the correct answer and if that student cannot explain their response, they have to put their card in the gremlin pile. This requirement keeps students from random guessing. Remember, hopefully, you have created an atmosphere where the students feel safe asking questions. If they do not understand a question they need to ask. Once a card is earned by a student or given to the gremlin, the original stack is rotated to the next player and play continues until the stack is done or time is called. The player with the most cards gets a prize. If the gremlin stack is the largest, no one gets a prize. When the activity is over, there should be few cards in the gremlin piles. Take the gremlins up and go over them as a class. You should find a lot of repeats so there should not be that many to discuss. I usually have a different color set of cards for each team so that I can quickly get the gremlin cards back to their rightful set. The gremlin stack lets you know what material is most troubling to the students.

THE ALAMO

Ask a question that has more than one answer such as:

1 What were the causes of the civil war?

2 Write down everything that you can remember about the Kreb's Cycle.

3 Tell me everything you can remember about a triangle including tests for congruence.

4 Give me as many examples as you can list of Shakespeare's use of metaphor in McBeth.

Now set the timer and let the teams work together to create one list per team with as many answers as they can come up with. You decide whether you want them to use resources or not. To me the Shakespeare question lends itself to resources and the other three do not. I usually give two or three minutes, but that will need to be determined by the question. Once time is called no more writing is allowed and *everyone stands* with the list in a position that everyone on the team can see it. I then shake up my chips and call a name. That student gives me a fact off of the team sheet. If they are correct, they remain standing. If they are incorrect, another student may challenge them. If indeed, they were incorrect that person must sit down. If the challenger was incorrect and the original student was correct, the challenger must sit down. Another chip is drawn and another student is called on. The students may not repeat an answer that has been given by another team. Someone on the team should be checking off the ones that have already been given, because if a student repeats an answer, they must sit down. You must be diligent in listening because you are the "judge and jury" as to what is relevant and what is a repeat. Once the chips are started, no team can add anything to or modify their list and students that are called on may only read something off of the list. The last team with someone standing wins the prize. I like this activity because it is a combination of knowledge and luck, and a great review of what has been learned.

PASS AND PONDER

This is a great activity to review for a test or a quiz. Give each student three minutes to write down everything they can remember that will be on the test or quiz. Encourage them to write down lots of information, not just topics. When the timer goes off, give the teams ten minutes to share what they have written and come up with five good questions. When the second timer goes off, have each team send one member to the board and write one question or problem. They should do this simultaneously not worrying about repeats. These questions should be answered and discussed as a class. Then, ask for another member of the team to write a second question on the board, being sure not to repeat anything that was discussed in the first set. Continue this pattern until everyone's questions are asked. Point out to the class if there are any topics or important concepts that they missed and review these. There is no prize involved here, just an active review.

SINK OR SWIM

This is a great activity to prepare the students to be positive contributors in any type of study group. In this activity, the team either sinks or swims based on every member of the team succeeding. Once a concept is introduced and some reinforcement has been given, it is time to check for individual understanding. Throw out a problem or question and have every student answer it on their own on a note card with their team number but no name on it. There should be no team discussion at this point. Take up the cards and quickly survey them telling the team if they "sink" or "swim". To "swim" everyone on the team must have the correct answer. Then instead of your going over the problem, each team does it in their group making sure that everyone understands. As you survey the cards, if you notice that no one on the team got the correct answer, be sure that you work with that group. I ask the students not to identify if they were right or wrong; if I catch a team revealing this information, I will penalize them a point. Each team gets one point for every "swim". I continue to call out questions and if done in the right spirit, the teams really put forth effort explaining the concepts in new and refreshing ways so that everyone will understand. Points are calculated until time is called and a team prize is given.

CYCLING NOTECARDS

This one is a little tricky and takes some exact preparation but it is a lot of fun. Mr. Tim Yoder introduced me to this and I love it because it is so fast paced and it really keeps everyone involved. First you must create a large set of note cards that has the same number of cards as students in the class. On the front in one color is a question and on the back in another color is the answer to a question on another card. Instruct the students to concentrate on the answer side of their cards. Initiate the activity by drawing a chip and asking the student whose name you drew to read the question on their card. The student who thinks they have the answer reads the answer and if they are not challenged they read the next question which appears on the other side of their card. Students must pay attention to the questions to see if they have the answer or the cycle is broken. If a student calls out an answer and is challenged by another student, the class discusses it with you as referee. Make sure that the discussions stay kind. Continue this process until all of the questions are answered. Time this whole process and when the first cycle is finished post the time on the board. Now take the cards up, mix them up and redistribute them. Draw another chip and encourage the students to beat their last time. Continue as long as time allows.

DOUBLE DIPPING

This activity works great for a long discussion question or a difficult math problem. Have every student get out a sheet of paper and writing instrument. Put one question or problem on the board. Have everyone start simultaneously and call time before anyone can possibly finish. Have the teams rotate the papers one time among themselves. Students look at what has been done on the problem or question and then they may correct it or continue. If a student completes the problem, they should stand and remove themselves from the rotation. After a reasonable amount of time, call "time" and have them rotate the paper again. Continue the rotation until it appears that most of the students have finished the problem. Go over the problem, being sure to give students with alternate approaches a chance to present their method.

EXPERT EXTRAVAGANZA

This activity works great for a concept that has four parts. I am going to use a mathematical example, but this can be adapted to other subjects. In geometry two lines can intersect a circle and each other in four ways. To use highly sophisticated mathematical jargon, I will call them "innies", "outties", "onnies", and "centies". The resulting angles have special relationships that I will not go into here. The point is, there are four facts that have to be mastered to meet the objective of being able to find the angles and arcs of the four types. Instead of my teaching the skill, I have each team number from one to four and send them to one of four stations around the room. All of the ones go to station one, all of the twos to station two, etc. At the stations, there is a self-guided discovery lesson, and the students at that station help each other go through the procedure making sure that all of them understand, because they are going to have to go back to their team and teach the concept. Each station is set up with measuring instruments and guides the students to the discovery of the concept. Students are then asked to write their findings in simple terms. Once they have their statement they practice a few problems to make sure that they can apply it. I walk around the four stations and monitor to make sure that they are all on task and on the right track. Once all four stations, have the correct concept, I send them all back to their own teams. I then have a worksheet which starts with five innie problems. The expert on that team shares what they discovered and teaches the concept to the rest of the team. The next section of the worksheet has five outtie problems and the process is continued until each type of problem has been introduced and each expert shares his/her knowledge. I then give the students a second worksheet where all four types of problems are mixed up and we work a few together and then some solo. This is a great exercise!

THINK-PAIR-SHARE

This is the old standby that is in every cooperative learning book ever written. It is also very simple and very effective. Give the class a problem or question and have them answer it by themselves with no help from their team. They may start when you say "Think". There should be absolute silence in the room. When you think they have had enough time, say "Pair". They should then consult with one other person on their team and if they do not agree, they should talk it out. When the time seems appropriate, say "Share. " At this point both pairs share their answers and if there is any disagreement they talk it out. By this point the problem or questions should be understood by all but still give the class an opportunity to ask questions. I use what I call quizlet boards to make this even more fun. (We will talk about quizlet boards in the management section.)

WORKSHEET WOES

That title does not only apply to the students who are on the receiving end of worksheets, but it also applies to the teachers who pass them out. As a math teacher, I have passed out my share of them. After many hours of standing in line at the Xerox machine, it is also safe for me to say that they are used a great deal in the other subjects. Worksheets are a practical learning tool. For some teachers they are a necessity for supplementing the textbook, and for others, they are a great way to help the students internalize the material. Used too often, and in the wrong manner, however, they become a boring instrument of torture for the students and a classroom management nightmare for the teacher.

Calling worksheets torture for the students is easy to understand. More often than not, they are passed out with the instructions to "do" the worksheet "on your own" and "see me if you need help". The teacher then either goes to her desk (usually in the hopes of getting some of her own paperwork done) or walks around the room and helps students individually. Those needing help are often too shy to ask and those who are not too shy, end up standing in line or at their desks waiting for help. It becomes busy work for the students. Those who "get it" finish quickly, and those who don't get it rarely finish at all, or they just give up, often copying their neighbors paper. The working of "it" is bad enough. Then there is the "going over it" phase. The teacher calls out the answers and asks if there are any questions. Once again those who are too shy to ask, have unanswered questions and those who don't care can remain anonymous and clueless. The ones who got it in the first place are bored as usual.

Now that we have established the torture element for the students, why do I say it is torture for the teacher too? From the teacher's point of view, it might seem like a good idea to reinforce concepts with a worksheet, but if handled in the usual manner it can become a class-room management challenge. First of all, you can not control the fact that students work at different paces and that some students will finish very quickly and end up with too much free time. Some students will not finish at all, no matter how much time you give them, and end up very frustrated. Also in the mix, are those students who simply put something in the blanks to make it look like they have done the work.

If students have to wait in line at your desk to get help, they are wasting time and you are answering the same questions over and over. If you go around to their desks, you lose sight of what is going on with the rest of the students, as you turn your back on the class. (Not to mention the unflattering part of your anatomy that is most prominent as you lean over a desk!)I also used to get very frustrated because I never could get to everybody who needed help. Another thing to think about is the fact that if you pass out a worksheet with 25 questions on it, some of the kids will finish it in 5 minutes! An activity that you expected to last 20 minutes results in too much free time for some and uncompleted work for others. I was also always very frustrated that so many of the students would so quickly ask for help and not really try to think it through themselves. If I was "too" available, they wouldn't try it on their own.

So what is a teacher to do? Once again, the idea is to use peer inter-action and teaming to accomplish the task of keeping all of the students "engaged'" in the learning process. You, as the teacher, cannot get to everyone who needs help, control behavior, and keep everyone on task. On the next few pages, you will find several approaches to worksheets that have worked for me in the past. These approaches use those who know how to do the work to help those who do not. With these tech-niques, there are many teachers in the room, not just one. Very few fin-ish early, and those who do, only have a minute or two before the "action" starts again. There are no long lists of answers to be called out, and the boredom factor drops several degrees. The teacher can su-pervise the entire class and no one feels "left-behind". The approach is fun and competitive, yet enough responsibility is put on each student, to make them accountable for really learning the material. I encourage you to try these new approaches to "the worksheet".

REGULAR WORKSHEETS

I use worksheets when I do not think that the textbook has enough practice or when I want to enrich a topic. If I make out my own work-sheets, I try to put as many problems or questions on the page as I can. No matter what, however, I never just pass out a worksheet and tell them to "do it". I also never go in order. I do not want the kids to know what problems I am going to assign in class or which ones are going to be for homework. If they do, a lot of them will get ahead of me, and I do not want that result because of timing issues. If I see a student getting ahead of me, I take the worksheet away and give them a clean one. After I do this once in each class, the problem seems to cure itself. I have many ways to try to be creative in using a worksheet, but the key issue is to only do a little of it at a time. Here are a few ways that I "do" a worksheet:

MAGNET PROBLEMS

I will teach a skill and then pass out a worksheet and instruct the class to do number 12 "for a magnet". They work on number 12 with their teams and put their team number and their agreed upon answer on a note card and bring it to me. If they get it correct, they get a magnet. I then go over the problem. I might repeat this two or three times before I expect the students to go solo. I will not help the teams during the magnet problems. I am trying to force the teams to help each other and figure it out by themselves. If a team cannot do the problem at all, I will assist them, but they know that they will not get a magnet. Most of my time during a magnet problem is spent walking around the room to make sure everyone is involved.

Once I feel like everyone has had enough practice with help, I call for a solo magnet problem. I call out another number off of the worksheet and each student must work by his/herself. When time is called, each student who got the problem correct gets a magnet. The kids know that this reward is coming, so they are better teachers when they are helping each other, because they know it will benefit the team if everyone knows the material. As far as I am concerned magnet problems are the best thing since sliced bread in a mathematics classroom because they provide multiple teachers at the learning stage and accountability on the part of the students. (Remember, if you don't have a magnet board, use dry beans, marbles, popsicle sticks…) I think the concept would transfer to any subject as you "hunt" for answers to questions in a social studies class or correct grammar in sentences in language arts, etc.

JUST FOR THE FUN OF IT

All of the work I have my students do is not rewarded with candy or magnets. Sometimes they must just work to learn with no extrinsic rewards. After we have done magnet problems, I will instruct them to do numbers 11-14 on their worksheet on their own. I will set the timer and go around the room and help those that I can get to. I will not give a lot of time. When time is up, I call out the answers and go over the problems requested. Often, I call students to the board, which motivates them to do their best when working on the problems. I use the chips to call students to the board, using a lot of "fudge factor". The fudge factor comes in when I draw the name of a student who I know is not ready to present at the board and I call out another students' name. No one ever knows whose name was on the chip!) I never assign too many problems without going over them. Students who are doing problems wrong are only reinforcing wrong work if they do too many before they hear the answers. The key here is only a few at a time. Every student will not finish and some will finish fast, but since you only gave the students a few minutes, time is not wasted. Once we have spent time in class on a worksheet, I will assign some of it for homework.

YOU CREATE THE TORTURE

If I am working on a skill that lends itself to student created problems or questions, I let them "create the worksheet". I have every student get a note card out of the boxes under their desk and write one problem on the front, work it out, and circle the final answer. I also have them put their name on it. I then have them create another problem on the back of the card, work it out and circle the answer. I then have each team rotate these cards among the teams to make sure they agree with their fellow student's work. To get them to take the problem seriously, I will give a shazaam to any student who finds an error on another student's card. I also ask them to look for problems that they think are not a good example and simply draw a small frowny face at the top of the card. After each team has had time to go through the cards for their team, I take them up and we move on. I take the cards and create a worksheet. I then use it the next day to practice, reinforce, or assign homework.

A great variation on this activity is to have students create the problems on notecards but a worksheet is never created. I have each student create one problem on the front of the note card and work it and circle the answer on the back of the card. Once again they put their name on it. I take up the cards and mix them up. I pass them back out, giving each student one card. Once everyone is ready, I say go and then about every 30 seconds or minute, depending on the difficulty level of the problems, I say rotate. A student must abandon the card to the next person when "rotate" is called. Students keep a list on notebook paper of the ones that they want to see worked. If they cannot finish a problem, it counts as a miss. After we have rotated all of the cards back to the original position, I call for questions, and we work the ones that were missed or not finished. If a student finds a mistake, they say "shazaam" and if they are correct they get a shazaam. If they are wrong the person who wrote the card gets the shazaam. There is a level of honesty inherent in this activity and I always look for students that are going to the back of the card too quickly. I usually do not give rewards for this one because it is too easy to be dishonest, but it is a fun way to do a worksheet without a worksheet. It is also a good idea to keep all of these cards in boxes so they can be used again.

50 CARD SWAP

This is another activity that will accomplish the same thing as a worksheet without being a worksheet. I prepare a set of about 50 note cards that have problems or questions on the fronts and no answers. I number them and create a blank answer key with 50 spaces. I give each student an answer key and then pass out one note card to each student telling the students to place the cards face down on their desk until I say go. Before we begin I instruct them to match the number on the card to the space on the answer key. For instance if their card is number 16, they should put their answer in blank 16. I place the remaining cards in a stack in the front of the room. When I say "go" they start with the card that I have given them and when they have the answer on their key, they are to quickly put their first card back in the stack in front and get another card that they have not done. They continue this process until time is called. They may never have more than one card at a time. This is a great activity to get them out of their seats and active. If they cannot work a problem, they put the card back and mark their answer key with a question mark. How long this goes on depends on how much time you have and how well the students are doing. You can call time whenever, because it is not necessary for all of the students to finish all of the problems. I rarely let this go past 15 minutes. Once time is called, I call out all of the answers and students score their papers. Sometimes I give rewards and sometimes I don't. I then call for questions and work several of the harder ones on the board. When the time is up for questions, I encourage those who are still having problems with the concept or those with unanswered questions to save their answer keys and come see me before or after school and we will pull out the cards and work some more.

LET'S RACE

Worksheet races can be a great change of pace and very competitive. Whether it is math problems; questions in literature, science, or history; grammar sentences to be corrected; or fine arts creators to be memorized this technique is fun and effective. Every student is given a worksheet and asked to keep it face down on their desk. I then call out a group of five to ten problems/questions. I never go in order so I usually start with something like 16-20, etc. I sit in a vacant student desk and when I say "go", I race the class and see if I can finish the problems before any of them. The first person finished stands up. Sometimes it is I and sometimes it is not. I continue the activity until I have about five people standing. I then ask everyone to stop and I call out the answers. We get a point for each one we get correct and we lose a point for each one we missed. The order you stand up does not matter in the points it is just fun to beat the teacher. Once scores are tallied and the winner is declared, I ask for questions and go over any problems in the set that need to be explained. I then call out another set of problems and we continue. The kids love this because I do not always win. Sometimes I never win. I am either too slow or too nervous or too careless.

This only enforces what I have told them from day one and that is that I am not smarter than they are, I am just wiser.

BLINDFOLDS, DUCT TAPE, AND HANDCUFFS

I give each team a worksheet and ask them to circle their desks with only one worksheet and one writing instrument per team. I then distribute two bandanas and a piece of duct tape per team. I have the kids number themselves off from 1-4. (If I have any two or three man teams they number themselves also, just lower.) I then ask #1 to put on one of the bandanas as a blindfold, #2 to put the duct tape on their mouth, and #3 to use the other bandana as handcuffs with a little help from their team. #4 becomes the writer. If there are only three people on a team, #2 uses the duct tape and writes. If there are only two people on a team #1 gets the blindfold and handcuffs and #2 writes. Once everyone is in position, I give them a certain amount of time, usually 10-15 minutes and tell them to work as many of the problems as they can. The blindfolded student cannot see and must be read the problem or question by their team and must be talked through it. The handcuffed student can only listen and talk and look but cannot write. The duct taped student can point and write, but cannot talk. While they are working, I walk around the room and keep things on the up and up. The duct taped students do not have to keep their mouths covered the entire time because it is uncomfortable, but they may not talk. If the blindfolded child does not want to put on the bandana, I let them just shut their eyes, but I do assure them that I have washed the bandana since its last use. When time is called, I read out the answers and go over the problems.

This activity is very good because the kids who talk all of the time may be forced to listen, and the kids who take over are sometimes the ones who are blinded. On rare occasions, I actually pick who I want to get the blindfold, handcuffs, and duct tape. It really changes team dynamics and allows the quiet kids to shine.

DRILL SHEETS

As a math teacher, I was always concerned about students knowing the basic facts. For me it was Algebra I and I needed to reinforce basic concepts such as integer operations and very basic skills. I created a template of blank spaces and numbered them from 1 to 80 on one sheet of paper. I Xeroxed several copies and put the sheets on a clipboard. On the way to and from school, which was about a 20 minute drive, I filled up each page with one specific skill. Let me quickly add here that this was when my son had just gotten his learner's permit and I was in the passenger seat. Not only did making out the "drill sheets" in the car help save me preparation time, it calmed my nerves! By the time he got his regular license, my blood pressure was back to normal and I had quite a collection of drill sheets. If I had been a history teacher, I would have probably done them on Presidents, constitutional amendments, states and capitals, etc. If I had been a science teacher, I would have done the periodic table, scientists and their discoveries, etc. As an English teacher, I would have done parts of speech, authors and their works, etc. The point of drill sheets it to use repetitive short questions to help students internalize facts. For instance, if my students were having trouble remembering the difference between "x" plus "x" and "x" times "x", I had a drill sheet that was nothing but those two concepts over and over again. Eighty problems with two questions asked over and over. Can you imagine how simplistic that seemed to the students? They thought that I had lost my mind! But I made my point; this skill is critical to learn before we move on! Did I hand out the sheet and say "do" this worksheet and see me if you need help? Of course not! That would have wasted the time of those who could do it and reinforced wrong work for those who couldn't. (I'll show you how to handle a drill sheet in just a moment-patience please!) Other drill sheets never repeat a problem. Some are very simple, some are a little tougher, but the point is, they are mostly designed to reinforce one skill. I had to put the word mostly in there, because sometimes they lead to a progression of skills. For instance in math, when you teach integer operations, you add, subtract, multiply and divide. First I made out an addition drill sheet. Then I made out a subtraction drill sheet. Then I made out a mixed addition and subtraction drill sheet. Then I made out a multiplication drill sheet. Then I made out an addition, subtraction, and multiplication drill sheet. Then I ...! I think you get the picture. If I were a social studies teacher trying to get the kids to learn the states and capitals, I might start with a drill sheet on the southeast, repeating the states over and over until I had asked 80 times. Then I would create a drill sheet on the Northeast. Then I would create a sheet on the Southeast and Northeast mixed up. Etc...

Now that the drill sheets and answer keys have been created, let's look at some ways to use them. I have listed a few variations here and I am sure that you can come up with some great ones on your own. The key here is to not be boring. Keep them interacting and helping each other. These activities also work well with regular worksheets. The directions may seem complicated but they are not once you get the hang of it. You may want to read through this quickly and then concentrate on how to do it as you instruct the class. This is really a great activity so don't be scared by the instructions.

THE CAROUSEL

STUDENT DIRECTIONS:

1   Get into your teams and move your desks together so that you are facing each other. You will need one writing instrument and a piece of scratch paper per team.

2   I am going to give one drill sheet to each team. Please keep it face down until I finish giving instructions and say GO.

3   When I say GO, the first person on the team will answer the first problem of the set that I assign. He/she will pass the paper to the next person on the team who will either correct the question just answered, or answer the next question. You may correct any other answer, not just the one before you, but you may not write down a new answer if you have corrected one.

4   The paper keeps rotating until I call time.

5   There can be no talking, and if someone writes a wrong answer there can be no gestures, etc.

6   You may not skip a person or skip a problem and you may not answer more than one at a time.

7   When the timer goes off, all writing instruments must go down.

8   Are there any questions? GO...

TEACHER NOTES:

1   Constantly monitor the class to make sure everyone is participating and that there are no talkers.

2   Start an electronic timer that has a loud beep and let it run for one to three minutes, depending on the difficulty level of the drill sheet.

3   Just before you say GO, tell them what number to start with. For instance, tell them to begin with 9. This keeps them from peeking ahead or trying to read thru the back of the paper.

4   When the buzzer goes off, make sure that every team stops and all writing instruments are down.

5   Ask the teams how far they got. For instance, start with a question: "How many teams got to 29? " and keeping making your number larger to see how high you need to call out answers.

6   Call out the answers, making sure that the team records the correct answer if they missed it. It is often good to have them correct it in a different color.

7   When the answers are called out, have the teams count the number that they got correct and place that number at the top of the page.

STUDENT DIRECTIONS:

1   Now I want you to spend about three minutes making sure that

everyone on the team understands how to do this skill. If you know that you are having trouble with these problems, ask someone on your team to explain how they do it. If everyone on the team is good at it, discuss how you could get faster at it, because we are going to try again and I am not going to let you correct anyone's wrong answers.

2   It is very important to your final team score that everyone on the team understands how to do this so please use your time wisely. Your team score will depend on everyone's success so please help each other! I am going to start the timer now and I want you to talk about this concept for three minutes and correct any that you got wrong. Do not try to work ahead or I will eliminate your team from the competition. Practice on the problems that you have already done.

3   GO…

TEACHER DIRECTIONS:

1   When you say GO, walk around the room and listen to their explanations. If they say that everyone on the team can do it, let them talk quietly about anything. They are only wasting three minutes. If you doubt their statement, drill them orally on one or two problems.

2   When the timer goes off, give them their next set of directions.

STUDENT DIRECTIONS:

1   When I say GO, and give you a number, you we will repeat the original process, but this time no answers can be changed. If someone misses one, you have to leave the wrong answer and answer the next one.

2   Only answer one question and do not skip problems.

3   Remember to keep the drill sheet moving and no changing answers.

4   When I say GO, start on number 38.

5   GO...

TEACHER DIRECTIONS:

1   Go thru the same grading process and add the number correct to the number already at the top of the page.

2   Give the team 3 minutes to try to find what they did wrong and help each other.

STUDENT DIRECTIONS:

1   Now that we have worked together, let's see what you can do on your own.

2   One member of the team should put the used drill sheet with your score in their desk for future reference.

3   Please get back in rows. You will not be working with your team this time.

4   I am going to pass out a clean drill sheet to each student. Please leave it face down until I say GO.

5   You must do your own work. I will be timing again, but please do not sacrifice accuracy for speed.

6   When I say Go, do column number three.

7   GO....

TEACHER DIRECTIONS:

1   Give the students two minutes to get as many done as possible.

2   Go thru the same grading process and add the number correct for each student to the number already at the top of the team page.

3   Have each team fill out a note card with their team number and team score and bring it to you.

4   While you are figuring out who won, have the students get back in their teams and correct the ones they missed with peer help.

5   Arrange the cards from highest to lowest scores.

6   The team with the lowest score gets one magnet. If you have a tie, all the teams with the lowest score get one magnet.

7   The team(s) with the next lowest score gets two magnets.

8   The team(s) with the next lowest score gets three magnets.

9   Etc… If you have eight teams and no ties, the top scoring team will end up with 8 magnets.

10 Call one person from each team to collect their magnet(s).

11 Give anyone in the class the opportunity to ask you one last question about any of the problems.

12 I usually assign column two for homework and have them do column one the next day in a magnet race.

When properly managed, this activity does not take more than 25 minutes and there is very little down time.

WHO'S NUMBER IS IT ANYWAY?

STUDENT DIRECTIONS:

1 The activity that we are about to do is an individual activity, but it will result in a team score.

2 Please put the drill sheet that I am passing out to you face down and do not turn it over until I say GO.

3 When I say GO, I will give you a column to work and I want you to work as quickly as you can. You will get a point for each problem that you get right and you will lose a point for each one you miss. Speed is not more important than accuracy.

4 When you finish, stand up and remember the number that I assign you.

5 If you have not stood up by the time I call time, you must stop writing immediately.

TEACHER DIRECTIONS:

1 Make a big production of writing a "secret" number, (no larger than about two-thirds of the number of students participating), on a piece of paper that only you can see. Make it big enough so that when you are ready to show it to the class, they can see it. This approach keeps the same students from being first every time.

2 As the students stand, count them off starting at one and continuing until they are all up or time is called. Remind them to remember their number. I call time when all but two or three are standing.

3 Call out the correct answers to that column.

4 Have the students give themselves one point for each one they got right and subtract a point for each one they missed. Have them put their score at the top of the column.

5   Now show the "secret" number. The student with that number becomes first and the next 5 consecutive numbers are 2nd thru 6th. (If there were eight teams in the class there would be eight places, 5 teams, 5 places, etc... One place for every team.) Those students whose numbers were selected may add their scores to the team score posted on the board.

6   Once scores are posted, have students look at the ones they missed and ask questions if they do not understand something.

On the next round have a different secret number. Once in a while let it be one so that the first kid standing can win. But once in a while pick a high number so that the not so fast ones can have a feeling of success. If you have 23 students in the class, pick 19 and then wrap it around so the first and second student up can still get some points.

Play as many rounds as you like. The more rounds you play, the more it will even out. I like this game because it can make heroes out of the guys who always finish last. And the smart kids who try to figure out the system and slow down on purpose can be outsmarted as the secret number changes.

When the rounds are finished, give out candy or magnets or whatever to the winning teams. This can even become a tournament with running scores over a six weeks period.

RELAYS

Relays are a great standby and are a great choice when it is "getting sleepy" in the room. This is not a team activity, because rarely are the teams on the same row and I think it is good to work with different folks once in a while.

STUDENT DIRECTIONS:

1   Line up in desks, single file.

2   I will give a worksheet to the player on the front of the row. Don't look at it until I say GO.

3   When I say GO, the first player in the row answers the first question assigned, and passes it back over his shoulder to the next student.

4   If you are the last person in line, when you have finished your problem, pass the drill sheet back up to the person in front of you, who will work another problem, and pass it forward. When it comes back up to the first person in line, they work a problem, and pass it back. The paper keeps moving until time is called.

5   You may only work one problem per turn. You may not correct anyone else's answers, and you may not skip any problems.

TEACHER'S DIRECTIONS:

1   When time is called, call out the correct answers to the problems. Each team should give themselves a point for each correct answer.

2   Then give the students an opportunity to ask questions.

3   Repeat as many times as time permits and add up team scores.

4   Reward with candy or magnets.

I'M STILL STANDING

I like to use this activity the day before a test. Up to this point I have taught the material and then had them review in teams or in pairs. Some students are over-confident and some are over-terrified concerning test material. I think it is a good idea on the day before the test for them to access their understanding and know how much they need to prepare for the test.

Students should clear off their desks and raise their quizlet boards. They will need pencil and paper. They may not use notes and whether or not they use their calculators depends on whether or not they can use them on the test. I have the song "I'M STILL STANDING" on my MP3 player and I have it playing as they enter the room. This becomes their cue to get ready.

Once everyone is ready, I write one problem on the board. (In lower level classes, I pick problems very similar to the test. In honor's class I use similar problems, but I don't work every type!) I watch, to keep them honest, but I will not help them. I survey the room and when most of them are finished I call time and work the problem for them. I answer all questions and then ask how many got it right. They stand if they got it correct. If it were not a math class, you would call out questions instead of writing problems.

I then put up the next problem. I repeat this process and after each problem, I ask "Who's still standing? " I keep putting problems up and keep asking the question. As soon as they miss a problem they can't stand up anymore, but they must continue to work the problems. When we are down to "the last man" or just a few, the students "still standing" `get a piece of candy. We then start over and repeat the process until we get a different winner. Once you win you keep working problems but you cannot win again in that class period.

By the end of the period, you have reviewed well for the test, the students have a good idea of how well they know the material, and best of all they stayed active and we had fun reviewing.

TOO GOOD TO PARAPHRASE

Over the years I have looked at many statistics that state how far the United States is behind other countries in their standardized test scores. I suspect this has something to do with the fact that we are "a land of opportunity" and include everyone in our educational system and as well as our test scores, but nevertheless, I always wondered how other countries have such high scores. How is instruction different in these countries and should we try to emulate them? Therefore, when I saw an article about Japanese education, I could not resist reading it. The title of the article is "How Asian Teachers Polish Each Lesson to Perfection. " I do not remember what magazine I tore it out of, but it was reprinted with permission from the authors of American Educator, Spring, 1992, 12-20, 43-47, copyright 1992 by the American Federation of Teachers. It is a wonderful summary of what good instruction looks like in a very precise amount of words and I wanted to share it. I wanted to maintain it's integrity so I declare it "much too good to paraphrase" and present parts of it in it's original form.

If we were asked briefly to characterize classes in Japan and China, we would say that they consist of coherent lessons that are presented in a thoughtful, relaxed, and non-authoritarian manner. Teachers frequently rely on students as sources of information. Lessons are oriented toward problem solving rather than rote mastery of facts and procedures and utilize many different types of representational material. The role assumed by the teacher is that of knowledgeable guide, rather than that of prime dispenser of information and arbiter of what is correct. There is frequent verbal interaction in the classroom as the teacher attempts to stimulate students to produce, explain and evaluate solutions to problems. Lessons are not rote; they are not filled with drill. Teachers do not spend large amount of time lecturing but attempt to lead the children in productive interactions and discussions.

Asian lessons almost always begin with a practical problem. It is not uncommon for the Asian teacher to organize the entire lesson around the solution to this single problem. The teacher leads the children to recognize what is known and what is unknown and directs the students' attention to the critical parts of the problem. Teachers are careful to see that the problem is understood by all of the children, and even mechanics, such as mathematical computation, are presented in the context of solving a problem. Before ending the lesson, the teacher reviews what has been learned and relates it to the problem she posed at the beginning of the lesson.

Chinese and Japanese teachers tend to use short, frequent, periods of seatwork, alternating between group discussions of problems and time for children to work problems on their own. Seatwork is thereby embedded into the lesson. After they work individually or in small groups on a problem, Asian students are called upon to present and defend the solutions they come up with. Thus, instruction, practice, and evaluation are tightly interwoven into a coherent whole.

Asian teachers do not spend large amounts of time lecturing. They present interesting problems; they pose provocative questions; they probe and guide. The students work hard, generating multiple approaches to a solution, explaining the rationale behind their method, and making good use of wrong answers. Incorrect solutions, which are typically dismissed by the American teacher, become topics for discussion in Asian classrooms, and all students can learn from this discussion.

In the United States, the purpose of a question is to get an answer. In Japan, teachers pose questions to stimulate thought. A Japanese teacher considers a question to be a poor one if it elicits an immediate answer, for this indicates that students were not challenged to think. One good question can keep a whole class going for a long time; a bad one produces little more than a simple answer.

AFTER SCHOOL "TORTURE"

I like to call it "after school tutoring". Other teachers call it "help sessions". The students refer to "it" with several expressions that are not nice to repeat. I have been told a gazillion times by the athletes that they cannot come because they have to go to "Bodyplex" to build those muscles. Therefore I have tried to put a new spin on "it" by calling it "Brainplex". The kids look at me like it was a cute idea, but it is still a wolf in lambs clothing and they will not be fooled. They approach "it" like entering a dungeon during the Spanish Inquisition! I see "it" as a golden opportunity for free professional help. They see it as <u>more</u> of what they do not already like. I see it as my time to provide more individual attention and they see it as a time when they can not hide their inadequacies among a classroom of other students. I see it as 45 minutes of individualized instruction. They see it as 45 minutes of academic misery.

With this is mind, how does a teacher create a "before" or "after" tutoring program that is "student" friendly, yet effective? I do not have any real answers because this remains a problem for me, but it is very important for us to try to create a welcoming tutoring atmosphere so I will share several tactics that help. The first thing I try to do is make sure that my body language and words express the fact that I am glad that they showed up. Sometimes this is hard for me because I usually have a million things to do and if no one shows up for tutoring it gives me time to get them done. It is very important that I am welcoming. The second thing that I think is very important is that nothing negative is said. If a student tells me they are going to be there at 7:15 and they show up at 7:30, I just smile big and tell them how glad I am that they could make it. I also give everyone who shows up for tutoring for at least 20 minutes a "shazaam". I keep a clipboard in my room and students sign in and out. This gives me a log which comes in handy during parent conferences.

Once they are in the door, it is very important to make them feel that any question is safe. Sometimes I get very frustrated when kids show up for help and do not know what questions they need to ask. Nevertheless, this is the time to be patient and caring. If they do not know enough to ask a question, that is definitely a signal that they are in the right place. Often students show up with a chip on their shoulder because their "mama made them come" and they deliberately come across as cool as a cucumber. I usually try the light hearted approach with a comment like "as long as you are here, we might as well make mama proud. "This is the time to be silly and do anything you can to help the students learn the material. Don't fuss if you have to really remediate and don't say anything to put the students down. Use personal examples if you can and take this time to be more warm and fuzzy.

My three biggest challenges, once I get the students to come to tutoring, involve the number of students seeking help, no immediate gratification, and timing. When too many students show up for help they do not get the individualized attention that they need. I have really struggled with this problem, especially when I teach several subjects. I have had mornings where I have 40 minutes to tutor and students show up who need help in three different subjects, ranging from Algebra I to Calculus. Talk about an impossible situation. This is when I go into "community" mode. I break the students into subject groups and I ask each group to pick a problem that someone in the group needs to see worked and work on it until I can get to them. I then go to each group one at a time to help them with the problem that they picked. If a group has two or three students in it, I often find that they explain it to each other and do not even need my help. They continue working problems selected by the group until they get stuck and I can get to them. If there is only one student in a group, they usually just struggle with the problem until I can get to them. If a group has no specific questions about problems, I simply give them a couple to work until I can get back to them.

My second challenge is when a student comes in for help and still does not do well on tests and quizzes. This is when I pull out my mercy card. If a student has shown up for several tutoring sessions and still fails the test, I allow them to come in for one or two more sessions and then retake the test and try to bring their grade up to a 70. I want them to know that I am more interested in what they are learning than their grade. If they are willing to come in for more help to clear up misconceptions, I am willing to give them another chance to pass the test. Students who try hard and do not get immediate results need extra encouragement.

My third challenge is my sudden popularity the day before a test. So many students wait until the last minute to receive help that I always have a crowd the day before a test and once again, I have too many to give out much individualized attention. To help solve this problem, I set up special tutoring sessions for specific classes. I offer tutoring for all of my classes every Tuesday and Thursday morning and afternoon. If calculus has a test on Friday, I will open a special session up on Monday afternoon just for that class. This does not totally solve the problem, but it helps.

In general, I think that it is very important that every teacher be available to help students outside regular class time. Making yourself available is one of the best ways to show the students that you really care.

CLASSROOM WHINING

To whine or not to whine; that is the question. I am a great believer in classroom whining. I think it is good for classroom morale, releasing stress, and perceived teacher empathy. I shared my opinion with another teacher once and she put me in my place quickly stating that whining is not Biblical. She stated several Bible references that clearly supported her opinion and I could not argue with her. Nevertheless, David sure did it a lot in Psalms and he was "a man after God's own heart". Therefore, I am maintaining my opinion on "whining" as a valuable classroom tool.

The first test of the year in one of my honors classes is usually the worst grade for a lot of my students. They are still trying to get used to me as a teacher and even though I try to warn them, they rarely spend enough time preparing for the test. Many of them have never had to "study" for a math test until they get me, and they are dealing with a little bit of "culture shock." Knowing that the test grades are not what the students had hoped for, on the day after the test I do my best to diffuse a "sad" situation. As they enter the door, I am wearing a large brimmed, black hat with a black net veil that comes to my shoulders. This is an immediate clue that something is up. I then have the students get a note card out of their boxes and have them answer four questions on the card.

1   Did you come in for extra help before or after school as soon as you had difficulty understanding something?

2   Did you pay attention in class and ask questions when something was not clear?

3   Did you seek help from your team or just let them do the work and you went along for the ride?

4   Did you do enough study problems, concentrating on what you did not fully understand?

I then invite them to whine on the back of the card about anything related to the test. I make sure that they know that I am going to read them so they will not get too carried away. I then set my timer for two minutes and have them whine in writing. I then have them turn in the cards. I only do this after the first test, because they quickly get the point. I save these cards for any future parent conferences.

When the cards are taken up, I pass out the test and listen to the chatter and watch the tears form in some of the girls' eyes. The boys usually just pout. I then give them my yearly speech on this being the first test and how they will have plenty more test grades to bring up their average. I call out the correct answers, give them an opportunity to see me if I have incorrectly graded their papers, and then work the three most

missed problems in class. The room is heavy with concern and disap-
pointment. It is time for some stress release. One of the problems on
the test required the students to use the formula for finding the area of
a triangle. We had not reviewed the formula this year. After I was finished working the problem, I asked them to pick a partner. I then got
out my stopwatch and told them they would have thirty seconds to
orally whine. I then suggested some whine topics such as how could a
teacher expect us to know a formula that we have not used this year. I
then started the stopwatch and the room buzzed with whining. I heard
some actual laughter and lots of complaining, but when the thirty seconds was up the angst was diffused. I later explained to them that they
learned how to find the area of a triangle in third grade and that there
were just certain things that I expected them to know because they are
juniors in an honors class.

I then told them to correct their test for homework and started a new
topic. I answered more questions on the test the next day for about 15
minutes and then took the tests back up. If they have any more questions they should see me after school. There is nothing more boring
than spending a whole test period going over a test. That is just something else to whine about.

I really believe that thirty seconds spent whining here and there is
valuable to get the students back on the track or give them an opportunity to vent when the going gets tough. It is also great after a long holiday!

PROPS

If you have not figured it out already, I believe that good instruction
has a lot to do with good entertainment and every good entertainer
needs their props. Elementary teachers use props all of the time, but
once again, as the students get older, we tend to get more "serious" and
the main props become the textbook, the worksheet, and the board. I
have several props that I have gathered over the years that have make
my instruction more effective. They are tucked away in boxes and drawers or hanging on a coat rack that I keep near my desk. They have been
collected over the years from every source imaginable. I have a reputation for using costumes so people bring me costumes of every descrip-

tion and I find a use for them. When my grandchildren clean out their toy boxes I find a lot of neat stuff. You cannot imagine how much you can do with a rubber roach, a stuffed python, or a slide whistle. The trick is to look at other people's trash as a classroom treasure and figure out how it will work for you. Sometimes I save stuff just because of its potential and figure out later what to do with it. Following are a few examples of some of the props that I use to beef up my instruction.

***I have a "magic cape". It is made of shinny material with an obnoxious purple swirl on the outside and gold lining on the inside. It has a hood. A parent made it for me many years ago before Harry Potter was even a twinkle in J. K. Rowling's eye. It is wonderful and I love to put it on. I save it for very special occasions when I have performed magic on a math problem and made something disappear. It simplifies the problem and helps them remember the concept!

***I have a "vampire cape". It is made of shinny material that is black on the outside and red on the inside. It was once part of a Halloween costume. It is very evil looking and I look great in it. When students try to cancel terms in a division problem or forget how to square a binomial, I have to get out my evil cape to remind them what an evil thing they are doing. Mathematically, these are two common errors that must be stopped before they can spread and destroy life as we know it on the planet. They are really just two common errors that cause students to lose a lot of points on their tests throughout their mathematical careers, but they pay attention better when I put it in exaggerated, world threatening terms. Just the act of my walking around the room and donning the cape is enough to strike fear in their hearts. They know that they have done something "majorly" wrong! On rare occasions I use it for discipline issues when an individual or class have really made an egregious error.

***I have Kaa, the stuffed python from the Jungle Book stories. He hangs beautifully near my Promethian Board and easily slithers around my neck when I am trying to get my kids to resist mathematical temptation. There are a few things in mathematical equations that are so tempting to do because they look correct, but they are not correct. When we get to one of these in a problem, I quickly put on Kaa, and the students identify where the temptation lies.

***I have a purple plastic roach. He sits in a drawer and comes out when I do limits in calculus. He is perfect on the board to demonstrate how a limit approaches from the left and the right. I have the students go to the board and use the roach to show me they understand what the concept means.

***I have a terrifying rubber dragon. He hangs on the front of my podium by the tail. He is the object of our ire and represents the motivational theme for the year for AP Calculus. He is the evil testing serpent. He is tricky and slimy, but we are being trained to slay the dragon and we will succeed!

***I have a big plastic blow up trophy. It hangs from my coat rack and on the front in big letters it says "champ". When a student does something especially great in any category, they get to hold the trophy for the rest of the period. I was so proud of one student for her great improvement on a test that I let her carry it around all day. She had worked very hard for her grade and loved the fact that I was making such a big deal over it.

***I have "cricket clickers" in the plastic boxes under the students' desks. I also have small plastic maracas. These are great if you are drilling the class on true false questions or any type of question that only has two answers. If the answer is true, the students click the cricket, if it is false, they shake the maraca. I train them to do it simultaneously so they just won't wait until they see what the rest of the class is doing. These noise makers are also great when there is a particular type of problem that I want the students to spot. They know to start clicking if they find that certain type.

***I have a lot of costumes. I keep these at home and when I am revealing the simplicity of the derivative I dress up as Isaac Newton. Teaching logarithims requires a visit from John Napier and al-Khwarizmi wanders in and out as we talk about the development of algebra. When I try to explain why boys are believed to "do" better in math than girls, we have a visit from Hypatia. There are several other characters I "do" throughout the year. On these days I have no trouble holding their attention!

***I have a roller coaster. OK, so it not quite a roller coaster, but it is pipe insulation cut in half long ways and duct taped together to form a trough about 48 feet long. We use it in calculus to explore position, velocity, and acceleration. We work in teams and see how far a marble can go by adjusting slopes, creating loops, and working on concavity.

I have lots more and continue to collect more as I teach. They are stored in every nook and cranny in my classroom and provide much excitement in my classroom.

THE RED BALL

One of my favorite props is a soft vinyl red ball. I think that it is very important to keep fun in the classroom and there is nothing more fun than a red ball. We all had fun in kindergarten, and as we grew older the fun just kind of got sucked out of education. By the time students reach high school they have to find their fun in friends and extra-curricular activities. They rarely find it in the classroom. When you teach some of the Advanced Placement courses, you don't have time for fun because there is so much material to cover and the test is so hard and unpredictable that every minute is crucial. Therefore, I often find myself in an ethical dilemma. To have fun or not to have fun, that is the question! In my opinion the answer is to have fun while working hard. In AP Calculus we had learned all of the basic derivative rules. The derivative rules are a little like having to know the alphabet in order to be able to read, so they are critical. I wanted to drill the students on them and needed a fast way to do it. Usually, as I throw the ball, I just call the rules out, but as my brain cells mutate into mush, I am finding that harder and harder to do in a swift manner. Therefore, I had each student create a set of derivative rule flashcards which we pooled and mixed up. The front of the cards has the original function and the back of the card has the derivative rule. This gives me a stack of about 120 cards that I rotate through. I then have the students stand in a "u"-shape around the room. If it is a nice day, we go outside. They throw the red ball back and forth and whoever gets the ball next, has to answer the question. At first we are very forgiving, but as we do this about once a week, if they miss it or hesitate too long, they have to sit down. The final winner gets candy. After they get good at the derivatives, I do it once a month to keep the rules fresh. Sometimes if my bursitis is kicking in I let them throw the ball, if not, I throw the ball. It is important to make sure that it gets thrown to everyone equally so if I see that they are not doing that when they are throwing, I make them go around the circle in order. The variations are infinite. I use this with my trig class when we are learning the basic functions and identities. This activity could be great in every grade and subject.

KEEPERS

One of the most valuable things, academically speaking, that a teacher can do for a student, is to show him/her how to separate the essential from the "nice to know", given the massive amount of information that is delivered to them each year in any given subject. This skill, begun at a young age, will help the student be a much better test taker. I do not get the students until their junior or senior year, yet I find that very few of them have been taught or developed this skill. Therefore, I start them out at the beginning of the year as if they have had no training at all. Initially, I point out the essential information to them. I call these important pieces of information "keepers". Even students who do not take notes, soon begin to copy material down if I call it a keeper. Nevertheless, I learned a long time ago that I cannot force every student to buy into my organizational methods. I have had some students that refuse to do keepers and I certainly don't make them, but they usually end up wishing they had at some point.

After they have written the keeper down in their daily notes and label it with a "k", I ask them, as part of their homework assignment for the day to copy their keeper into a bound composition notebook that is used only for keepers. At the end of each semester, they have a durable notebook full of mathematical essentials that I allow them to use on their final exam. The only exception to this is Advanced Placement Calculus. I encourage them to keep a "keeper book", but I do not allow them to use them on exams. It is about at this point that those who chose not to do keepers are wishing that they had! Three days before the final, I have students turn in their composition notebooks and I glance through them to make sure that there is nothing in there that is not allowed. I do not allow them to Xerox rules and put them in the composition books. Everything must be hand written. On the day of the final, I have their composition books laid out on the desks and those who did not have them have their names on a sticky note so they will know where to sit. (I always assign seats during a final to help the students stay honest.) I record in my grade book if a student turned in their keepers. A second benefit to the keepers is that those who have kept a good "keeper book" qualify for a small curve on the final if I find it necessary to curve it.

Probably the most important benefit is that the student has something to refer to in the future. My math department has agreed that we should all have the students do keepers and so the composition book begins in Algebra I and continues through Calculus. It is quite a valuable tool to take to college. In fact, I cannot count the number of students who have contacted me from college asking me if I could Xerox the Calculus keepers for them, because they got rid of their book, thinking they would not need them. I have also had many a graduate come back and tell me how they were able to help tutor friends because they had their keepers.

As the year goes on and they get used to picking out what is important, I begin to ask them to pick out what they think would make a good keeper. They tend to pick too many, because they want them in the composition books for the finals. They also want to put worked out examples in their books and get a little irritated at me when I won't let them. I encourage them to use colored highlighters in their regular notebooks to highlight keepers in yellow and good "study" examples in green. I work with them all year in listening for teacher clues and marking them in their notebooks. If I say that a topic is going to be on the test, they should put a red flag by it. If I say that something is important they should put a red flag by it. I am trying to train them to learn to get a "feel" for what a teacher thinks is important, so that when they get to college they will be able to "read" their professors. I do not think that you can start developing this skill too soon.

GARY TIFTON

Gary Tifton came back today. Gary graduated two years ago. Everyone loved Gary. He was the proverbial class clown and he was so cute and kind that even if he misbehaved, you could not stay mad at him long. It was very hard to discipline him with a straight face. He was not very serious about his grades either. Today he came back to visit and made a special point to come by and let me know how much he appreciated my having him do "Keepers". He was a business major and had taken one math class. He had an opportunity to take a test that would allow him to get credit for more math classes and he decided to take it. The night before the test he sat down, which was unusual in itself, and studied the keepers for about an hour. Gary had never been ignorant, just somewhat unmotivated and now that his motivation kicked in, he could refresh on a lot of material in a little bit of time. He passed the test with flying colors and was able to exempt and get credit for his next six math courses! I was so excited for him and so pleased that he came back to tell me how valuable his keepers had been, that I asked him to stay a few minutes and share his testimony with my next class, which he gladly did. High school students usually believe what college students say and any "speeches" that I can get in from college students are like gold.

SOME THINGS STICK BETTER THAN OTHERS

That is the subject line of an e-mail that I received from a former student. He had graduated from Georgia Tech and was presently working as a chemical engineer and working on a graduate degree. His email follows:

> Mrs. Sutton,
> I am currently sitting in a hotel room in Texas. I am working and trying to do some homework for grad school. I had a partial derivative of a second order polynomial over a first order polynomial. I am sure there was an easier way to solve it, but the only thing I could think of is Hi Dee Ho minus Ho dee Hi divided by Ho squared. It seems to be the right answer. I have taken no fewer than seven undergrad and

graduate level math classes since your class and it seems your method is what stuck. I also used a keeper while solving a problem for work recently.

Jim

I love it when I get emails from former students that let me know that they are still using some of the tricks I taught them! Using silly tricks and reinforcing the rules with keepers benefits the students for years to come.

SKILLS, NO FRILLS

The old adage "use it or lose it" not only applies to muscles and the mind, it also applies to most of what we learn. Most disciplines require the development of pre-requisite skills that are necessary building blocks for future success. Mathematics, science, grammar, foreign language, and music are three very obvious examples. "New" material almost always depends on the use of "old" material. Yet, as teachers, we just assume that once the students have covered skills two or three times over the course of their educational career, they should just "remember them. " This is not true for us as adults and it is not true for them. Students take in so much material in the course of a year that they cannot possibly be expected to remember all of it. It is the teacher's job to highlight the "skills" that they need to focus on that will be necessary for future success. This is a little bit like helping them create "Cliff Notes" for what is being taught. We have already discussed this concept of "keepers", but now I want to show you how to reinforce them.

Once keepers have been identified, it is wise to keep bringing these important concepts back up throughout the year. As a math teacher, these "keepers" are critical to me and I start class with three "skills" every day. I keep a laminated sheet under each students' desk that has the skills on them. On the next page is a part of one of these skill sheets. One set will be good for ten school days as I print on the front and back of the paper before I laminate it. Each sheet has six columns and two general problems for all classes, some of which come straight off of SAT practice sheets. They also have one specific problem for each class.

	One	Two	Three	Four
ALL BUT AP	An airplane flew for 8 hrs. at a speed of x miles per hour (mph), and for 7 more hrs. at 325 mph. If the average speed for the entire flight was 350 mph, what is x? How many Roman numerals are needed to write the year 1874?	Simplify $3a + 4b - (-6a - 3b)$ $4,500 was invested for one year. It earned $495. What was its simple interest rate?	What is the sum of the polynomials $3a^2b + 2a^2b^2$ and $-ab^2 + a^2b^2$? What is the smallest common multiple of 2 and 14?	How many ounces are in a pound? What's the smallest integer which has 3 different consecutive prime divisors?
CAL	Power rule	$\frac{dy}{dx}((2x^2 + 3)^2$	$x^2 \cdot x^3$	Product Rule

The students have a skills section in their notebook and when they come into the classroom, as soon as the bell rings, they begin working on these three problems. Music is on and it is a relaxed environment as they work. They may not consult each other, but they can use their notes, textbooks, and sometimes their calculators. (If I place an "NC" by the skill, they know they cannot use their calculator on that particular skill.) While I am checking attendance, homework, and dealing with make-up work, the students are working on their skills. So not only are skills good for the students, they are a great management tool to get the students on task while I do some necessary housekeeping.

When my chores are done, I ask them to bring their homework by and let me check it. When that is done, I stop the music and I am ready to go over skills. I pull out a chip and call on that person. They give me the answer or tell me that they do not know how to work the skill. If they give me the correct answer, I compliment them, give them a "shaz-aam" and ask if anyone needs me to explain that skill. If I need to explain it, I do so right then. If the student cannot work the problem, I guide them through it, using baby questioning techniques. I go through all of the skills in this manner. Since they are simple concepts it rarely takes me more than three minutes.

My goal here is to use that first few minutes of class wisely as I review my students on information that I do not want them to forget.

YOU CAN'T STUDY FOR A MATH TEST
(Study Problems)

As a young teacher, I never knew how to handle the student who insisted that they had studied hard for a test and yet they failed it. I was also confronted with students telling me that they could not study for a math test or that they did not know how. I do not know how long it was into my teaching career but I finally came up with a solution to both of those problems and it has worked beautifully for years. I am not sure how this could be adapted to other subjects, but with a little creativity, I am sure that it could. (For instance if you were giving a test on spelling, vocabulary, states and capitals, or parts of the body, etc. , you could have how many times they practiced writing these items count as study problems.)

I now give a handout to my students at the first of the year that defines study problems and we discuss how they are beneficial. On the first test, about half of the class will have study problems, but by the end of the first semester, more have "seen the light" and almost all of my students are doing them. I always have one or two die-hards that refuse to do them, but about the time they hit AP Calculus, I am able to convince them of their value. Here is what I give the students to put in their notebooks concerning study problems:

STUDY PROBLEMS:

*Study problems are the problems that you do to study for a test.

*You decide how many to do, based on how much you need to study. Everyone should do some.

*You decide which ones to do. It is not a good use of your time to pick the easy ones. Try one of each type and do more of the types that you are the least comfortable with.

*You should pick problems in your notes or homework or textbook examples that you already have the correct answers to so that you will know if you missed them. It is a waste of your time to work problems that you cannot check.

*Copy each problem and show all work. If you missed it, put a red "x" on it and try it again.

*If there is something to be memorized, you may write it five times and count it as one study problem.

*Study problems are due at the beginning of the period on the test day.

*You should start study problems about the week before the test so that if you are having trouble with a particular type of problem you will have time to come in outside of class for help.

*The night before the problems are due you should go ahead and prepare them to be turned in so that class time is not wasted on test day. Count them and then fold them like a "hotdog. " On the outside place your name and the number of study problems you did and place them in the box on my desk when you walk in the door, then get ready for your test.

Most of the students think study problems are a waste of time until we talk about homeowners insurance. I have been paying homeowners insurance since I was 23. I cannot begin to tell you how much I have paid over the years but if I had to guess, it would be at least $12,000 and that is a conservative estimate. I have never filed one claim but I keep paying it. Most of them are sitting there thinking what they could do with $12,000 and it usually involves a car! I then explain to them that I will never stop paying homeowners insurance because if I do need it, I want it to be there. Study problems are the same thing; they are insurance. If you do well on the test, maybe you did not need to do them, but who knows if you did well because you did them! If you make a 99 or a 100 on the test, you get no points so what is the point? My answer to that is INSURANCE! In my experience, the one time that you do not do them will be the one time that you wish that you had. I think it is some kind of law of nature!

On test day, as the students begin the test, I record the number of study problems they did in a column in the grade book. If I do not like the quality of their work, I put a negative below the number. I then throw the study problems away. If a student scores a 90-98 on the test, I will give them one bonus point on the test for doing their study problems. If they score 80-89, I will give them two bonus points. If they score 70-79, I will give them three points. There is not an assigned number of study problems that they have to do so all of this is very subjective. If they only do five study problems and make a 70, I may only give them one point and if they made a 95, I may give them no bonus points.

The real value of study problems, however, is when a student fails a test. If a student fails the test, I have no firm rule as to what I am willing to do to help them. I assign bonus points on an individual basis based on how hard I believe they have worked and the quality and quantity of their study problems. If a student makes a 60 on the test and they have come in for extra help and have lots of good quality study problems, I will give them a 68. They still fail the test, but it will be much easier to bring their average up. If there were special circumstances, I may even give them a 70. If a student makes a 43 on a test and they have come in for help and have good study problems, I will give them a 60 if they promise to continue to come in for help. If a student fails a test and they never sought help and did not turn in study problems, I will not raise the grade. It is a tough lesson for them, but most of them do not let it happen again.

Offering the opportunity to do study problems has made my life much easier as a teacher. Rarely, I will give a test and announce that study problems will not be turned in and will not get them extra points. The wise students do them anyway. There are truly some students who do study hard and just do not do well on tests and study problems allow them to prove that they had prepared. On the other end of the spectrum, students who insist that they studied cannot prove it to me if they cannot produce study problems. Study problems also help when parents call asking if there is not some extra credit their child can do to bring their grade up. I let the parent know that the student had multiple opportunities to get extra points and they chose not to. By the end of the year, almost all students are doing study problems. Not only are they doing better on the tests, but they are learning a valuable skill for college.

STUDY PROBLEM SNEAK

In AP Calculus today Sam, was madly working on study problems when he should have been getting ready for the test. I thought that he was finishing up on one but when he only turned one in I realized that he was just trying to get one turned in so he could say that he had done some study problems. I find this highly irritating because on the last test, I had several people fail, but those who did study problems received at least a passing grade. He did not want to spend his own personal time doing any at home, but he wanted to get that one in so he could have some "insurance". Too bad-so sad. . don't mess with the master. One study problem done in class won't get you anywhere. Sam made a 73 and he kept his 73.

FRONT AND CENTER

Students have been "going to the board" as long as there have been boards. This instructional strategy was probably one of the first after lecture and recitation, and has brought terror to the hearts of many an unprepared or shy student. Most students do not like going to the board and some are absolutely terrified by the prospect. Some students love it and would spend all of their time up there if you would let them. I strongly believe that all students need to be trained and encouraged to stand up in front of a group and talk. It is a valuable life skill and it helps them become more self confident. Going to the board is a great way to help build their confidence. Our task as teachers is to make this strategy less fearful and an effective instructional tool which benefits all the students. Once again, I am going to offer some guidelines and I encourage you to develop your own.

***The most important consideration here is to make board time safe. Do not let the other students heckle or make fun of the person or the work that they are putting on the board. Nip negative comments early in the year and let it be known that ridiculing someone at the board is a serious offense.

***Never let a student off the hook, but never leave them hanging. If a student goes to the board and says they do not know how to work a problem or what an answer is, guide them through the work with baby questions. Don't allow them to just not do it.

***Praise students at the board for their handwriting, oral presentation, and enthusiasm for their material. Find something positive about their board time. Encourage all of the students to be animated when they get to the board and tell them you expect them to present in a manner that is not boring.

***Be sure that the board work is spread around so that every student has the opportunity whether they want it or not. Use the chips to draw names to be sure that you are not calling on certain people. If you are drawing chips over several days and cannot remember who has been sent to the board; tell the students to say "no thank you" if they have already been called on that week.

***Use student board work as a small part of your instructional plan. Like everything else if this is over used it will become drudgery.

***Develop activities that incorporate board work with cooperative learning. Have students in each team number from one to four. Then throw out a problem or question and let the team discuss how to arrive at the answer at their desks. Give the teams the appropriate amount of time to come up with an agreed upon answer and then call out a team number and a number one through four. (Not only do I have chips with each child's name on them, I also have one container with numbered chips in it so I can stay impartial on team and position numbers.) If you call out team two, number three, that student goes to the board and works the problem or explains the answer depending on what type of question it is. If the student at the board gets the problem correct and does a good job presenting, the entire team gets a bonus point. Every team gets a point if they got it correct. If you have five teams in a class you should have at least five problems or questions. I always put my number chips back in after I call them out so a team or player may go more than once. It becomes a combination of skill and luck and the students like it. At the end of the designated number of problems, the winning teams get magnets or candy or both!

ASSESSMENT 101

I have really agonized over whether assessment goes in instruction or classroom management. Good assessment is an integral part of instruction, but at the same time if it is to be truly "good" it must be managed properly. Therefore I am going to put it in both. We will talk about assessment and its role in instruction in this section and save the logistics for the management section. In a perfect world there would be very little need for assessment. I have always thought that when I get to teacher heaven, learning will be so much fun for everyone that all are motivated and there will be no tests! Can you imagine the joy of teaching little sponges who just soak up the material with wonder in their eyes?

Testing would not be necessary! That is what my heaven looks like. For us mere mortals, however, we need to learn to use assessment as a teaching tool, not as a means of torture or revenge.

There are many forms of assessment and it is important to explore the different types and have a large array of possibilities in our tool kit. I looked up the word assessment in the dictionary to make sure that my perception fit the definition and at first I was very disappointed. Assessment is defined as "a way or schedule of assessing". How come my English teachers would never let me use the word I was defining in the definition when Webster can get away with it? I then moved to the word assess and all of the definitions deal with assigning a value to something for a purpose such as taxes or damages. It makes you think. When we assess, are we assigning a value to what the student has learned, or are we assigning a value to our ability to create an instrument that will fairly evaluate what they have learned? I do not want to wax philosophical here, because that is out of my league, but I strongly believe that we need to realize that it is hard to evaluate what students have learned by one or two instruments. If I am in the habit of just delivering material and then giving a test, I cannot fairly measure what has been learned by many of the students. I need more information. Grant Wiggins states that "research proves classroom feedback and instruction outweigh home environment in the learning process. " He is also very frank in stating that we are guilty of measuring what is easy to measure. Assessment is a lot more complicated than giving a test.

When I started teaching, assessment was pretty much relegated to the quiz and test. Of course we graded homework, sometimes notebooks, and if we were feeling brave we assigned projects. In today's teaching jargon, assessment is divided into two categories, formative and summative and encompasses a larger scope of possibilities. Simply put, formative assessment is anything you do during the unit to check and see how much learning is taking place. Summative assessment occurs at the end of the unit. Both are evaluations of student progress.

FORMATIVE ASSESSMENT

There are so many possibilities for formative assessment that there is no way to list them all, especially since I do not know all of them to list. Every teacher has developed evaluation tools that do not even re-motely resemble a test or a quiz that they use during the presentation of a lesson. Every formative assessment does not have to be connected to a grade. Hopefully, you are doing more formative assessment than you realize. This early assessment is important because not only does it let you know how the students are doing, it lets them know how they are doing. I have had students in the past that are confident they under-stand the material until they are asked to show me how much they know and then they realize how much they don't know. It is also important because it allows you to "readjust your sails" as you teach a unit. It is very rare that we can proceed exactly as we plan through a lesson if we truly want the students to succeed. We need to make timing and level adjustments as we go, and formative assessments give us direction. Below are the four formative assessments that I use the most. I am sure that you can add many to the list and if you collaborate with other teach-ers in your subject and grade level you will be able to make that list longer. Google "formative assessment" and you will come up with a gazillion more. Remember, anything that helps you gauge the progress of your students prior to the "big" test or project is formative assess-ment.

QUIZLETS. The formative assessment that I use the most is the qui-zlet. It all started with a weird little cow that is animated and plays music while it does the chicken dance. I found him in a drugstore a long time ago and it was love at first sight. He was just the thing I needed to spice up my habit of giving my classes one question "pop tests". I had been doing the pop test thing for a couple of years and found it kept the class on their toes, but it was more threatening than fun until I named that cow QUIZMOO. Once the cow became Quizmoo, the questions became quizlets, which sounds a lot less threatening than pop test. Any-time during the period that I wanted to see how the class was doing, I would push Quizmoo's button, he would dance, and the class would have until he stopped dancing to get ready for their quizlet. Quizmoo acted like a timer and everyone had to be ready by the time he was through with the dance. To get ready they clear off their desk except for a quizlet board (I will explain these in the management section), a writing instrument, and a notecard from the plastic box under their desks. I would then orally deliver or write on the Promethian board one brief factual question that was important to the lesson. I would give them 30 seconds to a minute depending on the difficulty of the question. They would then pass in their answers and I would go over the problem. When the quizlet was over, I put the stack of note cards on my desk. On my planning period, or at the end of the day, I went through the cards. If a lot of students miss the questions, I need to adjust. If everyone gets it right, I may need to speed up. I throw away the cards that are correct and keep the cards that are wrong. I put the wrong cards in a sorter by period and once a week, I record them in the grading system. Each student is given a quiz grade of 100 at the beginning of the semester. Each time they miss a quizlet, I take two points off of the 100. Once the cards are recorded, I file them in a box alphabetically and if I need to pull them out to verify a grade or use them at a parent conference I can. Throughout the semester, I can look at a student's quizlet grade and see who I need to keep a better eye on to provide more help. I love quizlets. They keep the students more engaged. I usually give at least one a class period and sometimes I give more than one. If I see that a class is having trouble concentrating, it is a great way to shake them up and get them awake. It is important to only count and record 50 quizlets a semester so I pick one of my OCD kids in every class to keep track of how many quizlets we have had that will count. I never tell them ahead of time whether a quizlet will count for a grade or just for practice.

SHOW ME! I have the students clear off their desks except for their quizlet board and a dry erase marker and a paper towel. I then ask a question and the students write their answer on their board. When I believe a reasonable time has been given, I say "show me. " The students then hold their boards up in the air facing me and I look at the answers. With a quick sweep of the room, I can see how they are doing. When you first introduce this activity be sure that you remind the class that you will not tolerate snickers, comments, or sarcastic body language directed to other students. If it occurs, come down hard.

TICKET TO RIDE. (This idea came from Mr. Tim Yoder, a wonderful middle school teacher who I admire and salute!) Line the students up, facing you, and give each of them a ticket. Start at the beginning of the line and ask a question related to the unit. If the first student is correct, ask the second another question and keep moving down the line. If a student misses, they have to give up their ticket and the same question in asked until it is answered correctly. The first time a student misses, they give up their ticket, the second time they have to sit down. Sometimes I deliberately pick hard and easy questions for certain students to challenge them or give them a chance to stand longer. This cannot be obvious! Keep asking questions until you have a winner. The winner has the ticket to ride which means they have 10 "free ride minutes" in class. They may sleep, work on homework for another class, or doodle, as long as they do not disrupt the class or another student. Free time is so rare this is a real treat.

SMILEY SIGNALS. I do this particular "check up" in two ways depending on the situation. When I want a feel for the level of understanding in the classroom, I either say "smiley cards" or "smiley wall". If I say "smiley cards", the students get one of the three cards from their box that fits their situation. I have three, three by five note cards in each box with a smiley face in the middle of each. One is green, with a happy face, one is red, with a frowny face, and one is yellow, with a mouth that is just a straight line. If the student feels good about the material I am teaching, they hold up the green card. If they are totally lost, they hold up the red card. If they just a little lost they hold up the yellow card. Once again the students must feel safe in your classroom if they are going to be honest. I survey the room and adjust if needed. If I say "smiley wall", the students get out of their seats and move to the corners that I have marked, each one with the happy, sad, or straight mouth. This gets them out of their seats for a minute, and gives me the information that I need. Sometimes I will then triple up the students, picking one from each smiley face group to form a temporary team. They grab their stuff and move back into seats in their new configuration. I then give them time to discuss and practice the concept in that group. I find that the student that was confident may be able to explain it better than I. If I find that a student is just going to the same corner with their peers or is picking too high or too low for the wrong reasons, a little private chat usually corrects their choices.

SUMMATIVE ASSESSMENT

In this section on instruction we will focus on designing summative assessments. Administering, grading, and returning them will be saved for classroom management. In my first years of teaching, I always planned my units and then made out my tests. My final assessments were always in the form of written tests and I was perfectly happy. I threw in a quiz once in a while which was basically a mini-test that was shorter and required less critical thinking. With a homework grade, a notebook grade, and an occasional project thrown in, I was confident that I was properly assessing my students. As I attended workshops and read educational literature over the years I realized assessment encompassed more than a test or a quiz and should be varied to meet the needs of the different modalities in students. I began evaluating what students had learned with small projects that were assigned instead of a test and oral presentations that allowed the students to become more comfortable speaking to a group. I started creating some take-home tests and occasionally allowed the students to take tests in teams. I will discuss these more fully a little later, but there are two important points that I want to discuss before I start. Point one was part of my paradigm shift caused by Grant Wiggins. Using his "backwards design" philosophy, I saw how valuable it could be to create the test before planning the lesson. I had always settled on my objectives, chosen my activities, started teaching and a week before the end of the unit, I would design the test. Once a lesson had been created, I would "tweek" it and improve it again and again throughout the years to the point that I could practically use the same test every year. Wiggins challenged me to rethink my lessons and I began settling on my objectives and then creating the assessment. As I began to do this, I found it harder to plan this way, because in the past I had just tested over exactly what I had taught, not necessarily on what I wanted to teach. This rearrangement of processing required me to fully think out what I wanted to accomplish and how would be the best way to go about it. I had to analyze my activities and instructional techniques to make sure they contributed to what I wanted to accomplish. In short, as Stephen Covey would say: "I was beginning with the end in mind" and it made all sorts of sense. I restructured my unit notebooks to accommodate my new way of planning. This does not mean to teach the test; it means to create the test and then plan the unit around it.

The second point that I would like to make is summarized in the statement by Wiggins when he said: "We measure what is easiest to measure. " Looking back over the years, I could see how many times I had chosen to teach mechanics instead of concepts, because it was easier to teach and easier to test. In a society where information is at our fingertips almost instantaneously, facts are just a duplication of what the computer can do for us. Application of that knowledge and critical thinking skills are what we should be focusing on. The problem arises because it is more time consuming to teach and much harder to create and grade assessments than just asking the students what they recall from a lesson. Once again, I had to seriously re-think my creation of assessments. Now when I start to plan a unit and my objectives are established, the first thing I do is decide what type of summative assessment I want to create for the unit. I use a standard written test most of the time but at some time during the year I try to use at least one of the following methods to provide some variety and become a more flexible assessor. Once again, a little research on your part will provide a myriad of summative assessments for you to choose from. Do not be limited by my short list.

TEST. Teaching upper level honors classes, I usually choose the written test because it is my job to prepare the students for college and that is what they see the most, especially in their core classes. After my objectives are in place, I start gathering as much already created material as I can find. I pull my old tests, tests that come with the book whether in supplemental form or on the internet, and anything else I can get my hands on. (Just a side note here; some assessments that come with the book are great, but I find they take up a lot of paper. At the same time it is important to take up enough paper that the questions do not run together. I have made the mistake in the past of trying to get too much on a page and that becomes a challenge to a lot of students.) I then pull questions at random making a list of what skills I have a question on and how many times. I like questions that embed the skills in higher order thinking but I believe it is also important to have some simple re-call questions. These simpler questions should be in the minority, but they should be there. Once I have gone through the collected "stuff", I check my list to make sure that every objective is evaluated on the test. If not, then I go back and create a question that will include it. I then look at all of the questions that I have chosen and try to get a feel for the length of the test. If I need more questions, I make up more and if I need to get rid of some I do, being sure to keep all of my objectives on the test and balanced. Once I am satisfied with the content and the length, I take the test myself to make sure that it is doable, to create a key, and see if I can discover any typos or bad questions. No matter how hard I try, I never can get it perfect the first time, but after I have given it to a class, I always make adjustments immediately, so I will not forget what needs to be fixed, added, or deleted. As I create the test, I try to use a combination of question types. Students need to be exposed to all types of questions. They especially need to experience multiple choice, because that is what they will get with standardized tests. They also need fill in the blank, problem solving, short answer, and true/false. It saddens me that so many teachers choose all multiple choice because it is so easy to put the score sheets in a grading machine. After the test is created, I use it to guide me in selecting my instructional techniques and activities. This is not teaching the test, it is teaching the objectives. My tests are designed so that students can use what I have taught them to answer the questions. I never let the students know ahead of time what the questions on the test are, and I make sure that they have to think. There is no way to teach the test without telling them the exact questions on the test and I refuse to do that. (I know I said that twice but I feel very strongly about that!)

QUIZ. Sometimes quizzes are formative and sometimes they are summative. If the quiz is short and only covers a portion of the unit material it is formative. Often times, however, I have very short units that do not warrant spending an entire class period assessing and I just give a quiz as the summative evaluation. These quizzes are usually around twenty minutes and contain a majority of recall questions with one or two "think" questions.

PROJECTS. A project turned in at the end of a unit, that replaces a test, is a form of summative assessment. I teach one particularly challenging unit on probability in one of my honors' classes. There are so many rules and so many different situations, even the good students get a glazed look on their faces. My objective is that they know when to use what rule, not that they memorize all of those rules. Therefore I assign a project. Fifty percent of the grade on the project comes from the creation of a mini-tri-fold board that contains all of the rules and a sample of when to use each. On the first day of the unit I pass out three pieces of card stock to each student and show them how to tape the three pieces together so that it will neatly fold into itself. I then give them the rubric for grading the project and we discuss the requirements and answer questions. Three days before the unit is complete, when I have covered all of the rules and I am mixing them up and reviewing, I pass out a set of twenty questions that will make up the other fifty percent of the project. The students are to answer the questions, showing any required work. They may not receive any help from any person, or computer, but they may use the tri-folds they have created. They sign an honor statement provided at the end of the twenty questions. These two elements make up the assessment.

ORAL PRESENTATIONS. Oral Presentations have some very important advantages but the biggest problem I have run into with them is that they are very time consuming, therefore I do not do them as much as I would like. Nevertheless, I think it is an important life skill for students to be able to make a presentation in front of a group of people. I would think that they would be easier to do in other disciplines besides mathematics, but I will not be outwitted by the rigor and structure of my discipline. I love math history and I have found that learning where all of those numbers come from helps the students view mathematics as a living developing thing and not a stagnant set of archaic rules. I have spent a lot of time studying math history and have created a set of 30 essay topics that fit into the curriculum throughout the year. When school starts, students draw a topic out of the proverbial hat and I tell them what unit their topic falls in. I cannot give them an exact date, but I will tell them a predicted month and let them know that they will always have one week's notice as to when their essay and presentation are due. I pass out the grading rubric, we go over it and I answer questions. The essays should be between 600 and 1000 words and the presentation should last from five to seven minutes. I also let them know that this grade will be recorded in the last grading period. I tell them that they will get a bad grade if they pick boring information on the topic or if they give a boring presentation. They are encouraged to be creative, dress in costume, and generally dig up as much "dirt" as they can on their topic. We want to be entertained! Most students like this type of activity. It terrifies some, however, and if I am aware that this is a real challenge to a student I offer to work with them to help them overcome their fear of speaking in public.

TAKE HOME TEST. Once in a while I will give a take home test. It saves a class period and takes the time pressure off of the students. When I design a take home test, I lower the percentage of recall questions and make sure that most of it requires higher level thinking skills. I usually give the students two nights to take it. The biggest drawback is honesty. No matter how hard you try there is no way to control cheating. I always have my students sign an honor code at the end, but some will still lie on that. I make sure that my students know what resources they may use and what will happen to them if I catch them using anything besides those resources. I also give them a brief lecture on integrity. Brief is the key word here because they have heard it all before, they just need to be reminded.

TEAM TEST. Once a year, I give a team test. The students never know when it will be and if they have never had me they don't expect one. Sometimes on the day before the test I tell them that tomorrow's test will be a team test but most of the time I do not. I am sure that they are expecting me to pair up a "smart" one with a "slow" one, but I let them know that partners will be picked totally at random. They may be with someone who knows more than them and they may not. I tell them when they enter the room for the test to turn in their study problems quickly but to stay standing until I can assign pairs. As soon as the bell rings I draw chips to pick teams. If I have an odd number of students I have one three man team. It is always fun for me to see how it turns out. A team may have two geniuses on it or two very slow students, but no changes are made. Two students who are like oil and water when it comes to getting along may be stuck together. This is a great lesson on being able to work with anybody. Once furniture is moved and everyone is sitting next to or facing their partner, I warn them that they must talk very quietly and that I will be monitoring them the entire period and they should have their eyes and ears on their own team. I also let them know that everybody will turn in their own paper, so if they do not agree with their partner, they do not have to both put the same answer. This choice is very important because each student will go away with an individual grade on the test, and I do not want any complaining that they had to choose a wrong answer because of their partner. I like this type of assessment because I enjoy watching the dynamics in the room as the students work together.

As you make your assessment choices, mix them up and be sure that you are fairly evaluating the student's "learning" of the concepts. Most of all make sure that you have taught the material. I will never forget a test that I took when I was in middle school in 1965. It was in a P. E. class and it was on how to keep score in bowling. Now at this point you have probably figured out that I am not gifted in the athletic arena, so I was always grateful when there was a written test because it gave me a chance to bring up my dismal grade from my physical performance. There was one question on the test that the teacher had never gone over. Everyone missed it and we told the teacher that she had never told us how to do whatever it was she wanted us to do. She said that she had taught it and not to argue. Being the sensitive type, I did not argue, but I was crushed and lost all of my respect for that teacher.

THE ALGEBRA TEST

(I wrote these two poems a few years apart after a class did poorly on a test. They were posted on the overhead when the students came in the next day. I never discussed the poems and their message. I just had them displayed when they came in with some appropriate funeral music.)

Today we are in mourning for our Algebra II test,
For the last two weeks my warnings were taken in jest.
It's not enough to copy notes and just stare,
You have got to really listen and act like you care!
You have to ask questions and work for understanding,
Albegra II is not easy and much more demanding!
Don't wait to study until the day before the test,
You must study daily to really do your best!!!!!!
~ Lizzy Sutton

THE TEST
Y'all really did do rotten
On yesterday's test
There's got to be a reason
You didn't do your best.
Could it be that you were sleeping
When something crucial was on the board?
Or were you the one studying for English
When a topic was explored?
Could you have been the daydreamer
When a point was made?
Or were you practicing your doodling
When the plans for a problem were laid?
Were you the one in the back of the room
Misbehaving whenever you can?
Making all sorts of sound affects

And missing an important span.
Were you one of the shy students
Who was scared to ask for assistance?
Who wanted to just be left alone
And keep the teacher at a distance.
Could it be that you didn't study
And just left your grade to fate?
Only you know what adjustments to make
Before it is too late!
~ Lizzy Sutton

LEVEL OF CONCERN
YOURS OR THEIRS?

An excellent, seasoned teacher came to me on Friday with tears in her eyes. She had been teaching sixth grade math for several years and is considered by all to be a master teacher. This year she has been moved to 7th grade and is teaching Pre-Algebra. She loves teaching Pre-Algebra and is very happy with those classes. She does have one high school class of Algebra I students who are a year behind. She was furious at them. She had spent a lot of time developing systems to use competition and other motivating methods for the classroom. She was teaching to build success and going out of her way to make these students feel successful. On Friday, they acted like they could care less about what she was trying to teach them. She was reviewing for a quiz that would be given immediately when the review was over. She had to stop repeatedly to take care of minor rule infractions like chewing gum. They were slouched in their seats and no one was responding to her questions. The students were simply not "engaged" and she was "enraged" at their "I could care less" attitudes. It permeated the classroom like a kid coming in from gym who doesn't have any deodorant! Since no one was listening anyway, she stopped the review and started the quiz. Some of the students did well, but there were too many failures.

Her frustration was not at the rule infractions, but at the apathy! She had worked herself to the bone, to be sure that this class was treated in a positive manner and they just did not seem to care. She was so mad on Friday that she couldn't talk about it without tears and threatened to go part time so she would never have to teach high school again! We did not have a long time to talk. I hugged her, listened to her, and encouraged her to wait until Monday to do anything drastic. She needed time to cool down!

On Monday, we met first period and I listened to her talk. As we both knew she would, she had her perspective back and the situation did not seem quite as dismal as it had on Friday. She had prayed about the class and a very timely sermon on Sunday morning had reminded her that she could only do her best; the rest was up to the kids and God. She really didn't need me to tell her how to "fix" the problem. She pretty much had figured it out herself. I did, however offer a few practical suggestions.

She was going to give the quiz back to them, go over it, and let those who did poorly, retake a similar quiz on Tuesday. I suggested that she not do this. I felt that the students needed to be held accountable for their lack of attention and that the quiz grades should stand. She was also going to talk to them again about their "apathy. " I suggested that she start over as if nothing happened and not mention the situation again. Students in lower level classes are so used to being given lectures on becoming "serious" students and being "disinterested" that lecturing them is like water off a duck's back. I also suggested that she not let them "get to her". Some of them probably enjoyed "pushing her buttons" hoping to get her upset. She was taking her job so seriously that she was taking their actions personally. If she had peeked into the rest of their day, she would have seen the same thing happening over and over. She realized that she could only do the best she could, and then it was out of her control. She needs to remind herself of this on a regular basis.

My suggestion to improve attentiveness was to raise the "level of concern" of the students. I recommended that she do this in two ways. First, I recommended that she use her fish bowl and chips. If a student was called on, they did not have the option of saying that they did not know the answer. They would be led to the answer by the teacher. The second thing I suggested was that she wake the class up with "quizlets" every few minutes until they started being involved more actively in the learning.

She was also concerned that they weren't getting what they needed as far as the curriculum went. After many years of teaching math, I have come to understand that they will not all "get it. " Despite what we tell them, I do not believe that they all "need it" to survive. Students in a lower level math class are not the ones going to Georgia Tech. They need to know the basics and how to use a calculator. Life will not be over for them if they can not successfully factor a trinomial! Those in this group who go to college will usually only take one or two core math classes. They will struggle through these, get credit and go on to what is important to them in life. Be sure that you understand what I am saying here. I did not tell her to expect less or "dumb down", I told her not to be upset if they did not accomplish as much as the other classes. She might need to go a little slower and practice a little more, but she needs to keep her expectations high. If a topic is important, she should continue to bring it up throughout the year. If she does not finish the entire curriculum, they will survive.

HOW LOW CAN THEY GO?

Anytime a student makes below a 60 on a major test and they have done adequate study problems, I will change their grade to a 60 in my grade book if they will come in before or after school for help in correcting the test. So many students give up when their averages get too low! It is very important to me that my students always feel that they have the hope of success, even if they are not experiencing it at the moment. Sometimes this is a hard pill to swallow when I know that a student has just blown off my class for a period of time and then gets scared and starts to work. Is there hope for a kid who wouldn't come in for help and has a 43 average at midterm? Yes! I will meet with the student and his/her parents and set up a contract for success. If the student honors the contract for the rest of the semester and demonstrates knowledge of the material on the final, the "magic grading fairy" changes those dismal grades at the beginning of the term to 60. A student who might have given up, starts working and we all win. Will they end up with a good average? No. Will they pass? Yes. I think it is very important to create as many win-win situations as possible.

THE BIG KAHUNA

Today was the day of the first "Big Kahuna" in AP Calculus. Four times a year, I give a test that covers all of the material on the four major strands of Calculus, derivatives, integrals, derivative applications, and integral applications. These tests are straight AP questions. There are too many of them, they are impossible to finish and the pressure is great. When I grade them, I put an actual percentage score on them. Today's test had a top score of 54. I then line them up from highest to least and give the top scorer a 97. I then score the following papers in increments of threes so the eight kids in my class got 97, 94, 91, 88, 88, 85, 82,78. The double 88 was because two students tied on their percentage scores.

Therefore the competition is fierce and the kids take it very seriously! They come in quickly and I already have their tests face down on the desk waiting for them. They start ASAP and don't waste any time. All except for Ronnie, that is. Now, Ronnie is what you would call a character. He is a very bright young man who has trouble taking life seriously. He is respectful, polite, and I love him, but once in a while he does not know when to get serious. He walked in the door on the day of the "Big Kahuna" with a Spiderman mask, the kind you would wear if you were robbing a bank, and was dancing to the music! (I was playing "Jaws" music as they entered the room to build confidence.) Everyone else started the test and Ronnie was still dancing in front of the class. It was before the tardy bell rang but I was irritated that he was not in a hurry to start the test. I just gave him the evil eye until the bell rang. When it rang, I turned off the music, he took off the mask with a flourish, and he seriously began the test. He ended up in the top half of the class on the test. He is a bright boy who doesn't' always pick the more serious things in life, but I am sure that he is going to live longer than all of us, because he is full of serendipity! ! Oh how I wish for more serendipity in my life. Maybe I should not be so quick to give the evil eye. You can be too serious...

BITS OF GLASS
It's All About Instruction

***The man who can make hard things easy is the educator. Ralph Waldo Emerson

***It is not necessary for students to like something to perform positively.

***There is, in fact, no teaching without learning. Freire

***In sports, constant drills and no game is no fun!

***Teach tough, grade easy.

***Video tape yourself teaching as much as you can. It is very instructive.

***Email from a former student: I just wanted to tell you a BIG THANK YOU for my keepers. They have really come in handy. I was able to finally have calculus "click" for me tonight. . the night before the test. They are amazing. Tell your calculus class to keep those things they will need them.

***Email from a former student: I just want to thank you once again for being such an incredible teacher. All of your AP tests have really helped me be a better test taker—I feel like I'm able to pace myself so much better and I don't linger on a question that I'm unsure of. So even though AP Calculus didn't give me college credit, it taught me such valuable study and test taking skills. I do not regret taking the class! It might have been hard, but it taught me to never give up.

***Email from parent: I've wanted to thank you for teaching Valerie this year. She looks forward to your class and is particularly impressed with your teaching skills. "Mom, she's clear, methodical, and doesn't waste time so when we get home, we don't know what we're doing. " That pretty much says it all. We too are happy to retire what has become the norm of hiring a private math tutor and buying supplemental books. Your offer to help students after hours does not go unnoticed. What a servant's heart.

***Don't block the overhead. If you have a white board or a smart board move from side to side so you are not always standing in the same place. Most students will never tell you that they cannot see the board because you are standing in front of it!

　***Use lots of color in your work on the board or overhead. Putting different things in different colors helps separate it and organize it for the students. It also teaches them a valuable skill in taking notes.

Chapter Seven
IT'S ALL ABOUT COMMUNICATION

Dedication

This section of the book is dedicated to my son, Scotty. He taught me how to talk to teenagers and that prayer is the most powerful form of communication there is.

SOCIAL IQ ? ? ?

IN THIS SECTION we will discuss how to improve communication in the three areas that are critical to teaching; "the students", "the parents", and "the staff. " Good communication is vital to your success as a teacher. I have seen so many good teachers create difficult situations for themselves because they did not communicate well, when a little "verbal awareness" could have made their lives so much easier. Before we begin with specifics, however, I would like to talk a little about something called your "social IQ". As school teachers, we all know what IQ stands for and it may seem strange to use "social" and "IQ" in the same phrase. I have often seen cases where the higher the IQ, the lower the social skills and, forgive me for saying this but, vice-versa! I know this is a stereo-type on my part and that it is not always true, but I have seen enough of it in my teaching career to know that it is common.

So what is your "social IQ"? Very simply put, social IQ is the ability to connect with others. It is being able to empathize with the person you are trying to communicate with. As school teachers, it is critical that we develop our social IQ. It may not come naturally to all of us, and if it does not, we have to work at it. I have had to work at it a great deal. I am always more eager to tackle a new book than a new friend, and I feel very awkward "mingling" in a crowd of people that I do not know very well. Put me behind a podium in front of 500 people and I can function with only a few inner butterflies. Put me in a room with ten people that I do not know and expect me to socialize and it is more like dinosaurs dancing in my tummy than butterflies! I have had to practice a great deal to improve my own social IQ and I am learning all of the time! Not only is it important as teachers to learn to connect with people, I also believe that we should help our students develop their own social IQ.

In an article titled "Boost Your Social IQ", (Positive Thinking, Jul/Aug 2007), Jessica Kraft lists six behaviors that add up to a high social IQ. When I read her article, I was amazed that what she had written for the social world was so applicable for the classroom. The specific behaviors that she listed fit beautifully in the classroom environment. I decided to use them as part of my introduction to communication, because they summarize so succinctly what I want to say about classroom communication. The first behavior is situational awareness. Kraft defines it as "a radar that helps read social situations accurately and respond appropriately". Oh, how I wish that I could tell you that I have responded appropriately to all of those situations that come up in the classroom! Unfortunately, my "radar" is not always on and I jump in with both feet! I certainly do a better job of "awareness" than I did when I started teaching; experience, as painful as it is, is a very good teacher. Awareness is the ability to quickly analyze what is going on and choose the action or in-action that will handle the situation in the most efficient manner with a minimum of disruption. Simply put, it is knowing when to do what. It is the ability to take two identical classroom situations involving two different students and knowing that you cannot always handle them in exactly the same way, yet coming across as "fair" at all times.

This behavior is very closely linked with the second behavior, attunement. Attunement is the ability to sense what the other person is feeling or experiencing and responding with an attitude that will put them at ease. This is why it is so important to be aware of the person you are dealing with and not have one "pat" solution for every problem that might occur. It is "tuning" in to a student's personality type and making adjustments in our approach to them. If, for instance, I know that a student "bows up" and becomes belligerent at any form of correction, I handle that student a little differently than the compliant student. If the "crime" is the same for the two, the "punishment" will probably be the same, but my approach will be different.

The third behavior is listening. Are you a good listener? I am not. True listening is giving the other person your un-divided attention and making them feel like they have been heard. It means stopping what you are doing and focusing on them. I have really had to work on this one. I am especially guilty of being in the middle of doing "something" and not wanting to stop and just listen. As a teacher, you need to make yourself available. You need to make eye contact and be willing to give the student your full attention. This is often hard in a classroom setting, when you are responsible for thirty other students. Just finding a quiet place where you can listen is often a challenge. If I feel like I need to talk to a student privately, I try to find them during my planning period and arrange for them to come back to my room. Once in a while, I invite them to eat lunch with me, or come by and see me after school. I often call them at home at night if I did not have time to talk to them during the school day. When I talk to students, I also make sure that I do as much or more listening than I do talking. This one is really hard for me, but it is essential. Not only should our students be "well listened to", but this strategy also applies to other teachers and parents. If we would truly listen to our peers and the parents we could get more insight into our students.

In Kraft's article the next skill is: "knowing the etiquette for different situations". Some teacher's have an instinct for knowing how to act in certain situations and some have to learn the hard way. There is no book of etiquette for the class room teacher. I do not act the same on field day as I do on test days! It is very important that you know when to be their friend and when to be their teacher. I believe that one of the most common mistakes that first year teachers make is: "wanting to be their friend". There will be plenty of time for that, once you have established that you are first and foremost, their teacher. I think that this is also a very important skill to develop with parents. As I work with parents in helping their children, I become their friends. I am always mindful, however, that I am their child's teacher first and I try to separate business from friendship. (i. e. Let's not talk about school if you invite me to dinner!)

The fifth of the social IQ skills is called "presence". For a teacher it is the ability to see that "how I act and appear determines how others see me. " When you are standing in front of a class on a daily basis, are you able to perceive how you are coming across to the students? I have seen some teachers that I just wanted to cry for. They were working very hard and really loved what they were doing, but the students thought they were a joke and they never figured that out. A video camera can be very helpful in making sure that you are really coming across, like you think you are. Developing your own style of teacher "presence" is so important to your control of your classroom.

Teachers must be "masters of self-control, able (if need be) to hide their true feelings so as to project an image of self-confidence. "This statement from Kraft, which I have modified for teachers, is so critical to teaching success! A teacher can not let a student, or a class, know that they have "gotten" to them. No matter how angry or hurt you become, you must stay in control and not let your emotions run the classroom. You have to be so careful of what you are communicating. I am not trying to say that you should never let a class see you angry. I am saying that you better be careful how you manifest that anger. Every teacher needs a hobby like kick-boxing or weed pulling to help them express their negative emotions so that they do not have to "share" those feelings in the classroom.

The last of Kraft's skills is the ability to "feel and act on genuine concern for others. " How many times have you heard that a good teacher is the one who really cares? In fact, students will forgive you for almost anything if they know that you care. This is all about having the ability to "walk in another's shoes". We can only begin to imagine the situations that some of our students come from. Just the fact that we are teachers means that we have a college education, and that someone in our lives valued education and believed in us. Some of the young people we teach do not come to school with the same mindset. They come from every walk of life and every possible situation. Even the affluent and well cared for are often under great stress to perform and excel. Teaching and caring should be synonyms!

So how is your social IQ? Mine is improving with age, but I find it helpful to remind myself on occasion of the six strategies:

1 situational awareness-read situations accurately and respond accordingly

2 attunement to others-put others at ease

3 attentive listening-focusing on the speaker with full attention

4 etiquette for different situations-exhibiting the proper behavior for the given situation

5 presence-understanding how others see you and acting accordingly

6 genuine concern for others-caring and acting upon that concern

As we teach, we mature, and these six strategies will become part of who we are and we will not have to think about them quite as much. I always find it helpful, however, to review! ! !

THE PARENT TRAP
(HOW NOT TO FALL INTO IT!)
HANDLING PARENTS 101

I would now like to take the six general pieces of advice that I found in "Boost Your Social IQ", and apply them directly to parents. We will review each one briefly and then see how it helps us "handle" parents.

The first is situational awareness and suggests that we read situations accurately and respond accordingly. There is no place for "knee jerk reactions" when dealing with parents. A great example of this is the five boys in one of my upper classes that "messed with one of my systems". I consider that a serious offense because I believe it shows a lack of respect for me and my authority. When I found out about what they had done, I wrote a letter to all of their parents letting them know what the crime was and how I had decided on what the students would have to do to make up for their lack of judgement. I was just before sending the students out in the hall to give them their letters and "what for", when one of them stood up and told me that they would like to apologize to me and the class. They did so and came up with their own punishment, which was tougher than I had decided on. I thanked them for their willingness to accept the consequences and asked them to step out in the hall. I handed each one a copy of the letter that I had written to their parents. When they read it, they did not look happy. They were willing to pay for their crime, but they would rather their parents did not find out about the situation. After they had read the letter, I told them that they did not have to get them signed since they had apologized before I even had a chance to talk to them. They were all very relieved and most of them tore up the letter and threw it away before the end of the period. They went back into the classroom and apologized to the class.

Early the next morning, I walked to the end of the hall to get some water for one of my plants, and I saw one of the young men coming down the hall with his Dad. The young man had a strained look on his face and both of them, being over six feet tall, towered over me and I felt cornered at the end of the hall. I had no idea what was up until the Dad started talking. It seems that the boy showed his father the letter that I had written. That was a serious mistake on his part because his Dad was furious with him and gave him a very strong lecture in front of me about how I was such a great teacher and how I only deserved his respect not his dishonesty. His Dad made him apologize and let him know that if anything like that happened again, he would be in more trouble than he could imagine. This conversation went on for at least five minutes and I was more or less standing there with my mouth open because I did not know what to say. My immediate reaction was that the Dad was being too harsh and I wanted to let him know that the boys had apologized in an honorable manner. I decided that the best thing for me to do was keep my mouth shut! The father then apologized to me and stormed back down the hall. I was still standing at the water fountain. If I had tried to defend the boy, or made light of the situation, I would have been interfering in his parenting skills. His dad needed to make a big deal because he was desperately trying to teach his son about being honorable. I could not interfere with that.

The second piece of advice involves becoming attuned to others and putting them at ease. This is so important in dealing with parents when they are at the end of their rope in dealing with their child. I once taught a young man who was very bright but had some mild learning disabilities. His mother was also a teacher and she was very frustrated. Jack did not always do his best, but he was also very frustrated by his inability to do well when he did try. He was a "B" student in my classroom but he was badly failing Spanish. The Spanish teacher was out of patience with Jack and, in my opinion, was a little too in-flexible considering the situation. The mother asked for a conference with all of Jack's teachers. We knew that it was going to be a bad one because Jack had problems in several areas and the Spanish situation was just before becoming a crisis. His mother worked for the school system and some of us knew her personally and we knew that she would be very defensive concerning her child. I was the team leader and it was my job to lead the meeting. I was nervous going in but determined that we could accomplish this without anger. I talked to the Spanish teacher and found out how far she was willing to compromise and developed a private signal. I then asked each teacher to be prepared to say something positive about Jack to help defuse the mother. When the conference began, I asked each teacher to tell us what Jack was doing well and every teacher was able to say good things. This approach took the wind out of his mother's sails and she relaxed. We then went around the table and kindly and gently said where we felt Jack needed to make improvements. The Spanish teacher was generous and Jack was given hope for passing. The mother had come prepared for a battle and had found peace and compromise. Everybody won, especially Jack.

The third piece of advice is to be an attentive listener, focusing on the speaker with your full attention. I am not very good at social networking, but it is such an important skill to have when dealing with parents that it must be developed. Over the years I have had many "chatty parents" and I have always been kind and tried to be attentive. June, however, was my greatest challenge. She was a wonderful mother who had done so much for the school. She practically lived at school at times, volunteering even when her children were not involved. She was a true asset to the school and I often felt that she was under appreciated. She was so good to me. One morning she came in and I was feeling so bad and my throat was so raw it was like swallowing barbed wire. I should have been home, but since that is against my principles, I vowed to survive the day. She immediately ran to the store and brought back hot tea and ice water. At lunch she delivered chicken soup and more hot tea. I would have never survived the day without her. She was always bringing me surprises and was always there if I needed something. I loved this woman! The problem is, she was a social butterfly and loved to talk. She knew when my planning periods were. I was truly ashamed of myself, but I knew that I was not going to get anything done when she entered, and dreaded her frequent visits. Nevertheless, I stopped what I was doing and gave her my full attention. It was hard, but it was the right thing to do.

The fourth and fifth items on the list of good advice run together in my mind. One is choosing the proper etiquette or behavior for different situations and the other is understanding how others see you and acting accordingly. As a teacher, it is critical to be able to go back and forth from serious to silly and know when to be what. It is easier to do in the classroom than in the rest of the school environment. In situations where parents are present it is so important to be aware of your behavior. I do not act the same way at a basketball game that I do at a Baccalaureate. Nevertheless, I am always aware that parents are present and even though they do not expect me to be a super serious mature adult all of the time, they do expect me to be a role model for their children. I will not talk about problems at the school or other personnel or students around parents. I will not holler negative comments or lose my cool at ball games. I will get in dunking booths, dress up in silly costumes, and climb on jumpy things, but I will not show any disrespect for anyone or present myself in a negative manner.

The last thing on the list is to show a genuine concern for others by making it obvious that you care and acting upon that concern. There is nothing that a parent wants more than to know that you care about their child. The best way to communicate to your parents that you care is by being there for their child in the good times and the bad. When a child is in academic difficulty, being there is providing extra help, keeping in contact with the parents and letting everyone know that you have the best interests of the child at heart. When a child is facing physical difficulty, being there is going out of your way to help them keep up academically, making adaptations if needed. It is moving furniture to accommodate a wheel chair or crutches or dimming the lights as much as possible for a student with a migraine. Being there is keeping up with a kid that you taught last year even if you will never teach them again. Being there is going out of your way to be nice and give chances and help each student succeed.

THE PARENT IS ALWAYS THE PARENT

In the retail community there is an expression that goes something like this: "The customer is always right. " Now if you talk to any person who works in retail and handles returns and customer complaints, they will be the first to tell you that the customer is not always right and is often very wrong. I had a very short career at the customer service desk at K Mart when I was young and poor. My husband and I wanted to buy a house, and we both took on a second part time job until we could come up with a modest down payment. (Teacher's salaries back then did not cover such frivolous luxuries as savings.) I was quickly trained in "the customer is always right" philosophy and did my best to treat everyone with dignity. It was very hard sometimes. I remember one time when a guy brought back two gallons of paint that he claimed were the wrong color. I was so eager to please him and give him his refund that I failed to notice that the paint was not a K Mart brand. Fortunately, I was being watched by an observant supervisor who very kindly informed the customer that he must be a little bit mixed up as to where he bought the paint and pointed out the brand. Even though the man was trying to take advantage of the store, he was still treated with respect.

I am sure that you can see where this little story is going. I am going to modify the "philosophy" a little as I move it into the realm of education. My philosophy in dealing with parents is simple and is based on the fact that "THE PARENT IS ALWAYS THE PARENT. " It does not matter how right or wrong I believe they are, they are still the parent and it is my job to treat them with respect. This is not always easy, when I believe that some of them are "clueless" as to what is going on with their child, but it is always beneficial. When it comes to parents, I have had some "doozies" over the years, and of all the ones that I have dealt with only two left me feeling like I had not communicated properly with them. These two were so un-reasonable that the only thing I could do was lick my wounds and try not to take it personally. I fell into the "parent trap" twice and it was not a comfortable place to be. When it happens, the student loses, the parents lose and you lose. Therefore it is essential to avoid misunderstandings with parents, if at all possible.

I am always grateful when I survive a year with no irrational moms or dads. The thing that I try to remember is that no matter now I feel about them, I am the professional and they are the parents. I often cringe that students have to live in families with parents that I deem too permissive, too strict, or too entitled. Nevertheless, I always try to remember that the parent is always the parent whether I agree with their parenting skills or not. I learned very early in my career that we cannot change where the students come from, we can only change where they are going to.

As I finish this section, I must say that parents who physically, sexually, or emotionally abuse their children are *never* right and we must report these activities to the administration.

SAY IT TO THE CHILD, SAY IT TO THE PARENT

Never say anything to a child that you do not want the parent to hear. Even when you are dealing with teenagers, who are famous for not talking to their parents, this rule should stand firm. Do not confide anything in a student that you do not want shared with the world. I learned this the hard way after I had been teaching about fifteen years. I had been out of school a great deal. My husband was dying of lung cancer and I missed two consecutive weeks of school. I had left lesson plans and had good subs but it was just not the same. I had one young man that was failing my class and I had not been communicating with his mother.

She was a difficult mother who kept a lot of teachers in hot water and called the board of education at the drop of a hat. After the death of my husband, on my return to school, I met with this young man after school and made a comment to him that I regret to this day. It was time for report cards and I did not have a lot of grades for his class. I decided to give him a "C", which was not the problem. The problem was that I was honest with him and told him that I was giving him a "C" because I had been out so much and it would keep him out of trouble with his mother. That last part was a very unwise thing to say to a student. Naturally, he told his mom and she called the board of education. An assistant superintendent came to talk to me and I admitted that I had said that and explained the circumstances. I offered to apologize to the parent, but was told that would not be necessary. This woman was well known for being difficult and I had to be "dealt with" to satisfy her, but there were no repercussions except for my feelings of stupidity.

INITIAL CONTACTS

At the beginning of the year it is critical to make contact with all of your parents. There are many ways to do this. During pre-planning, my school has an open house and we have a large turn-out. I have the parents sign in as they enter the room, and I try diligently to speak to all of them. I introduce myself and welcome them into my room and hand them a class syllabus which has all of my basics on it. After the open house, I try to call any parent who did not show up before the first day of school. If this is not practical, I email them. I think it is very important at the beginning of the year to let the parents know a few basics. If practical, I schedule a brief meeting during the first week of school, inviting all of my parents to attend. I make sure the meeting is humorous and informative and I give them a taste of my philosophy. I make sure that I cover my basics. These basics will change with the teacher, the grade level, the subject , and the situation, but these are my basics:

1   I make sure that they have my home phone number and are comfortable using it. I give it to the students also and I have one simple rule: no phone calls after 9:00pm. In all my years of teaching, I have never had a student or parent abuse this privilege.

2   I make sure that they know when I am available for extra help
     if their child has any difficulties.

3   I make sure that they know I am serious about their child's
     education and will use their class time wisely.

4   I make sure that they understand that their child's daily atten-
     dance is important and should not be taken lightly.

5   I make sure that they understand that I am really into critical
     thinking and problem solving and that I intend to challenge
     their child.

6   I let them know that I believe what the students learn is much
     more important than what they "make".

THE GRADE IS THE THING

<u>TO A PARENT, GRADES ARE MORE IMPORTANT THAN
LEARNING, UNTIL IT IS TIME TO TAKE THE SAT.</u> I know that
this sounds cynical, but in my experience, I have never had a parent call
me and complain that their child was not learning enough. I have however, had many calls wanting to know how their child, who has never
made a "B" in their lives, has an 87 in my class. Parents want their children to learn and succeed. The problem is they assume that they are
"learning" if they have an "A". If you gave everyone in your class an
"A", I am confident that you would have very few parent calls. (You
would probably get a call from a competitive parent wanting to know
why you gave all of those "inferior" students the same grade that their
"prodigy" got.)I think it is sad that we, as teachers are not questioned
about how much we are teaching. Parents often ask a child: "What did
you make on your history test? " They should be asking: What did you
learn for your history test? "

Therefore, I believe it is necessary to communicate grades to parents
on three levels. These levels are the actual grade, the progress, and the
learning. We will begin with the actual grade. Where I teach, the students
get an electronic progress report twelve times a year. It is hard to measure how many of the parents actually see the reports. If you send home

paper reports that have to be signed and returned the chances improve, but I have been teaching long enough to know that many of them get signed by a friend during PE and the parent never sees it. In an ideal world, a parent would alert the school if they did not receive a progress report, but that is not what happens. It is critical as a teacher that we do not let any parent be surprised by a grade. It is unconscionable to let a student get to a point of failure, where there is little or no hope of passing, without parental contact. This is also true of an "A" student who is working down to a "C". I do not make as many parent contacts with the parents of seniors as I do with 9th graders, but if there is any radical change in grades or the possibility of failure, the parent must be notified ASAP! Even if a child is a straight "A" student, there should be at least one personal contact a year to talk about grades.

Progress and learning are not easily graded, and very hard to communicate to parents. Straight "A" students often score low on the SAT and parents cannot understand why. Average students who are motivated and work very hard perform well in school, but do not have the higher order thinking skills that are needed for high scores on tests similar to the SAT. If a teacher has never communicated with the parent about their child's progress and learning, this outcome confuses parents and catches them off guard. I believe that at least one personal contact should be made with every parent at least once a year to discuss their child's educational progress, promise, and/or problems. It is very difficult to tell a parent that their straight "A" child is an over-achiever and a very hard worker, but they are not an "out-of-the-box" thinker. It is a very common cop-out to say how bright the student is, but that they do not test well. Students with higher level thinking skills usually test very well. I know it is very hard to tell parents how you feel about their child's ability or effort level, if it is not good. They have the right to know and it is cruel to let them find out later as opposed to sooner. They need to form realistic expectations for their children. On the other hand, informing parents that their child is performing high on Bloom's taxonomy is always such a fun experience! (I think every student and parent should have "Balloon's" taxonomy explained to them!) For every difficult contact you have, there will be many more great ones, and they are just as important. Parents love to hear positive things about their kids that are not followed by a "but" …

I know that grades are important. Society has put a top premium on them. Good grades usually mean a good college. Good grades mean honor roll stickers for the car bumpers and proud relatives at graduation. Good grades mean scholarships and pats on the backs. The problem with good grades is that they do not necessarily reflect the level of knowledge and thinking skills a student has acquired. Even though it may create some problems for you as a teacher, always communicate with your parents that you are teaching students how to think and how to learn and that grades are secondary. The higher level thinking skills that are the best learning experiences usually tend to bring down grades. Students who have always "had "A's"" suddenly become students who are making "B's" or are struggling for those "A's". I find it very helpful to communicate with the parents about this early in the year. I explain my expectations and let them know that I am more interested in what the students are learning than what their grades are. I explain that I will be teaching the students how to think and problem solve and grades usually go down when I challenge the students thinking. I talk to them about students who are good memorizers and therefore have good grades, but then they go to take the SAT and they do not do well. This plan smoothes the way for a challenging year. Parents still expect good grades but they are a little bit more understanding when they realize it is ok to make a "B" if the learning is real and problem solving is the goal.

PARENT CONFERENCES

If email, phoning, or written communication is not effective or does not seem appropriate, a parent conference is in order. Parent conferences should include both parents, if possible, and I usually insist that the student be present, unless there is a special reason why this might not be wise. It is critical to set the participants at ease, which is not always successful, but should be attempted. Chairs or desks should be arranged in a circle so that everyone is on "equal footing'. I often tease the student and ask them if they would like for me to sit between them and their parents. I start with thanking the parents for coming and then I always start with something positive. I then approach what I see to be the problem and ask the parents if they have any questions about what I have presented. I also ask the student if he would like to add anything to what I have said. I never go into a conference without a list of possible solutions in my brain. I then offer the solutions and ask the parents and the student to respond to each one. It is critical that there be no raising of voices, lost tempers, or unkind words between any of the parties involved. It is your job as the teacher to moderate the conference in the friendliest way possible. If things begin to get out of hand, you need to suggest that the problem needs to be handled in an appropriate manner with meaningful dialogue. If a parent gets too angry, you may need to ask a parent to step outside and talk to them privately. Be kind and let them know that you realize that their explosive behavior is a result of their frustration and concern for their child, but that it accomplishes nothing. Give them a minute to pull themselves together and then invite them to rejoin the conference. If you anticipate that a conference may be difficult, it might be wise to invite an administrator to attend.

I read an article once about a "student led conference". This idea intrigued me and I have tried it and it worked pretty well, but I only use it for special cases where mature students are involved in the conference. If I feel that a conference is needed and that it would be a good idea to let the student be in charge, I speak to the student privately, ask them to invite their parents, let them know some times that I am available, and have them make the arrangements. I make sure that the student knows exactly why we need a conference and ask him or her to let the parents know what the conference will be about. I then challenge the student to come to the conference prepared with solutions to the issue. I also insist that they make a list of positive things about themselves in regards to my class and to be prepared to share everything that they have prepared with their parents. I welcome everyone and then pretty much let the student lead. On a couple of occasions, I have had to take back over, but generally this has worked well.

PHONE CALLS
Since the "coming of email" I have cut down greatly on my telephone conversations with parents. Over the years, I find that they are rarely at home when I call and usually in the middle of dinner if I do reach them. Therefore, I handle as many messages as I can through email. It is im-

possible however, to avoid phone calls completely, and you should not want to, because sometimes you need that verbal communication. Often it is much better to call a parent than to send an email and only knowledge of the family and the situation will dictate what is most appropriate. The phone is more personal and if the situation is delicate, it is probably the best option. I love to call home when a student has done something great in class. If the student was the only one that figured out a tough problem or their oral presentation was exceptional, I think that it is a great idea to call home and let the parents know how proud of them you are.

Some of the rules for calling are the same as for emails, which we will discuss in the next section. Always return calls promptly and always start with a positive comment. If you initiated the call, explain the situation very clearly and do not assume that the parents know all of your classroom procedures. Give the parents plenty of time to respond and ask questions and be prepared with possible solutions to the problem. If the parent initiated the call, it is wise to let them say everything they want to say before you start your end of the conversation. You may want to jot down brief notes, so you can remember what you need to respond to. Be patient with parents who are upset and try to soothe them so you can carry on a normal conversation. I have found that most parents who are upset have gotten wrong information from their child or another parent. After acknowledging their concerns, I usually start with the statement: "I am so glad that you called me so that we could get this straightened out. " I then proceed to tell them my thoughts and facts on the situation. We usually end up with the mis-understanding worked out and proceed to find a solution to the problem. It is usually a good idea to make the parent feel like they are making the decisions in the problem solving process. I try to offer several possible "fixes" and ask them which one(s) they think would be the best for their child.

If the misunderstanding is the result of something you did wrong, admit it, apologize, and explain how you plan to remedy the situation. Never be afraid to apologize to a parent. They can forgive you most anything as long as you are sorry. If I have not been able to reach a parent on the phone, I usually email them and ask them to call me.

One of the neatest discipline experiences I had involved a phone call home. I had a young man in class who had misbehaved in a certain way that was not appropriate. I cannot even remember what he did, but I will always remember the phone call. When the mother answered, she sounded funny to me and I realized that she had food in her mouth. I apologized and asked her to call me back when she had had an opportunity to finish her dinner. She agreed, but hesitated and asked me what Eric had done. Not wanting to get into it before we really had time to talk, I asked her to get Eric to tell her and then she and I could chat about it later. She called back in about an hour. She apologized for Eric's behavior and assured me that it would be dealt with. Just out of curiosity and to make sure that our stories were straight, I asked her what Eric had confessed. She rattled off a list of transgressions half of which I would have never told her because I had forgotten them! We both had a good laugh, but knowing the family, I knew that Eric's sins would not go unpunished!

I have only had a mother scream at me once and it was over the phone. She was a stay at home mom and she was old enough to be the child's grandmother. Our team was scheduling parent conferences and she was one of the first to sign up. Another mother, who worked and was on a tight schedule, could only come in the time slot that I had given the first mother. I gave her the slot, thinking that the first mom would not mind rescheduling. Boy was I wrong. I called the first mother back to explain the situation and she started screaming at me and told me that she had that time slot and expected me to honor it. She would not be calmed down and I ended up letting her keep her original time. I called the other mother back and apologized profusely, and we made other arrangements that were very inconvenient for both her and us. She was very gracious. I explained the situation to the principal and we decided that it would be a good idea for her to sit in on the conference with the screaming mother. The mother never mentioned the phone call or the effort to move her appointment, but she had plenty to say about the school and the teachers and none of it was good. The principal had all she could take and thanked the teachers for their input and dismissed us from the meeting, staying in the room with the irate parent. I do not know what she said to that parent, but I did not hear from her for the rest of the year.

EMAILS

I taught for 30 years without email and got along great, but I must admit it has its advantages and is a great way to communicate with parents as long as it is not the only way that you communicate with parents. I am going to classify emails in two ways. I will start with group emails and then we will look at individual emails.

I enjoy being able to send out a mass email when I want to communicate with a large group of students or parents. Here are some ways to use email to help with parent communication:

1   When I have a big project, test, or assignment due, I often email home a week ahead of time to remind everyone.

2   When I "hear" through the "grapevine" that a senior skip day is coming up, I email my senior parents and let them know that I will be doing important stuff in my class and that I expect everystudent to be present.

3   When a class has done a great job on a test or assignment, I like to email that group of parents and let them know how proud I am of their children.

4   When I am out of Kleenex, paper towels, or other classroom necessities, I will email a group of parents and ask for donations.

5   After Halloween, I email all of my parents and ask them to send any leftover candy that they would lie to donate to the school. I use it all year as a motivator, and they are very generous!

Often, individual emails are called for and should include good ones as well as bad ones. It is just as important to contact a parent when a student does something "good' as when they do something "bad", maybe even more so!

1   I usually start with an email if I am concerned about a student slipping academically. It is standard procedure for me to email a parent when a student has missed their third homework assignment, or fails a test.

2   If a student has a great improvement on a test, I always email the parents.

3   If a student works especially hard on a test and does not do well, I always contact the parent and let them know that I am aware of the effort.

4   If a parent, donates something to my classroom, or helps me out in any way, I always send them a thank you email.

There are five very important email rules that I always follow in communicating with parents. Rule number one, the most important, is to always reply to a parent email and do it punctually. This is critical to parent respect and communication. . Rule number two is to always start a "negative" email with some positive comment about the student. Rule number three is to always follow up with a phone conversation if the parent does not acknowledge your email when it concerns the student's academic standing. Rule number four is to always print a copy of any emails that you think should be kept on file if a difficult situation might arise. Rule number five is to always word emails carefully and have another teacher proofread it if you are concerned about the wording or the tone.

WRITTEN CONTACT

I love to use the surprise element of this method of communication to make a big impact on a parent. Can you imagine going to the mailbox and getting a handwritten note from your child's teacher on nice stationary, telling you of some wonderful thing that your child has done? If I had ever gotten one of those, I would have shed a few tears and pressed it in my son's baby book! Just the fact that the teacher took the time and spent $. 45 to mail it makes it special. It shows that you really care about the child. It is old fashioned, but it is special.

Written communication can also be helpful when you have a parent that is so unreasonable, they won't listen to you. Once, before email, I had an irrational parent and the only contact I had with her was the phone. She ended one of our conversations by hanging up on me and

I was not able to explain the situation fully. I did not feel that calling her again would help, so I wrote a very long formal letter to her. I talked to my principal about the situation and asked her to read the letter to make sure that I had responded in a professional and appropriate manner. I then asked an English teacher to read it to make sure that I did not make any serious errors that would jeopardize my credibility. I then mailed the letter in the hopes that she would respond in a more positive manner. I never heard from her so I am sure that she is still taking my name in vain, but I felt a whole lot better, because I had the opportunity to say what I needed to say.

I also like to shock the students by writing directly to them. Imagine the impact of a student going home and finding a written letter of encouragement from the teacher. This is also useful if you are having issues with a student. It allows you to say what you want to say and let it sink in before you see them again.

COMMUNICATION LOG

I have found it helpful over the years to keep a communication log. This does not have to be fancy or formal, just something you can refer to if the need arises. I keep this in a notebook with copies of emails that I might need again. I simply date the entries with a brief description of what the communication was about. The log is good insurance if you are ever accused of not communicating!

ONE LONELY PARENT

At the beginning of the year, I send home a letter to all of my parents inviting them to sit in on my class, unannounced, anytime they would like. I really meant it. There are very few times that I would not want a parent in my classroom and I just hoped that those times were not when one actually showed up! I knew the numbers would be low because a lot of my student's parents work and since I teach Juniors and Seniors, the kids did not encourage them to visit. (It bothers me that we are anxious to get involved at school when our kids are in the elementary grades, but we spend less time there as they go through their teenage years. They need us just as much or even more as they navigate those puberty years.)Imagine my surprise when a mom walked in the door during my AP Calculus class. She is one of my quizbowl moms so I am very comfortable with her, and she fit right in with the kids. She listened intently while I taught and when I had them working in teams she walked around the room and interacted with the kids in a very positive manner. She did not understand what we were doing, but she was fun to have in the room. She also got a real appreciation of how hard her son had to work. I wish I had more parents that would take the time to observe. I know that there are a few "whacko" parents out there, but they are rare and hopefully those won't take you up on your offer.

I admit that it makes me a little nervous to think of parents freely coming in and out of my room, but the benefits in perspective are wonderful. I think the trust between school and home would increase greatly if we had more visitations. It is like there is some kind of invisible wall between school and home that needs to be crossed. I also have a problem getting my students and parents to call me at home at night because there is some kind of "understood" rule that you just don't call a teacher at home. I pass out my phone number and encourage its use. I let them know that if they call me after 9:00pm they flunk, but otherwise I welcome their calls. It is very rare that I get a call and most of the time the reason given to me is that their mother said that you just don't call a teacher at home. Maybe if we could get more parents to visit the classroom, they would feel more comfortable communicating in other ways.

COREY

Corey made a 66 on his advanced placement calculus test last week. He is a very bright young man that has trouble sitting still. His writing is horrible and his hands can never keep up with his brain. Sometimes his brain can not even keep up with his brain because he gets so far ahead of himself that he makes careless mistakes and his grades do not reflect his abilities. He is also not the world's greatest at following directions and often loses points on logistics. By the end of the semester his grades always even out, but his mom expects good grades on all assignments. She emailed me and let me know how disappointed she was and asked what I thought the problem was. I emailed her back and let her know that Corey had no evidence that he had studied because he had turned in no study problems. I let her know that this class is probably the biggest math challenge that he has had to face so far and that he needed to step up to the plate. I also let her know that he did an excellent job participating in class. She emailed back that she was taking everything away from him. Now when this mom says she is taking everything away from him, she means anything that requires power. So if it plugs in, runs on batteries, or gas, it goes. Not only does she restrict Corey from these things, she carries through. I know this mom well and I felt comfortable in playing "let's make a deal" with her. It was early in the semester and so far the test was the only grade. I emailed her; Do you have to take it all away? I am the queen of second chances. She emailed back: He can keep his broken phone then. I emailed back: You are so generous, can't you do a little better than that? She emailed back: O. K. I gave him his truck. I emailed back: Great now throw in some food and I can live with it. She emailed back: Never withdrew the food, he needs that to think! I love this exchange. She has a great sense of humor and is holding her child to task. I hope I calmed her down, and yet did not interfere with her discipline. I wish my students had more parents like her.

ALL THOSE EXTRA TREATS!

One of the most valuable skills you can develop as a teacher is learning to be what I call an ethical opportunist. I am always looking for opportunities to benefit my students, even at the cost of groveling and swallowing my pride. For instance, at Halloween, there is often left-over Trick-or-Treat candy in most homes. It is way too expensive and good to throw away, yet for most people, way too tempting to keep in the house. I consider it a service to relieve my students' households of this temptation. All they have to do is send it to school and share the joy! Every year on Halloween, I send out a mass e-mail to my parents and suggest that if they are looking for a good cause to support, sending their left-over candy to my classroom will give them a warm "fuzzy" feeling. I explain that I use it all year for motivational purposes and I would be grateful for any small contribution that they would be able to make. By November 3rd, I have enough candy to get me through most of the rest of the year. I keep a record of who brought in candy and I then email a brief thank you. Gratitude is essential.

I have been begging for candy most of my educational career but it was not until I begin private education that I started begging for more. I noticed that several teachers were putting sticky notes on their boards just before open house. I took a peak and found each sticky note had the teacher's name as well as one object that they needed for their room. For instance if the teacher needed five rolls of paper towels, there were 5 sticky notes that said paper towels on them posted on the board. Other things that I saw on the notes were kleenex, notecards, candy, pencils, pens, notebook paper and many other items. During open house if a parent wants to contribute something to the classroom, all they have to do is take a sticky note. I immediately caught on to this plan and have had to spend very little on classroom supplies since. I like this approach because it is a completely voluntary activity and I do not have to say a thing!

In addition, many times throughout the year, parents ask if there is anything they can do for me. I never pass up an offer. I always keep my request cheap, but I never turn down an offer. I ask for a roll of paper towels, a box of tissue, or a bottle of antiseptic hand gel. I usually end up getting a huge package with more than I asked for. If they insist on being more generous, I ask for colorful dry erase markers, or a bag of fun size Snickers, which I give out on birthdays.

SPONGES, FORCEFIELDS, AND JUDGE JUDY

I am going to use three analogies to try to get a very important point across. This concept is so important that it is a "make it or break it" point for many teachers. Whether they realize it or not, students are a combination sponge and judge all rolled into one which requires the wise teacher to handle them with an invisible force field.

Sometimes it seems like students are little sponges and soak up everything we say and do except the material that we are trying to get across. We can teach a concept until we are blue in the face and it will not have the "mental holding power" as one slip of the tongue that we wish we could take back. I found out at the end of the year that a young lady in my calculus class was keeping a list of what the class called "Suttonisms. " I had no idea that some of the things I said were being recorded for history. Most of them were very benign but a few of them were slightly embarrassing, especially when the students wanted to put them on the back of a calculus tee-shirt. It is not only what we say it is how we act. We are being watched no matter where we are or what we are doing and we need to be sure that our behavior and conversation are worthy.

Not only do students absorb messages from what we say and do, they also are very much in tune to our appearance and body language. I cannot emphasize enough the need for us to dress professionally. Female teachers in skirts that are too short or tops that are too low are not being a good influence on young ladies and worse than that they are a distraction to young men. Male teachers who wear flip flops and dress too casually do not put forth the proper image to young males. We have to set ourselves apart. This does not mean that we have to wear panty hose or neck ties, just that we have to look like a teacher and not a student. As society has changed over the decades and dress is getting more casual, it is reasonable for "teacher dress codes" to get a little more relaxed also, but we still need to maintain a level of authority in our appearance. Students respect a teacher who rises above social standards in their appearance. It is also very critical that we do not try to dress like our students. If the only thing that distinguishes you from the teenagers at school is your nametag, it is time to update your wardrobe to a more professional level. Not only is our appearance important, we also need to be very aware of the signals we send with our body language. Students have radar. They know when the teacher is as bored with the lesson as they are, or when a teacher can be easily distracted.

Not only are the students sponges, they are also like judges sitting on the bench pointing out any areas of "unfairness" that might exist in the classroom. If the teacher can chew gum, why can't they? If the teacher can drink coffee in class, why can't they? If the teacher can eat in class why can't they? If the teacher can use a cell phone in class why can't they? I have heard all of the arguments in the world from teachers that they are the adults and have gone to school for blank number of years and they should be able to do what they want to in the classroom. Call me a spoil sport if you like, but you will gain a lot of respect if you will impose the same rules on yourself as you do on your students. Trust me, this one action goes a long way with the student's sense of justice.

Finally, I would like to talk about that force field. If you want to be a great teacher, you need to develop student-teacher relationships that demonstrate mutual love and respect. You want to bond with them as much as you can and you want each student to feel comfortable with you. Nevertheless, there should be an "invisible force field" around each student that should never be crossed. Every school district has its rules concerning physical contact with students and teachers should adhere to these rigorously. Teaching high school students, I am very careful that my touches are on the top of the shoulder or on the back of the hand and that my hugs are always sideways hugs with no frontal contact. But the force field I am talking about goes a lot deeper than that. It is not our job to be their friend. It is our job to be their instructors, mentors, coaches, and encouragers. There must be something that separates "them" from "us". This does not mean that we cannot have fun with them, cry with them, and laugh with them. It does mean that we are in charge of the relationship and that for their own good we remain the adult.

CRAZY IDIOT

I have been teaching long enough to know that sarcasm can get you in a lot of trouble. I am very careful how I use it. I also know in my heart that if I say it in class, there is a good possibility that it will get home so I always have my inner radar up to keep my mouth from outpacing my brain. I have one exception to that rule and that is when I am discussing preparation for my final exams. My exams are not hard but they are thorough and require preparation. It is a competitive test that is graded on the curve. For 90 minutes, students try to remember and apply everything that they have learned in a semester. The grades are never good and I always take the highest grade and add enough points to get it up to a 98. I then add that many points to the grades of every student in class who has "earned" the curve.

A student "earns" the curve by doing some pre-assigned study problems. Three weeks before the final, I give the students a list of about 50 problems that are good practice to prepare for the final. When I hand out the list, I tell the students that anyone who does not do the study problems would be a real "idiot". I explain that they have to do them to get the curve and how important they are. I really make a big deal out of it and use sar-

casm and the use of the word "idiot" to convince the students how important the study problems are. Several times before the due date, I remind
the students and laughingly challenge them to not be "idiots". Nevertheless, on the day that the study problems are due, I usually have one or two
students in each class that have not done any of them.

I spend three days reviewing for the exam by going over the study
problems. I need to be able to check the problems and give them back
immediately so I can start answering questions. Therefore, I have everyone line up in alphabetical order with their study problems and I check
them off in my grade book. I scan them and put a plus, check, or minus
depending on the quantity and quality of their work. This allows me to
apply the curve when the final is graded. Those with a plus get the entire
curve; those with a check get most of the curve; and those with a minus
get some of the curve. Those with no study problems get no curve. As
they pass by me, if a student has no study problems, I look at them and
smile and say: "I hope that you do well on the final so you will not be
an idiot". Most of them just smile back, confident that they are smart
enough to "ace" my test without doing all of those study problems,
which they perceive as busy work. Almost all of them wish that they
had heeded my "idiot" warning after the exam is graded.

Two days after the study problems were due, I got an email from a
mom asking if we could have a conference about her daughter, Hillary.
I was clueless as to why she wanted the conference. Hillary is an A student who does B minus work, but I had not heard from the mother all
semester and was not sure what the conference was about. I guess I was
just dense, but it never occurred to me that my "idiot" comment was
about to come back to bite me. When the mom walked in I asked her
what the conference was about and she very politely told me that she
had problems with me calling her daughter an "idiot". She explained
that a comment like that was made to her when she was a child and it
had affected her even to the present. I listened intently with no interruptions until she was finished telling me how her self-esteem had been
crushed and was never restored. She was quick to point out that she
knew what a respected teacher I was and that she wanted to hear what
I had to say before she decided if any further action on her part was
needed. When she had finished saying what she had come to say, I im-

mediately apologized to her for any anguish that I had caused her or Hillary. She graciously accepted my apology. I also told her that I would apologize to Hillary at the first opportunity I had. Then I asked her what exactly Hillary had told her that I said. She told me that Hillary had told her that I called her an idiot. I explained to her that I said that I hoped Hillary would not be an idiot. Just those few extra words made a total difference in meaning. I explained the whole process and what I was trying to do and that I had not treated Hillary any differently than any other student that had not done the study problems.

After my explanation, she agreed that Hillary did not deliver the exact story and that she had been irresponsible in not doing the problems. She suggested that in the future, I should use the word "crazy" instead of "idiot". I am not sure that "crazy has the same impact as "idiot," but if there is going to be miscommunication, I would rather deal with "crazy. " After we agreed on this new approach we discussed why an "A" student had a "B" minus. I showed the mom all of the homework cards that Hillary filled out saying that she had just forgotten to do it. We talked about Hillary putting forth more effort. When we parted, we hugged and I reiterated my apology. I also thanked her for coming and talking to me before she decided if she needed to take any other action. She was satisfied and I felt grateful that I had been given an opportunity to explain without having to involve an administrator. The next day, I spoke to Hillary privately. I apologized, yet told her that I did not believe that I had ever directly called her an "idiot". She agreed and told me that her mother was the one who was upset, not her. I talked to her about her capabilities and encouraged her to study hard for her final so that the curve would not be needed.

As a footnote, Hillary did not do well on her exam and ended up with a high "C" in the class.

TRUTH OR CONSEQUENCES

One of the hardest things to tell a parent is that their child is not as intellectually gifted as the parents think they are. This revelation is a very slippery slope that has to be maneuvered with the greatest of care. It is also my opinion that it should never be done in the presence of the child.

I teach a young man who is new to the school this year. He was home schooled by his mother thru the 10th grade. He then moved in with his father and step mother and was enrolled at our school. At the beginning of the year he struggled in my class and I scheduled a conference with his father. It was a good conference at which the father and son were both present. We talked about what he could do to improve his grades and that he needed to come in for tutoring before and after school. His dad made it clear that Tucker was Ivy League material. At the time, I had not taught Tucker long enough to know what his true abilities were, but I had not seen any evidence that would fulfill his father's high expectations. Tucker started coming in for help and his grades did improve, but I started noticing behaviors that I felt kept him from doing his best. His homework did not show effort and in class when I gave out an instruction like "get out your calculators" or "be sure and get these notes down", he was always behind. It was like he would sit there a minute and process the instructions and then slowly begin to comply. On some occasions he did not comply at all and I had to go to him and repeat the directions. His performance on tests was passing, but not good, and he had trouble answering questions in class when called on.

We had a test that was half take home and half in class. On the take home test the students were encouraged to form study groups and work together on the test. I emailed the parents ahead of time to let them know what was coming and encouraged them to host a study session with refreshments so that the students could get together. I got an email back from Tucker's dad letting me know that he would not be in class on Friday to take the "in class" part or to receive the take home part because of a trip to Florida for a family wedding. I let him know that Tucker could take the in class part on Monday afternoon and that he could pick up the take home part on his way out Thursday. Tucker forgot to stop by and pick up the test so I emailed his dad, and his stepmom came by and picked it up for him. Tucker turned in his take home part on Monday and took the in-class on Monday afternoon. I graded the in class part over the weekend and got them back quickly. The take home part took longer to grade, and the students got them back on Thursday. Early Friday, I sent the following email home to all of my parents:

Honors Advanced Math Parents:

    I finally got those take-home tests graded! Some of the students rose to the occasion and I had some excellent papers. Some of the students did not take the test seriously enough and their grades reflect their efforts. I have returned the tests, and I would like you to ask your child to see it. It is important to me that everyone understands what I am trying to accomplish. I know that grades are important, but they are not as important as being able to problem solve and being able to use what has been learned. I believe that grades will gradually come back up as students learn that they have to do more than just memorize and give back in the same way that the material was given. As the year progresses there will be more tests that require the students to go beyond spouting back what was learned in the classroom. I will continue to expect excellent work and hopefully everyone will deliver.

    As always it is a privilege to teach your children and I will continue to expect great things from them. Please feel free to contact me any time that you have a question. I will be sending out up-dated progress reports today.

    Thanks,

    Lizzy Sutton

Friday just before lunch, I got this reply from Tucker's dad:

    Hello,

    I understand and appreciate your email, but still feel there may be a dis-connect…and I definitely do not agree with your suggestion that everyone who did poorly are getting what they deserve because they did not put in the effort. This is very strong, direct language, that yes may apply to some, but nonetheless is a very broad negative statement, in my opinion.

I see Tucker working as hard or harder than he ever has on math, and I like this. It has been his favorite subject forever, but now he really dislikes it, is frustrated and this I do not like. Not sure I can accept this much longer.

I'd like to meet again with you and Tucker- but would like to talk to you prior to. Please let me know your availability next week, I'd prefer to meet before school begins.

Kind Regards,
Thomas Smith

I was shocked and had another teacher read my original email to see if she thought it sounded negative. She did not, but I knew that she was my friend and might not say so, if it did. I answered his email that afternoon before I left school:

Mr. Smith:

I have read my email multiple times to make sure that I did not word it poorly, because I never wish to offend. I said that some of the students did not take the test seriously enough and their grades reflect their effort. I never implied that all of those who did poorly did not take the test seriously. I did not mean for it to be a broad negative statement. I am sorry if my choice of words has caused problems, but my intentions are to help all of the students become better prepared for college and whatever lies ahead for them. I am also sorry that Tucker is not enjoying my class. Would it be possible for you and I to meet Friday morning, November 12th? This is my first free morning. I would like to talk to you personally and then if you would like a conference with all three of us, Tucker can join us. I can meet as early as 7:00 or as late as 8:00. Let me know if this is convenient for you.

Sincerely,
Lizzy Sutton

I immediately got back this reply:

> Friday at 7 is fine.
> Kind Regards,
> Thomas Smith

Thursday afternoon, I got an email stating that the youngest child in the family was ill and Mr. Smith would not be able to attend the conference. He said that he would get back with me. He never did. About two weeks later, I emailed him and asked him if he still wanted to meet. He told me that he was out of town a lot on business and would get back with me. He never did. I emailed him again but he never had time to meet.

Tucker ended up with a "C" for the semester. He continued to come in for help occasionally, but still did not participate or follow directions well in class. He was a very likeable and respectful young man, he just could not focus. His homework showed none of that effort that his dad said was apparent at home.

Second semester Tucker continued to make "C's" and, I never heard from his father. As the year passed, he became more comfortable with me and I with him. He got involved in soccer and did not come in for tutoring so I tried to be more diligent in class to see that he was concentrating on the math. I assigned him a young lady that he seemed to work well with and instructed her to help him "stay engaged". If Tucker were ever in danger of failing, I would have immediately called his father and schedule another conference. I do not know why Mr. Smith never tried to come in for a conference. His dissatisfaction with me may have been frustration at his son's performance. I will never know if he still blames me or if he has accepted the fact that his son struggles with mathematics. Telling a parent that their child is not a "stellar student" is always difficult. Some of them would rather avoid you than find out something that they don't really want to know. Tucker did not come back the following year.

CYBER COUNSELING

I am one of those old dogs that has had to learn a lot of new tricks. I remember the "olden days" when everything was done by note and phone, and I do not want to go back. I still believe in phone conversations and I use them often, but I find that I spend a lot more of my time consoling parents through email. It seems more effective than phone conversations for a couple of reasons. First of all, it allows me time to think, re-think, edit and get my thoughts in order. I can spend time developing what I really want to say before I actually have to deliver it. Once a statement is made on the phone, there is no taking it back, but with an email you can be sure the tone and content are correct before you push send. Communicating with parents is critical, and one trend that I have noticed growing over the years is the amount of time I need to spend encouraging parents, that despite their child's work ethic at school, the child will not turn out to be a bank robber or serial killer after high school. How you communicate with parents is a delicate balance of truth and diplomacy. Raising children is hard work; parents need encouragement from their children's teachers. They want what is best for their children and have to balance dreams with reality. Below are two cyber conversations that illustrate my point:

The first conversation is about a young man that is very intelligent, yet very social. It is not that he doesn't want to study; he just has never had to before in order to keep good grades, and he just has more important things to do!

*Mrs. Jones:
Kirk was the only one in class to make a 100 on yesterday's quiz. He is so smart!

*Mrs. Sutton:
Thank you so much for your encouraging words. Kirk came home last night and told me he had a lucky day. Then he proceeded to tell me that Michelle told him Mrs. Sutton had told her class that he was the only one to make a 100 on the quiz. (It really boosted his ego that you told his peers.) Then, of course, I proceeded to tell him it had nothing to

do with luck; He was just smart and a good listener in class. I really don't think he understands the potential that lies within him, Mrs. Sutton. I have struggled with this his entire school life and everyone just keeps telling me it's a boy thing. But, Kirk knows I expect him to make A's because I know that is his potential. However, he's just as happy with a 90-A without having to work hard, than to put just a little more effort into studying and making a 98-A. I know this comes from within, and I had decided this year I would not push him to get high A's. However, now with the HOPE requirements changing I don't want him to get penalized for taking challenging classes. (I realize this is a totally different subject than I started out with and maybe we can talk about this in a future forum.) Bottom line...thank you so much for recognizing Kirk and the other kids too. You definitely make a HUGE impact in their lives! We feel so blessed to have you in Kirk's life!

*Mrs. Jones:

Kirk has a world of potential and is smarter than he gives himself credit. Please allow me to share my perspective as a teacher who has taught a lot of kids. I have known many students that were as smart as Kirk that concentrated on high A's and were miserable and had no "people skills". Kirk is not only going to be a great success at life because of his smarts, but he is going to succeed because he is kind and never meets a stranger. He also seems happy and content! I am not saying that you should lower your expectations. I believe in high expectations. Kirk has met most of them. He is drug and alcohol free, respectful, knows the Lord, and is a joy to be around. With more work, Kirk could be making high A's but at what cost? Low A's (and I think you should expect these even in the challenging classes) might not get Kirk valedictorian status but they will get him HOPE, and I have seen the stress and turmoil caused by trying to motivate from "without". You know Kirk much better than I, and although I like to "tame" the high spirit, I never want to see it broken. Does the world need more nuclear physicists or do we need more folks like Kirk? My vote is on the Kirk's of the world and if he ever decides to buckle down and be a nuclear physicist, how fortunate we are to have a future Albert Einstein with people skills! Just some random thoughts…

*Mrs. Sutton:
Your perspective means the world to me! Thank you so much.

My second example is concerning a young man who has a lot of difficulty in school. It is hard to tell if there are learning disabilities or if he has just been so unmotivated from the beginning that he can't catch up. I taught Adam in 8th, 9th, and 10th grades and spent many hours trying to tutor him and help his mom motivate him. We had many conferences and phone chats during that time. Adam is a great kid, he just wants to exist and not perform. I received these emails from his Mom at the end of his 10th grade year. They cover a two month period.

*Lizzy:
I hope you don't mind my sending this note, but… I am in need of some guidance, in regards to Adam. Problems remain the same as always, however just letting him handle the situation is driving me crazy. To be honest, some believe I should just let him work out his school/grade situation on his own, but I cannot find any reason to just sit and wait for something magical to happen. I have done virtually everything imaginable, but I struggle with the fact that college is around the corner, and I know that missing that particular boat will be devastating. Do I just let Adam do what he thinks he wants; which is virtually nothing, to improve grades? While virtually every teacher has called and/or emailed numerous times in the last six weeks. I have made contact with Mr. Griffin (the principal) and at this point

don't think he feels a need for any major intervention. At this time, I will not contact him again in regards to Adam and his grades or status at KCA. Also, I thought that being on the football team might help his self esteem, but that was a fantasy and has probably hurt, with only seconds on the field in the past three weeks. Anyway, I know how busy you are. I want to help this child and not sure if I should let him flounder or force him to bring home books and study. Adam is a smart child, but rarely applies himself in his school work. Let me know if you have any ideas on the subject.

*Dear Jinny :
I never mind hearing from you and I am never too busy. Focus on building Adam's character and work ethic in an area that he is motivated. Don't give up. Worrying about our children is the most natural thing in the world and it never stops no matter how old they get or how old we get. Just try to turn that worrying into prayer. It is much more constructive.

I wish I had some answers for Adam. I hope that some of the things we did in SAT Prep will motivate him. I agree that Adam should be handling this on his own, but if he is not, as a parent, I would continue to "help him make the right choices". I would not micro-manage his school work, but I would stay on top of his grades with Ren-Web and intervene in any grade that is totally unacceptable. Deciding what is acceptable is up to you and your husband. I suggest that you have Adam take the SAT this year and see how his score is. If it is good, then straight "A's" will not be necessary to get in a good college. If it is bad, then with his grades, he needs to make alternate plans. He could go to a good technical school or the military. The Marines were great for my son Scotty but it almost killed me, and I praise the Lord that he never had to go overseas. I could never recommend the military with that in mind, but I do know it taught Scotty a great deal.

What does Adam want? If the answer is nothing, then it is going to be hard to deal with motivating him. If the answer is college, I suggest that you might take him on a couple of college visits and talk to admissions officers and let them tell Adam that he better get on the stick. If he has a career in mind, expose him to the realities of that career. I would never just sit back and let him fail without very specific consequences. You should never give up, but you should change your tactics to accommodate for his age. As to football, Adam needs to understand that the best players spend the most time on the field. If he wants to be best at something he has to work very hard at it and be very patient. As a sophomore he has time to build his playing time for the future by spending more time in the weight room and working hard at being the best. He needs to learn to be the best bench warmer he can be until his dedication has paid off and he is skilled enough to take his place on the field. What else does Adam enjoy? Is he musical? Is he great at Frisbee? Help him build his self esteem by encouraging what he is good at.

I know that I am just rambling, so if you would like for us to get together and just talk, I would be glad to help you come up with a specific "plan of improvement" for Adam and his school work. I will pray for Adam and continue to try to motivate him in SAT Prep.

Lizzy:

I don't think I responded to your wonderful note. I can't thank you enough for your words of wisdom. Thank you for taking the time to spill your guts regarding the Adam situation. By the way, Adam will be tutoring with Renee Jordan, a senior, beginning on Friday. Mrs. Brewster has been pushing for this for a few weeks now, and has finally thought this might be the answer. Anyway thanks again. Also, notice the interesting grade on the last notebook check: I am sure you beat him for that!!

*Jinny:

Glad to see Adam with Renee. She is a wonderful student and very motivated. I guess you know that she will probably be going to West Point. If he can gain motivation by osmosis, she is the one to spend time with. He is really doing well in SAT Prep. I hope some of that will rub off on him too! Just remember how long Sarah had to wait for God to answer her prayers for Issac! Keep the faith...

*Lizzy:

Hope your Thanksgiving was a great one, with all the little ones running around. We had a great week off, we went with my entire family to Disney; it was terrific. First, thank you for the accolades for Adam, the last time we spoke in the parking lot. I can never get enough of that; especially this year! I need to get your baseball bat out and do some damage to this boy. Things are getting worse by the minute with school; teachers are calling and e-mailing on a regular basis. This is it in a nutshell. If the teacher has any type of tutoring session; he never studies for the test. He will go to the session prior to the test and hope for the best, which is usually a "D"! ! ! He actually only went to one session with Mrs. Matthews for math; he did not get the help he needed, so refuses to go any other time. I mean the woman has been in the dog house since day one, for no reason. At this moment his math grade is; I believe a D. Spanish is simply down the toilet; not sure if he has passed one test or quiz in that class. I have actually met with Mr. Griffin and he seemed to understand. Then no follow-up, so I sent an e-mail and he asked for Adam and his grades to be in his office the next morning. I know he spoke to some of the teachers, and that was about it. So I don't need/want to go there again. What Adam needs is some sense put into him. He needs someone besides mommy/daddy to be on to him, every single day. What do you think about Sylvan or some other place like that? Thanks again for listening to me ramble.

*Jinny:
I do not know how expensive Sylvan is, but I think it would be a great idea if they would work with him on what he needs in Spanish and math. I agree that he needs the one-on-one supervision and that mom and dad are not always the most effective. Adam has got to get over not liking teachers and therefore not performing. He needs to get mad at the teachers and do well just to spite them! ! ! ! I will be sure to address this in SAT Prep when we go over study skills and college preparedness. Have you talked to Mr. Richards (the guidance counselor)? Adam could report to him once a week and go over grades. Mr. Richards is a very encouraging person, and he takes a personal interest in the students. I wish that I were not so full on my tutoring days, but I have so many calculus and trig students that I would not be able to get to Adam and he would become frustrated with me. Have you thought about peer tutors for math and Spanish? I know that Brice and Adam get along well, and Brice would be an excellent tutor. You might want to pay him to stay after school with Adam a couple of afternoons a week to work together. As to Spanish, it takes so much memorization! I do not know what the answer is there. Have you had a conference with Mrs. Alvarez? If you talk to Mr. Richards, ask him about some other diploma options. If Adam were removed from Spanish, maybe he could concentrate more on geometry. He would not get a college bound diploma but he could get a diploma and still go to college, just not a research university. I know you do not want to lower your expectations but at the same time it is important to be realistic. I will pray for Adam and try to continue to encourage him and do as much geometry in SAT class as we can squeeze in. Let me know what you decide.

Both Kirk and Adam graduated. The last time Kirk came back to visit, he was doing great at the University of Georgia. I have not heard from Adam.

GOTTA HAVE A "B"

Trent's mom made it clear from the very beginning that he had to have a "B" in my class. She never mentioned his learning anything or doing his homework or studying for tests in our first meeting, just that he had to have a "B". As I got to know Trent, I quickly realized that he was not into learning, just playing, and doing as little work as possible. It became a constant battle to keep him engaged in class. I moved him directly in front of me and had to keep an eye on him every minute. He forgot to do his homework, forgot to study for tests, and always forgot to take notes. He doodled in class, daydreamed and was ready for any distraction that came his way. The amazing thing was that Trent was a senior, not a third grader. Trent was not any different from many students I have had in the past that will do great in life once they manage to get out of school. He was personable, a great "schmoozer", and a real charmer. I didn't trust him any further than I could throw him, because he was sneaky and did not always speak the truth. He was fortunate to be a "C" student based on his work ethic and classroom presence. The problem was the fact that his Mom needed that "B".

She emailed me at least once a week lest I forget that Trent needed a "B". In her defense, she definitely did her part. She made him come in for tutoring and checked to see that he showed up. He always showed up, but usually for the last 5 minutes because he had somewhere else he needed to be. I suspect Mom thought he was there the entire time. She badgered him about homework and study problems. She was a mom on a mission to get that "B", but due to the lack of motivation on the part of Trent, it was a "mission impossible". In his defense, he was just not wired for math or sitting still… He was marvelous on the basketball court and that is one of the reasons that it was imperative that he get a "B". He needed it for a basketball scholarship.

At the end of the semester he had exactly an 80. This grade was the result of several acts of grace on my part and a very persistent mom. I made it perfectly clear that he had to make a "B" on the final to keep the "B". Trent does not test well and a comprehensive exam would be a real challenge for him in the best of circumstances. He made a 50. He did some study problems so I gave him a 70. His average ended up a 78. I got an email from his Mom asking what else I could do. I explained to her that since the final counted 15% of the grade, I would have had to give him a high "B" on the final to get him back up to an 80 and I could not do that. She reminded me that he had to have a "B", and I told her that I had done all I could do. I then got an email from Trent's Dad telling me that he appreciated what I had done for Trent but that he knew that Trent had put forth 100% effort in my class to earn that "B" and that it is extremely important for him to make a "B". He wrote: "Is there anything that can be done for him to make a "B". I really feel bad for him because he does try hard. It's only two points. "

As hard as I tried to communicate Trent's lack of motivation with these parents through emails, conferences, and calls, they truly believed that their son was doing his best and deserved a "B". I was always patient with his parents but over the course of the semester I ran out of things to say and dreaded the frequent emails. Nevertheless I replied to them all. Despite making a "C" in my class, Trent got his basketball scholarship at a very small college. He lasted one semester. I guess he didn't get his "B" in college either!

IVORY TOWER PARENTS

One of the toughest types of parent to deal with are those I call "ivory tower" parents or grandparents or any other assorted relative who works in education or is a highly educated professional. They have the best interests of the child at heart and are sincere in seeking the best possible education, but they often do not see the reality of the situation and are making unreasonable demands on the teacher and sometimes the child.

These demands are often in the form of a request for a more challenging curriculum. If these requests are legitimate they should be honored to the best of your ability if the child and the parent are both motivated. In my experience, however, I have found that most of the students would have been happier if the parent had just let them do what the class is doing. The student does not want to be treated differently and usually does not carry through with the independent work. The child must be self-motivated for independent curricular enhancement to work. In a class of 25 students it is hard to meet the demands of an overzealous parent, especially when the child just wants to be "one of the kids" and does not want to be treated differently. Never-theless, I have found that this situation often takes care of itself when I cooperate with the parents and come up with an alternate individual-ized project. More often than not, the child does not want to work alone, and they make the parents so miserable that I do not have to say a word. Requests for individual projects cease. The more persistent parents keep asking and I keep providing, but it is almost always a lot more work for the parents and the students so eventually it tapers off. If the parent in-sists on an enhanced curriculum, I always insist on a conference with the parent and child to lay out my expectations for their individualized work and to emphasize that they are expected to be self motivated and conscientious. I put them on probation for a certain period of time and let them know that if the work slacks off, the individualization will stop.

Sometimes it is not a matter of adjusting the curriculum, just a lot of free advice and "constructive criticism". In that case you cannot do much but "grin and bear it". I had a grandmother that was a retired teacher who called and emailed me at least once a week to let me know how I could have done something better or how I had not given enough partial credit on a test. I was very patient but firm, with her. I was hoping that she would tire of calling me, but she never did and we went the entire year with her questioning my methods and my trying to be nice. I had no problems with her grandson, but I was not sorry to see him move on to another teacher because I was really tired of grandma.

On rare occasions you will get a parent that is so sure that they have all of the answers that they start quoting educational studies and drop-ping names. Most of them are very sincere, but they have trouble seeing the big picture. Our mathematics department wanted to start placing students according to their abilities and spent many hours coming up with a plan that we believed would enhance the entire math curriculum. We had a three tiered approach. Students were scored on a carefully constructed placement test, their present test average, and a teacher rec-ommendation. The students would be grouped into three levels; accel-erated, honors, and regular. We also offered Advanced Placement Calculus and Statistics which were entered by invitation. A letter was prepared and sent home to the parents, which carefully explained the process. It was well received by the parents. We also scheduled an open forum where we discussed how we were going to implement the program and answered questions. Prior to the forum I received a letter from a father who was a teacher. He stated that we explained clearly the procedures the school would use to place students but "the explication is not aligned with the current trend of academic achievement and lifelong success of young learners". He then quoted several academic sources and dropped several names including Mr. Duncan, the Secretary of Education of the United States. His letter was most sincere and I agree with him that all students should have the opportunity to be challenged and work at their best level. The reality is, however, that all students do not work at the same pace and are not all mathematically capable at the same level. They can all learn, and should be challenged to move beyond their level of understanding, but they should not all be in accelerated classes. I replied promptly and tried to address his concerns, but I knew that I had not succeeded when he came to the forum and raised the same questions. Philosophically, this parent and I will never agree, but I understand where he is coming from and I respect that.

Parents with educational backgrounds are a valuable resource to the school and are usually your best supporters. Some will cross the line and when they do, they just need a gentle nudging back to the other side.

Chapter Eight
IT'S ALL
ABOUT "OVER"

Dedication

This section of my book is dedicated to my Father, Charles Sikes. He taught me that growing old is a privilege not shared by everyone. He showed me how to age gracefully and just do the things I love to do a little differently!

YOU'VE COME A LONG WAY BABY

QUITE A FEW YEARS AGO there were two commercials on T. V. that had catchy themes that sum up how I feel as I finish my book and am on the downhill side of my teaching career. The first was the Virginia Slims slogan "You've come a long way baby. " Oh yes I have! When I think how young and ignorant I was when I first started teaching, I am embarrassed. When I left college I was sure that I was going to educate the world and solve all of its problems, one student at a time. I would only want to go back to that point in my life if I could take all of my wisdom with me. I am a much better teacher now than I was then because of my experiences and those only come with time. It is very possible to be a great young teacher but no matter how good you are, you will get better with age and experience. Age and experience bless you with perspective, which is easy to lose in the daily struggles of being a teacher.

I believe that the second slogan was from a Clairol hair color ad: "She is not getting older, she is getting better. " I really like that! My hearing is going, my age spots are standing up and saluting, my eyesight is dimming, and my one remaining "name call recognition brain cell" requires an electron microscope to be found, but I feel like I am in my teaching prime. My body is failing me and my brain is a little slow, but my will is as "iron" as it ever was and I charge forward knowing that with a few adjustments and modifications I will continue to teach. There is much to be gained from us "old fogies" and as long as we are effective in the classroom we should be given the chance to share our wisdom and experience with others.

I hope I will never stop learning and welcoming change. Young people need wise old people. My senior status is not a curse it is a blessing. Therefore I present this last section which includes a few of my ramblings; a few good books that I would like to recommend; and if you will forgive me for not being humble, a few of my favorite things that others have said about me.

LET'S MAKE A DEAL

It is a beautiful Saturday morning in early fall. I just got out of bed and it is early. I am sitting at my computer looking out the window at a tree that is turning from green to orange. It is a beautiful sight and I am enjoying the serenity. It reminds me of my favorite growing old quote. "How beautifully leaves grow old, how full of light and color are their last days. " I found this quote by John Burroughs on the back of a Garden Gate Magazine. It really spoke to me. I want my last days to be full of light and color. As I write this, I am 62 and most people would tell me that I am not old. My body is telling me otherwise. I have survived "the change" without drugs; I try to work out to keep my body in shape but I do not eat well and sometimes my negative personality traits keep me from enjoying life. You know, things like worry, perfectionism, and unrealistic expectations. These things interfere with my "light and color".

I am up so early on a weekend because last night I had a dream and it unsettled me. I am not sure if it was a blessing or a warning; maybe a little of both. You see, I was having my usual issues with a lack of moderation in the food department and I ate too much last night; that might explain the dream. I dreamed that I had been diagnosed with cancer and that I was dying. It is not always easy to remember a dream, but I distinctly remember two things. The first impression I am left with is that no one has any expectations of you when they find out that you are dying. They just love you, and try to help you. How freeing that was! The second one is that when you find out you are dying, you savor every moment and regret not living your whole life like each day is your last.

I remember somewhere in the early 1960's when I was a young teenager, trying to cross a busy intersection in my home town. I do not remember if I was being stupid or the driver was being careless, but I almost got hit by a car. It scared me enough that I made a deal with God. I am sure that it would seem like a very strange deal to most people, but all I begged God for was at least twenty years to teach. Back then I did not know that I had to teach thirty years to be able to retire or I might have made a more fiscally responsible deal, but I only asked for twenty. Why such a silly request by a thirteen year old? Because even then, I was sure that I wanted to be a teacher and the passion and planning had begun. I was taking notes in class as to what the bad teachers and good teachers do and I created a list of things I would never do when I became one. (I wish that I still had that list!) I loved school and I knew that it was my future. I was so ready to start and I had about eight years of my own schooling in the way before I could begin my life's work. I still had a lot of intersections to cross, and I was ready to deal. I really don't remember what I offered God as my part of the bargain, but I can assure you that He more than kept His end, and I suspect I did not.

So this morning when I dreamed that I was dying, it was time to do some dealing again. This time I did not ask for any time, I asked God to help me teach each day like I am dying! I want to be so conscious of the moment that I grab each one to instruct, care, advise, empathize, laugh and share. I want to interact with my students like it is my last chance to make a difference in their lives.

I do not know how many more years God is going to give me in the classroom, but I do know that I want to savor them all. I am living my dream and that makes me a better teacher.

Last Day of Post Planning

It is the last day of post planning. I left school two hours ago and I am sitting at my neighborhood pool, grateful that the rules in this retirement community do not allow kids and teenagers at this particular pool. I love teenagers and 180 days during the year, I want to be in their presence, but it is the end of the year and I am tired. I am so glad that there is a long break. In about a month, I will be all excited and ready to go back, but this year is at an end and I am glad. I am always grateful that we get to "end" every year. It is very rare to have a "job" where you get a chance to start over every year and correct your mistakes. I do not care how long I teach, I always make mistakes, and I made some hum-dingers this year! Therefore, it is my habit at the end of each year, during post planning, to go through my syllabi and make changes to correct things that I want to do differently. I know that I will forget by August. I also take notes of things that I want to do differently that do not involve my syllabus. I then start my calendar for next year and my steno "to do" list. There are always things that I wanted to do and did not have time to get done; by going ahead and starting my next year's list, I do not lose them to the ravages of that stray brain cell. After I have thus preserved my thoughts for next year, I usually celebrate my survival of another school year by giving myself the month of June to rest and recreate.

In my opinion we are a very fortunate profession. We have the opportunity to recharge our batteries before we go again. The year closes out and we get to re-group!

DAY OF DISCOURAGEMENT

Once in a while I wonder if I will know when it is time to quit teaching. I have seen a few teachers that were way past their time of effectiveness. I believe that older teachers have a lot to offer in wisdom and experience and there are many effective "senior citizen" teachers. It is just very important to know when to quit. I worry about my own personal knowing. I do not want to be ineffective in the classroom.

Today I had one of those days that made me wonder if it was time to think about "my leaving". My brain was playing tricks on me and my ears were helping with the charade. It all started with my SAT Preparation class. I had a young lady absent who is Hispanic in origin. I have had trouble learning names in this class because I only teach them every other week. I feel like the main area that I am loosing brain cells is in remembering names. It is so important to get their names right that, given a choice, I would rather lose a different brain cell! The young lady who was absent was named Arelye. It was a study skills/time management day in the class and I gave them some study tips for about 20 minutes; then, I gave them the last 30 minutes to catch up on work in any of their classes. (SAT Prep is not a math class and therefore I actually do give free time! We have one of these days about once a month and I find they are very appreciative of that "catch up time".) During this last 30 minutes, I was sitting at my computer while the students worked. I had my back turned to the class when a young lady walked up behind me and asked if she could take pictures for the annual staff. When I turned around I saw a young Hispanic lady and immediately fussed at her for trying to miss my class. She looked at me sadly and said that she was in my class last year. Her name was Talia. I was mortified that I had gotten those two girls mixed up. I apologized to Talia. I was mortified that she stood behind me for a couple of minutes before I knew that she was there because I could not hear her. But I was most mortified at the sympathetic look that Talia gave me. It was kind of like the look that you would give a beloved grandmother when she called you by the dog's name.

I hope that this was a brief moment of dementia and not a sign of what is to come.

RESENTED SELF-EXILE

I am at the age that I am generally respected as a teacher and asked to be on committees and be at decision making meetings. My opinions are generally valued and respected because I have the experience to back them up. If I had a dime for all of the committees I have sat on in my career, I would not necessarily be a rich woman but I could at least have a nice cruise to the Bahamas.

Recently, I served on a committee that revamped the dress code in an effort to make it simpler to understand and more enforceable. We worked long and hard and came up with a reasonable policy. By the time the dress code was presented to the students however, several fundamental items had been changed. I quickly asked the Dean of Students not to put me on any more decision making committees because I had too few brain cells left to waste if our recommendations were not going to be seriously considered. I am sure that he thought that I was just being a pain in the behind but he is young and has more minutes and brain cells to waste than I do. The older I get, the more protective of my time I have become.

My request was soon forgotten until I talked to Tammy and she told me that she would need a substitute because she would be at a leadership meeting. I asked "what leadership meeting" and she told me she wasn't sure what it was about. The next day, I walked by the media center and it was set up in conference style and a meeting was going on. It was hard to see exactly who was there without being obvious. I do know that the headmaster, principals, CFO, and several teachers were in there. I especially noticed that the newest member of the math department was in there! I was very miffed that I had not been invited and truly got my feelings hurt. I huffed and I pouted for about two hours and then I had a revelation. I had specifically asked not to be put on any decision making committees. Now I was irritated when my wish was honored. I guess I expected them to offer again so I could turn them down, or could I have possibly not meant it when I wanted to be overlooked when decisions are to be made? The answer was very simple, I wanted to be in on the decision making and have all of my recommendations approved.

It is hard to give up any perceived power that I have. My reputation and the respect that I have earned are important to me and it makes me feel good when people ask my opinion. But, I am too old now to waste all of that energy and I need to concentrate on my classroom. It is time for me to retire from "educational politics" and let others play that game. I just want to be content to teach. That, however is never going to happen. I still have valuable insights and I just need to be grateful when my opinion is asked and stop being so "put out" when it is ignored. It is very important that "teacher" input be sought in policies that affect them in the classroom and we have to be willing to be listened too at the risk of being over-ruled

TO HEAR OR NOT TO HEAR

I left school after my last class and headed to the "ear" doctor. I have been having trouble hearing and knew it was time to get it checked. After an interesting session with the audiologist, I was told that I had 30% hearing loss in each ear. It had not affected my teaching up to this point, and the doctor told me that at this time, the decision was mine as to whether I thought hearing aids would improve the quality of my life. After researching the cost of hearing aids I decided that the quality of my life was just fine for now! I do believe though that it is important to let the students in on anything about me that may seem strange to them. I told all of my classes today, we had a good laugh, and then I stressed how important it was to me that they speak loudly and clearly. I am confident that most of them will respect my "condition" and comply.

I think it is especially important to be up front and honest with your students if you have any obvious physical limitation. Students will not make fun of you if they understand the problem, but if it goes unexplained you may become the "butt" of many cruel jokes.

Postscript:

I held out about five months and decided that I needed to bite the bullet and get the hearing aids. I prayed hard that I would adjust to them because I have heard stories of people who bought them and then would not wear them. My prayers were answered as I adjusted very quickly and oh what a difference they made! I want to teach as long as possible and they helped remind me that there are a lot of wonderful inventions out there that will allow me to keep on keeping on. I may become the first bionic teacher!

AUDITORY CLUTTER

I had another one of those moments today when I wondered how long I am going to last in the classroom. In Advanced Math I was talking about "end-behavior" and positive and negative infinity. I had my back partially to the class and every time I said an answer to a particular problem, I heard some members of the class saying something else. We played this back and forth game on the same problem for about 30 seconds and then I went over to the side of my Promethian Board to explain it again on the white board because I just didn't think that they were getting it. (This is kind of like where you say it louder the second time if they don't understand it the first time.) After I explained it again, they said that my answer is what they had said and that they agreed with me all along. Why had I heard something else? Am I losing my mind? I felt like one of those movies where an elderly person gets lost in the woods and can't find their way out. Are you old enough to remember "On Golden Pond" when Henry Fonda got lost? Great movie!

Staring out into a sea of perplexed faces, who were mostly concerned that they might have to deal with my insanity, I knew that I had to take the bull by the horns. Now my classes know that when I have something serious to say I make them all stand up. It helps them focus their attention on me. I do not do it very often, so it remains an effective technique. I told the class "all rise" and spent about 3 minutes explaining the functionality of hearing aides and their limitations. We talked about all of that background clutter noise that I always hear and how if my itty bitty microphones are not pointing in the right direction, I can be confused by what is being said. I then told them that they needed to speak one at a time, which is a good rule anyway, and that they needed to speak loudly and clearly.

They agreed that this was not too hard to do and looked relieved that my handicap was physical and not mental. I think that it is very important to have these types of discussions in front of the class because if you do not, they will have them behind your back and they won't always represent the truth.

AIRPLANE PILOTS DO IT!

Once again, I have to make an adjustment for my longevity. Recently, for the first time I can remember, I am having trouble remembering where I left off and what is next in each class. I teach five different classes and remembering where I left off was always a challenge, but I solved that problem with sticky notes. Now, however, I sometimes cannot remember what I have done or where to go next and sticky notes can only do so much. I do not use many notes. I teach off the top of my head, and I take pride in the fact that I am so prepared that I can do that. But now, sometimes I am confused and skip something or do something twice in the same class. Now, I know what the term "absent minded professor" really means.

In my never ending quest to keep teaching and be effective, I came up with another system to help me stay on track! Every airline pilot has a check list in the cockpit that they go through to make sure that they have checked everything before take-off. Nobody makes fun of them or tells them it is a waste of time. Therefore, to improve my efficiency, I have created a checklist for every unit I teach. It includes, in order, each topic, activity, textbook assignment, worksheet, technology enhancement, quiz, and test. By each item there is a blank to be checked off when completed. I still do not need my notes to teach the information, I just need my check off sheet to be sure I go in the right order and do not forget anything. I keep my check off sheet in my very special, leather bound notebook and I refer to it before, during and after each class and it keeps me organized. No one has made fun of me yet!

BOOKS, BOOKS, BOOKS

I wish that I had kept track over the years of all of the wonderful books that I have read that helped me become a better teacher. It is impossible for me to remember all of them. I wish I had kept a list. There are a few, however, that I would like to recommend to you because they really stand out. Once again, I am going to have the English teachers frowning, but in this day and age with the magic of Google, all I am listing is the title and the author. That should be enough information to find one if you are interested. I used to hate writing papers for English because of all those commas and semi-colons and that very particular order to a bibliography, so I am expressing my rebellious nature and making this easy on myself: my book-my rules!

Category One: Very Practical

I have the same opinion about a book that I do about a staff development workshop. If I get one good idea for my classroom, it was worth the time. These books are definitely worth the time and have lots of good, practical ideas. They are also "easy reads".

The End of Molasses Classes by Ron Clark

50 Ways to Improve Student Behavior by Annette Breaux and Todd Whitaker

Every Minute Counts by David R. Johnson

How to be an Effective Teacher the First Days of School by Harry K. Wong and Rosemary T. Wong

Making Minutes Count Even More by David R. Johnson

Motivation Counts: Teaching Techniques that Work by David R. Johnson

Never Work Harder Than Your Students and Other Principles of Great Teaching by Robyn R. Jackson

The Essential 55 An Award-Winning Educator's Rules for Discovering the Successful Student in Every Child by Ron Clark

The Teacher, Teacher Joke Book by Jennifer Hahn

Category Two: Very Inspirational

Sometimes I need to read a book to fill up my empty tank. These books do the trick!

A Treasury of Courage and Confidence edited by Norman Vincent Peale

Chalkdust by Elspeth Campbell Murphy

Chicken Soup for the Teenage Soul by Jack Canfield, Mark Victor, and Kimberly Kirberger

Escalante The Best Teacher in America by Jay Matthews

* *God's Little Devotional Book for Teachers* I have the book in my hand and cannot find an author or an editor anywhere, but it is published by Honor Books and well worth looking for.

Recess: Prayer Meditations for Teachers by Elspeth Campbell Murphy

Smiles for Teachers (Second Edition) Walnut Grove Press

The Teacher's Quotation Book: Little Lessons on Learning collected by: Wanda Lincoln and Murray Suid

The Falconer/What We Wish We Had Learned In School by Grant Lichtman

Category Three: Older than Dirt

Several years ago I was looking for some antique math books and found a book entitled *Manual of Methods for Georgia Teachers 1911*. This little book was falling apart, but it was too good to resist and only cost two dollars. I would have paid twenty. It was wonderful in every way. I laughed at the expectations of teachers in 1911 and was amazed at the difficulty of the curriculum. This little book is a treasure trove of sound teaching advice as well as a thorough overview of what needed to be taught to all grades in all subjects. I was hooked. I began looking for other antique books and found several that intrigued me. Thus began another book collection. Antique teacher education books are harder to find than antique math books and I doubt if you will have much luck finding another copy of my *Manual of Methods*. I also found a book entitled *The Teacher's Speech*. It was written by Wayland Maxfield Parrish and published in 1939. It has six chapters with the titles: The Teacher's Responsibility, The Teacher's Personality, The Teacher's Voice, The Teacher's Pronunciation, The Teacher's Expression, and The Teacher's Rhetoric. I doubt if you can find this one either. I do not know about you but I never received any instruction in voice, or pronunciation. The point I am trying to make here is that most of what was true for teaching in the early 20th Century still holds true in the early 21st century, and these antique books are wonderful treasures worth the search. I encourage you to rummage and see what you can find. Here are some older books that you can find. They are oldies but goodies;

Good Morning, Miss Dove by Frances Gray Patton
Goodbye Mr. Chips by James Hilton
Great Women Teachers by Alice Fleming
How to Survive Your Native Land by James Herndon
Present Day Standards for Teaching by F. Burke Firzpatrick (1926)
The Heart Is the Teacher by Leonard Covello with Guido D'Agostino
Up The Down Staircase by Bel Kaufman

Category Four: Instructional Development
These books are not "quick reads", but they are well worth your time to investigate. I have already referred to The Understanding by Design series, and they have changed my teaching paradigm. Imagine making out the test before you plan the unit! The discipline book by Gibbs and Haddock is full of useful advice for all schools, not just Christian schools.

Classroom Discipline-A Management Guide for Christian School Teachers by Ollie E. Gibbs and Jerry L. Haddock

Collaborative Peer Coaching that Improves Instruction by Dwight W. Allen and Alyce C. Leblanc

Differentiating Assessment Strategies by Carolyn Chapman and Rita King

Differentiating Instruction with Style by Gayle H. Gregory

Madeline Hunter's Mastery Teaching by Robin Hunter

Schooling by Design: Mission, Action, Achievement by Grant Wiggins and Jay McTighe

Understanding by Design Expanded 2nd Edition by Grant Wiggins and Jay McTighe

Understanding by Design: Professional Development Workbook by Jay McTighe and Grant Wiggins.

All of these books are like one grain of sand on a beach. There are so many more good ones and it is impossible to read them all. The important thing is that you keep on reading and keep on learning. As a teacher we must continue "growing". It is not acceptable to stagnate or decay.

TAKING THE BULL BY THE HORNS

What makes a person a hero? I am confident firemen, policemen, military personnel, surgeons, and astronauts all fit into that category. They are always rescuing folks at their own peril, facing the unknown, and giving hope for a future. As a teacher, however, I am rarely called a hero. What I do is so ordinary in the eyes of others that I could never qualify for the title. As I gain age and I gain wisdom, I know in my heart that I have indeed rescued many students (not usually at my own peril); I face the unknown every day; and I have given many a hope for the future. I do not say this in an arrogant way, every teacher who is worth their salt has done the same thing, I am just old enough to look back and recognize it. But am I a hero? The answer to that is yes because I have two pieces of physical evidence to prove it.

The first piece of evidence is somewhat of an illegal activity. Students know that they are not to write on their "quizlet boards". You can get into serious trouble if you get caught. Nevertheless, once in a while a "doodle" will pop up and I can rarely catch the perpetrator so I make a blanket "reminder" announcement to the classes. Last time that happened, however, I made no announcement because I loved the "doodle". If that is the kind of graffiti they want to put on my boards, bring it on! Someone who I will never know wrote: Mrs. Sutton is my hero. It may not seem like a big deal, but that one little statement made my day and every time I saw it, it encouraged me to keep fighting the good fight. Unfortunately it was in dry erase and with time it disappeared. I thought about putting it in permanent marker when no one was looking but I decided that would be a little self-promoting.

The second piece of evidence came from a less than dignified activity. Every year our school has an auction for education. It begins with a silent auction followed by a live auction. Volunteers are needed to "walk" the silent auction tables, man the many check in and check out tables, and a lot of other necessary duties. Some of the teachers also volunteer to take the students on "auction trips" during the school day. When the call came out for volunteers, I signed up for three activities. The first was simple. All I had to do was walk the silent auction tables for two hours. The second was easy also. Another teacher and I volunteered to take Juniors and Seniors on a day trip which would include laser tag, frisbee golf, and lunch. These "auction trips" raise a lot of money for the school and having survived the laser tag last year, I was not hesitant to volunteer again. Caught up in the spirit, I brazenly volunteered for one more activity that was so outside my comfort zone that I agonized over my decision for a month.

During the silent auction, a mechanical bull is placed on the gym floor. All it takes is a dollar to prove your ability to hang on to that whirling dervish and the line is always long, especially with elementary students. The auction organizer, Betty, wanted to increase high school participation so she asked me if I would ride the bull. At this point in my career, I am 62, with high blood pressure, high cholesterol, type 2 diabetes, and arthritis. Mind you I am not decrepit by any means. I work out at Curves three days a week, walk regularly, and play with my grandchildren, but I know what happens to people my age who break a hip, and I was not ready to inhabit the nursing home yet. To say I was anxious was an understatement but I had made a promise. Fearing that I might come to my senses and change my mind, Betty put my name on flyers, and quickly made it public knowledge that I would be riding the bull. Now I have done a lot of crazy stunts in my teaching career, and compared to the high ropes course this should have been a breeze, but I was very concerned that I would be jerked so badly that I would have to be put in traction. My arthritis is in my back and neck, and I began to question the wisdom of my choice. Nevertheless, there was something inside of me that wanted to prove that this old girl still "had it in her. " I am not sure what "it" is, but I needed to prove to myself that I still had "it. " I also needed to show the kids that their hard driving, nononsense math teacher still had a little "fun" left in her and her passion for teaching sometimes outweighed her common sense. At this point I am sure that some of you are thinking that riding that bull had nothing to do with my passion for teaching, but trust me it had everything to do with it. If you want to communicate your passion to your students you have to take a few risks and ride a few bulls.

The dreaded hour came. I had taken three ibuprofen, donned comfortable clothes, and said my prayers. I had even gotten to the young man that was working the controls on the bull and let him know in no uncertain terms that he was to keep that thing on low speed at all times. It was all I could do to prepare. I was instructed to get in the long line of elementary students who were waiting to ride the bull. When I got close to the front, the master of ceremonies would announce my ride and unfortunately, all of the folks in the gym would direct their attention to the bull riding arena. I got in line for a rather lengthy wait and I watched carefully as one kid after another was thrown from the bull. The bull was in the middle of a soft jumpy thing and there were no injuries, just squeals of delight or terror as the kids were thrown from the bull. I watched those who were staying on the longest and planned my strategies. I studied and I prayed. I had been standing in line for about ten minutes when the young lady in front of me turned around and very politely asked me if I knew that this ride was not for old people. I assured her that I was aware of that but I wanted to give it a try anyway. I was a little concerned about actually getting on the bull, but as I watched some of the smaller kids bounce themselves up, I figured that I could maneuver it.

After waiting about twenty minutes, I took my shoes off, climbed onto the jumpy thing and faced the bull. That bull felt like it was twenty feet up and no matter how hard I tried I could not get on it. I know it was only a matter of seconds, but it felt like an eternity as all of those people all over the gym had directed their attention my way. I could not get on that bull. The lady taking up the money tried to help me but she kept falling every time we tried. Finally the young man operating the bull got on one side of the bull and she got on the other and she pushed and he pulled and I finally got on. I was already exhausted and totally humiliated and the bull had not even gotten into motion. (I can only imagine what the bull was thinking at this point.) The operator put the bull on kindergarten speed and away I went. I hung on for dear life, using all of the strategies that I had watched, and I actually managed to hold on for 52 seconds. If the truth be known, I could have held on longer, but I was ready to get off so I just let go and fell onto the jumpy thing. A lot of kids were around the bull screaming faster!, faster!, faster!, but fortunately the operator saw the look of terror in my eyes and kept it on low. As I tried to regain some composure walking off the jumpy thing I was shaking so bad that I had to sit on the bleachers and had trouble tying my shoe laces. I got a lot of congratulations and high fives and looks of incredibility. I loved that part. The adrenaline rush for me was not the anticipation or the ride; it was the respect that one brief moment of time gained me with the students and parents. Sometimes you have to get just a little crazy. A week later Betty sent out an auction update to every family in the school. In the letter she thanked all of the volunteers that had worked so tirelessly to put the auction together. She said that there were many heroes Saturday night and then she listed several. I was on the list; "Mrs. Sutton on El Toro the Bull! Now that was a sight and to top it all off, she rode the full 8 seconds." My new motto is: "Never say Never!"

You do not have to ride a bull to be a hero. You just have to love your students and show it; inject your instruction with energy and passion; and treat your career as the wonderful profession it is.

MY HERO

A parent brought me a gift that I want to share with every teacher in the universe. This gift validates all of the things that I believe as a teacher. It motivates me to go further. At a time in my career when it would be normal to start winding down, I find myself wanting to work harder, be better, and excel in ways that I thought unimaginable at my age. This gift is helping me to do that. It seems strange to me that I am writing a book when I have nothing to offer compared to what I have found in this gift. I am thinking that you would be better off putting my book down and running out and purchasing this gift for yourself. Enough with the "gift" theme and the mystery; my gift was an inscribed copy of *The End of Molasses Classes* by Ron Clark. Every teacher and parent in the world needs to read this book. It is absolutely energizing! It is all about parental and teacher expectations and how education works for every student.

I had admired Ron Clark ever since I read his first book, *The Essential 55*. He is an extremely gifted teacher who uses old fashioned values and new fashioned techniques to empower teachers and students. He is changing the face of education for those who are willing to listen. The parent who brought me the "gift" knows that I am a little weird and knew that Ron Clark would be one of my heroes. After reading *"Molasses"*, he is not only my hero, he is my "mentor unaware" as I strive to emulate his energy and enthusiasm in the classroom. The book was signed by Ron: "To: Lizzie (Who cares if he spelled my name wrong, when greatness writes it matters not how they spell your name...) I hear you are a phenomenal teacher that would make me proud! Keep up the great work! Ron Clark 10-11-11. " He used two exclamation points and a smiley face. I will cherish this book forever.

I do not remember being this excited about a hero since the Beatles in 1966. Even though I do not have posters of Ron all over my bedroom, I feel the same sense of adoration and irrational need to breathe the same air as he does, as I did when I was fifteen and the Beatles were on the Ed Sullivan Show. The difference is that now, I was able to have my dream come true. I have already shared my visit to the Ron Clark Academy. It was a like a trip to Disney World for me. You are never too old to improve and never too good to be better.

DRAGON FLIES

I think that the hardest part of writing a book is "knowing" how to begin and how to end. The beginning is tough because you have so betweenies". Thank you for investing yourself in them and your other students. I feel very privileged that all three of my children benefitted from your considerable talents for many years.

***And my all time favorite from a very difficult student: Keep up the good teaching; it makes a difference.

***Ancora imparo! I am still learning! Michelangelo's pronouncement at the age of 87.

***Part of an essay written by a student for an English class:

> There are a lot of teachers today who are very old. Mrs. Sutton is one of the best teachers to ever live and she is very old. I have learned a lot from Mrs. Sutton and she has a lot of useful advice to tell.

Chips
Doorbell
Hall Pass

"Refrigerator" (Name only)

245 sticky
"who has
I have" Note

254
Store
Name - personal
out in hall
- outside please -
students w/issues
& those to compliment

264-
Kids need
attention - not
blurt out

Cover
Sheets -
Cardboard

"Starter"
isi
RBL - Seating
Chart

Birthday

227-
Substitute
Dr. Y